Beautiful Monsters

CALIFORNIA STUDIES IN 20TH-CENTURY MUSIC

Richard Taruskin, General Editor

1. *Revealing Masks: Exotic Influences and Ritualized Performance in Modernist Music Theater,* by W. Anthony Sheppard

2. *Russian Opera and the Symbolist Movement,* by Simon Morrison

3. *German Modernism: Music and the Arts,* by Walter Frisch

4. *New Music, New Allies: American Experimental Music in West Germany from the Zero Hour to Reunification,* by Amy Beal

5. *Bartók, Hungary, and the Renewal of Tradition: Case Studies in the Intersection of Modernity and Nationality,* by David E. Schneider

6. *Classic Chic: Music, Fashion, and Modernism,* by Mary E. Davis

7. *Music Divided: Bartók's Legacy in Cold War Culture,* by Danielle Fosler-Lussier

8. *Jewish Identities: Nationalism, Racism, and Utopianism in Twentieth-Century Art Music,* by Klára Móricz

9. *Brecht at the Opera,* by Joy H. Calico

10. *Beautiful Monsters: Imagining the Classic in Musical Media,* by Michael Long

Beautiful Monsters

Imagining the Classic in Musical Media

Michael Long

UNIVERSITY OF CALIFORNIA PRESS
Berkeley · Los Angeles · London

University of California Press, one of the most distinguished university presses in the United States, enriches
lives around the world by advancing scholarship in the hu-
manities, social sciences, and natural sciences. Its activities
are supported by the UC Press Foundation and by philan-
thropic contributions from individuals and institutions.
For more information, visit www.ucpress.edu.

University of California Press
Berkeley and Los Angeles, California

University of California Press, Ltd.
London, England

Library of Congress Cataloging-in-Publication Data

Long, Michael, 1952–
    Beautiful monsters : imagining the classic in musi-
cal media / Michael Long.
        p.   cm.—(California studies in 20th-century
music ; 10)
    Includes bibliographical references (p.   ) and
index.
    ISBN 978-0-520-22897-9 (cloth : alk. paper)—
ISBN 978-0-520-25720-7 (pbk. : alk. paper)
    1. Popular music and art music.   2. Popular
music—History and criticism.   3. Motion picture
music—History and criticism.   I. Title.

    ML3470.L64   2008
    781.6'8—dc22   2007051009

Manufactured in the United States of America

17   16   15   14   13   12   11   10   09   08
10   9   8   7   6   5   4   3   2   1

This book is printed on Natures Book, which contains
30% post-consumer waste and meets the minimum requirements of ANSI/NISO Z39.48–1992 (R 1997) (*Permanence of Paper*).

For Sheldon, Bob, Stephen, and Maia

Contents

Acknowledgments ix

Introduction 1

PART ONE · *Registering the Classic*

1. The Expressive Vernacular 11
2. Making Overtures 44
3. Yiddishkeit and the Musical Ethics of Cinema 73

PART TWO · *Envisioning the Classic*

4. Hearing Monsters 109
5. The Fantastic, the Picturesque, and the Dimensions of Nostalgia 121
6. Listening in Dark Places 157
7. Concertos, Symphonies, Rhapsodies (and an Opera) 196

Conclusion: Sitting Down with Mnemosyne 233

Notes 241

Selected Bibliography 287

Index 299

Acknowledgments

In making my way through the wide range of topics and repertory addressed in this book I profited from conversations—sometimes casual or merely in passing—with colleagues, friends, and students within and outside the discipline of musicology. For their helpful suggestions concerning relevant bibliography, repertory, and conceptual details, I would like to thank Karol Berger, Daniel Chiarilli, James Currie, Lawrence Earp, Kai Fikentscher, Christopher Gibbs, Lorena Guillén, Martha Hyde, Michael Martin, Peter Schmelz, Charles Smith, Peter Otto, and Albin Zak. Caryl Emerson, Christopher J. Long, Harold Rosenbaum, and Jayson Rodovsky each shared specific expertise on matters of language, linguistics, or Yiddish song. My thanks also to William Rosar for his generosity as an interlocutor and as a repository of details related to the early years of sound cinema. Some of the material in this book was developed while teaching seminars at the University at Buffalo and as a visitor at the Eastman School of Music, and my work has profited from discussions with graduate students in both those contexts. I am grateful to the music librarians at both institutions for their assistance and cooperation, especially John Bewley, Rick MacRae, Nancy Nuzzo, and Gerry Szymanski.

For the provision of illustrative material, I am grateful to the Birmingham Museum and Art Gallery; also to Arnold Berlin (www.stafford shire.org). Special thanks to Trevor C. Bjorklund who, during a very busy phase in his own life, volunteered to prepare the musical examples, a task he carried out with expertise, efficiency, and good humor.

I thank the anonymous readers for the University of California Press for their many helpful comments. Special thanks to Richard Taruskin, the most formidable reader I know, for his detailed review of the manuscript and for the enlivening conversations that followed. His insights and suggestions were invaluable in making this book significantly better than it would have been otherwise. I am further indebted to him and to Elaine Sisman for their many years of service as colleagues, friends, and cheerleaders. My work has benefited from their unwavering encouragement and especially from the models provided by their distinguished and inspiring scholarship.

For their hard work, congeniality, and expertise I thank also my production editor at the University of California Press, Jacqueline Volin, and copy editor Julie Brand. I bear full responsibility for any stylistic or conceptual infelicities that remain. I am especially grateful to Mary Francis, who has shepherded this project since its inception with wisdom, generosity, and patience.

Finally, I have to thank Robert W. Marion, MD, for having unknowingly (to either of us) planted the seeds of this study in our childhood by a remark about Procol Harum's "A Whiter Shade of Pale" that I have always remembered. Suggesting with breathless enthusiasm (and thinly veiled impatience), "Michael, even *you* will like this song," he may have initiated my contemplation of those processes of appreciation and communication explored in the pages that follow.

Introduction

Prompted by the "crisis" of devaluation and delegitimation of (mainly) European literate art music over the course of the previous generation, Julian Johnson fired a question into the apparent cultural void with his 2002 monograph *Who Needs Classical Music?*[1] If there is an answer implicit in the following study, it is that classical music is and will likely continue to be fundamental to everyone who has confronted or been confronted by it, even or perhaps especially when it has taken the form of a reconfigured fragment. Since the crisis to which Johnson's book responds appears to be bound at least as much to institutions as to sounds, and is linked more to received modes of framing, evaluation, and analysis than to other varieties of musical perception, mourning the supposed decline of the classics strikes me as maudlin. For Johnson, classical music (including twentieth-century modernism) constitutes a language—a word that turns up with some regularity in his text—that differs fundamentally from the plurality of musical languages he grudgingly welcomes but ultimately dismisses. His insistent, if understated, taxonomy of language is built upon a discursive foundation he has grounded in the elements of music most germane to his evaluative arguments, elements such as musical form and harmony. (Thus his enthusiasm for the aesthetically bracing challenges of musical dissonance.) Focusing on music's nuts and bolts, and specifically those easily demonstrated and enumerated by reference to printed musical scores (however much all of this hardware may transport us when presented in performance), Johnson argues for the discouraging "simplicity" of a great deal of twentieth-century popular song, along with other types of main-stream music.[2]

I agree (as most everyone will) that it is not easy to talk about what music does without recourse to a vocabulary linked to our understanding of language, of how we use it and why we use it at all. In the pages that follow I will refer at times to the academic sciences of language, but any borrowed concepts are not rallied to support the promulgation of structural models or analytical systems. They are selected instead for their relevance to concretizing the human need for particular modes of expression and are dependent upon nothing more technical than a kind of situational linguistics.

Johnson's position regarding the special qualities that inhere in the literate art-music tradition will be clear to anyone reading his work; his arguments have little to do with the substance of mine, and their usefulness as a foil will not extend much beyond this introduction. But in situating the music I treat in the pages that follow, one of Johnson's formulations is particularly relevant. Referring to Simon Frith's work on the sociological implications of musical valuation, and to Frith's reporting of a mode of dismissive criticism often employed by "mass" audiences in assigning the adjective *stupid* to music that consumers sense "demeans us through our involvement, however unwilling, in the collusive act of listening," Johnson appropriates their same tone. His position, hardly unique, is based, again, on a language analogy: for music to have value it should possess coherence, continuity, and challenging originality, rather along the lines of a nicely composed essay. With an eye toward provocation, Johnson expresses his own perspective on Muzak and its degenerate kin, the whole clan of sounds regularly served up by radio or in clubs, on television, in film, and as an accompaniment to video games: "Much of the music that surrounds us acts as a kind of aural tranquilizer. So-called elevator music is not confined to elevators: music that expunges any unfamiliar element, any hint of complexity or self-development saturates the private and communal spaces of modern life. This music is inane, stupid, and empty in the same way that repetitive and undeveloped writing is stupid, full of clichés and non sequiturs, attempting to pass off empty and worn-out phrases as the vehicles of genuine thought and emotion."[3]

This book addresses what Johnson characterized as the hollow and predictable fakes. The musical and textual clichés, fragments, non sequiturs, and undeveloped iterations of twentieth-century media, specifically those that are related to the noise of "genuine" art and its consumers, form the core of this study. It is largely devoted—by Johnson's definition—to *stupid music,* a construction that brands the conventionality of his musical aesthetic and that I appropriate therefore with some seriousness of purpose. My intent is to bring a methodologically flexible—that is, a "generalist"—perspective to bear upon music that has often been represented even by its adherents and its devoted analysts as something essentially distinct from that which lay at the heart of academic musical discourse prior to the last decades of the twentieth century.

With the advent of historical and critical studies of popular musics and film music, it has seemed that even as items formerly residing at the artistic periphery (within the discursive and aesthetic constructions of the old academy) were being moved toward the foreground, this repositioning demanded mastery of specific methodological and critical strategies. Particularly when approaching rock and pop, scholars have regularly turned to academically sanctioned paths of enriched sociological contextualization (by which I mean disciplinarily defined methodologies), as if to underscore such music's privileged ties to the century's material culture—in the ethnographic sense—which concert hall music did not enjoy.[4] This has encouraged, in some cases at least, the abdication of historical perspective for descriptive culturology.[5]

While the musics associated with Hollywood cinema and with mainstream rock and pop that serve as the focus for my discussions have been on the musicological table for some time, scholars have not encouraged conversation among works originating within different media (or different genres within the same medium). Nor has there been much call for the integration of historical, critical, and intellectual apparatuses regularly brought to the historiography and criticism of concert hall music. Even Nicholas Cook's broad and innovative *Analysing Musical Multimedia* usually addresses a single topic related to a single work, medium, or genre in each chapter essay.[6] And while in recent years practitioners of film-music criticism have repeatedly addressed the so-called use of popular music in film scores (also so-called in many such cases), these analyses usually amount to narrative glosses. And so I attempt in this study to bring a wide range of items closer to a single conversational and methodological center as it continues to be imagined by many scholars working in the ever more ghettoized realm of European musical museums with longer histories. In drawing together musical material from film, rock, and the concert hall, I have tried to acknowledge but not rely upon the idiolects and approaches linked only to methodological, terminological, or repertorial ghettos of more recent design.

The embarrassment academics daily confront when we halfheartedly recite categories of "art" and "popular" that we know are meaningless or wrong, and the extent to which we still regularly frame our own language in air, scare, or typographical quotes, suggests that if we could comfortably recategorize the objects of our discourse we would likely do so. Replacing old chestnuts is no less problematic. Many of our systematic markers of classification, including even those derived from vocabularies of recent vintage such as "hegemonic" and "counter-hegemonic," demark the rest of what in other respects might be legitimate and fluent expositions (demark in the Deleuzian sense, since they crash into our otherwise nuanced conversations as clumsily as Hitchcock's seagull into Tippi Hedrin's forehead).[7] I tend to ignore most such distinctions except in those cases where they are decisively called for by the object under consideration, hoping to expose and emphasize the links between items formerly stored in different cabinets. In many cases the links are forged by musical gesture, in others they are suggested by broader cultural readings. Direct relationships between Andrei Tarkovsky and Procol Harum, T. S. Eliot and Michael Jackson, or Bugs Bunny and Freddie Mercury, might be trivial or even nonexistent; the webs in which they have been mutually implicated are not, however, and these transcend directional associations of influence, imitation, or referentiality.

While my text is bookended by Dante and the Sony PlayStation, respectively, there is no continuous chronological trajectory to its organization, and some individuals and musical works will be examined from more than one perspective. So, for example, musical motives associated with the composers Richard Addinsell and Bernard Herrmann are considered within a particular frame in chapter 1, where their resurrection as rap samples is shown both to link and to differentiate their presence in late twentieth-century recorded music in revealing ways. Each "original," however, will return later in the book, reconsidered against the backdrop of some broader contexts for its creation and reception by different audiences in other generations.

Even though this study considers musical or multimedia works that were widely circulated by the machinery of twentieth-century commerce, my choice of "media" rather than "mass media" in the title derives from my sense that the massness of mass media—the feature that has rendered media products artistically, economically, politically, and sociologically suspect—is largely an academic digression. In fact, the consumption of mass media even prior to the digital age, as far back as the period of music-store listening booths and pre-surround-sound theaters, or even the makeshift viewing environments of earliest cinema I describe in chapter 6, made room for new forms of individual apprehension unfettered by social mannerisms and public graces. This grand shift in musical reception was at least as significant as the new tendency to meddle with the supposed integrity of classical music's authentic content and mode of presentation; and while driven perhaps by the availability of options linked to commerce, it was not configured by commerce at the level of the individual human experience. For the most part this phenomenon was historically unimaginable except in unusual cases linked to practices of *musica secreta* or *reservata* such as that associated with the solitary keyboard players of the eighteenth century recalled in chapter 5. Processes of reception provide one thread that may be usefully traced through the webs of historical linkage associated with the repertory of (stupid) music considered here.

Although my title flaunts the term "classic," this book is concerned primarily with a collective, not quite definable, yet inescapably powerful "vernacular imagination." Vernacular here is intended simply in the sense of something commonly shared or understood by a community. Since my emphasis throughout this book will be on items that are drawn from among the most commercially successful and widely consumed products of twentieth-century musical media, that community must be taken to consist of what from a sociological perspective is likely a problematically broad, amorphous, undifferentiated demographic: American and in a few cases European media audiences of the last century. What I think of as the "imaginative" classic is generated from within the space of an artist's imaginary and reflects a creative or re-creative process typically related to a slate of priorities (aesthetic, ethical, sensual) that intersects with a prioritized sense of the past. Calling upon a concept based in the memory arts of the European Middle Ages, I would suggest that the imaginative classic also denotes a particular collection of boxes associated with the imagination's reliance upon memory and the essential function of imaginative memory as both a filter and a repository.[8] Thus my attention turns to Mnemosyne, maternal guardian of memory, in the book's conclusion. These tracks and processes are significant. The imaginative path taken by an auditor to judge that an item—however fragmentary and in Johnson's terms insufficient with respect to the syntactical or grammatical proprieties of "language" as the stuff of forms—marks an intersection with the classic is as relevant as the classic's reinvention by that item's creator.

This classic, then, embraces historical and contemporary products as well as states and operations of mind, in the latter instance providing a taxonomic umbrella for a particular mode or trail of reception. By the activities of evaluating objects to distinguish the classic from the merely vintage and, for historical works produced in the fifteenth through the nineteenth centuries, critiquing in retrospect the means by which such evaluations were recorded, the attention of scholars is typically diverted from the process of the classic's imagining and the forms taken by its imaginative promulgation. I examine many items in this book from perspectives of both creation and reception. If any single theoretical or disciplinary position informs my approach to the diverse materials explored in this study, it is an intention to practice and perhaps extend the potential of a kind of musicology of the whole that Richard Middleton called for from a rather different perspective more than a decade ago, an optimistic proposal that for the most part has remained unrealized within the arena of specialized musicological discourse concerning the musical media of the twentieth century.[9]

Chapters 1 and 2 examine the ways in which the musical classic, so labeled, has been heard and understood as an object of reception in a variety of contexts. I mean hearing the classic literally: by what means does the classic announce itself as an aural presence or a force in operation outside its own time and context, within a mediated environment, perceived and comprehended by unscreened or unprepared audiences? Drawing upon notions of "register" as understood within the domain of historical systems of poetics and rhetoric, and more recently in the arena of sociolinguistic discourse that gave this expressive practice its musical name, I suggest a conceptual frame for the creative and receptive processes associated with hybrid music. Tracing a single gesture through multiple registrations in chapter 2 underscores how, unlike taxonomies of genre or audience, registers function within living systems of expressive discourse. These are often oral (and aural), but even when literate they tend to be powered by the implicative presence of aural markers. Chapter 3 extends the registral function of the musical classic in a particular rhetorical direction and considers the role of media (not only musical media but all in which music has resonance, including mass-market literature) in promoting and embodying vernacular or domestic systems of ethics, political and spiritual.

In this and other cases the recourse to classical gestures within a conventional system of ethical rhetoric is linked to the expressive practices of economic, ethnic, aesthetic, or social outsiders. Taken to particular extremes of affectation and representation, they may eventually intersect with the traditional aesthetic null sets of kitsch or camp, often associated with creative artists—some of them encountered in this book—who were Jewish (like Al Jolson and Max Steiner), gay (like Jimmy Somerville and Freddie Mercury) or both (like Allen Ginsberg). Such labels are linked to perspectives that are more sociological (that is, bound up with the definition of groups) than artistic or musical.[10] Even in discussing these zones of cultural activity, I have tried to maintain the focus on specific intersections of musical and visible gesture positioned within culturally and chronologically broad categories of expression. I have tried to analyze even these categories not as touchstones for social theory but as regions within a general musical history of commercial media and artistic production.

Chapter 4 introduces the second part of the book and attempts to open up the acoustic, topographical, and temporal spaces of the auditory imagination addressed in the remaining chapters. Throughout these, I address the potential relevance of historical aesthetics and cultural practice to the creation and reception of twentieth-century musical media. My point here is not to suggest that twentieth-century media merely reiterate or revisit aspects of these environments. I am more intrigued by the possibility that such cultural analogies might offer unexpectedly relevant frames for our own imaginatively critical hearing of mass-market works that are usually assigned to more predictable categories. The emphasis throughout is on "cinematic" listening, a process of simultaneous audiation and envisioning; this concept extends beyond film to the soundscapes of classical and vernacular musics and especially to their hybrids. In my discussion of acoustical nostalgia in chapter 5, I suggest—with the help of visual-art analogies—that by extending our understanding of music's expressive capacity to aural features beyond those of its fundamental elements (like pitch, harmony, timbre), media items of apparently insignificant aesthetic value often take on a sense of remarkable depth (in both literal and evaluative understandings of that word). I consider music's implicit visual dimensions and its occupation of conceptual space within more literally cinematic contexts in chapter 6. There, and again in chapter 7, I return to matters of gesture and the expressive function of musical registers described in the first part of the book; the emphasis here, though, is on the ways in which aural gestures can trigger the construction or recall of particular image registers and the reverse.

In essence, the position on the musical classic in the twentieth century set forth in these pages is not far removed from that of Wilhelm Heinrich Riehl's assessment of folk music in the century before: "Folk songs are not once-and-for-all finished things, but are in a constant state of becoming. . . . Our ancient folk melodies are not dead 'reliques,' history lives and breathes in them."[11] Radical as it may seem to replace "folk songs" with "classical compositions" in the face of Johnson and other treasurers of the notated canon, the move, as I argue in the first chapter, would in fact reflect the flavor of most thoughtful expositions on the nature of the classic since such a thing was first put into words. As for the "beautiful monsters," even though the phrase in my title is borrowed from a journalist's comment on Procol Harum's song "A Whiter Shade of Pale," discussed in the second part of the book, these extraordinary yet strangely familiar creatures begin to materialize much sooner. Cinematic projections—realized or imagined—of musical utterance, musical hearing, and musical reception, they lurk throughout the conceptual spaces described in this book.

Registering the Classic

The Expressive Vernacular

What we call the common tongue is that which we acquire
without any rule, by imitating our nurses.

> Dante Alighieri, *On Eloquence*
> *in the Vernacular (De vulgari eloquentia)*

At the beginning of the fourteenth century Dante proposed—radically,
for his time—that not only classical Latin but vernacular languages as
well might serve as agents for eloquent and even elevated poetic expression. Even if his case was strategic, since he intended to promote his native Tuscan idiolect as the most "literary" among the many forms taken
by what we now call Italian, his methodology foreshadowed in a general
way the enterprise of modern sociolinguistics. In his unfinished treatise
on the eloquent vernacular, the medieval poet attempted to describe
broadly and systematically how language is acquired, and how it strikes
the ear. Suggesting that some languages and their verbal forms and gestures could provide models for meaningful imitation or refashioning outside their original ethnic and cultural environments, he argued that the
expressive features of a language resided in its sound, and might even be
grasped without command of its grammar, a "second" and less essential
form of language. His observations constituted a watershed of cultural
practice: vernacular literature would soon take off, not only in Italy but
in France and England, where poets like Machaut and Chaucer were
ready to embrace Dante's modernist perspective.

Dante's sense of how language works is especially relevant to musical
media repertories of the twentieth century (including some of the monster hits of rock and pop), in which concert hall music, as it was popularly imagined and characterized by those whose experience lay primarily outside the walls of "classical" music venues, played a significant

expressive role even though its musical grammar did not. How have so many musical works in our own time indulged in reference and citation without compromising vernacular intelligibility and, most important, expressive immediacy? Modern academic readers are familiar with notions of cultural register, a term that appears often in discussions of such hybrids, usually alongside the scalar modifiers "high" and "low." I would like to bring this commonplace into sharper focus, by invoking register less as a general indicator of cultural location than in a more specific sense familiar to scholars of medieval poetics who have linked the *sensory* aspects of cultural products to the *expressive* value of the registers (i.e., collections) in which they are understood to be located.[1]

In the case of poetry, the bearer of register will be words, of course.[2] Their sensory apparatus can include a range of qualitative and quantitative elements such as phonemes, number of syllables, and resonance with other words; this understanding might be amplified to include, in the case of song, the acoustical components of musical settings. Register, particularly in its expressive function as outlined below, is related to the broader fields of acculturated styles and genres in which it functions as a signal and marker and thus may be (and, especially in literary criticism, has been) expanded beyond the measurements of a simple scale to a system of classification based on words, syntax, form, and sounds; it often serves in place of more general notions of, for example, tenor, tone, and style. Indeed, once they have been sufficiently registered (or registrated) as normative practice, sounds in general may be expressive in this sense with no textual linkage. I see some potential in an expanded approach to the implications (especially for reception) of defining registered objects, borrowing from the sociolinguistic models wherein the concept was first cultivated some additional critical tools related both to register variation and to register formation. Late twentieth-century linguistic criticism, which thus far has been confined primarily to literary studies, provides a model for such an approach.[3] But I would suggest that even if the current terminology and the taxonomies of register theory belong to the field of mid-twentieth-century sociolinguistics, *hearing* register—whatever we might call it—as a concretization of shared cultural values, categories, and word relations is hardly limited to the twentieth century; neither is the tendency to frame this phenomenon within a theoretical or scientific matrix.

LISTENING BACK

As a theorized listening practice, the origins of the concept lie in the cultivation and simultaneous intellectual framing of an expressive vernacular literature centuries ago, as reflected especially by Dante's treatise. Such early approaches to sound and syntax still bear implications for analysis and criticism of vernacular cultural products in the twenty-first century. In this instance I am using *vernacular* only in its most neutral sense, as a thing that is standard or shared, ordinary or everyday, intending no implications of naturalness or ethnological circumscription, pace Dante, whose project included the characterization of languages according to geographical and ethnographic groups based upon each group's way of expressing the simple affirmative "yes" *(sì, oc, oïl)*.

Scholars of medieval poetics often preface *register* with the modifier *expressive*, thus pointing to the lexical and syntactic arsenal of gambits and gestures that define and encode particular styles or genres and their expected performance, reception, and audience.[4] While characteristic word types contribute to the establishment of expressive register in the works under consideration in this book, I extend the literary understanding here, embracing additional phenomenal levels such as vocal and instrumental timbre, harmonic and melodic structures, and, in the case of multimedia, visual images. Expressive registers reflect "the extreme formalization of tradition."[5] They are collections that contain the established landmarks of convention. The idea of poetic register embraces an inherent verticality: one speaks, for instance, of the high expressive register of the medieval *canso* versus the low expressive register of the *pastorela*. Crucially, these poetic (or rhetorical) registers were constructed from sound types; oratory and lyric, whether or not fitted with a musical setting, were for hearing more than reading.[6] As "texts," poems were, and still are in some cases, stand-ins for the real thing. This is worth recalling as we set out to "read"—as so many late twentieth-century academic titles characterized it—modern musical media. Medieval markers of register include, at the high end, convoluted syntax and abstract or exotic polysyllabic nouns; at the low end, one encounters simple syntax, concrete and mundane nouns, nonsense syllables, and childish words. Dante, who already in the early fourteenth century dealt extensively with the classification and status of words according to their phonemic structure, cited as cases of lowest aesthetic weight the simple infantile bilabials (humanity's *ur*-words): for him, the Italian *mamma* and *babbo*.[7] These resonate, it might be noted, with the low-register bilabials of English-language rock, rhythm and blues, and

country musics, particularly the conventional expressive vocatives
"mama," "babe," and "baby."[8] High register, in contrast, evoked more
unusual and even disorienting aural and linguistic strategies.[9] The effusive
polysyllabism of later psychedelic and progressive rock represented,
among other things, a shift in the generic operations of register within
rock's communicative systems.[10]

Rock's expressive registers were under construction from its earliest
mass-market phases. A less than classic effort, at least according to the
current canon, "Surfin' Bird," by the determinedly low-register 1960s ensemble the Trashmen, took these phonemic strategies to their extreme,
essentially ventriloquizing Dante's linguistic position almost seven centuries later. Instructing listeners through the lyrics that "bird is a word,"
"Surfin' Bird" demonstrates the power of the smallest phonemes to invoke register and to capture and hone the ear of pop consumers as the
song proceeds to effectively disassemble the components of its own language into nonverbal timbral abstractions. The Trashmen's bilabial
fantasy reached as high as the no. 6 position on the *Billboard* charts in
January 1964. Featuring a repetitive ("bird . . . bird . . . bird") and eventually stuttering vocal ("pa-pa-pa-pa-pa . . . ," "mau-mau-mau . . .")
that, it might be argued, presages more recent percussive effects in rap
and hip-hop, the song's strategy derived from similar nonsense syllable
insets that characterized the earlier California surf music of the influential Jan and Dean.

While many of these gestures were no doubt meant to invoke for surf-
crazed listeners the phonemes particular to native Hawaiian, it is relevant
that Jan and Dean's first trip to the *Billboard* Top Ten was in 1959, with
a love song bearing no coastal references, but full of the same form of bilabial vocalizing on Dante's markers of low register, *m* and *b*. The song
was titled, appropriately, "Baby Talk."[11] Early rock was associated (dangerously, for some) with low-order sexuality and linked to relatively explicit and apparently nonchoreographed, asocial (i.e., infantile) types of
dance and bodily motion. From this perspective, Jan and Dean's alliterative and self-consciously infantile vocalizations were intended as sexual
incantations that might register beyond any lyrical context. Their theoretical position with respect to the power of rock phonemes was clarified
in another hit wherein the duo answered, for the edification of their adolescent male peers, their own musical question, "Who Put the Bomp in
the Bomp-ba-bomp-ba-bomp?" with "We were those guys / I hope you
realize / we made your baby fall in love with you," underscoring the relationship between low-register language formants and the imaginative

realm of informal sexual relations. Akin to the nonsense exclamations that mark the registral collections of medieval pastoral—a genre that often deals with the unritualized "love of peasants" (as Andreas Capellanus described it in his twelfth-century treatise on courtly love, *De amore*)—surf music's expressive vocal register was hardly as new as it may have seemed.

Poeticians had borrowed register as something approaching a "scientific" tool for analysis from the disciplinary arsenal of the sociolinguisticians, and I call upon that model at times but by no means systematically or exclusively throughout this book. The study of register variation in sociolinguistics proceeds from the assumption that "a communication situation that recurs regularly in a society (in terms of participants, setting, communicative functions, and so forth) will tend over time to develop identifying markers of language structure and language use, different from the language of other communication situations."[12] One could imagine a dialect-word forming an item within some special expressive register, but registers are distinct from dialect in general. According to the theory posited in sociolinguistics, "In dialects we say the same thing in different ways while in registers we say different things in different ways."[13] Constituents of registers, including special terms and formulas, provide communicative shorthand in some cases; in others, they might serve as markers or signals of the register or might create rapport between conversational participants. For music, to the extent that it may be said to communicate (as in fact it *must* do in some instances, for example in film scoring), aural collections based on gesture-type, texture, timbre, and more must be added to the phonetic content of texts, if present.

Although the concept of language specific to situational context well predates the introduction of the term, *register* appears to have been coined in the mid-twentieth century by T. B. W. Reid, who already had in mind a wide application, linked to genre and style in writing: "Among the most generally applicable registers are those of familiar intercourse, of administration (in the widest sense), of religion or ceremonial, and of literature (with various subdivisions)."[14] There was, in this early phase, a suggestion of verticality with respect to register distinctions. Reid cited J. R. Firth's work of the late 1940s and early 1950s; Firth had referred to situation-appropriate "levels of diction." When he elaborated register theory in the 1960s, M. A. K. Halliday seized upon the musical analogy inherent in the term, further emphasizing its scalar aspect: "All speakers have at their disposal a continuous scale of patterns and items, from which they select for each situation type the appropriate stock of available harmonies in the appropriate key. They speak, in other words, many registers."[15] More recent linguistic criticism has largely abandoned the vertical-scale metaphor in its understanding of the way registers function in language, particularly in literature, but some vertical scales of distinction are so deeply inscribed in the Western view of literary products that their impact must be acknowledged. Indeed, word register as a function of genre registers implying literary status or rank was already the theoretical frame for Aristotle's *Poetics* and was transmitted in medieval doctrines of poetry, notably those of John of Garland's thirteenth-century *Parisiana poetria* (which, following the Virgilian categories established in the *Eclogues, Georgics,* and *Aeneid,* speaks of "words cognate to the subject"), along with Dante's later *De vulgari eloquentia.*

Rock's conventional registers were occasionally distorted by the introduction of materials—or, "objects"—appropriated from a "higher" expressive register, typically one associated with the concert hall (in the case of music) or the "literary" (in the case of lyrics). These shifts in the tectonic norms of song appear, from the perspective of a two-node scale, to represent a process of "inversion," a simple juxtaposition or substitution involving the high and the low, and for much of the late twentieth century, theorizing inversion was a significant and popular intellectual undertaking. Musicology is familiar with Barthes's theories of *inversion* and *renversement* and with Mikhail Bakhtin's concept of the "carnivalesque."[16] Seemingly hybrid works might also be theorized as "camp" objects that seek refuge in the "hopelessly, and thus safely, dated" elements of certain period styles, but camp is usually associated more with social typing and group definitions than with analysis of dynamic processes in music and text.[17] In practice, these processes of juxtaposition are various and highly differentiated through expressive nuance; to describe them requires more than an all-inclusive tag.

PLAYING WITH REGISTER

Opening gambits generally provide the locus for the encoding of pop "genre," often through a nonvocal introduction or "hook" that triggers in the listener what Leonard Meyer—referring to other musical styles— called the "internalized probability system."[18] Significantly, in some cases songs that play with register assert their noncompliance with pop genre codes right off the bat. By not adhering to this standard, these works break the implied contract between song and audience before it has even been signed.[19] This might be effected through suggested or out-right borrowings of concert hall music to introduce a song. For instance, characteristic girl-group register is deflected at the opening of the Toys' 1965 "A Lover's Concerto" (discussed in chapter 7) by concertizing, pianistic gestures. A more extreme case is Barry Manilow's 1975 hit "Could It Be Magic," which begins with a full performance of Chopin's C-Minor Prelude, which Manilow will use as the basis for a harmonic contrafact structure.[20] While Manilow's songs often call attention to his own musicianship, the Chopin citation is not primarily a reference to concert hall practice. In the song's refrain Manilow draws not upon the supposed elevation of the classical-piano register collection from which it is taken but upon what he hears as a vocative quality inherent in the rhetoric of the prelude.

Forcing the listener into a specific analysis of Chopin's expressive register he clearly hears as embodied in the work's inflexible rhythmic patterning, Manilow lends orality to an explicitly Svengalian imperative suggested by the music, one strangely at odds with the saccharine romance of the song's verses. The effect is rendered especially vivid by the ultimate abandonment of verse material in the second half of the song in favor of constant reiteration of the refrain's core words ("come, come, come . . . now, now, now"), layered upon a harmonically manipulated fragment of the prelude that serves as a quasi-cinematic underscore. Each successive utterance is marked by the typical Manilow bump-up in dynamics and orchestration, but it functions as more than a nightclub gimmick here, for it turns the text into a screenplay that must be realized in the listener's imagination. Structurally, the multimedia impression (dramatic monologue, implicit visual, repetitive yet incrementally expressive musical background) is virtually identical to those of "real" cinema, for example the famous threefold farewell embrace scored by Max Steiner for the airport scene of the Bette Davis vehicle *Now Voyager* (1942), a classic of conventional Hollywood scoring. In the end, the song's coda—a replay of the last bit of the Chopin original—forces the listener to reinterpret the prelude as a vehicle of cinematic potential. In another 1975 Manilow effort, "I Write the Songs," there is no classical-style musical content, but the text borrows from the discourse of oratory and rhetoric, specifically in the song's prosopopoeic climax, "I am music," no more overblown perhaps (in terms of twentieth-century media bombast) than Francesco Landini's identical ploy in the fourteenth-century madrigal "Musica son," today inscribed in the musicological academy's registers as a work of high art and technical prowess.

In some cases musical citations of classical music in rock borrow from the text registers of essay rather than narrative or dramaturgy, and these can be rather clever (appropriate to the essayist's enterprise), featuring provocative text/music play often buried beneath the surface. Rather than emphasizing musical alterity, these essays often underscore the universality of music's expressive registers. Two reinterpretations of the slow movement of Beethoven's Pathétique sonata, Billy Joel's "This Night" (1983) and Kiss's "Great Expectations" (1976), intersect with Manilow's music-centric perspective in calling attention within the song to musical traditions outside pop genres. Kiss's number opens with a rock orchestration of Beethoven's theme. The text, addressed in part to an imagined female fan, frames the topic as music (in the abstract) by the deliberately reflexive phrase "our music" and describes the arousing sight of the guitarist's fingers in motion. In brief, "Great Expectations" reconsiders—in rather amusing fashion—the dynamics of all staged musical virtuosity and concert performance.

Joel's treatment of the same Beethoven material is even more literal than that of "Great Expectations," although he withholds the melodic quotation until the refrain. But the song is shot through with wordplay linking Beethoven's nineteenth-century practice to that of the self-described "piano man" Joel and to the expressive registers of historical doo-wop ballads that the song references. Indeed, the love lyrics at times seem to suggest the solo pianist's relationship with the keyboard; distortions of musical time and imaginative space are effected through the utterance of words that possess meaningful implications outside the conventional subject matter of the song. These include "ready for romance" (code word for nineteenth-century repertoire), "only a slow dance" (the slow movement, outside the context of the full sonata), and the notion of an expressive historical musical continuum delivered at the end of the Beethovenian refrain music ("this night can last forever"). Joel sets up the first citation of the theme when his doo-wop rocker persona admits at the end of the verse that he can no longer "remember the rules," launching the song into a different registral collection from which the melody and harmony of the refrain are borrowed to create an effectively expressive hybrid.

BIRD: WORD OR SIGN?

Studies of mass-market media that have been informed by language models draw primarily upon the field of semiotics, often relying on a pared-down subset of its essential elements, or an unsystematic mix of terms related to imprecise notions of meaning and its indicators. Philip Tagg's analyses regularly spotlight small musical units, often in multimedia contexts, of precisely the sort I use to generate some of the discussions in this book. His characterization of such units as *musemes* reflects the post-Barthian semiotic framework for his systematic perspective. Tagg's language, accordingly, relies to no small extent on matters related to "units of meaning," connotative codes, "the indexical quality of much musical discourse."[21] And meaning is often, in his analyses, essentially "ideological." For Tia DeNora, Tagg's musemes are signs denoting "emotional significance."[22] Barthes and Lévi-Strauss provide the background for Royal S. Brown's concept of the *mytheme* in film music, a term, discussed in his *Overtones and Undertones: Reading Film Music,* that invokes not merely meaning (in its latter Barthian part) but the broad text belonging to a culture (in its primary, Lévi-Straussian root).[23] Scholars involved above all in film-music criticism continue to privilege music's role as a bearer of "meaning," a formulation that has survived for several decades.[24] I would argue that film music, like other vernaculars, is an especially expressive mode of discourse, and— adopting the position of literary register theory—that language-based modes of contemporary critique that neglect the operation of registers inappropriately homogenize their subjects.[25]

Brown's discussion reveals the tendency in the last two decades of the twentieth century to think of film as a particular sort of textual entity, and the business of film-music scholarship as one linked to explication of music's role in (and as) the text. That position (with appropriately Barthian punctuation) is rendered apparent in Brown's first chapter title: Narrative/Film/Music.[26] Our widespread acceptance today of film's implicit narrativity, and thus of all "-emes" as constituents of textual systems, may be credited above all to the enormous influence of Claudia Gorbman on this corner of musicological practice. Her *Unheard Melodies* not only encouraged the application of "meaning" to the hearing of filmmusic "texts" but placed meaning within a specifically narrative and more precisely narratological context at a time when narratology was upon the minds of many scholars interested in musicodramatic forms. Had it not been for Gorbman, and her highly accomplished application of Gérard Genette's theories of narrative to film sound, would so many writers still relish exploring the tensions and ambiguities related to the presence of "diegetic" and "nondiegetic" music in a single multimedia work?[27] Genette's systematic narratological perspective on texts—on dialogue versus reportage, on narrative voice—remains, via Gorbman, a guide to the overhearing of the off- and on-screen conversations, mechanical music, voice-overs, sound effects, and orchestrations that make up film's complex soundscape, everything that contributes to, in Rick Altman's intelligent coinage, the filmic mise-en-bande.[28]

There is nothing wrong, of course, with using diegetic and nondiegetic as pretty, slightly more nuanced substitutes for the old "source" versus "background" music distinction. Once implicated in the landscape of a theoretical discourse of film music, however, they limit the range of potential approaches to multimedia objects. The point may be illustrated by comparison with the discourse of film in general. Shots are fundamental to the language of film visuals; low- and high-angle shots especially can transmit understandings to the audience that are unavailable to the characters in the so-called narrative. These cannot "see" the perspectivally skewed images any more than they can "hear" the nondiegetic (i.e., background) musical content. Yet few will find it useful or appropriate to found much film analysis upon the division of the visual track into diegetic versus nondiegetic components. Understanding film music as a parallel narrative tracking a novelistic text seems to be based mainly on the popularity in the last quarter of the twentieth century of the notion that all music narrates (or might narrate), a position that is hardly central to most understandings of cinema's image track.

Our shyness as scholars or our difficulties as viewers in approaching films abstractly is by no means attributable entirely to the narratologists. Early twentieth-century kinotheks (libraries of "silent" movie film music), like that of Erdmann discussed below, attached meaning to film accompaniments (an early musical hermeneutics). This meaning was thought of as tracking a film's dramaturgical structure. We have substituted for that stage-based perspective a more novelistic one. Consider, for example, two analyses of the meaningful aspects of Steiner's 1942 score for *Now, Voyager*. At the time of the film's release it was reviewed in terms that suggest not merely its classic elements but their relationship to the dramatic trajectory of the film: "Once again Max Steiner assists mood and dramatic intent by giving this picture a symphonic musical background of impressive strength. The love poem filtering through the superb action is a symphonic tone poem of great beauty, stressing a great spiritual quality. The ratio between dialogue and music and action is well defined at all times, yet music is an important dramatic element, eloquently supporting description, emotion, action, mood and pace. The work is heavily orchestrated in keeping with the weight of the story, varying in range to contrast with the production structure."[29] The reviewer—clearly a Steiner apologist—heard the music dramaturgically, although he does invoke the term "story" in a general rather than linear sense. In her annotated leitmotivic catalog of the film, Kate Daubney seems to hear pretty much the same thing but reveals the influence of Gorbman's model for the apprehension of musical meaning:

> From the opening of the film, with its bold orchestral statement, to the quotation of popular hits of the day, the score for *Now, Voyager* relishes the power of music to be expressive. Steiner has seized the opportunity to create a score which, though largely non-diegetic, emphasizes our experience of the characters from points of view both within and outside the narrative space. Where the diegetic choices for the cruise ship cocktail bar, the party, the cafe near Cascade and the Vale mansion evoke quite particular atmospheres and contexts for the action, the non-diegetic score seems to traverse and transcend the narrative boundaries that can make a post-production score seem objective and wise after the event.[30]

We might, though, approach Steiner's music and its expressive operations by way of its particular registers. This would place much of the score, I would argue, in that of the "Puccinian-operatic."[31] I will address this characterization in its specifics in the next chapter, but simply put, the orchestral background score is—despite the on- and off-screen intrusions of Chaikovsky's Sixth Symphony—unambiguously vocal in its expressive gestures, and these gestures embody a form of musical expression that in the nineteenth century was mimetically linked to certain forms of conversational expressive gesture (particularly with respect to dynamic range and the phrasal caesuras that imitate natural, high-emotion respiratory events). My point is to suggest not a wholesale replacement for the language of conventional film-music criticism (journalistic or academic) but only that a slightly different approach to scoring "language" might supplement our currently rather narrow and inflexible range of discursive options. In assigning meaning to a musical bit, writers tend to emphasize the significance of the link to an object's original associated text (literary, musical, social). Steiner's Puccinianism, conventionally addressed, would more likely be taken exclusively as miming Puccini rather than as a mimetic realization in music of the expressive potential of most Western languages, something that any attentive Western listener might hear in Puccini's music. Missing in these analytical positions is much accommodation for the scale of expressive performance involved in the real iteration of such musicolinguistic "signs."[32]

Even before Dante, Occitan poetics—and Occitan was the first language for "composed" vernacular song in the West, the one Dante
looked to as his model for the new Italian—emphasized that each vernacular genre demanded a particular mode of expressive performance, a
special vocal and perhaps gestural demeanor. These prescriptions offer
a glimpse into the expressive component of registral collections. They are
part of a continuum of practice that survives in twentieth-century vernacular lyric genres. Emotive and motive elements appropriate to estab-
lishing expressive register in a blues performance differ from the laid-
back, expressively flat vocalizations that characterize and registrate most
surf song. However impressive the chronological gulf between the pre-
modern and modern repertorial nodes I am citing, more impressive are
their points of conceptual intersection: lyrics composed with an eye toward live and—within certain registral limits—individually flexible performances and geared toward reception based on aurality rather than an
inscribed text. In film music the score's performers are physically absent
but their expressive gestures resound.

One advantage of defining registers, especially for something like film
music, which is usually historicized as a single continuous strand, is that
doing so provides conceptual spaces in which signifiers or markers are
understood to be alive and in flux. Register theory invites diachronic exploration of "the life of signs." Beyond this, by locating conventions in
registral systems that may be shuffled in any number of ways to create
meaningful loci of intersection (as in a linguistic topography constituted
of movable Venn diagrammatic circles, with each circle representing a
register), we may expose and account for differences in implication that
have been attached by vernacular listeners to objects that look or sound
nearly identical. I would hardly argue for a "system" of registers, a sociolinguistic grid against which all vernacular cultural products may be
placed and interpreted or through which we might arrive at understandings somehow imbued with the scientific spirit of sociolinguisticians. I have introduced the subject primarily to foreground the importance of acoustical-phonological formants in musical communication,
and to underscore the potentially transitory aspects of the conventional
meanings attached to the signs that make up living systems of discourse.

Strategies for cultural critique that emerged in the last third of the
twentieth century located critical interest primarily in moments of rupture, or in structural relations of inversion or reversal. As I have suggested, these descend in many cases from the principles of structural linguistics and semiotics, and they must necessarily direct their focus

toward the original or intentional content of the constituent parts of cultural objects, with such content offering meaningful positions on critical-relational maps. Register, while it may be silently implicated in such analyses, is taken as a function of a "dead" language (or a multiplicity of dead languages), in which word values (or image values or sound values) and cultural content are fixed. Postmodern bricolage or pastiche is often read against such values, which are normally located on a vertical scale in standard evaluative systems. If register is primarily a vernacular shorthand, the deciphering of which proceeds from a shared cultural or linguistic understanding, then it must be considered at least as much, perhaps more, a feature of the act of reception as one of authorship, intention, or performance. By focusing on this fluid aspect of register, and by locating its field of operation within *standard* cultural discourse, we can largely avoid invoking the cumbersome bipolar signifiers that demark and deaden the meaningful or live-ly critique of mixed-register, pastiche, or middlebrow works and genres.[33]

Bipolarity has been a particularly dominant aspect of conversation and criticism regarding mass-market, mass-media productions; its constructions may be academic, journalistic, or anecdotal and may include, in addition to high versus low, the old music-appreciation standard art versus popular, along with new markers and their associated positions. Steven Feld's catalog adds, "'inside' versus 'outside,' 'elite' versus 'vernacular,' . . . 'progressive' versus 'mainstream,' and 'hegemonic' versus 'counterhegemonic.'"[34] Since standard language is in a process of constant transformation, locating all registers in the zone of common practice, or at least close enough to it so that intersections can be charted, permits readings that take into account the diachronic dimension of register formation, along with the potential for reregistrations, like those considered in chapter 2.[35]

THE PARTY OF THE FIRST PART

Film music—particularly for mass-market studio productions—is a mass-media discursive arena in which shorthand communication is key. Music for movies must communicate something to justify its eternally tenuous position in the eyes or ears of both the producers and consumers of film; it must accomplish this quickly, even instantaneously. In film, the range—subjective and objective—of communications is broad; mainstream filmic discourse is primarily novelistic, albeit abbreviated and telegraphic. With respect to the score, this leaves much of the burden of the act of musical communication to the audience, who must decipher the language of the composer. How, then, does music that either reproduces or imitates the sounds of the Western concert hall canon communicate to a noninitiated listener? First, I would emphasize that by drawing upon registered elements that were collected or deposited in the arsenal of vernacular listening over time, film music, and by extension all "cinematic" musics, are ultimately heard in the vernacular.[36] Few American filmgoers, for example, would be able extemporaneously to quote the text of an entire legal contract, but almost all recognize the registral connotations of the phrase "the party of the first part." Had that phrase not found its way into the register of "legalese" in common practice, the vaudevillian set piece enacted by Groucho and Chico Marx in *A Night at the Opera* as they argue over the percentages due the agent in an artist-representation contract would be neither funny nor brilliant.

Musical parameters that lend themselves to registration are those that are most easily transformed on the fly into visual images (i.e., contour and trajectory) or those most easily sensed as significant in a linguistic sense. If my own language here and above appears to teeter dangerously close to the brink of declaring, more naively than the author cited in my introduction, that music might constitute *a* language, this is hardly my intention. We might better say that language, in its components, is very much like music. Some acts of nonanalytical or nonstructural hearing, though certainly not all, correlate with the interpretative acts of linguistic hearing.[37] Timbre and attack are the primary acoustical correlates to the phonemes of the poetician. Dynamics and isolated pitch values need no translation; they work the same way in speech as in music, at least for the cinematic listener.[38] Often, it seems, even a "noncompetent" listener can hear unfamiliar music in precisely the way it was intended, or in the same way—with respect to its communicative, if not its technical, elements—as a trained musician.[39] Reuven Tsur suggests that there is a physiological basis for the human capacity literally to feel the textural or volumic implications of timbre.[40] Tsur's emphasis on the phonological dimension of poetics, and his notion that musical tone color is experientially correlative with aspects of the letter sounds of spoken texts, suggests that these factors may participate in the registration of phonological and acoustical content in the reception of music with or without text.

These are precisely the elements that, by their immediacy of perception and their potential applicability to a range of registers simultaneously, point to a weakness in the assignment of "meaning" to the traditional film score. Timbre or tone color, for example, is such a powerful signal in acoustical communication that it may outweigh other musical nuances and lead not to misreadings but, more to the point, to false registrations based on recalled experience. An example is provided by Frank Nugent's review in the *New York Times* (February 17, 1940) of Lewis Milestone's film version of Steinbeck's *Of Mice and Men*. Nugent mentions Aaron Copland's score just once: "We noted but one flaw in Mr. Milestone's direction: his refusal to hush the off-screen musicians when Candy's old dog was being taken outside to be shot. A metronome, anything, would have been better than modified 'Hearts and Flowers.'" Both Copland and his friend Paul Bowles responded in the next issue of *Modern Music*.[41] Enumerating the "three important ways in which music helps a picture" (intensifying emotional impact of a scene, continuity, and "neutral" backgrounding of dialogue), Copland characterized the first as "no more than the Hearts and Flowers tradition, but still, perfectly legitimate."[42] Bowles was more direct. Suggesting that the critic "objected to the idea of using music at all to foster emotion for such a patently sentimental episode," he pointed out that "it is quite obvious, even to the layman, if he listens to Copland's score, that there is not the slightest musical connection between the blatancy of that old tune and the sensitive music for this scene."[43]

Nugent's review applauds the authenticity of Steinbeck's vision and its realization in the film: "As in 'The Grapes of Wrath,'" he wrote, "we have the feeling of seeing another third, or thirtieth, of the nation, not merely a troupe of play-actors living in a world of make-believe." He perhaps felt that the particularly harsh realism of this particular scene, rather than its sentimental flavor, was, in an already heavily realist diegetic environment, overly mitigated by the presence of a music cue. In any case, what he *heard* was the legato string subject, as well as the egregiously filmic sound engineering applied to the dynamic level of the background score (instantaneous and unnatural fades) to accommodate the few, halting moments of conversation in the bunkhouse. To make matters worse, the scene ends with an equally conventional "expressive" increase in dynamic level, a musicodramaturgical stinger employed once there is no chance of its interfering with dialogue or other diegetic sounds. What he missed, though, was not only the unusual intervallic and rhythmic features of the string material but, more important, the affective ("poignant," according to Bowles) interruptions by the solo, monotone flute.

Copland's flute marks, like an involuntary intake of breath (neither a sentimental sob nor a melodramatic gasp), the temporal units of that excruciating delay during which we, breathless listeners, await the horrid

but inevitable sound of the diegetic gunshot. It aurally embodies in a temporally collapsed span the inexpressible and immeasurable aloneness of
Candy who, as soon as the dog has been led outside, finds himself for the
first time without the companion through whom his own existence was
defined and signified. Yet the sound of a flute, for the nonspecialist listener, is simply not, as an aural object, textural or tactile enough to com-
pensate for the connotations of the conventional orchestral "presence"
and its registral implications, which are those not literally of "Hearts and
Flowers" but of the lyric, symphonic expression, grounded in late
nineteenth-century concert repertoire, of high, and most often romantic,
emotional utterance.

CLASSIC'S REGISTERS

Within the nested matrices of vernacular registers, then, in which some
are more inclusive, and some more specialized, we might position a
register bearing the label "classic." "Classic register," while it may include any number of items literally borrowed from concert hall musics,
is not a *Bartlett's* for musicians. Classic register, as I conceive of it, is
specifically a region *within* normative cultural discourse. I will employ
this construction without attempting to provide it with a simple
definition—for it is too broad and in too constant a state of live flux to
admit fixing. In vernacular contexts, the terms or objects of the classic
collection will tend to be registrated as such on the basis of mnemosynic or metonymic apprehension, or both. This is to say that a
speaker (I am pressing the linguistic model here; I mean, of course, a
song or a film sound track) drawing upon this register will trigger a
recognition response that tends to proceed from the listener's experience (memory) on one hand, or from an intuition that beyond what has
been heard, its phenomenal portion, lies a greater whole, with
"greater" intended in the dimensional rather than the evaluative sense.
Among those "musicolinguistic" possibilities embraced by the classic
register is a special register, that of "the classic" per se. In mass-market
musical discourse, "the classic," or "the register of the classic," possesses a special flavor; it is often associated with the invocation of death
and the dead on the one hand, and reanimation on the other.[44] By this
I refer not merely to a condition of pastness, of being dead, but to the
state of being monumentally dead, or in a *monumental* state of being
dead, emphasizing monumentality to call attention to the architectural
implications of invoking the register. Such architectures may be meta-

phorical (i.e., formal) or actual (i.e., plastic or sculptural). Monumentality in this sense plays a part in some of the territory I shall explore later in this book.

Emphasizing the notion of a register of the classic, as well as the generality of the classic register, frees both from any enforced participation in the Western cultural tradition of the classic, which typically has stressed the deathless aspects of the aesthetic objects so identified, although this by no means excludes that tradition from inclusion in vernacular communication structures. Some of the classics of the twentieth century have been elevated, to whatever ends, by critical or, more often, commercial forces that have sought to locate them outside the streams of societal or artistic flux ("classic rock," "a classic car"). That positioning is crucial. The classic in any case will be framed and discrete. It may be borrowed, with its outsidedness intact, for vernacular use. An analogy from standard language would be the situation in which, locked in a face-to-face stalemate with a pedestrian walking from the direction in which one is heading, an English speaker recites, "*Après vous Alphonse.*" Items situated in "the classic register" of the vernacular, by contrast, have been integrated and absorbed, as in the construction ". . . *du jour,*" which will be encountered in a range of written or spoken circumstances, invoking any number of intersecting vernacular registers, including "turnpike diner-menu register," "authentic bistro chalkboard register," or "academic in-joke register," each of which contains special, register-specific features, while sharing this linguistic formula in common as part of the register collection.

As I have suggested, the typical implications of wearing the brand of the classic are those of longevity, incorruptibility, or universal value. Sainte-Beuve held such a view of Virgil in the middle of the nineteenth century, in an essay whose title is cited at the beginning of many subsequent discussions of the question *("Qu'est-ce qu'un classique?"),* in which forum he opened the term up for the first time (although Dante had hinted at something similar centuries before in his *De vulgari eloquentia*), allowing that the word "classic" might embrace literature of any epoch, if so judged by men who have reached the stage of "maturity": "It is at this age that the word *classic* takes on its true meaning and defines itself for every man of taste by the irresistible predilection of his choice . . . whether it be Horace or someone very different, whatever favorite author gives us back our own thoughts ripened and enriched, we shall then seek from one of those fine old spirits an unfailing intercourse, a friendship that never declines and cannot fail us."[45] T. S. Eliot's 1944 essay, bearing the same title, begins with Sainte-Beuve (and Frank Kermode's *The Classic* with both).[46]

Sainte-Beuve's flexibility, as well as his having chosen a metaphor related to alimentary consumption (specifically, the improvement and appreciation over time of fine potables like brandy and cognac), would eventually permit the word to encompass such pantry items as Classic Coke and Johnson's Saran Wrap Classic, those "fine old spirits" singled out among mounds of competitors and multiflavored or multicolored variations. The latter, interestingly, was abandoned shortly after its introduction at the turn of the millennium when—with technologically linked Y2K anxieties momentarily stilled—the product was renamed Saran Wrap Original, in keeping with its traditional position as a techno-utopian alternative to its nonclinging ancestor, Reynolds's Cut-Rite Wax Paper. Wax paper, most appropriately, turned to the classic tag in the early years of the twenty-first century in a different sense, one we encounter in other popular media constructions. Recognizing that its target audience fit Sainte-Beuve's circumscription of the category as one appropriate to the realm of the "mature," the new design played upon the product's capacity to trigger in that group a sentimental, perhaps morbidly Romantic reminiscence of generations past and passed, emblazoning their new box with the nonsensical heading "A Kitchen Classic for Over 75 Years." Thus, it seems wax paper was classic from birth, a view Eliot held regarding his own poetry.

Sainte-Beuve maintained, as did Eliot, the position of Virgil at the top of the heap. And so, when Eliot describes the classic as possessing elements of commonality, comprehensiveness, maturity, and universality, he draws that model from his understanding of Virgil, simultaneously laying the groundwork for reception of his own work.[47] Regardless of the name Eliot gave it, Virgil's "common language" is elite, not vernacular. The classic, that is, the "absolute" (in contradistinction to the "relative") classic, as Eliot put it, remains, as I have suggested of items in the register of the classic, outside the practice of vernacular language and experience. One may aspire to it, and one may invoke it, but one may not act upon it. Eliot's imperialist absolutism on this issue was no doubt the object of Groucho Marx's jibe in a letter of 1963, written during a period of correspondence between the two men that eventually led to dinner at Eliot's home in London in 1964. Groucho, who was somewhat familiar with literary criticism as well as literature, wrote: "I have just finished my latest opus, 'Memoirs of a Mangy Lover.' Most of it is autobiographical and very little of it is fiction. *I doubt whether it will live through the ages,* but if you are in a sexy mood the night you read it, it may stimulate you."[48]

Yet Eliot did acknowledge the possibility for intuitive reception of something outside the realm of one's personal experience, something bearing aesthetic weight and absolute value, although the direct communicative power he had in mind was not necessarily that attached to *the* classic. It does approach, however, my concept of the metonymic apprehension of the classic register in musical products by listeners who are not necessarily familiar with its referential aspects through personal experience. Addressing the British-Norwegian Institute in 1943, Eliot described having found "sometimes that a piece of poetry, which I could not translate, containing many words unfamiliar to me, and sentences which I could not construe, conveyed something immediate and vivid, which was unique, different from anything in English—something which I could not put into words and yet felt that I understood. And on learning that language better I found that this impression was not an illusion, not something which I had imagined to be in the poetry, but something that was really there."[49] Eliot's experience of unfamiliar poetry (Norwegian or otherwise) was, it would seem, a response to register as it resides in phonological, rather than significative, content.

There is no need to rehearse the extent to which fragments of concert hall and opera house music—"real" classics—constituted much of the treasury of film-music vocabulary in the days of the kinothek pastiche scores attached to silent movies in the first decades of the twentieth century.[50] But less has been said, from a theoretical perspective, regarding the reception end of the multimedia equation in these "primitive" citation-patchwork scores. A tentative step, however naive by today's standards, was undertaken in an extraordinary two-volume *Allgemeines Handbuch der Film-Musik,* produced in 1927 by Hans Erdmann, with the assistance of the film-music composer Giuseppe Becce, which offered students of the subject a theoretical framework for the enterprise that emphasized the hermeneutic elements of film-music practice.[51] Erdmann engaged with the film-music problem head on, insisting that the increasing demand for film music on a daily basis required the establishment of a hermeneutic foundation for the practice. He achieved this by way of a registral edifice of monumental proportion, rather in the spirit of Friedrich Ludwig's musicological monster the *Repertorium.*[52]

Erdmann's first volume is devoted to his wide-ranging and learned general essay, and to instructions for use of the second, *Thematisches Skalenregister,* a library of musical examples surrounded by elaborate systematic notes and symbols. Presented in regular type with Friedrich Ludwigian small-font glosses running concurrently along the outer edges of every page, the approach—users are told—is based on a sort of "musikalische 'Hermeneutik'" that puts into words the principles of musical expression fundamental to the practice of film accompaniment. The *musikwissenschaftliches* format of the book notwithstanding (indeed, the copy I consulted contained an autograph inscription from the author to Otto Kinkeldey), Erdmann warned that his was not a precise or complete "scientific system."[53] Clearly, though, it was an attempt to systematize for the sake of professional pedagogy the communicative act between composer and audience, based on a hermeneutic system of register variation. Musical excerpts in the second volume are taxonomically classified according to subjective qualities (passionate, melancholy, religious, etc.), dramaturgical function (music for dramatic climaxes, low points, etc.), musical elements (mainly expressive markings familiar to most keyboard players, such as *lyrisch, ruhig, ruhig bewegt,* etc.), and markers not unlike those of early linguistic register theory (e.g., music appropriate to a religious setting, a scene of royalty, etc.); most of these elements are indicated by a graphical system of letters and geometric shapes, the tome's most charming, and bizarre, feature.

Critiques of Erdmann's creative model (essentially a scholastic summa of existing practice) were, and continue to be, inspired by the tenuous status of two canons, one of which was undergoing a process of Osiris-like dismemberment and another that was being generated from the parts of the first. The classics, so named, had been subjected to the hatchet jobs of theater musician-recomposers, while the film score was aspiring to a location among the genre fields constituting the classic domain. Louis Silvers, in the kinothek-style score for *The Jazz Singer* plays with Chaikovsky in the classic register, operating within the standard hermeneutic system of 1920s movie music, and commits, the critics would maintain, an aesthetic violation. Max Steiner's invocation of Chaikovsky in the register of the classic in *Now, Voyager* (the citation is introduced by an on-screen orchestra in a concert hall) was something else: an inset within Steiner's continuous, "original" film score. At either end of this musical Osiris myth lay the integrated body of the canonized art work, framed by the doctrines of high-art genre, most especially those linked to creative, rather than receptive, authority.[54]

THE MUSICAL HUMANISM OF MICHAEL JACKSON

When in the second century Aulus Gellius propounded the notion of the classic, his selective approach was no less slapdash than that of the modern executives hawking "classic" paper products. The classic was from its inception a grab-bag miscellany of items whose value was (perhaps) literary and linked to specific linguistic turns but also judged by its value to move a reader in an ethical direction, in other words toward a life well lived. Ethical resonance in the apprehension of the classic will be considered further in another chapter. For now I would emphasize that the classic's origins lie in the notion of citational pastiche, precisely the aspect of quotation "outside the hall" or—recalling Julian Johnson's implicit criteria—outside the grammatical, formal aspects of the systematic whole of a work. Gellius's classic possessed the features that now move musical and social critics to target especially vernacular music's aesthetic insignificance, inauthenticity, and commodified or culturally retrogressive posturing. As Leofranc Holford-Strevens put it, "who are we to throw stones" at Gellius or his enterprise? Gellius gathered bits of material he deemed appropriate for his *Noctes Atticae (Attic Nights)*, a haute-bourgeois florilegium that was—in the words of another scholar— a "Reader's Digest of antiquity."[55] Gellius's *classicus* was sewn together from fragments meant to inspire, through an abundance of worthy *sententiae* (the quotational stuff that came to enliven much of later medieval rhetoric), new confrontations with the past and the sound of its messages, sometimes flavored by atypical words or syntactical forms. Gellius did more than define a new sense of the word; he laid the foundation for what would be known as "humanistic" study, and he understood, before Sainte-Beuve or Eliot, that exposure to the right fragments might render a citizen "better." If the classic has been defined in no small way by hinting at some inherently ethical quality, the question will arise at each invocation: whose classic and whose ethics?

Contemplation of the eternal scope of the issue is enriched by remarks recorded in Julie Shaw's now notorious 2003 documentary *Living with Michael Jackson*. In pointing out the amusements of his Neverland estate to interviewer Martin Bashir, Jackson described the music he programs for his carousel, explaining that he preferred the ride to be accompanied by "classical music" and citing by way of exempla several familiar standards, including "Childhood," "Smile," and, in his words, "'People' by Barbra Streisand." As an act of hearing classic implications this might seem even more inscrutable than Eliot's appreciation of Norwegian poetry. All of

Jackson's selections are movie theme songs and thus drawn from the twentieth-century's main repository of classic bits, but they are hardly of the kind patched together in early kinothek practice.

The first, his own song from *Free Willy 2,* suggests an aesthetic position close to Eliot's in a creative sense: the notion that a classic aesthetics might be defined by the practice of one's own work. "Smile" is the song David Raksin elaborated upon Charles Chaplin's tune for *Modern Times,* and Jule Styne's "People" is from *Funny Girl.* In the concert hall of the conventional musical museum, the classical style—that of Mozart, Haydn, and Beethoven—was, according to Charles Rosen, marked especially by a group integrity, and so Jackson's elevation of the repertoire for his merry-go-round lies perhaps not so far away from E. T. A. Hoffmann's evaluation of the conventional triumvirate (even if he called Mozart and Haydn "romantics") cited by Rosen in the opening paragraphs of *The Classical Style.*[56] For Jackson's classical repertoire, that integrity, it seems, lies first in the sermonistic or aphoristic elements of a song, particularly as expressed in its lyrics (in terms medieval rhetoric would borrow from Gellius's notion of the classic, its moral *sententiae*). In this, his position is fundamentally Gellian: he hears song as an expression of an ethical position, however rudimentary. Moreover, all three of his merry-go-round tunes share a certain acoustical profile in their standard realizations. Jackson's remarks suggest that being classical is largely a matter of reception, but even here his "classical" music shares certain aural markers of register we have encountered before.

A close analysis of "Childhood" and "People" reveals that Jackson has reiterated many significant gestures (melodic, harmonic, lyric) in his own song for *Free Willy 2,* not the least of which is the high registral placement—in the ordinary musical sense of "register"—of the word "people." But more significant for register in the linguistic sense is the acoustical environment produced by Jackson's choice of vocal timbre (as close to Streisand as any male singer is likely to get) and the arrangement that relies on symphonic strings supplemented by a concertizing piano, eschewing big concerto-style chords (a register marker found throughout hybrid vernacular musics), however, in favor of a lyrical expressiveness characteristic of concerto slow movements. Streisand's performances of "People" were also usually embedded in a wash of strings, and the original Broadway score in fact intertwines with that a discreetly concertizing piano. If Jackson's own performance of "Smile" (included with his "Childhood") on the *HIStory* album is less conventionally classical in its acoustical wash, this is mitigated by the fact that the song's register was securely established long before, when it was appropriated by Liberace as a signature tune.

When Liberace performed the Chaplin number on his television show in 1956, his classical-style pianistic virtuosity was supplemented by the sudden appearance halfway through the song of a strolling violinist (his brother, George), thus filling out, in abbreviated form, the timbral environment expected in "concerto register." The song's lyrics, of course, are aphoristic and didactic; a classical utterance that Gellius himself might have recognized. Visually, Liberace's performance provides a remarkable snapshot of media's claim to transmission of the classic and its related registers, marking the song as a literal classic while underscoring the freshness of its mediated presentation: the pianist's trademark candelabra is fitted with safe and efficient electric bulbs while behind him rests the blank, expectant screen of a television upon which sits an Emmy award, testifying to Liberace's rank as a new kind of laureate. "Smile" was sufficiently registrated through decades of media awareness and televisual reiteration that Jackson could take liberties with his arrangement without fear of sacrificing the song's access to the expressive register of the classic.

RAPPING UP REGISTER

Embedded musical entities may signal the classic register regardless of their original intention or context (i.e., they needn't be literally classical in the conventional sense) so long as the material operates within or projects the communicative parameters of the register, as witnessed by Jackson's position and by Frank Nugent's "Romantic" hearing of Copland mentioned earlier. Since the advent of digital sampling, subversion and shuffling of registral expectations has metamorphosed into one of the fundamental creative options in vernacular music genres. Choice of material and its expressive registers can be manipulated with increasing flexibility and acoustical effectiveness.

Some examples drawn from a particular corner of the "new" museum of late twentieth-century historical reception—the field of rap and hip-hop sampling—reveal two strands of "rapport-response" situations such registrations may initiate.[57] For rap musicians, sampling involves a relationship with the source that is intentionally "meaningful" and often respectful: most practitioners of digital sampling are serious "collectors." In any case, the spectrum of potential relationships between original and borrowed sound is extensive.[58] From a wide range of possibilities, two help to illuminate an important distinction between the classic register, *generaliter dictum* (i.e., in the general sense as medieval word theory might have it) and the register of the classic, *specialiter dictum* (in the specific sense). "What's My Name," by DMX, and "Gimme Some More," by Busta Rhymes, both successful products that circulated just prior to the turn of the twenty-first century, commence with introductory samples that "classicize" the sound environment and emphasize their own remoteness from the sound world of the main rap.

This is mainly accomplished through the presentation of registrated timbres. In fact, for "noncompetent" listeners (those who do not "recall" the original source of the sample), acoustical color provides the only registral marker. In each case the introductory sample will reappear as part of the number's long-term form. They follow dramatically different functional paths, though, each revealing the operational dynamics of a new cultural product, in which the nature of the sample's registration as intended and presumably received prefigures the shape and reception of the rap as a whole. Neither sample originated as what might be termed, in general parlance, a piece of classical music, but the first considered here, Richard Addinsell's *Warsaw Concerto,* is a sort of liminal classic residing since its introduction in the mid-1940s on the borderline between the popular imagination and "authentic" concert hall consumption. The second is borrowed from one of the most lauded Hollywood film scores, Bernard Herrmann's music for Alfred Hitchcock's *Psycho.*

In rap, the opening sample often serves a psychological and aesthetic goal parallel to that of title music in the cinema. Sometimes characterized as "mythic" or "spectacular" (i.e., linked to the historical tradition of "spectacle"), film title music does (or at least did, prior to the subversion of opening title conventions in the last decades of the twentieth century) provide the accommodative imaginary space in which a viewer-auditor recalculates the relationship between "real" sensory input and the interior envisioning required for successful reception of a filmic environment.[59] Raps are, for the most part, intentionally cinematic.[60] Indeed, a cinematic aspect, in which music promotes novelistic constructions in the listening imagination through reference to multiple registers, became the norm for popular music forms beginning in the second half of the 1960s, prior to which time pop and rock songs ordinarily projected a single register and a unitary affect. Introductory samples can invoke the same registers as film scores; some are even, as I've indicated, borrowed from the film-music repertory. While the mainly original portion of the work—the rap and its accompaniment—is, musically speaking, mainly about movement and beat, the listener's body is held at bay in the kind of sample-intro construction encountered in these works, akin to the straitjacket of a concert hall seat, until the drum-kick and the bass slip in.[61]

In this, rap rehearses an experience that might have been savored by European listeners to fifteenth-century polyphonic structures in which the familiar, grounded, and grounding material of a tenor cantus firmus was characteristically withheld from the listener's ear for an indefinite period of two-voice "free" compositional fantasy, during which expectations and envisionings were the only psychological and aesthetic possibilities. Among these anticipations is that of the moment when the tenor drops, to lend a palpable weight to the soundscape. Prior to the bass drop in rap, the sample is essentially "background" music with no foreground (remember Manilow's introductory performance of the Chopin prelude). Yet it possesses the impetus, the potential, to lay a foundation for and set in motion the envisioned diegetic world against which the text and rhythms of the rap will be projected. Such samples can, at this point, only be registered in an absolute context, outside the range of the still unencountered work "itself."

"What's My Name" confronts the listener immediately with an excised bit of piano music implicitly framed by aural quotation marks. In popular media of the mid- to late twentieth century, the manifestation of nonintegrated piano sound was often associated with the registers of the heroic or the demonic. Its first utterance here is disfigured by an editing "cut" that effects a double amputation. DMX's source, the first bars of the *Warsaw Concerto,* was firmly fixed in the register of the heroic at the time of its composition, but especially because of its decontextualized status in the song and in the realm of rap effects in general it takes on the darker aspects of a "severed hand," a horror-genre topos encountered more than once in this book.[62]

The piano's timbre seems unnaturally sharp and dry against the background of the dark, smooth outlines of the bass sounds when they enter, further emphasizing its resonance in a dimension outside that of the real or the mundane.[63] One of the most enduring fetishes shared by artistic and anthropological cultural practice, the severed-hand topos was fully inscribed in aesthetic literary products by the nineteenth century (e.g., in works of E. T. A. Hoffmann and Gérard de Nerval) and in Hollywood by the mid-1930s (e.g., *Mad Love* and later *The Beast with Five Fingers*).[64] DMX's musical soundscapes, according to *Rolling Stone* magazine, were imbued with precisely such an atmosphere. They are described, through a chain of timbral-sensory analogies, as "*skeletal*, drawing on the *brittle* sounds of dance-hall reggae, the pulse of old-school hip-hop and *ominous* keyboard swells that resemble horror-movie scores."[65] DMX's musical poetics here are clear: by selecting from the register of the classic an item that bears resonances in its own and other repertoires that are both oratorical and annunciatory (i.e., the standard big-chord piano concerto opening), he capitalizes upon its high expressive value potential. This stands in marked difference to other forms of "theosophical" rap that represent death in homelier or more sentimental fashion.[66]

In "What's My Name" a kind of prophesying is set in motion by the piano's voice, conjured, whether from the grave or the realm of the divine, and authorized by precisely the aspect of "classic" technique, in this case the pianistic "power chord" that, two generations before, allowed the film *Dangerous Moonlight* to sell the short, one-movement work as both an act of musical heroism and a special aesthetic object: a concerto. The "imaginary" power of the chords, in registering Addinsell's work and others like it, cannot be underestimated, and I explore this power further in chapter 7. One would be hard-pressed to distinguish the melodic substance of the opening material of Addinsell's composition and the main theme, composed by Bronislau Kaper for Victor Saville's film *Green Dolphin Street* (1947), were it not for the invocation of concerto register as understood by mainstream consumers in the piano chord flourish of the former.[67] No surprise that Kaper would turn to that model for Saville's adventure. Kaper was a pianist himself, born in Warsaw. Conservatory-trained in Berlin, he left Nazi Germany for Paris in the early 1930s. Al Tinney's performance of "Green Dolphin Street," a melody that has become a jazz standard, exploits the aural confusion between the two works. Tinney begins the song not with the "Green Dolphin Street" tune but with the first section of the Addinsell.[68]

As the rap proceeds, the opening chord (repeated three times by the piano soloist in Addinsell's original) is here thrice reiterated jerkily and artificially through cuts and short loops, producing a new rhythm that will serve as the background for the rapper's recitation of his name, "D-M-X," and the title command/interrogative "What's—My—Name." Architecturally the piano sounds serve as columnar supports for the monumental temple of dark prophecy on which DMX raps, while within this implicit mise-en-scène Addinsell's chord remains stiff and unnatural, a reanimated Frankenstein monster, a sonic Karloff analogue. DMX plays the role of the charismatic, an agent of divine revelation, supported by the sample. Addinsell's aesthetic (abstractly "beautiful") chord, prior to the launching of DMX's rap, is a "monster" in its literal and original connotation: a divine, if terrifying, omen that points the way. The scriptural elements of the album on which the song appears, . . . *And Then There Was X*, elaborate upon scriptural originary mythography, starting with the title paraphrase of Genesis. The cover art features a giant papyrus fragment in the form of the letter X (the *chi* of Christomythic orthography). Upon it is inscribed a fragmentary text that includes references to the Nativity ("a star") and the Crucifixion ("if it takes for me to suffer for my brother"), along with a prayer of thanksgiving. Self-sacrifice (for the sake of one's "brethren"), in its aspects of spirituality and violent carnality, is central to the thematic content of the collection, as it was—perhaps coincidentally—to Addinsell's inspiration for the wartime "concerto," and DMX positions himself as both priest and prophet with respect to its message; he is an interpreter and a vessel. His acoustical assembling of effects that conjure sensations of terror, sacrifice, and ethical positioning is representative, however—whatever DMX's personal faith—of the musical melodramatist. The track projects to listeners a sort of ethical drama that, as Peter Brooks has argued, is fundamental to the melodramatic gestural mode of authors operating outside a social environment grounded in common acceptance of a single "true Sacred."[69]

René Girard has stressed the fundamental importance of sanctioned acts of sacrifice, in antiquity, in Old Testament narrative, and in more recent third-world cultures, as a balance to societal violence: "In a universe where the slightest dispute can lead to disaster—just as a slight cut can prove fatal to a hemophiliac—the rites of sacrifice serve to polarize the community's aggressive impulses and redirect them toward victims that may be actual or figurative, animate or inanimate, but that are always incapable of propagating further violence."[70] The form taken by the "Dead Sea Scrolls" *chi* of the cover art on the DMX recording sends the consumer a signal of this thematic element by applying to the visual register of the scriptural a violent inflection. Resembling crossed daggers that take the shape of scissors or shears, the image of the *chi* mitigates the born-again aspects of the rapper's poetry (in particular, the prayer recited on track 16 of the CD), and maintains the mythography of urban chaos, real or imagined, that has been consistently re-created in rap music imagery. Similarly Addinsell's borrowed chord is momentarily reregistered in the domain of the urban rap vernacular at one point in the song where it backgrounds the phrase "suck my dick," while its registration is ambiguous, or double, in the phrase "I shed blood," evoking both the street and the deity.

Envoiced on the three competing tiers of textual identity: the subjective ("What's *My* Name" and "DMX"), the universal or divine ("*What's My Name*"), and the profane, the concerto chord offers a musical field on which the rapper may experience several positions of power or, alternatively, the potential for a terrifying loss of subjective self in something greater. Such awareness—of being in the presence of some force (the intuitive apprehension by metonym I mentioned previously)—is simultaneously projected onto those listeners who buy into DMX's cinematic construct.[71] In the end, though, despite the elements of co-optation expressed in DMX's scissors-job on the concerto flourish, the rap, in fact, straightforwardly rehearses a number of (pace Feld) "hegemonic" features of classic Western music, including those of contrafact, refrain, and concerto ritornello structure. Addinsell, in his home register of the classic, is not "acted upon" but recited; the recitation is tweaked by no procedures other than abridgement and wholesale transposition (the sample appears at two pitch levels separated by a tritone), which is to say, by no process at all. It remains, true to the register of "the classic," a pure quotation operating within a melodramatic expressive mode not far removed from the literal citational accompaniments of pre-sound cinema.

In Busta Rhymes's highly successful "Gimme Some More," those elements that tend to impose form in the classic sense are subsumed under the "counterhegemonic" impulse of Rhymes's rap, which is percussive and antivocal; the rap's contrary position is not with respect to high art or concert practice, however, but to the conventional practices of pop and mainstream vocality.[72] The song is distinguished especially by its quite effective illusionary projection of an unconstrained (infinite) cyclic looping of the digital sample, by the restrained and potent use of cuts, and, especially important, by the wholesale incorporation of the sample into the rhythmic lifeblood of the number. In drawing on Bernard Herrmann's classic score for *Psycho*, Rhymes chooses not the ubiquitous shower-scene music but eight measures first heard in the film's title sequence, music that within the body of the film was eventually associated with Marion Crane's anxious preoccupation with having stolen some money from her employer. (I discuss Herrmann's own references here to the music of Stravinsky and Antheil in chapter 6.) The musical cue backgrounded the visual of Marion's famous (seemingly endless) drive along the highway that brought her to Norman Bates's hostelry and to the end of her road. As in DMX's rap, there is a narrative appropriateness to the selection. The sample amplifies, or at least complies with, the meaning of the song, another instance of the fundamental cinematicism of the genre. In an interview, Rhymes indicated that the song is about "what people want more of," a terse summary of Hitchcock's dramaturgical set-up for Marion's demise in the first part of *Psycho*.[73] But with respect to the real dynamics of the musical environment, there is more.

Rhymes and DMX shared a similar understanding of or at least adherence to a practice based in the implicit cinematicism of sampling from past classic referents. In terms of musical language (as a language system), both samples are, in Julian Johnson's terms, "undeveloped." The interesting distinction between them rests in the register invoked not by the originals (they are both classics) but by each rapper's musical discourse, Rhymes calling on the classic register—rich with expressive implication—and DMX on the register of the classic, that is, the literal mode. Each register determines a particular approach to pre-existent material. From the standpoint of the reimaginative workings within each, DMX's Addinsell, a decapitated architectural artifact, remained uninvolved in the process of DMX's song. Conversely, Busta Rhymes truly co-opts Herrmann's music, nurturing the cyclic germ inherent in but never realized in the original, owing to the constraints of the visual to which it was attached. Along the way, but not primarily, they perhaps specifically highlight the ambiguous status of repetition as a "cultural force" in African-American musics, as outlined by Tricia Rose.[74]

In "Gimme Some More" Herrmann's theme is not just reanimated but reincarnated and set loose. More a musical Osiris than a Frankenstein monster, the amputated original here has been "re-membered."[75] Most extraordinary about the metamorphosis is that Herrmann's music already seemed, in the original, a perfect complement to Marion's state of mind, wherein the music resided.[76] As a body, she was—as Hitchcock indicated by those memorable windshield shots with Marion dead center—*frozen* in place, *constricted* by the car, *tight* with fear, *motionless;* her forward trajectory was effected only by the agency of the machine in which she was imprisoned. This aspect of Hitchcock's exploration of a novelistic topos of time and space that Bakhtin called the "road" chronotope—in this case the physical and mental distance she traverses prior to her arrival at the Bates Motel—was effectively enhanced by the music, whose repetition patterns are long-range.[77] She, in her mind, moves backwards, as her gaze is directed consistently toward the rear-view mirror, and she recalls—as realized within the mise-en-bande—echoes of past conversations.[78] In "Gimme Some More" that backwardness of gaze is reproduced through Rhymes's recitation-remembrance of childhood that precedes the bass entry. Creating a cross-registration, it is a nostalgia element inflecting the classic register elements of the sample away from the neurotic model of Herrmann and Hitchcock and more toward earlier cinematic Romanticism. Elements of register that allow for this substitution include the legato orchestral strings, the classically balanced 4 + 4 phrase structure, and the "artfully" chromatic line.

Musical cyclicity is released from the grinding wheels of the mind, its rhythmic force paramount and directed at the body and the body's natural rhythms: an extraordinary sense of short-range ebb and flow emerges from Herrmann's music. Rhymes accomplishes this by framing and relocating the sample's pinched strings in the environment of rich bass and the percussive attacks of his vocal phonemes. Still a classic register object, to be sure, Marion's music now operates in a new field of somatic, rather than interpretative, reception. To borrow from Bakhtin's analytical terms of novelistic authorial discourse, I might say that both rappers are "in the *zone.*" Whatever register that phrase occupies in late-twentieth-century vernaculars, for Bakhtin it is the area of authorial negotiation between present audience and past stylistic and generic referents. DMX, however, also plays within the sample's *field,* Bakhtin's frame of form and genre, on which the original "concerto" had been deployed.[79] Busta Rhymes's Hitchcock sample retains only its psychic energies, redeployed on an entirely new field: that of the vibe of movement.[80]

As I suggested with respect to Steiner's Puccini, the classic register of Herrmann's procedures borrowed from Stravinsky and Antheil is now classic cinematic, but the quotation in "Gimme Some More" is mined for its inherent expressive potential in a linguistic sense, invoking an effectively psychographic environment involving recollection and motion, indeed the very circularity Herrmann had cultivated decades earlier. In *Psycho* the score's participation in its multimedia environment was rendered insistently graphic by the jagged visuals of Bass's title sequence, and later psychographic by the image of Marion to which the music is eventually attached. Marion's road curves back on itself and drills into her psyche, stifled by the music. Busta Rhymes reinterprets not just the music but the music-visual mediation, maintaining its core aspect of self-reflection by invoking in his opening words an autobiographical narrative stance, that is, a cinematic voice-over. Throughout, the sample's value is its sheer expressionistic capacity, accessible without any interpretive strategy or intellection of meaning.

Sampling, and the consumption of music containing samples, raises issues related to familiarity and the cultural capital that pertains to acculturated objects in different social sectors. That is, we are handicapped—it might be maintained—in judging some sorts of referential reception if we can't be certain of the consumer's familiarity with the original. The narrative aspects of Marion's musical anxiety will be lost on the "noncompetent" listener, for example, as would any of the cinema-history details of the Addinsell I described above. In these cases, I have emphasized the presence of other nonspecific, acoustic markers of register; this, in fact, is one of the virtues of invoking the concept. But how to approach the measurement of "competence" with respect to a broad and only generally defined audience base? Pierre Bourdieu's statistical, sociological approach to class habitus and its construction seems to offer one way in.[81] In the end, though, it leaves little room for accidents and thus little for history.

MAINSTREAMING

"Let Joyce be unconfined," punned Groucho Marx in a 1960 letter to Leonard Lyons of the *New York Post*. Lyons had written the comedian to inform him that Thornton Wilder had identified a Marx Brothers "Napoleon" sketch, in which the trio wore three-cornered hats, as the source for Joyce's "three lipoleum Coyne Grouching down in the living detch" in *Finnegan's Wake*.[82] Groucho and his brother Marxes were accustomed to parodistic discourse on literature: they participated at times in Alexander Woolcott's Algonquin circle in New York, as well as in his Neshobe Island Club in Vermont, and had maintained throughout their careers social and epistolary contacts with many of the now classic literati and theater artists that intersected with Manhattan and Hollywood society.[83] Groucho's response satirizes a particular variety of literary criticism that his sometime correspondent T. S. Eliot had described in "The Frontiers of Criticism," where he linked *Finnegan's Wake* with John Livingston Lowe's *The Road to Xanadu*, a monograph in which Lowe "ferreted out all the books which Coleridge had read . . . and from which he had borrowed images or phrases to be found in *Kubla Khan* and *The Ancient Mariner*."[84] Groucho answered Lyons's and Wilder's speculation:

> Tracing this item down from the "Wake" could be a life project and I question whether I'm up to it. Is it possible that Joyce at one time was in the U.S.A. and saw "I'll Say She Is!"? Or did a New York policeman, on his way back to Ireland to see his dear old Mother Machree, encounter Joyce in some peat bog and patiently explain to him that, at the Casino Theater at 39th and Broadway, there were three young Jewish fellows running around the stage shouting to an indifferent world that they were all Napoleon?

Marx in this text may reveal to us the fundamental silliness of our critical-historical enterprise; but, simultaneously, his presence within the field of such heady conversations reminds us of the elusive and often un-expected paths that reception of individual canonical works, in this case *Finnegan's Wake,* may follow.

In the daunting statistical analysis provided in Bourdieu's study of class-based taste distinctions, Stravinsky's *Firebird* appears among the collections associated with middle-class lower-income groups of high cultural aspiration such as teachers.[85] He is, in fact, especially sensitive to the subversion of "art" toward pedagogical service through main-stream presentations.[86] The mainstream, however, derives its flow from more than a few tributaries. In a famous tale, director George Cukor re-lated that Katherine Hepburn, Olivia de Havilland, and Bette Davis were being treated to Stravinsky's drawing-room performance of *Firebird* at the same time Groucho's cigar was accidentally setting fire to the dining room tablecloth during a "witty" evening in the composer's honor at Cukor's home.[87] Apocryphal or no, and whatever the personal aspira-tions behind Cukor's big dinner parties, *Firebird* is lodged in this tale within the conversational register of a group well outside that charac-terized by well-intentioned schoolmarmishness, a group whose musical experience—one that would be passed along to generations of audiences—was configured by the odd assortment of creative individu-als who contributed to the accidents of Hollywood history (which in-clude many of the most important accidents of twentieth-century music history).

While the incorporation of concert music into film scores has ac-counted for a certain mode of circulation in vernacular culture at large, original film scoring has played a significant role in widening the range of expressive options for vernacular music. David Raksin, a favorite among Schoenberg's students, surely expanded normative musical regis-ters via his wildly popular score for Otto Preminger's 1944 classic *Laura.* Its most famous scene, the build-up to Laura's on-screen appear-ance, is accompanied by a psychodramatic barrage of background music in the composer's early style. Over the top in its expressionism (not merely in the melodramatic but in the music-historical sense as well), clear as a bell in its Schoenberg references, Raksin's own music for this portion of the film lodged something new in the standard registral col-lections of audience expectations through the accident of the film's spe-cial success (a success linked in no small part to Raksin's famous open-ing theme music, which drew upon an entirely different musical register associated with the harmonic conventions of jazz). This new sound was intense, mesmerizing, even breath-taking attached to an otherwise normative multimedia context. Neither a safe space for petit-bourgeois escapism nor a pretentious collectible in an unused record library, Raksin's Schoenberg served as a node between existing registers, between those of "real" expressionism and of the familiar melodramatic expressiveness of older Romantic film scoring. As imitators filled that in-between space with more vernacular practice, some musical gestures were reregistrated, while extremes found their way to the middle, leaving room for other musical gambits to enter registrated, and thus intelligible, expressive collections.

No question that Hollywood—especially as it formed a haven for émigré composers—represented its own odd "culture elite," and that the "consumption" of Stravinsky's music, accidental or otherwise, at a dinner party thrown by a culture maven like Cukor is only one short step removed from the concert hall or museum gallery or its domestic imitation. But the special blend of artistic and commercial motivations, of authenticity and pretension, that characterizes media-centric socioeconomic aggregations invites material that is not necessarily bland, "lite," or pointedly pedagogical to enter the stream: cultural efflux that otherwise would never find its way into our vernaculars.

CHAPTER 2

Making Overtures

Historians of Hollywood film, and of film music, have had a hard time keeping their paws off *Laura* (to paraphrase one of the acerbic remarks aimed by the journalist and aesthete Waldo Lydecker at the earnest, hunky police detective Mark McPherson in the film scored by David Raksin). I will address here only its opening moments, quoting Kathryn Kalinak's characterization of the gesture by which the aural dimensions of *Laura* are first inscribed. In a critique that contrasted the title music with the image it accompanies, one that Kalinak saw as ideologically gendered, she wrote: "The score opens with a typical technique for attracting the spectator's attention and signaling the nature of the images which follow: string *glissandi* and a cymbal crash. (This is similar to the musical gesture that opens *Captain Blood*.) This musical flourish activates certain expectations about the narrative content—that it is heroic, romantic, epic—which rest uneasily with the ideological message of the portrait."[1]

Kalinak's description of the music's effect constitutes one of the commonplaces in film-music criticism and underlines one of its weaknesses. I am thinking in particular of the way in which critics of film music, in their pursuit of meaning, move breezily through the slippery territories of style and genre. There is no reason to fault Kalinak especially; her book represents an early and important contribution to the study of mainstream film scoring. But a literary historian might point out that "heroic," "romantic," and "epic" cover an awful lot of ground, whether one has style in mind, or genre (as Bakhtin, for one, understood especially well).[2] The musical gesture recalls Korngoldian swashbucklers like *Captain Blood,* yes. But what does that imply, generically, about the music? Those scores embodied heroic adventure, identifying and encoding the genre of their host films, but now with their principal features recycled in John Williams's *Star Wars* music of 1977, Korngoldianism may lie closer to the field of epic.[3]

Furthermore, there is another representational "gap" in the title's presentation, which includes, after all, not just music and image but the titles in their graphic sense. The glissando and crash prepare the appearance of the title *Laura* in very large print, with the original novel's author appended; what we read is not "Laura" but "Laura by Vera Caspary." In its writerly aspects—projected by terminal balls and serifs associated with typeset and typewritten texts—the graphic register of the title does not follow romantic cinematic convention. The normal curvilinear and cursive forms associated with Hollywood's romantic register appear only later, when the credits begin to chart *Laura*'s specifically filmic components (first the screenplay credit, and then the long list devoted to the music, editing, costume, and art departments). The design gambit foreshadows the first scene of the film in which we (along with the film's detective hero) will encounter Waldo Lydecker typing in his bath. His occupation as a newspaper and radio critic is, in fact, crucial to the drama. And so, among the weighty if not epic elements of the opening multimedia construct is a representation of the film as one that draws upon registers of literariness, or at least the mass-market literariness within which the novel was situated. Caspary's book was more overtly sexual (including uncensored innuendos of Waldo's homosexuality) than the film. As literature it reads like a gentler cousin to the sexually charged low-register crime novels of the French *Série noire,* and indeed *Laura* sits on most French journalistic lists of the later 1940s as an example of what French film criticism had begun to label Hollywood noir.[4] In its role as an acoustic chiffon draped across the silkily formal yet undeniably come-hither image of her décolletage, especially in this literary context, Laura's signature tune must hint at something else as well. Jazz renditions of "Laura" in its pop-song incarnation (fitted with lyrics by Johnny Mercer and put into circulation in response to audience demand shortly after the film's release) torque the music in that direction, providing a telling link between the spectacular and sexual implications of the gesture's potential registers. In his early Verve recording of "Laura," Charlie Parker launched his saxophone solo with a subtle and highly suggestive glissando.

And so perhaps what we should be talking about here is not the music's role in the fixing of any sort of genre, or in the transmission of a single meaning by way of a musical sign, but the identification of its position within a complex of intersecting registers all of which belong to the language of vernacular music. Since all are normative possibilities, which one (or two or three) among them might take priority in a listener's apprehension of the moment will depend not on group initiation or class habitus with respect to the musical gesture but rather on individual experience. A mystery fan, a romance fan, a newspaper editor, and a nonreader might perceive the opening differently, as might women compared with men. The reminiscences or intuitions prompted by visual cues like the portrait could remind the mystery fan of her rich parents' living room or a cheesy magazine advertisement. Even mood and circumstances (e.g., those of daters versus loners) play a role in the deciphering of communications. What unites these potentially disparate acts of interpretive reception is the music's insistence on its expressive potential, generated by its acoustical formants.

ROCKETS

Laura's is not a single grand gesture; it is actually bipartite, consisting of the string glissando followed by its point of arrival, the cymbal crash on the downbeat. Is the crash any different, in its musical parameters, from those featured in Max Steiner's title music for *King Kong* (1933)? As one of several signals of that film's register, or of some of its registers, the strings' surging scalar ascent to the cymbal crash on the downbeat will be heard differently here. This difference results from the gesture's being delayed until a few measures in, after the three-note "Kong" motive. The resonant gong crash accompanying the first downbeat of that motive is register-specific: it immediately locates the music to follow within the frame of the exotic. An intersection of the exotic with the horrific is at the same time registered by the monster's short chromatic signature, featuring the low brass. A critical approach through register helps to distinguish between categories, and to spotlight the variations between apparently similar objects (in this case, musical gesture), without which criticism or analysis cannot realistically proceed. Register is really what Kalinak has in mind when she rightly indicates that the opening move "activates certain expectations." Outside the sphere of regular spoken discourse the expectations excited by gesture are often linked both to genre and to style, and while all three concepts are related, they are not quite the same. To locate the characteristic glissando within the communicative system that permeates the classic Hollywood film score calls for some historical anchor points.

For the familiar gesture that launches the score, one that might well be characterized as the "Hollywood rocket" (a coinage that would emphasize by music-historical analogy its gestural familiarity within a particular category of musical production), awareness of the diachronic aspect of register formation illuminates its use and function as a marker. Admittedly not all writers who have adopted the term register when addressing elements of artistic (i.e., artificial) as opposed to natural language recognize a significant difference between a register and a genre, or between a register and a style.[5] In this particular case, though, we are dealing with an item—a musical correlate to a word, phrase, or phoneme—that might appear, and has appeared, in a range of generic contexts, filmic and other, passing through multiple registers and registral variations over time. All of them, because of the acoustical content of the original unit and the strength of its original registration, are arguably subsumed under the broad heading of the "classic register" even if, as I have already suggested, others are relevant to its reception.

Most Americans of the twentieth century derived their film-music expectations from exposure to the works of Max Steiner and his contemporaries—among them Erich Wolfgang Korngold, Alfred Newman, and Franz Waxman—or their heirs who serve the contemporary mass media. Even in today's mediated environments, television's increasing flirtation with precious self-consciousness and film-school media procedures has had little impact upon the communicative strategies of its musical scores, which for the most part are discount (now usually digital) reiterations of old Hollywood practices. To suggest that such scoring conventions are tenacious would be an understatement. A familiar example is the compositional trope attached to sexually active or experienced women, as so often noted by film-music historians including Kalinak.[6] Is it an aspect of scoring style?

Stylistic gestures tend to advertise their age; they don't possess the longevity of a marker of register. An audience watching *A Summer Place* in 1959 was unlikely to register anything especially antiquarian in the moment when Max Steiner's music backgrounds a teenager's confession to her father of a virtual relationship with a young, handsome voyeur. The style of the music, including its salacious saxophone gliss (slipperier—more lubricated—than *Laura*'s "spectacular" rocket or even Charlie Parker's reregistration) was, if not exactly cutting edge, not significantly out of line with 1959 norms. More than a decade later, amid the orientalist posturing of Lalo Schifrin's score for *Enter the Dragon* (1973), the on-screen appearance of Han's sex bomb consort is spotlighted by the weak dialogue ("Oooo, would ya look at that? . . . A woman like that could teach you a lot") that triggers breathy undulations, less jazzy and more modernist than Steiner's, served up by an alto saxophone. Its sound has fantastically materialized within the musical background score that on either side of the musical intrusion consists of static pentatonicism and zitherish chinoiserie. A sore thumb in its immediate context, the gimmick will nevertheless come across as perfectly natural to film audiences, even those of a younger generation. Yet both share something historically with another, earlier Steinerism of markedly different style, through which he had inscribed in Hollywood's (and America's) ear this particular approach to the register of women's sexuality: a leitmotif attached to the prostitute Kate, the girlfriend of the title character Gypo, in his score for John Ford's 1935 classic *The Informer*.

Kate's leitmotif is Gershwinian, rather like a swingier version of the C♯-Minor Piano Prelude of 1926, a fairly modern model for a 1935 film. Scored for strings in its first presentation in the score, the jazzy gesture had still not collected the timbral, and more immediately identifiable, details—the saxophone- or "Summertime"-style mute trumpet—that would, along with the filmic elements of appearance, dress, and vocal timbre, come to characterize the femme fatale or streetwise woman in the conventional matrix of noir character types during the 1940s and 1950s.[7] These were already finding their way into normative vernacular register, however. The reiteration of Kate's motive later in the film is scored for saxophone rather than the flute Steiner originally intended there. Kalinak reported that the original manuscript of the score contains an attachment from the orchestrator Bernard Kaun, who suggests using the solo sax, because "it will make more sense."[8] The "woman of experience" music is not a convention of style; it is one of a number of related gestures that came to form a register of sexuality in the twentieth-century mass-mediated vernacular. That register's eventual acoustical components were not instantaneously fixed, at least for a Wagnerian like Steiner. Kate's music in her first appearance in *The Informer* is now insufficiently sexy, that is to say, it is too quaint, to get across a truly expressive message. (We can of course still comprehend the motive as a sort of emblem, even if we don't feel it as an expressive gesture in the way a listener of 1935 may have done.) For later twentieth-century audiences it was increasingly timbre, the shortest of shorthands, and not bluesy intervals or rhythms, that marked the register of sexuality, as evidenced by Schifrin's ability to conjure the sexual register through a melody that, if analyzed purely as a pitch series, is in fact rather high-toned and academic. A saxophone's registral associations via timbre carry more weight in this instance than contour or rhythm (see the discussion of Nugent's response to *The Grapes of Wrath* in chapter 1).

As in all vernacular registers, even these components will continue to be subject to transformation, a process that usually entails some form of reduction. Among the many contemporary vestiges of this particular practice, I would call attention to two multimedia genres that have tended not to invest heavily in nondiegetic scoring save for musical interjections at moments of dramatic weight: the television soap opera and Japanese anime.[9] On the daytime drama *All My Children,* for example, an erotic moment featured tycoon Adam Chandler seductively embracing the mature, powerful, and oft-married former sex kitten, Erica Kane. Registering not the woman in this case but the pure sexual content of the scene, the sound of a saxophone abruptly slipped in between the words of the dialogue (reflecting the timbre of Kenny G more than Jerry Mulligan). The brief musical interruption lasted no longer than the length of a single swooping glissando. It seems that the marker of this register may have shifted at last from timbre to pitch bending, now that the timbre has become hackneyed and, in light of the ubiquitousness of the jazz saxophone in media contexts throughout the second half of the century, less subject to this specific registration.

In a scoring move somewhat reminiscent in its more developed melody of Schifrin's old cue, but one in which many more individual notes provide excuses for the execution of sexy glissandi, Iku Suzuki's anime production *Fake* (2000) even transferred the pure eroticism of this truncated gesture across typical cinematic gender lines. Here again the utterances are related not to character but simply to the sexual content of a cinematic moment. *Fake* represents the *shonen-ai* genre of printed *manga* books and televisual anime, gently homoerotic but conventionally romantic in both narrative and cinematic senses (such products are in fact aimed primarily at pre-teen girls). In this case the reiterated glissandi permeating a brief musical cue acoustically elaborate the first kiss between the male protagonists, the New York City cops Dee and Ryo.

Idiosyncratic linguistic text forms, like cookbook language, provide vantage points for assessing the diachronic dimension of registers. They are comparable to such vernacular musical registers as that of the femme fatale. Text registers are more easily controlled and traced than those invoked in music that was not meant to be analyzed or even read, like film music, pop music, or any other category Julian Johnson might label "stupid." From the pages of real linguistic research, Charles Ferguson's synopsis of Christopher Culy's study of cookbook-recipe register provides a useful example of register formation over time:

> Several observers have noted that a striking feature of recipe language is the omission of definite object noun phrases, or—as Culy puts it—"zero anaphors as direct objects, for example in 'Beat [Ø] until stiff.'" Culy examined English-language cookbooks from the fifteenth century to the present and found that "the use of zeros . . . increased dramatically over time," especially in the period between 1830 and 1880. A speculative interpretation might be that the language of cookbook recipes was at first not very different from other written varieties of English, that it began to develop as the circulation of books increased, and that it took definitive form in the mid-nineteenth century with mass literacy and the popularity of cookbooks; such an interpretation would require of course a great deal of evidence to validate. Kittredge too notes the omission of definite articles in recipe language, a feature that characterizes many so-called simplified registers of English . . . French recipe language shares both of these English register features to some extent, but the incidence of the omissions is much lower, and the history of the register, to my knowledge, has not been studied.[10]

A similar transformation, I suggest, took place in the iterations of gestures of sexual innuendo as well as of the original Hollywood rocket, whose historical position in film practice might even point to its eventual blending of sexual implication with the marks of Kalinak's "romantic-epic-heroic." For musical items—even as their details are subject to metamorphosis while remaining potent within their original registers of expressive communication—may also be transferred from one register to another. In the 1940s the sound of the theremin in film scoring was associated exclusively with the register of psychopathology.[11] After Bernard Herrmann's 1951 score for Robert Wise's *The Day the Earth Stood Still*, it became the shorthand marker for the science fiction genre. Pitch content delivered via the theremin is always nondiscrete: this is one of its peculiar charms. Today, with the theremin itself out of the picture, this single element of "weird" musical sound, especially when linked to a nonconventional source (electronic or pointedly ethnic, like an Asian or Andean flute), serves on its own as a musical phoneme related to registers of aberrant psychology (especially as linked to sociopaths and murderers) or to the supernatural.[12]

When the Hollywood rocket first appeared in a sound film it was as part of a quotation of the kinothek variety in *The Jazz Singer* (1927).

Touted as the first talkie, since the synchronization of sound and visual for the first time included not just music but dialogue (or monologue), much of the film operates within the parameters of the old silents. Among more than eighty musical cues in his pastiche-style background score, music director Louis Silvers included the "love theme" from Chaikovsky's *Romeo and Juliet* Fantasy Overture. Though symphonic, this music, for audiences of the 1920s, was not really representative of specifically high-brow symphonic musical style or culture, of "art music," or even of the classic-lite consumption patterns of the *culture moyenne,* but rather a marker of a specific "musicolinguistic register, one that followed a path of transference from the original work to the film sound track. Like the nonprofessional chef faced with the construction "beat until stiff" who is unlikely to be thrown off by the linguistic zero, most American filmgoers, including the Al Jolson fans who flocked to *The Jazz Singer,* were unlikely to have much familiarity with nineteenth-century musical repertoire in its own context as a sort of specialist musical practice. But Chaikovsky was already common currency in the period: he occupied a place in the filmic imagination through multiple reincarnations as a staple of kinothek movie accompaniments. Chaikovsky's *Romeo and Juliet* theme (mm. 388–91 of the standard version) appears as item no. 404 in Erdmann's *Thematisches Skalenregister,* embraced by the systematic folds (moving from the highest to the lowest level of his dramaturgical pyramid struc-ture) of: *dramatische Expression/ernst; ruhig bewegt/Höhepunkt-Appassionato/leidenschaftliche Erregung.*[13] For the theater musician seeking something to accompany a climax of passion (as opposed to other sorts of dramatic climax), Erdmann proceeds to deeper levels of expres-sive nuance in his hermeneutics. He suggests that the theme registers not passion but specifically passionate *excitement.*

Which register(s) did Chaikovsky call upon in *Romeo and Juliet?* In an engaging and masterly exploration of musical invocations of an "iconi-cally erotic" orientalism, Richard Taruskin has located the "big love theme" at the Venn intersection of the musical registers (this is my, not his, terminology) of the sensual and the oriental, in a discursive region as-sociated with the Russian *nega* (amorous lassitude).[14] But *nega,* as Taruskin explains, resides particularly in the "undulating," "chromatic passes" embedded—too deeply, I would say, for the noninitiated listener to pick out—in the theme's pitch structure and in the timbre of the En-glish horn that introduces it the first time around (not the statement that film scorers usually invoked). Erdmann and his contemporaries seized on the more accessible register of "highest emotion," one appropriate to the dramaturgical *Höhepunkt* and particularly inflected toward the passionate. The register is marked by crescendo, unambiguous melodic erection, and eighth-note triplets whose nervous energy is finally released in the vocalic half notes set to a frictional semitone when the theme, per se, arrives; in short, the kind of structure that exhibits what Susan McClary, following Carl Dahlhaus, has termed "lyric urgency."[15] If we hear the string glissando in *Laura* as a relative of this gesture, as it most assuredly was, then the message of the glissando in *The Jazz Singer* begins to illuminate the difference that I am getting at between a vaguely genre-indicative sign and the shorthand communication of an expressive register marker. It also points to the incremental process of shorthanding that such markers may undergo over time, as did the elements of English-language Cookbookian.[16]

Only once in *The Jazz Singer* does the love theme sound as a complete statement. Following his success on the road, Jack Robin (Jakie's stage name) returns to New York to appear on Broadway. Visiting the home from which he had fled, Jack entertains his mother in an extended sequence of audio-visual synchronization using the new Vitaphone process. He sings "Blue Skies," accompanying himself on the piano, and provides his bewildered mother with a lecture-demonstration of the musical elements of "jazziness." When his father, the cantor, appears at the door, the sound track (which has been perceptually located within the zone of the diegesis) slips with an audible thunk back into its standard location, farther back in the field of perception, a position it had occupied during those portions of the film that are "silent" (i.e., in which dialogue was provided by intertitles). The fallback to silent-movie aural space is triggered by the last sound-synchronized, so-called diegetic event: Cantor Rabinowitz appears in the doorway (a visual recall of his earlier discovery of young Jakie singing in a saloon). Communicated by a series of facial gestures shot in close-up, he processes what he is seeing and hearing and finally shouts "Stop!" He seems to address not just Jack but Jack's sell-out counterparts in Jewish Hollywood, along with their technology that will soon put an end to the theatrical conventions alive in the film and its silent predecessors.[17] Afterwards, with the sound relocated outside the frame, the audience, too, slips back into a mode of reception in which music was heard dramaturgically, that is, the kinothek pastiche model. When Chaikovsky returns in this context, the love theme gains its climax not in a moment of passionate excitement in the romantic sense but in the heated argument between Jack and the cantor.[18]

Any sweet sensuality residing in the Romeo theme here will be lost on anyone who isn't a Russian or a devoted fan of Russianicity. The rapport response is triggered by the upward trajectory of the rocket and its corresponding increase in volume, the broadening of the discursive pace at the point of arrival, and the triplet accompaniment figure. The last, in its insistent throb, which for the cantor and his son is located in the neck or temples rather than elsewhere, seems to match the inflamed rhetoric (provided by the intertitles) and finger-pointing (provided by the visual) of Jack's diatribe against his father for his refusal to acknowledge that all song, from *Kol nidre* to "Toot, toot, tootsie," is a reflection of the voice of God. It also must be heard as envoicing some high-intensity name-calling ("You . . . You jazz singer!"). Whatever Chaikovsky's meaning, his register is still perceived instantaneously, as in any common-tongue register, to be that of "extreme high-emotion utterance." If one insists on an intellected meaning, as do most writers on film music, one runs the risk of misdirection and false registration, since how could *Romeo and Juliet* mean anything other than love? Some, remembering their schoolroom Shakespeare, might further position it in the region of "generational conflict:" a love diverted toward the particular elements of the movie's scenario of *parental* love, a love thrown off track by the generation gap.

But these readings are red herrings. Kalinak was wrong in characterizing the love theme as a representation of Jack's feelings for his parents, and Alan Williams works from a misremembering of the scene when he writes that "Jackie's [*sic*] feeling for his mother . . . is evoked on the sound track by a full-blast rendition of the love theme from Tchaikovsky's *Romeo and Juliet*."[19] In his analysis he emphasizes the "ultra-sentimental" aspects of the presentation, invoking the term *melodrama* rather loosely and in the manner of an epithet. On the basis of this same apparent weakness, a trait it inherited from the story by Sampson Raphaelson that inspired the screenplay, professional journalists were already criticizing *The Jazz Singer* upon its release. While as drama neither *The Jazz Singer* nor Raphaelson's story "Day of Atonement" push the envelope of convention very far, the film's genre features and the precise nature of Silvers's scoring gambits have gone largely unremarked.

CANTUS INTERRUPTUS

Like Jakie/Jack and the real Jolson, Lou Silvers was caught between competing musical identities, and he appears to have approached his position as a musical Jew in Hollywood with seriousness. The relationship of Jewish theater and Jewish music to sentimental modes of expression is rich and complex, and I will consider it (and Silvers's score) again in the next chapter. Silvers went on after the film to become head of the music department at Fox and in the late thirties was central to mounting the first performance (with members of the Fox orchestra) of Schoenberg's highly unconventional *Kol nidre;* the evidence for his involvement is revealed by a belated thank-you note (in the end, a "please return the parts and score to me" note) from the composer.[20] The conventional *Kol nidre* is, of course, one of the musical signatures of *The Jazz Singer* and the centerpiece of its dramatic conflict.

Silvers's treatment of the Chaikovsky is revealing on several levels. When Jack confronts his father to the accompaniment of the love theme, we have arrived at the moment of highest emotion in the drama (there are other climaxes to come, but they belong more to the realm of dramaturgical pathos). Jack's diatribe, presented in intertitles, is an argument for the universality of music, for music's implication in whatever form it takes within a world governed by a system of ethics. His exaggerated acting gestures combined with the "full-blast" music might appear operatic, with words projected on the screen almost like modern supertitles. But this is not opera. It is pure melodrama: melodrama as genre, not as antiaesthetic epithet. In the absence of any diegetic noise, Silvers's Chaikovsky does not merely render some form of musicodramatic "emotional" expression. Not only the dramaturgical climax but also melodrama's particular modes of acoustical excess are rendered here—silently. The sound of Chaikovsky's music is, in fact, a substitute for the *fait feu,* the foot-stomping gesture that Peter Brooks has remarked upon as one among the catalog (perhaps the registers) of what he characterized as the "expressionistic" gestures of staged melodrama.[21] Even though Jolson is not shown in a full body shot in this scene, the trajectory of his body's movements and his hand gestures unambiguously reveal the actor's engagement with this sort of expressionistic convention, especially in light of the moment's particular significance.[22]

Once invested with the markers of melodrama as genre, we can hear Chaikovsky's music, in all of its dynamic excess, in the same light in which Silvers probably intended it, wherein the excess of melodrama is linked to its recognition and exposure of essential social and ethical conflicts.[23] Indeed, in the performance on the sound track there is a noticeable silence interposed between the end of the ascending surge and the explosive statement of the theme, in which we might hear the same melodramatic, pregnant moment attached to characters in the melodramatic contexts associated with Henry James and the ethical dilemmas of his characters that Brooks explores in his study. Calling upon one of the author's characteristic formulas attached to moments that prepare for the exposure of ethical positions through dialogue, the acoustical gap in the sound track between the surge and the melody might be taken as the inaudible sound of Jack "hanging fire."

With this in mind the other appearance of the love theme (much ridiculed by modern film-music listeners) makes sense as part of a musicodramatic whole. The eleventh music cue, falling in the first portion of the film (which depicts Jakie's childhood), presented all of the preliminary material of the Chaikovsky leading up to the surge, but the arrival of the love theme was diverted into a musical deflation composed by Silvers. On screen, to the undulating preparation for the big tune, Cantor Rabinowitz brandishes his belt. He drags Jakie into the bedroom for a beating while his frantic mother tugs and pleads, demonstrating what acting theory will term the "histrionic code" that survived in cinema until the introduction of panchromatic film rendered the human image too natural to support the code's reliance upon excessive artifice and it was replaced by the new "verisimilar" style.[24] (Indeed, it was likely her training in that mode and its inherent excess of gesture that rendered Eugenie Besseler, playing the mother, so clearly uncomfortable during the naturalistic synchronized-audio scene with Jack at the piano.)

In this early sequence we witness and we *hear* the heart of melodrama: the ethical dilemma that lays the groundwork for Jack's eventual *fait feu* when he returns as an adult to register his ethical position. It is, as required, a moment of injustice involving the characteristic struggle between blind institutions of power (the empty conventions of the patriarchal synagogue and the bickering of the kibbitzers) and those who might eventually transform ethical insight into social change. Unjust, since Jakie is being punished for having performed in a saloon the music that he loves. In addition to providing insight into Silvers's method of constructing the patchwork score as melodrama, we also begin to sense how a classical music reference, by its location in a group-defined "universal" tier of expression, may function as an ethical talisman.[25]

Young Jakie's position as a social outsider within his own ghetto community in these early scenes is underscored by a small detail of costuming: his American-style urban garb is ornamented with round pins. In the 1920s and 1930s these were usually acquired as premiums associated with food products, that is, American mass-produced food products (like

breakfast cereal) and often associated with radio programming of a sort
that had taken hold in a significant way in the years just prior to the film's
production. Jakie's assimilation, then, extends beyond music and beyond
his miming of black minstrelsy in his youthful dance moves observed in
the saloon by Moisha Yudelson, the "man of influence in the business
and religious affairs of the ghetto." Indeed, that the synagogue in the
early phase of the film stands in melodramatic opposition to a socially
equitable community is clear when Yudelson races back to the cantor to
inform on Jakie. Yudelson's arm is held vertically, and he waves his hand,
mimicking not the moves he has witnessed in Jakie's performance of
"raggy-time music" (including an interesting prototype for the Michael
Jackson moon walk) but rather one of the characteristic pictorial representations of the dancing Jim Crow.[26] At the other end of the melodrama
comes the reverse assimilation, privileged by the author's (perhaps rudimentary) social perspective: Jack sings *Kol nidre*, employing his characteristic expressionistic gestural style (associated with Jolson's Broadway
performances), and his Jewish mother makes her way to a theater to hear
him sing "Mammy" in blackface.

To return to the question of genre and register as these may be encoded or revealed, respectively, by the Hollywood rocket or
Chaikovskian surge, it should be reiterated that there is nothing of the
"romantic" or of the "epic" in the images that accompany Chaikovsky's
Romeo and Juliet theme or its fragments in *The Jazz Singer,* where it appears at moments of verbal and physical confrontation between
Jakie/Jack and the cantor. Silvers's first surgical move on the theme was
prescient, and perhaps originary, for eventually there would be nothing
left of Romeo but his musical erection that, once abstracted, might serve
as an equal-opportunity gesture attached to a range of emotions or even
to the expressive gestures of women. Except in those cases of direct citation in the register of "the classic," this unit could serve as a more general communicative signal, making its way through other registers of vernacular musical discourse with no specific implications of the original
affective profile.

As Chaikovsky's theme continued to resonate in the sound film after
The Jazz Singer, it revealed a significant element of register formation
and the potential flexibility of registered items to participate usefully and
expressively in a pluralistic vernacular. As I suggested earlier, the extent
to which such items have been made available to common-language users
in vernacular contexts may, depending on their potential expressive
range, result in reregistrations, and some items may in fact function sig-

nificantly in multiple registers. For example, Yiddish words like *meshuggeneh* (crazy) and *tsuris* (trouble, woe) were originally confined to the linguistic register of "urban immigrant Yiddish" (using register in its most global linguistic sense, where it is indistinguishable from a "language" belonging to one sector of a diglossic group).[27] Both words eventually found their way into an expanding register of "familiar Yiddish expressions" interposed in normative English conversation. But *meshuggeneh*, whose nuances are descriptive whether used as a nominative or a modifier, does not possess quite the generally expressive communicative value of *tsuris*, which doesn't just name or describe something. To say it ("I've got such *tsuris*" or "Don't give me *tsuris*") is vocally to enact a state of being.

Now, whether declaimed with exaggerated borscht-belt inflection or not, many non-Jewish English speakers will draw this term not from a register of potential alien interpositions but from one of standard emotional nuance. Uttering *tsuris* in a casual conversation may now commonly and implicitly invoke the subjective content residing in the nonverbal cue of the burdened sigh, the roll of the head (which probably originated as an aping of the original word and its speakers), without either having to be performed explicitly. Cognitive poeticians like Tsur or Roman Jakobson might locate some of the expressive potential of the word in its "dark" or "round" principal vowel, the "oo" sound, that the word *meshuggeneh* lacks.[28]

In Silvers's score, it is clear that while Chaikovsky's tune possessed translatable meanings as outlined above, its register connotations for cinema came to reside principally in the surge to climax, a flexibly expressive gesture that throughout the so-called Golden Age usually exhibited another element, one of structural functionality, particularly in the extent to which it was drawn upon for opening gambits. These were located not only at the beginnings of films but also at transition points within. That the cinematic power of the gesture was deemed especially "communicative" is clear: Silvers's trick of musical truncation in the first Chaikovsky passage of *The Jazz Singer* wouldn't have "worked" if he hadn't been able to count on his listeners' absorbing the message of imminent climax. Erdmann, who was putting together the *Handbuch* at just about that same time, makes the message even clearer. While Chaikovsky (no. 404) was able to express *leidenschaftliche Liebe* (passionate love), the item above it in the *Skalenregister* (no. 403), a made-up classic-style theme taken from a kinothek of dramatic musical gestures composed by Domenico Savino, says it even better. Identified as *Liebesleidenschaft* (note the difference in emphasis), this little phrase provides two rockets in the space of three measures, each time traversing the dynamic range from *f* to *ff*. [29]

CASTLE SPACE

I have argued that in making sense of *Laura*'s opening as multimedia we must look beyond the visual impact of the portrait to the implications of the superimposed titles, and that these lead elsewhere than to the genres represented on film in *Captain Blood, The Sea Hawk,* and *The Charge of the Light Brigade. Laura*'s apartment—the container for the "mise-en-shot"—is so crucial to the film that follows, however, that it too calls for some consideration. The music's register is received through the filter of the entire collection of visual cues, all of which mitigate the grander (classic timbre) aspects of the orchestral surge but not exactly in the way Kalinak suggested. Gaston Bachelard suggested that we learn to imagine the spaces we can't inhabit ourselves through reading: "George Sand said that people could be classified according to whether they aspired to live in a cottage or in a palace. But the question is more complex than that. When we live in a manor house we dream of a cottage, and when we live in a cottage we dream of a palace. Better still, we all have our cottage moments and our palace moments. . . . And when reading has given us countless inhabited places, we know how to let the dialectics of cottage and manor sound inside us."[30]

Filmgoers learn to inhabit and reenvision such spaces by watching as well as listening. Laura's living room, shown in the title visual, will in fact turn out to be a sort of psychic trap for the characters, as rendered especially vividly in the brilliantly scored sequence of Mark's "silent dialogue" with Laura's spectral presence just prior to her appearance on screen. The tenuousness of the apartment's conceptual space leading up to her materialization and its sense of claustrophobia (closets, drawers, scents, chiaroscuro lighting) may intersect with other genre fields, notably those of the medieval dream vision and nineteenth-century reverie, but not those of the monumental. Such cinematic spaces as this unquestionably play some role in the way that the music attached to them might be heard. *Laura* is a special and familiar case, and its spectacular surge is a feature only of the titles; Raksin's theme famously recurs in a range of stylistic guises throughout the score, starting in each case on the downbeat that followed the rocket. We can borrow Laura's contradiction as a point of departure for considering the gesture and its grand implications in another structural context, one in which its discourse is still within the parameters of the classic Hollywood tradition but located within the frame of film time rather than at its edge.

Emotional topographies of palace and cottage lie at the heart of one of the most celebrated "women's films" of the early 1940s, *Now, Voyager*. The film and Max Steiner's score, including original and borrowed material, embody Bachelard's representation of the poetics of domestic spaces. Throughout *Now, Voyager,* Chaikovsky wanders through both spaces, diegetically and nondiegetically (even ambiguously, in fact, to the delight of film-music scholars). Steiner worked with a portion of the first movement of Chaikovsky's Symphony No. 6, the *Pathétique*. That material, including Chaikovsky's crescendo surge occupies a communicative space somewhere between that of *Laura*'s abstract graft in the titles and the "significant" citation of the composer's Romeo material in *The Jazz Singer*. A fragment, reiterated in several positions with respect to the screen space, and with no way to reach a satisfactory musical conclusion, Steiner's Chaikovsky in *Now, Voyager* defines the reductive and out-of-place that so irked Julian Johnson in his assessment of valueless music, particularly since the work—unlike *Romeo and Juliet* in most of its appropriations—is cinematically represented first as classical music per se, and then treated with what a committed highbrow will consider disrespect for its integrity. (In both E. M. Forster's *Maurice* and the Merchant-Ivory film version of the novel, Durham pumps out a movement of the *Pathétique* on the pianola, after which Maurice calls without success for an encore as Durham chastises, "A movement isn't like a separate piece—you can't repeat it.")

In *Now, Voyager* the symphony is featured in a four-scene sequence that adds up to a somewhat elaborate montage of conceptual multimedia spaces. In the first, Charlotte aka Camille (Davis), the spinster daughter of a wealthy and domineering mother, encounters at a cocktail party the married architect Jerry (Paul Henreid), with whom she had had a secret fling while on a cruise where she had adopted her romantic pseudonym. As an on-screen pianist performs Cole Porter's "Night and Day," they carry on a two-tiered conversation, one public, the other sotto voce. In the next scene the partygoers move on to a concert (the studio orchestra led by Steiner with a great deal of arm-flinging is presumably meant to be the Boston Symphony Orchestra, since the story is set in Boston), where she is seated between Jerry and her fiancé Elliot, an up-tight and well-bred doctor. After the concert, Charlotte/Camille returns home. She receives a phone call from Jerry, who tells her that he is leaving Boston immediately. She makes it to the train station in time for a grand farewell and another big Hollywood screen kiss. The fourth and final unit is set back in the house. Charlotte is in the small parlor with Elliot, whom she informs—after determining that he is insufficiently "Bohemian" for her new tastes—that she intends to break off the engagement. She is not, she tells him, "the marrying kind."

Chaikovsky's music, starting right at the bottom of the surge to the *fortissimo* statement of the first theme (measure 134 in the score), leaps into the aural field at the juncture between the first and second scene, its point of arrival accompanied by a big, fat close-up of the conductor. All this excess contributes to an intentionally bumpy transition from domestic to monumental architecture, from salon to concert hall. (The musical transition is not so bumpy; the Porter song was transposed to A Major, so that its cadence serves neatly as dominant to the opening of the Chaikovsky excerpt.) Our brightly lit crowd of Back-Bay salon revelers is transformed into a dimly illuminated congregation of respectful high-art consumers, with the pathetic and tortured Charlotte/Camille (Davis) planted in a seat between her two lovers (one a spiritual and sexual partner, the other a potential domestic mate). The "pathetic" aspect of the musical selection, though appropriate to the tone of the scene, is perhaps lost on most of the audience; Steiner regularly engaged in subtextual connections like this.[31] But that registral content has been supplied by Davis's facial gestures, which lend a particular expressive register back to the music. And so to comprehend the scene and its reception we must add to the registral potential of Chaikovsky that of Davis's gestural mode of expression.[32] At the scene's opening, her eyes are cast down and she holds Elliot's hand. Charlotte is resigned to her future and she has, at least in her love life, arrived at Erdmann's *Tiefpunkt/ Resignation;* she appears uninvolved in the music. Jerry begins to speak to her: Davis enacts a short intake of breath, the beginnings of a quivery smile, and her gaze flashes back and forth between Jerry's eyes and the orchestra, which is to say, Chaikovsky. Both of them, the architect of Charlotte's dreams and the architect of music, the audience is signaled, are the *real* thing.

When the director Irving Rapper aimed the camera at Davis in the concert hall, he was framing another bit of register information that audiences would learn during the war years and that would be encountered for some time after in a broad range of film products, regardless of genre. A vernacular register of the aesthetic sublime, unlikely though it may seem, seems to have found its way around that time into the filmic vernacular collection of registrated types. This item relies on multimedia presentation: unlike nondiegetic register markers (background music cues), its expressive value lies in an inflexible conjoining of on-screen music with a fixed image type. The trope usually involves a concert performance, with the camera focused on the transfixed, immobile face of a central character as s/he becomes lost in a sometimes sexually tinged "aesthetic moment."

A cinematic register of the sexed aesthetic sublime (still a subtype of the classic register) may intersect with others, for instance the cinematic registers of the fantastic, the purely sexual, and, in *Now, Voyager*, of both pathos and high emotion. Scenes of this type transmit a potent message to common-language audiences concerning the power of musical "art" and suggest that music can even project "ordinary people" into extraordinary moments of ennobling engagement.[33] Often, as a visual detail, the protagonist's eyes will water or a single tear will flow down her cheek, a sign that the experience has grown into some sort of confrontation with an ineffable presence—the essence of the sublime—the flavor of which will vary depending on the relationship (in the drama) between the participants engaged in this two-way on-screen musical communication. Examples are found in other "women's films" of the 1940s; these include Davis in *Deception*, where, having just committed a murder, she watches her cellist lover (Henreid again) on stage, and Joan Crawford watching "violinist" John Garfield in *Humoresque*.

That this form of cinematic sublime continued to operate as a trope of register in the later twentieth century is attested by Jean-Jacques Beinex's *Diva*, in which Frederic Andrei, playing a young postman, watches Wilhelmena Wiggins Fernandez sing Catalani's "Ebben, n'andro lontana" early in the film. Beinex, in this 1981 production, took care to let the camera linger over Andrei's perfectly formed aesthetic tear as it trickled down his cheek. Steven Spielberg's *Close Encounters of the Third Kind* includes, in its climactic Kodalyan "communication" scene, a moment in which the player of the electronic keyboard who has been attempting to send "pitched" messages to the alien ships is bombarded by a musical performance issuing from the mother ship. His stunned reaction and frozen gaze, eyeglasses notwithstanding, revisits the tradition of the "aesthetic moment" close-up, while the immeasurable volume and complexity of the music projects, as surely as did Mozart's Jupiter finale, a sense of the Kantian mathematical sublime; the alien musicians, too, are "beautiful monsters" of a particular kind.[34]

In the case of Chaikovsky's Sixth, the overwhelming aspects of the human confrontation with sublime "input" is musically registrated

through the double rockets in measures 134 and 138, the octave transposition of the theme from its original pitch level (and now *senza sordini*), and the extreme echo-fade of measures 155–60, whose invocation
of the *pianississississississimo* dynamic suggests just the sort of "unimaginable" ranges of aesthetic experience that mark the domain of the sublime.[35] All of this intersects with the principal diegetic register of pathos
(signaled by Davis's expression) and the principal musical register (within
common discourse, one of high emotion, or lyric urgency). Steiner allows
the whole passage (through the first half of measure 157, where the clarinet is interrupted by the ringing of Charlotte's telephone) to sound as a
continuous cue, but the scene change occurs during the transition to the
Adagio mosso, when Chaikovsky migrates from the diegetic field to the
background score.

Steiner's own music for the farewell scene at the train brings to climax
the dramatic Puccinian "love theme." Its contour reminiscent of "E lucevan le stelle" (note especially the way both melodies hang suspended
midway through their first utterance, then free themselves by a down-
ward leap), the *Tosca* model probably occurred to Steiner because of
Davis's now famous concluding line, to which he eventually affixed the
theme's grandiloquent peroration, "Don't let's ask for the moon . . . we
have the stars." This is, naturally, followed by closing shots of a star-
filled night sky. As the leitmotivic sign of the Camille-Jerry romance, this
material cycles throughout the nondiegetic score at times of climactic
high emotion.[36]

In the last scene in the four-unit sequence I have been describing,
Chaikovsky makes his way back to the acoustic space of on-screen hearing. Charlotte sits on a plush sofa in the cozy parlor of her Boston home,
next to the bland Elliot. They are listening to a reproduction of the "real"
symphony that issues, small and tinny, from the elaborate wooden box
in which the mechanical sound device is hidden, reflecting the fashion in
American domestic technology prior to the information age. Radios,
phonographs, and many early televisions were disguised as furniture,
hiding their odd functions from the moment they left the factory (now
the secret places in which we hide our machines—armoires and storage
"systems"—are custom built and we do the secreting ourselves).

Issuing from the box is the symphony's theme, but in its earlier, more
tentative form (measures 89 and following, *con sordini*). The message is
unambiguous, and accordingly Charlotte opts not for the stifling doctor
in the drawing room but for the unconventional affair. She was, it would
appear, a Frankfurt School sympathizer. Eisler's and Adorno's critique

of film music was still a few years off, but Steiner must have seen
Adorno's essay on the radio symphony published a year before the release of *Now, Voyager*.[37] Charlotte's two confrontations with source
music in the sequence of scenes under consideration reproduce via the
film sound track the principal arguments of Adorno's essay, in which he
compared symphonic live performance to radio broadcasts of the same
musical matter. Of particular interest to my argument concerning the
cinematic sublime, and conceptually linked to Bachelard's metaphor of
the mnemosynic spatial imagination, is Adorno's high-culture cathe-
dralism. Charlotte, while "at" the symphony, enters the music—as
Adorno would have explained it—as she would have a cathedral. Once
inside, she experiences "symphonic space." Radio sound "is no longer
'larger' than the individual . . . The 'surrounding' function of the music
also disappears." As *Now, Voyager* shows us, to the accompaniment of
the meager Chaikovsky reproduction, the work itself has become "nothing more than a piece of furniture."[38] Indeed, the director has taken care
to lay that message on with a trowel: the parlor scene opens with a peculiarly long close-up of the large, square, heavy, and lovely (as domestic furniture goes) wooden radio or phonograph cabinet, complete with
the requisite vase of flowers—marking Bachelard's "cottage space"—
resting upon its doilied top.

STAYIN' ALIVE

Eventually the nineteenth-century rocket would live an independent life
in vernacular musical media, sometimes acting grand or sexy (but not
necessarily either). Even when not attached to a film at all it remained
nevertheless primarily cinematic in its musicolinguistic aspects. Multiply
reincarnated, with or without discrete pitch values (i.e., as scales or glissandi), the surge found an especially happy home in the repertoire of
disco music, among the most cinematic of all registers in vernacular
music. Lighting effects in dance clubs, whether involving the disco ball
or strobes, specifically underscored the filmic aspects of participation in
the disco scene. Reflected light from the ball triggered associations with
the excessively choreographed romance fantasies of 1930s musicals, and
the strobe could make dancers view their own movements as if from
within the flickering screen space of a silent movie projection. As disco
reached its most theatrical and decadent phase, club space became associated with mise-en-scène: the elaborately staged coke-snorting moon at
the heart of Studio 54's staged version of life is emblematic. Visitors to

the same club were confronted in the entrance space by another reminder, a camera boom left over from the space's previous life in the service of television production.

Disco songs per se as well as other (especially later) disco-influenced
mixed-genre works are often launched with some form of rocket, which
might either be the first acoustic event or follow after an introduction
that establishes the beat, groove, or vibe. From the lighter side of the
repertoire, "The Hustle" is perhaps the classic example of the initiatory
scalar string ascent. An edgier manifestation is the synthesized ascending swoop at the opening of Freez's "I.O.U," and the arrangement of
Stephanie Mills's "Put Your Body In It" employs the unison string ascent
as a sort of romantic foil to the disco-funk register of the song: the ascending string scales in their first appearance lead into the most romantic part of the song's lyrics ("Don't be afraid now / I'm waiting just for
you") and thus bear the imprint of past cinematic registers. In cases
where the gesture consists of a synthesized and uninterrupted ascending
pitch bend it fulfills its expressive promise: Tsur's pure vocalic "uninterrupted streams of energy" lacking the "obstructive" features of conso-
nants, and by analogy, articulated pitches and attack points. Love Un-
limited Orchestra's "Love's Theme" (1973), tagged by Peter Shapiro "the
perfect disco record," opened with an elaborately ornamented ascent
through the strings (discreet pitches rather than a glissando, but no less
a take-off), while the synthesized rocket had already made an appearance
by the time of Sylvester's "You Make Me Feel (Mighty Real)," one instance of the intersection of the gesture with registers of the gay vernacular culture (compare also the elaborated rocket that forms the bridge
between the intro and first verse of Village People's "YMCA"). Shapiro's
discussion of "Love's Theme" and its introduction within the Fire Island
community prior to its mainstream commercial circulation points toward a likely pop-cinematic model for the song's particular orchestral
arrangement (including the prominent French horns, and the emphasis
on the high strings heard at the beginning): Percy Faith's deathless version of one of Max Steiner's cues for the oceanside drama of sexually
driven familial angst, A Summer Place (recorded and circulating in pop
as "Theme from a Summer Place").

If, in disco, the surge intersects with a sexually charged expressive discourse involving the pure vocalic, no rendering of this component of its
registral collection was likely more effective than "Don't Leave Me This
Way," a song that has been covered by many well-known artists over the
span of several decades. A 1975 hit for Harold Melvin and the Blue

Notes, Teddy Pendergrass's vocal was distinguished by a nuance that came to serve as the song's emblem, a pure vocalic *(aaahhhw)* glissando performed by the group in unison, leading into the refrain. It also looks back to Pendergrass's untexted presentation of the melody (on a nasal *mmm*) that had preceded the first statement of the lyrics, a ploy that locates the notion of vocalizing as the conceptual core of the song's expressive language. Considering the musicolinguistic units I have been exploring, the singer's ascending surge is particularly interesting from a structural perspective; a vestige of high-emotion romantic practice filtered through cinematicism, it gains its climax in an explosive iteration of the word "Baby," one of the low-register components (again, in the purely linguistic sense) of the musical vernacular. In 1977 Thelma Houston scored a hit with a more purely disco-style cover of the song. Not surprisingly, her approach to the song takes advantage of the vocalized surge, which clearly provided the trigger for the song's successful reception, by condensing the lyrics—eliminating one of the verses so as to arrive more quickly at the big moment. She also added another sound (a vocalization on *ah*) to the introduction, drawing further attention to the significance of the expressive voice in communicating the song's musical content.

In 1986 the Communards scored their biggest hit with a cover of "Don't Leave Me This Way." While disco may have been dead, elements of its characteristic registers and even full covers of disco songs continued to serve as expressive vehicles for gay musicians, like the Communards' Jimmy Somerville, and their fans. That intersection was in part supported by historical circumstances too complex for consideration in a musicological essay. What interests me especially about the expressive content of Somerville's cover of the song is the extent to which it displays an intelligent and effective manipulation of a registral element. Somerville, employing his trademark falsetto voice, extends the ascent to three times its original musical length in its last electrifying utterance. Unusually, he does not perform solo here and is joined in the number by Sarah Jane Morris. Play and even confusion between the two voices provides a rich field (too rich for my context here) for contemplation of the sexual and gender connotations of disco conventions.

If it were the only business of musicology to do so, each of these three interpretations of "Don't Leave Me This Way" might be dispensed with as examples of music's response to presumed audience tastes and group habitus. Houston's cover transformed the original into more conventional disco music. Somerville's reworking might slip comfortably into a sociocritical dress of gay camp, especially characteristic exaggerations of (disco-) diva posturing and performative style. But there are real, and really interesting, musical processes at work in each finished product and in the expressive gestures shared by this apparently trivial group of musical offerings.

In both its terseness and its power as an unambiguous genre code, the nineteenth-century erotic surge cut a wide swath across the landscape of twentieth-century cultural discourse, rather like such initiating code phrases as *l'autre* or *l'autre jour* of medieval French that I explore further in chapter 7. The evolution of the erotic surge into a cinematic fetish is perhaps best indicated by its availability to parodistic reinterpretation in cinematic contexts. Warner Brothers' *Merrie Melodies* cartoons explode onto the screen in bright colors, accompanied by the trademark ascending "sproing," which corresponds to the wind-band and calliope timbres of the series theme music just as film drama's Chaikovskian rockets corresponded to its musical register's essential symphonism.[39] These cartoons, especially those featuring Bugs Bunny or Daffy Duck (unlike their MGM competitors, the Tom and Jerry series), were replete with references to Hollywood conventions and personalities. The field on which the Warner animated short subjects were enacted was one that mirrored, in the literal sense of inversion, the standard studio product. Bugs's musical sproing may well be heard in this way, as a low-register parody of the characteristic "cinema register" linked to the original gesture.[40]

WHAT'S IN AN OVERTURE?

Title sequences and their associated typeface styles can be crucial markers of genre, register, dramatic content, and historical context. No one can misinterpret the archeological and monumental visual register of the chiseled *King Kong* with its inclined perspective, an incline of architectural magnitude that was to be set in parodistic motion decades later with the scrolling text at the opening of the original *Star Wars* episode. Over the last two decades of the twentieth century, the title—as such— was intentionally removed from its standard location at the beginning of films, usually replaced by a gradual unfolding of credits, often with multiple interruptions, projected against some aural background, typically diegetic, that might occupy the first five to ten minutes of a film.[41] An early, somewhat different example of the standard model's circumvention is the silent title that precedes Orson Welles's *Citizen Kane* (1941).

The first portion of Bernard Herrmann's score comes after the title. Accompanying Welles's extraordinary images of a neglected Xanadu at the moment of Kane's death projected in a quasi-archeological pastiche, this "prelude" serves the same function as title music (even though the mood and mind-set it engenders are quickly deflected by the high-volume newsreel episode that follows). It provides the zone of accommodation delayed by the uncomfortable image of a full-screen title *in vacuo* (looking, in its letter style, like a cross between a newspaper headline and a college letterman's sweater); uncomfortable because audiences had come to expect a cozy musical cushion between their world and that of the diegesis.[42] Far less common are those Hollywood productions in which on-screen text is linked with nondiegetic music prior to the appearance of the film title. Cases include *Gone With the Wind* (1939) and *2001: A Space Odyssey* (1968), which are particularly relevant for this study, as both manipulate audience perception through special registers of sight, sound, and temporality.

David Oliver Selznick's *Gone With the Wind* was advertised and reviewed not merely as "larger than life." Here was a film, it seemed, that, like the enormously popular (and, at 1,000-plus pages, simply enormous) novel by Margaret Mitchell that it fairly faithfully transferred to the screen, was too large to be contained by any standard frame. Everything about the film, and the conversations surrounding it, fed the impression that this thing was bursting at every seam, a beautiful monster too big for its cage. "THE MOST EAGERLY ANTICIPATED FILM IN THE HISTORY OF MODERN ENTERTAINMENT," the trailer displays; the voiceover broadcasts that it "has captured the imagination and acclaim of the entire world." Words like "gargantuan" and "spectacular," and endless superlatives of magnitude ("the most expensive;" "the most florid color"), pepper the language of contemporaneous criticism, even that of film sophisticates like James Agee and Frank Nugent.[43] As Nugent reported, the Gallup Poll had estimated the film's "palpitantly waiting audience" at 56,500,000. Agee's remark that "*The Wind* blew for four hours" gets to the heart of the matter, for *Gone With the Wind* is about scale. Nowhere is this more apparent than in the main titles, where the letters are so large that they must sweep across the screen a few at a time, too grand to be corseted into the frame of a single human eyeful. It was apparently the final visual element in the studio's strategy to build overwhelming anticipation at all stages of the project, up to the ultimate moment of presentation to an audience. The title was even too big to fit within the parameters of other title-related conventions. *Gone With the Wind,* like "grand" opera—as all opera has been so frequently mislabeled by nonattenders—begins with a preparatory, anticipatory formal gesture: a two-and-a-half minute overture.[44] The screen presents a motionless snapshot of a single mature tree of many branches silhouetted against a semi-dark sky (which might be read as "dawn," "sunset," or "approaching storm clouds"), a space-time marker (a chronotopic snapshot) that director Victor Fleming revisits throughout the film.

There's not much of opera in the music for the overture, certainly nothing "grand." Its register is unambiguously pastoral: the natural setting embraces a series of themes that don't exceed a *piano* dynamic level, with quiet "sentimental" strings meandering through ideas too vague, with perhaps the exception of the syncopated, dotted-rhythm "country dance" music, to be "registered." All the more so as ambient noise in the theater (while patrons found their seats and settled in for the show) would have mitigated any concentrated engagement with the music. In filmic hindsight, though, that is, looking back at the overture from the titles, we can recognize it as a sort of recitative: the set-up and the clue to Steiner's vision of the "real" music, the grand sweep, that he kept in check until the main titles. Steiner's approach in selecting his "classic" models, it should be recalled, was in full accordance with one of the main principles of classical poetics, John of Garland's medieval doctrine of "words cognate to the subject."

John was, as mentioned previously, an early witness to the communicative power of expressive register and called for the incorporation of words that, when sounded, would invoke the genre of the poem in which they were embedded. Steiner extended the notion to a kind of pun-code that extends throughout his scoring praxis. I have already suggested the selection of Puccini's "E lucevan le stelle" as a model for *Now, Voyager*'s stellar love theme. There are other similar instances: his near citation of Wagner's *Liebestod* music throughout the score of *Dark Victory*, another Davis vehicle about a woman whose inevitable death is transfigured by love, and the reliance upon the effects of Wagner's *Ring* in the fantastic, multiplaned universe of *King Kong* (especially Wagner's use of chromatic harmonic sequences to initiate imaginary motion up and down through his diegetic planes or worlds). While there is a bit of *Tristan* perhaps in the sentimental turning figure of the last portion of *Kong*'s title music ("beauty" to the monstrous beast), and—as other have pointed out—a resemblance between the three-note Kong motive and *Tannhäuser*'s Pilgrim's chorus, most of the score seems to depend especially upon *Das Rheingold*.[45] It was a perfectly sensible choice, since the film's action embraces settings that are aquatic, terrestrial, and of impossible altitude (e.g., Kong's mountaintop lair, the Empire State Building). Most careful listeners will, I think, recognize the writhing Fafner when Kong confronts the land serpent of Skull Island.

But in *Gone With the Wind*, when the "Tara" theme finally blows, there is something of a bait-and-switch, for it would appear that the musical model is not so "grand" after all: I would say that it's likely Handel, and specifically *Serse*, a mock-*seria* and "antiheroic" work. Approaching the *Wind* from this side, we can observe how a composer, while feigning compliance with the shorthand communicative standards of kinothek registers, might simultaneously engage in a quietly subversive act of multimedia banter with the monoglossic vision of a director or studio. Steiner's famous Tara theme sits in the same pastoral-register key (F) as its model, *Serse*'s pseudo-*seria* opening aria, "Ombra mai fù," and reaches a virtually identical majestic climax with a leap to a high f, bumping up Handel's already expressive register by a small realignment of pitches that resulted in dissonances even juicier than those of the original. We need only recall the fixed image of the grand, dark, lonesome tree that had been on screen during the film's overture to understand the associative connection that inspired Steiner's choice of Handel's shade tree as a model. That link is audibly drilled home in the title sequence when the Tara music finally arrives toward the end, blown in not by Handel's quivery breeze but by a symphonic musical gale. At precisely this moment in the score, the tree from the overture reappears on screen and the giant title letters begin to scroll. It will reappear, in an even more melodramatic context, about ten minutes into the film, framing the crucial scene of Scarlett and her father (once again in silhouette) looking down on the family manse. *Serse*, like *Gone With the Wind*, is about family in a time of civil war, and so the "cognate" elements that link the music to the film are not only visual but extend to the components of the diegesis. Finally, Steiner, whose sense of humor was never highly nuanced, could not have failed to enjoy the pun-relationship of "Atlanta" and *Serse*'s soprano, "Atalanta."[46]

Meaningful as all of this may have been to Steiner on some level, what of the audience? Could any of this have filtered through into the vernacular understanding of the sound? Perhaps. Little known as *Serse* would have been (it was not even revived until the 1920s), "Ombra mai fù" was a staple of the musical amateur and, presumably, of the movie theater. "The plane tree," as it was known, was a sheet-music standard in the first years of the twentieth century.[47] Handel's "Largo from *Xerxes*" or "Famous

Largo," arranged for piano, is often encountered in elementary pedagogi-
cal anthologies. More specifically relevant is the appearance of Handel's
"Berühmtes Largo" as item no. 1572 of the 1927 Erdmann-Becce *Skalen-
register,* where it has been classified (along with the "Meditation" from
Massenet's *Thaïs*) at the core of an impressive taxonomical onion: *Lyrische
Expression/Incidenz/gesangsmässig-ruhig/Religiös-Kulthaft/ Meditation.*[48]
The register reflects Erdmann's hermeneutics, that is, the translation into
words of the meaningful content of the original music.

If moviegoers in the late 1930s had heard the piece before in the pre-
sound films of their younger days, it was perhaps in the dramatic contexts Erdmann suggests were appropriate and could have invested the reception of the Tara theme with a nonsecular flavor, and thus with a
grandeur surpassing the secular epic, containing hints of an ethical or
moral aspect (which in American culture has been defined primarily in
churchy terms). All this would hold true only if they "got it," of course;
whether the musical correspondence between the "Famous Largo" and
the Tara theme would have been noted, unconsciously or not, by anyone,
I cannot say. (I can only relate anecdotally that I first noted the similarity as a young and unaccomplished amateur piano autodidact growing
up in the New York area, where I regularly heard the Tara theme as the
signature music for a local afternoon television program called *Million-
Dollar Movie.*)

Stanley Kubrick, in *2001: A Space Odyssey* (1968), reawakened in the
public imagination that sense of size as an icon previously reserved for
Gone With the Wind, which everyone knew, and Tolstoy's *War and
Peace,* which most did not but knew about. By abandoning Alex North's
score and affixing to the film his own selection of preexistent "art
music," Kubrick eliminated the bothersome "dual-author" aspect of
sound film production, ensuring that the path of the sound track, as copi-
lot in the process of guiding audience reception of the film's messages, remained under the control of the *auteur* mechanism, as in a driver's-edu-
cation car. Kubrick's sense of scale was a product of, and made for, his
time. *2001* doesn't strain at the seams. Something different from the
grande bouffe of *Gone With the Wind* (as film or novel), it lacks the sense
of cultural tonnage popularly associated with those earlier register icons.

Its magnitude is boundless, thus weightless (as the outer-space visuals
will remind us), expressing, in Max Kozloff's formulation "the puzzling
gravity of the heavens."[49] The rapport-response that Kubrick intended by
invoking this category of limitlessness is one that he expected to emerge
from the domain of interiority; it is not imposed by phenomenal input

from without. As he put it in an interview, "I intended the film to be an intensely subjective experience that reaches the viewer at an inner level of consciousness, just as the music does."[50] Kubrick's own linguistic register in this remark is one that was of particular cultural currency in vernacular jargon of the late 1960s. But if his language is dated, the exploration of scope and scale that it describes is not. It looks forward, and it looks back. As Kozloff wrote, "Big as it is, the screen is but a slit through which to comprehend immensities that always escape the frame. The film is haunted by imminences always outside, left and right, above and beneath, its depth of field—imminences which make even the most complete local information look arbitrary in face of the scope now opened up.[51]

Yet, metaphysics aside, one of the most remarkable details of *2001* as an audiovisual "text" was its reinvention of the Fleming-Steiner model that had marked the "epic" register of *Gone With the Wind*. Accordingly, Kubrick's film also began with an overture and a screen in stasis, the featured typeface only marginally different from Fleming's 1939 model (Kubrick opted for an appropriately chunkier three-dimensional metallic). Its dimensional aspects with respect to the frame are virtually identical, as is the equal-sized all-capital type (i.e., OVERTURE, not Overture or OVERTURE). Just as Kozloff's observations suggested, the frame's corporeality—that is, as an object within the real architectural space of the venue—has been mitigated by the black background behind the text. In a darkened theater this creates the effect of an "infinity edge." An excerpt from György Ligeti's *Atmosphères* provides the aural environment, and it lasts just fifteen seconds longer than Steiner's overture pastiche. *Atmosphères* finishes with a string "fade." As multimedia, the whole package corresponds to the monumental frame of *Wind* (whose sharper edge was marked by a stable cadence at the end of Steiner's music).

Kubrick's, though, is a frame of no substance, its contents subject to individual exploration. Ligeti's music, too, is, as Kozloff wrote of the director's visuals, "an exercise in haptic orientation."[52] *Atmosphères* provides the "vast" and "ominous" presence in this filmic abstraction, a presence assigned to the visual component in *Wind*. Ominous though it may be, we are encouraged (as Kubrick indicated by the "inner level of consciousness") to lose ourselves in it; indeed, we have no choice in the darkness and stereo sound of a theater setting.[53] Fleming's darkening war clouds and technicolor skyscape over the cotton fields was impressive in 1940, but viewers three decades later required more to satisfy their increasingly self-conscious sense of their own fields of consciousness. Ligeti's "planes" and "fields" of clustered sound ("white-note" collections, "black-note" collections) played by large complements of strings, or strings and winds, account in the first portion of *Atmosphères* for the terrible beauty of this otherwise blank filmic page, the music's anti-structure standing as the perfect cognate to Kubrick's vision of unbounded space and time.[54]

In both films, the overture was followed by the MGM studio logo (in the styles of 1939 and 1968, respectively), after which the sound track relaunches. Kubrick, as everyone knows, kicks off the musical program of the "background" score with Richard Strauss's *Also sprach Zarathustra*, now known commonly as "the *2001* music." In the "Dawn of Man" sequence, the ambiguous dark-light, dawn-dusk sky of Fleming's visual world of enormity has been recast as the light and shadow play of sun and planets. Like the black tree silhouetted against the diurnal heavens in *Gone With the Wind,* the black background field of *2001*'s overture helped effect a transition into the film proper. Here the empty, unfathomable blankness of Kubrick's overture screen turns into an interpretable image of the black vastness within which the planets position themselves, to the accompaniment of Strauss's *Sonnenaufgang,* in "Dawn of Man."

CHAPTER 3

Yiddishkeit and the Musical Ethics of Cinema

Few orchestral musicians are likely to hear in Lalo's 1873 violin concerto, the "characteristic" *Symphonie espagnole,* any expression of Jewish communal identity. Neither would many Jews of the past seventy years recognize in the off-putting musical surface of Schoenberg's 1938 *Kol nidre,* with its pointed rejection of the more familiar expressive outlines associated with the Yom Kippur chant's nineteenth- and early twentieth-century arrangements, any musical embodiment of their annual ritual of atonement. Whatever musical spirit of the early twentieth century might have accommodated both musics under a single umbrella of Jewishness would have to have been imbued with a substantial dose of musical catholicity. Less flippantly put, such a position would have required a commitment to an ideology of expression (with respect to Judaism as faith and as culture, either or both of which may be taken to constitute "Jewishness," and to music per se) that academics will perhaps now find uncomfortably naive or hyperbolic. But at this fulcrum, teetering between the goyish Iberianisms of Lalo and the Schoenbergian return to roots, sits Louis Silvers. Because of his involvement in the production of *The Jazz Singer* of 1927, he is surprisingly well known to practitioners of film studies and historians of film music—surprisingly because his musical endeavors have passed with very little remark. If his visual trace as an on-screen credit in the title sequence (which he scored, mainly in the pastiche style) marks him as historical, a more remarkable trace renders him real, for he is embodied within the screen's frame in one of the talkiest portions of the so-called first talkie.

73

By the end of the twentieth century Silvers was accessible (only on VHS, alas) for perpetual re-view, visually realized in one of his many capacities. Seated at the piano, he leads the on-screen ensemble that accompanies Al Jolson's first synchronized jazz performance in the film during the Coffee Dan's scene. Right after that epoch-making and over-rehearsed "ad-lib" utterance ("Wait a minute . . . you ain't heard nothin' yet"), which introduced his rendition of "Toot-toot-tootsie" and skewed the direction of emerging sound cinema toward speaking rather than musical performance, Jolson had acoustically engraved Silvers's name upon an unintentionally weighty historical instant: "Lou . . . give it to 'em *hard and heavy.*" And Silvers, rarely invoked by those writing on this landmark film beyond recitation of his credit as music director and conductor of the Warners Vitaphone orchestra, modestly obliges on screen (presumably to Jolson's satisfaction). It was Lou Silvers, then, who invested Jolson and his protagonistic alters, Jakie Rabinowitz and Jack Robin, with whatever energy audiences may have felt emanating from the screen; Silvers who mapped the interaction of intra- and extradiegetic voices constituting the synchronized jazz performances and the melodramatic background scoring (discussed in the previous chapter) that was heard in the "silent" portions of this silent-sound hybrid.

To remember and to remark upon him is significant to my project for several reasons. First, while *The Jazz Singer* has been universally installed in film and film-music historiography by virtue of its sequences containing synchronized vocal music, Silvers's orchestral score for the film has been confined to the academic discursive margin, cited only as a vestige of practices that were quickly eradicated by the transition to sound that was set in motion by the film's surprisingly enthusiastic reception. Next, whether the "Jewish" aspects of *The Jazz Singer* have been largely ignored (by scholars of film music) or addressed within the broad outlines of issues related to immigration and assimilation (by cultural historians), little attention has been paid to the representation of Jewish music within the film's unprecedented multimedia context or to that music's dynamic and meaningful relationship with the musics surrounding it. Finally, the historiography of Hollywood as a twentieth-century Jewish "empire," even while it has included Jewish composers and musicians among its roster of mentionables, has not prompted similarly detailed investigations of the extent to which the Jewish background of personalities or repertoires in the area of film music played a crucial role in the reception of most non-indigenous musics, including that of the European orchestral concert hall, in a broad range of twentieth-century American mass media.

BODY ENGLISH

I have suggested that a primary distinction between classic and other registers in media lies in the imagined dimensions of spaces in which acoustic events are judged to be more properly located. The sphinx was not merely a very large, tantalizing, and lovely entity but also a prompt for the mental construction of something even greater: a space big enough properly to hold it along with others of its kind, the flock of deities who chose to remain invisible. This architectural distinction, the property of magnitude both ponderable and imponderable, is common to our apprehension of literally monumental edifices but also to their stand-ins, both "halls" (museum, opera house) and the most proximate models for them "temples." The same may be said of the rituals of special dress and special behaviors associated with each; these may be unnaturally restrained (captured in Bugs Bunny's famous assassination by gunshot of the concert hall cougher in 1946's *Rhapsody Rabbit*) or unusually demonstrative and expressive, as in certain evangelical traditions.

In *The Jazz Singer* we hear three human voices: those of the actors Al Jolson, Eugenie Besseler, and Warner Oland (who shouts the single word "stop"). That of Besseler, simpering and indistinct, reveals her discomfort with acting while being recorded as a sound source. Jolson projects two voices, each derived from his real life as a stage entertainer. One, his supposedly ad-libbed patter about the Goldbergs and Guttenbergs, marginally funny one-liners derived from Jewish vaudeville, targets a Jewish audience. His second voice has a somewhat wider base, in that it is an imitation of such African-American vaudevillians as Joe Britton, whose signature line "You ain't seen nothin' yet" Jolson appropriated for his historic media moment.[1] In this moment he used his speaking voice to remind consumers of his race-based musical praxis. To disentangle the threads related to cultural assimilation, racism, and universality of musical expression (linking the "negro's tears" to the "wail of the *chazan*," rendered explicit in the confrontational dialogue between Jack and his father) remains a problematic and important task, albeit one that cannot be addressed here. Interpretations put forward by scholars like Mark Slobin and Michael Rogin, among others, have laid out many of the significant features of this difficult cultural topography.[2]

Silvers's largely neglected score adds several specifically musical voices to the mix. In some sense they speak as much as they sing, belonging to Jewish liturgical music, other Jewish musical items (that locate the New York community within the Eastern European Ashkenazic strain), popular

Example 1. *Kol nidre*

tunes, and, of course, classical fragments. Not only Lalo's but also Chaikovsky's voice emanates from Silvers's pastiche score. I have discussed the latter at some length already, suggesting that its musical content was intended in large part abstractly and that it served a specific purpose linked to the film's association with the effects of melodrama. The *Symphonie espagnole,* however, is a different matter. Listeners unfamiliar with that work will have a hard time, unless they have seen the cue sheet, distinguishing this material from that of the *Kol nidre* chant whose diegetic performance it prepares (Example 1). Indeed, the Lalo fragment is linked throughout the film specifically to *Kol nidre* and more generally to the cantorial household (Example 2).

Often a musical score constructed by an intelligent musician—however dated it may appear from an insufficiently contextualized perspective—projects a coherent reading or assessment of a film's contents that extend beyond the range of a director's vision. (A famous case in point is David Raksin's monothematic score for the final version of *Laura.*) I would suggest that for Silvers—who, as I pointed out earlier, brought Fox studio resources to bear upon the presentation of Schoenberg's "new" Jewish music a decade later—there was likely more at stake here than a simple matter of harmonic or melodic convenience.

One of the principal currents in the academic and theological enterprise surrounding Jewish music in the 1920s was the new ethnographic form of study brought to bear upon Jewish musical repertoires, represented especially by the pioneering work of A. Z. Idelsohn. The spirit of the enterprise prompted the collecting of essential tunes and their variants, linking them to the social aggregations and geographical boundaries

Example 2. Lalo, *Symphonie espagnole,* 4th movement, mm. 17–26

that distinguished them, and at the same time implicating all in a single network of Jewish musical practice by revealing salient commonalities and thereby "museumizing" vestiges of the authentically originary.[3] In *The Jazz Singer* the Jewish milieu depicted was that of the New York Ghetto; it was Ashkenazic, Eastern European. As the "classical" tie-in to *Kol nidre,* Silvers chose a pointedly, characteristically Spanish violin concerto from among any number of possibilities (including Jewish song) that might share its melodic and harmonic features.[4] The fourth movement of the *Symphonie,* of course, possesses the kind of general "oriental" features that have been discussed by Western musicologists in the last several years ("oriental" here as opposed to the specifically middle-eastern application of the term to Jewish music by ethnomusicologists).[5]

Raphaelson's story makes much of the distinction between Jack's movements in dance and those of the "whites" around him, linking it not to black minstrelsy but to Jack's ethnic heritage, his "Oriental instinct for undulation." Kinothek collections classified Jewish music amidst other "exotics" linked (in the case of Erdmann's *Handbuch*) to the expressive register of "Volk-Gesellschaft."[6] But in this particular selection Silvers may well have been hinting at a spiritual association with Idelsohn's position and those others intent upon comprehending, rather than simply reiterating, Jewish musics in their traditional contexts, thus extending the expressive (and indeed expressionistic) musical language of the film's background score pointedly to embrace the ethnographic terrain of the Sephardim (or the Sephardim and Mizrachim, the orientals in the specific sense). In what has been taken as simply an old-style pastiche score Louis Silvers drew together the principal cultural frames for Old World Jewry in a conjoined and coherent multimedia utterance (especially in the succession of cues 15–16).[7]

A move of this sort would nicely, indeed thoughtfully for the time, reflect the spirit of the script's central message concerning musical expression. In the case of melodic conformance, both the chant and the symphonic fragment reach their expressionistic zenith on the minor third
above the principal note, emphasizing not only what Silvers heard as a
universally perceivable marker of a particular communicative register
but also one that conjoins the music of the temple to the music of the
hall.[8] Implying on the one hand Silvers's own commitment to Jewish
music as an object linked to personal belief and intellection, it also stands
as an argument for the universality of art's expressive potential (a position shared by Erdmann and other serious proponents of pastiche scoring, as evidenced by the extensive discussion of dramaturgy and the morphology of emotion and expression in the commentary portion of
Erdmann's *Handbuch*).

To press the general sense of my reading a bit further, we might hear
Silvers's device as an extension of the musical commentary upon the ethical failings implicit in the religiosocial machinery of the ghetto I described in the previous chapter. Cantor Rabinowitz is a good man, but
(as Chaikovsky tells us) his treatment of young Jakie is based on an ethical glitch, a particular attitude shlepped especially by Eastern European
Ashkenazic Jews to the new American Ghetto: the notion that there is no
fundamental distinction between Judaism and Jewishness, between the
Jewish religion and the Jewish people. Within these populations, social
and political interactions were governed by a shared understanding that
religion (along with its associated institutions and laws) functions as an
inexorable cultural regulator; therein lies Jack's, the "new" Jew's,
dilemma.[9]

Jolson's verbal formulas, however authentic a representation of the idiolect shared by popular-music insiders, were conceits of his performance
to the new invisible audience. They served as a reminder of his stage
act—for which *The Jazz Singer* served as an electronic surrogate—in
which he had appropriated not just the look and the repertoire but also
the signature phrases of African-American entertainers.[10] "Hard and
heavy" will seem to the modern listener an absurd misrepresentation of
the tame musical content of Jolson's act. As an expressive construction
it is now as quaint to us as the essentially analogous words recorded in
Martin Le Franc's famously enigmatic and equally alliterative attempt to
invoke the musical essence of his fifteenth-century Burgundian contemporaries Gilles Binchois and Guillaume Du Fay. Their music did not
strike courtly ears as hard and heavy (or perhaps it did); in any case Le

Franc advertised it as *faire et frisque,* reminding us of the unavoidable reliance upon the metaphor of nonaural sensation as a means of communicating the ineffable to the musical consumer and, at the same time, of the
temporal nuances of all such tropes (compare, for example, "hard" rock,
"heavy" metal). But the jazzer's terms, like those of the courtier, resonated
with a particular feature of Jolson's mode of presentation and, significantly, of his expectations with respect to its reception. They encapsulate
both his appropriated Africanism and the Jewish core of his performance.
For all the emphasis on Jolson's appropriated Africanisms, it is interesting
that Raphaelson—moved by seeing Jolson in performance—emphasizes
the oriental aspect of his body movements.

For our time, academic interest in Jolson's choreography has, not surprisingly, focused on its racial problematics, a region of discourse inscribed quite effectively by Krin Gabbard.[11] His analysis of Jolson links
blackface minstrelsy to later modes of jazz and rock "presentation," emphasizing white musicians' fascination with the acculturated sexual connotations of black bodies.[12] For those watching Jolson in his time
though, the effect by most reports was not so much erotic as ecstatic, in
the original sense, something hardly imaginable to a modern viewer of
the film. As Stephen Whitfield describes this element of Jolson reception,
"There was something demonic about him, something that could not be
contained within the thin membranes of Victorian order. His performances emitted something so raw that he seemed possessed. 'John the
Baptist was the last man to possess such a power,' critic Robert Benchley told readers of *Vanity Fair.* 'It is as if an electric current had been run
along under the seats.' The emotional voltage Jolson could unleash was
so high that [Gilbert] Seldes saw corybantic equivalents only in religious
exaltation, only in mob hysteria, only at the stock exchange."[13]

Hollywood was well aware that there was potential cinematic value in
capturing that aspect of musical experience, for example in the revival
scene of *Hallelujah* (1929), where the same unbridled hand motions that
Yudelson mocks in *The Jazz Singer* are linked to evangelical hysteria.[14]
And yet, all jazz aside, perhaps the most significant point of intersection
between ecstasis and Jolson's expressive mode may be seen in the performance of *Kol nidre* late in the film, a performance that has often been mis-
read or misheard. Chion renders the scene uncomfortable and impossible:
"When Al Jolson is supposedly performing the Kol Nidre at the synagogue, the film forgoes Jolson's own light and fluent voice, which we
heard singing 'jazz.' He lip-synchs to the voice of a real cantor—but we
are not supposed to know."[15] Gabbard recognizes the voice as Jolson's

own but refers to the performance as "jazzy."[16] There is some resemblance between the singer's movements and those employed in his stage presentations. We should recall, however, that Jolson in preparing the scene had been coached by a cantor.

In early twentieth-century practice, the voice of the *chazan* was hardly restrained; in fact the best Jewish liturgical singers were known for their extreme expressionism. As mediators between text and congregation, and lying outside the realm of rabbinic authority—cantors are selected and supported by the laity—their job allowed for and tended to promote musical exaggeration, not to mention distrust on the part of those who feared that vocal prowess and effect might obscure or overwhelm the significance of liturgical texts.[17] Like the business of jazz singers, that of the cantorate focuses largely on *ex tempore* expressive nuance. Mark Slobin records an interview with Samuel Vigoda, who spoke of his early experience at a Rosh Hashanah service in the 1920s: "At the Shir hamalos before Borchu I let myself go; I poured out my heart. Somehow it came out so that people couldn't get over it . . . it was improvised."[18] And *Kol nidre*, despite its liturgical familiarity, remains a musical zone for "Oriental" (here in the specific, ethnomusicological usage) individuality.[19]

Chasidism, which even includes ecstatic dancing as a mode of religious expression, had made its way from Eastern Europe to America by 1915, and the cue sheet for *The Jazz Singer* includes an item, cue 57, identified as "Chassidic Dance."[20] However many affectations drawn from the African element of the American South's musical culture were added to its surface, American East-coast Jewish orientalism was undeniably a significant—and perhaps the more significant—element in Jolson's "bilingual" encoding of the expressive content of *Kol nidre*.[21] His performance adds to the arsenal of musical elements in the film the nuances of expression that are mustered to enable the faithful (quoting the movie's decidedly non-Jewish intertitle) to listen to "the voice of *God*."

While the lives of many cantors (most famously, Richard Tucker's) intersected with opera, others participated in the vernacular musical culture of Yiddish theater, for example the "Yiddish Broadway" of Second Avenue.[22] Within the frame of Yiddish performance, variety shows, or melodramas, the tunes heard within the mise-en-bande of *The Jazz Singer*—from the liturgical *(Kol nidre)* to the melodramatic (*Bar kochba*, associated with the late nineteenth-century theater piece by Samuel Goldfaden, used for cues 37, 56, and 65)—had already found a place in popular entertainments. Both circulated in the second decade of the twentieth century in popular sheet-music arrangements. Mark Slobin, in

Tenement Songs, reproduces the covers of two versions of *Kol nidre* (published in New York on Canal Street and Delancey Street) and a piano arrangement of *Bar kochba* (published by the Hebrew Publishing Company).[23] Where along the spectrum of genre and its registral implications can we position an item like *Kol nidre,* confronted by its multiple personalities and its seamless transitions from synagogue to theater, parlor, film, Bruch, Schoenberg? Max Steiner had an answer.

WHICH CLASSIC?

In 1932, a few years after the national release of Warner Brothers Studio's *The Jazz Singer,* RKO Studios (aka Radio Pictures) released *Symphony of Six Million,* a sound film based on a story by Fannie Hurst. *Symphony* has not attracted much attention from film or film-music historians, aside from Royal Brown's *en passant* remark that the film "probably contains more musical evokers of Jewish culture than any narrative film score in history."[24] Hurst, whose novelizations of life in the Jewish neighborhoods of the Lower East Side and Brooklyn were enormously popular, was already familiar to movie patrons by the time of the film's release. Many of her short stories circulated widely in mainstream magazines like *Cosmopolitan.* Hurst's "Humoresque" received its first (silent) screen treatment in 1920 by Cosmopolitan Productions, a company that a few years later mounted another pre-sound film in the Hurstian vein, *The Nth Commandment,* which in a bow to local color featured transliterated "Brooklynese" in its intertitle dialogues. A year after the premiere of *Symphony,* for which he had provided an innovative original score, and in the midst of that transitional period during which the presence of extradiegetic music in sound films was still hotly contested, composer Maximilian Raoul Walter Steiner described his work on the project as "an idea in musical underscoring never used before."[25]

Max was not merely the product of musical privilege; he was the gifted godson of Richard Strauss and had grown up in a Viennese household that had hosted such musical notables as Jacques Offenbach and Gustav Mahler. These biographical details (and their resonance with those of other émigré film composers descending from families involved in the promotion and production of concert music) no doubt have contributed to our insistence upon locating the principal models for film scoring within the practices of opera: nineteenth-century opera, early twentieth-century opera, or even the eighteenth-century pastiche opera.[26] Steiner's own recounting of the score for *Symphony* a year after the film's release appears to reinforce the assumption, but a closer reading suggests some ambiguities regarding his frames of reference and the role of Selznick (then at RKO) in developing the new scoring procedure: "The suggestion was made by David O. Selznick, then executive vice president in charge of production here. The music in this picture, much of which was composed by myself, and some of which is my own arrangement of the Jewish Classics, is handled like opera music. It matches exactly the mood, the action and situation of the scene on the screen." Elsewhere the composer related: "David said, 'Do you think you could put some music behind this thing? I think it might help it. Just do one reel—the scene were Ratoff dies.' I did as he asked, and he liked it so much he told me to go ahead and do the rest."[27]

Providing special music for a single scene was hardly unusual for the time (see, for example, the discussion of *The Mummy* in chapter 6). This is one of the features of the new sound-cinema praxis that might argue against any wholesale appropriation of opera aesthetics to the mixed media form. If not in opera, then the model—it has been argued—lies in melodrama. Peter Brooks drew attention to the similarities between cinema and the musical component of melodrama, a notion that was further elaborated by David Neumeyer. Brooks had offered his remark as a generality, applicable as much to the ineffable music of literary genres (like the novel) as the real musical accompaniment of silent movies.[28] His primary interest lay in the hyperbolic elements (i.e., the rhetoric) of melodrama that music has the capacity to invoke or embody.[29] When Neumeyer examined the early sound film from the perspective of melodramatic models, much of his analysis featured examples of such acoustically hyperbolic effects, upon melodrama's use of music to "turn the volume of the drama up" and draw attention to particular moods and characters.

Treating at length Max Steiner's score for John Ford's *The Informer* (1935)—the first for which the composer received an academy award—Neumeyer drew upon models that included *Fidelio,* Sigmund Romberg's *Maytime,* and Rudolf Friml's *The Three Musketeers.*[30] *The Informer,* although not terribly familiar to present-day film fans, is a staple of film-music historians. When Steiner famously remarked of his scoring procedures that "every character should have a theme," he cited Gypo, this film's protagonist, as exemplary.[31] The web of leitmotifs in the film is extensive, their long-range manipulation technically impressive, and the musical fabric at times decidedly operatic in that sense. In a passage in which he obliquely apologizes for having once described in print a scene in the film without ever having viewed it, Michel Chion emphasizes this aspect and cites a possible model in Debussy's *Pelléas et Mélisande*.[32] (Kalinak, writing in the post-Gorbman era, considers Steiner's contribution from the perspective of "the junction of narrative action and music," invoking the *n*-word three times in her introductory paragraph.)[33] Neumeyer wisely attempted to look past the academic clichés that represent film music as a form either of "narrative" or of "virtual opera."

As a widely accepted model for Steiner's full-blown discursive and formal style, *The Informer* may be usefully invoked as a control before entering into any hypothesis regarding Steiner's first extended essay in "original, continuous" scoring in *Symphony of Six Million* a few years earlier. *The Informer* is a model for the mickey-mousing variety of close synchronization of music and image (the term was used by Steiner himself); Neumeyer made a compelling case linking some of these instants to the expressionistic gestures of mainstream European melodrama. Arguing against a wholesale representation of Steiner's technique in those terms here, however, is the notorious imitation of footsteps in the opening sequence by precisely synchronized musical sounds, for it turns out that the mimetic function of Steiner's music extends beyond the simple two-track environment of the sound film. Both mise-en-bande and mise-en-scène seem to reflect some of the specific textual effects featured in the novel upon which the film was based.

In the pages of Liam O'Flaherty's novel *The Informer,* the brevity of Frankie McPhillip's death is striking: it is described in (or as) chapter 2, the full chapter taking up less than half a page. Whether the decision stemmed from Ford, Steiner, or both, it is suggestive that the musical score absents itself during the film's death scene (in fact, all diegetic sound as well disappears at the moment of Frankie's death), that is, the medium is marked by a sudden and drastic economy of means. An even more compelling argument for the "novelistic" aspect of the film's multimedia design is Ford's and Steiner's repetitious footstep motif. It has been critiqued from both visual and musical perspectives as an example of melodrama at its worst, a superfluous demonstration of the potential of music to clarify filmic motion and filmic content that require no clarification. However, chapter 3 of O'Flaherty's text—following immediately upon the death of Frankie—clarifies the origin and significance of both acoustical and visible gestures. After a brief opening paragraph, the next two paragraphs lodge footsteps in the reader's ear as a verbal idée fixe:

He walked quickly along a narrow passage into the dark lane. . . . But as Gypo stood hidden in the doorway of an old empty house, piercing the darkness with wild eyes, he heard a footstep. The footstep made him start. It was the first human footstep he had heard, the first sound of his fellow human beings, since he had become an informer and . . . an outcast.

Immediately he felt that the footstep was menacing. . . . Within the course of ninety minutes the customary sound of a human footstep had, by some evil miracle, become menacing.

The passage is strange, and one could, I think, make the case for its essentially melodramatic aspect; it possesses its own gait, as much stop-and-start as that represented on the screen. Most interesting for an analysis of the film's working parameters is that the synchronization turns out to be not one of sound and image but one of image and text, sound and text. Novelistic as the correspondence may be, it realizes a melodramatic gesture in the novel rather than a novelistic approach to the telling of a story.[34] But it warns us against relying too much upon stage melodrama as a formal model for all such effects; here the multimedia melodrama reflects a literary device, one of the genre's categories advanced by Brooks.

Additionally, the models of music melodrama cited in scholarly interpretations of early film scores are most often melodramas of a particularly high-toned sort, not that far removed from opera practice and consumption. Their musiconarrative or musicodramaturgical gimmicks (especially with respect to character and plot emphasis) have been analyzed with respect to the implicit understanding of stories as continuous wholes. And so, despite theatrical melodrama's reliance upon music as a hyperbolic interjection, the models themselves (i.e., the works of Beethoven, Friml, or Marschner cited by Neumeyer and Brooks) that have been brought to the table exhibit precisely those elements that are least like melodrama's essence: they exhibit elements of "continuity." While discussing details of the score for *The Informer* Neumeyer invokes that term five times in a single expository paragraph.[35] In the end he admits rightly that the continuity aesthetic was fundamentally at odds with the commentary aesthetic of melodrama, and thus that melodrama accounts for only a single part in the complex mix of early sound-film scoring practices. In looking for a conceptual umbrella of form and style that might provide a broader surface area, we might look not to the repertoire of art musics that film-music history has always invoked but rather to the history of early movie theaters, film's early practitioners and audience, and the clues provided by *The Jazz Singer* and—eventually—*Symphony of Six Million*.

KOL NIDRE REVIVIT

One of the most telling moments in *The Informer* will be heard by most as supremely trivial. As Gypo and Katie, Irish to the core and poor Irish at that, view with frustration and resignation a poster advertising steamship passage to America, the "musical continuity" is interrupted by a low-prominence quotation of the first phrase of "Yankee Doodle" in the underscore. Several years later, in *Now, Voyager,* Steiner used a virtually identical cue—although one of greater acoustic prominence, since it serves in this case more as a musical postcard than as a reflection of protagonistic psychology—for the return to America (accompanied by a shot of the Statue of Liberty) directly following the airport farewell scene. In other films, for example *Casablanca,* Steiner relied on anthems to establish a sense of place or—in the case of the minor-mode fragment of the "Marseillaise" heard early in that film—of a place's subjection to inappropriate or unethical force. ("Yankee Doodle," however, will be shown to possess a particularly significant pedigree.)

I referred earlier to a "particular" register that Silvers might have heard in the minor-third utterance that forms the expressive cell of the familiar version of *Kol nidre.* Schoenberg, complaining about the tedious melody and conventional harmonizations of *Kol nidre,* criticized especially their reliance upon what he called the "sentimental minor." Writing to Paul Dessau in 1941, he expressed satisfaction with having reorganized some of the conventional pitch material from several versions of the standard melody for reorganization into rows, explaining that this rational approach might burn away *Kol nidre*'s associations with Bruch's sentimental cello and the sentimental minor mode in general.[36] Schoenberg expanded upon this critique of conventional hearing of *Kol nidre* in another, undated (English) typescript preserved in the Schoenberg Center collection: "This melody in spite of its very striking beginning suffers from monotony which is principally caused through the minor key in which most of its parts are composed. Minor has become during the last century an expression for sad and touching feelings."

The composer had legitimate theological concerns about the chant's transmission and the text's meaning, concerns shared by many other Jews. But one has to wonder whether it was only the symphonic sentimentality of "Bruch, etc." that rankled, for by the time he and Rabbi Sonderling undertook their revision, *Kol nidre* had long been a fixture in mass entertainment media, including sheet music, musical theater, and cinema. Its cinematic profile was drawn in *The Jazz Singer,* where it was sure to sound sentimental. More specifically, by virtue of the special characteristics of audiovisual conjunction, the tune was lodged for future Hollywood practice and audience expectation in a particular expressive register, linked to the demise of ethical men.

Kol nidre was among the Jewish Classics that Steiner brought to the score of *Symphony of Six Million,* providing the musical background for the death of Meyer, the father of the brilliant surgeon Felix Klauber; this was the scene that Selznick felt cried out for scoring. Meyer is portrayed from the opening moments of the film as warm, gentle, humorous, and ethical. He is above all a good father to his children. To accompany his passing, Steiner wrote a cue that begins with the *Kol nidre* tune played by low strings. It was a logical choice, for only a few years earlier, the same classic had served as the plot hinge for *The Jazz Singer* and marked the moment of Cantor Rabinowitz's passing, content and reconciled at last as he seems to hear (in a special effects vision) the voice of Jack singing the Yom Kippur service. He was not as warm a soul, of course, as Klauber, who is more of a new Jew, a semi-assimilated American. Rabinowitz, in spite of taking the strap to young Jakie, emerges at the end as a rather more heroic figure in Raphaelson's original story when crowds gather around the house to mourn and celebrate their respected "chazon" and Jack takes up his father's position at the Hester Street Synagogue.

From at least the time of *The Jazz Singer, Kol nidre* was ensconced in Hollywood's imagination as a musical utterance of lamentation, a collection of—in the words of Raphaelson's story—"grief-laden notes." And as late as 1939, in the MGM short feature *Sons of Liberty* starring Claude Rains as the Jewish freedom fighter Haym Solomon (a hero of the American Revolution), *Kol nidre* appears as a significant leitmotif and, I would say, registral cue. To mark the patriotic fervor of the screenplay, the score is shot through with interjections of "America" (i.e., "God Save the King") skewed in a dizzying array of modulatory directions depending on the spirit of the moment, although the title music is the more iconic and less nationalistic "Yankee Doodle." Directed by Michael Curtiz, with Leo Forbstein credited as musical director, the film only slightly predates *Casablanca* (a better-known Rains vehicle, also directed by Curtiz but scored by Steiner). *Sons of Liberty*'s anthem-based scoring practices and hammy nationalist message serve as a kind of microcosm for Curtiz's collaboration with Steiner in the later, more extravagant production. Both *Casablanca* and *Sons of Liberty* share the same big-boned MGM sound elements of the period. (Indeed, the superimposition of the tolling liberty bell upon a ramped-up presentation of "America" at one point rivals the noise being made by Quasimodo at rival RKO in the same year.)

Kol nidre enters the background discreetly (again, played by low strings) as Haym Solomon comes upon his old friend Jacob in a British prison. In a marked Eastern European accent, Jacob bravely but resignedly warns that he expects soon to be "freed" by the soldiers "with their rifles." He requests that, after his own execution for being a patriot, Haym take it upon himself to watch over (he gestures to another prisoner) his "good Christian" friend. The Christian prisoner asks Haym to help him recall the words of the twenty-third Psalm, and they engage in a simultaneous recitation. With the Jew's theological position thus clarified as explicitly normative and nonthreatening, "regular" Americans in the audience were more likely comfortably to enjoy the effective (and melodramatic) revelation that followed moments later. A guard enters and calls out the name of the Christian prisoner: "Nathan Hale!" Eventually General Washington himself enlists Haym Solomon's aid: his messenger interrupts a synagogue service. The congregation wears three-cornered hats rather than yarmulkes, while the cantor sings expressively in what appears to be modern temple regalia. Perhaps surprisingly, Forbstein's leitmotivic score keeps *Kol nidre* out of the scene, reserving it for a more expressive destination.

On his deathbed Solomon expresses to his wife, Rachel, his faithfulness, his love of his children, and his understanding that these will be enough even though he has nothing of material substance to leave them (he has donated all of his time and money to the war effort).[37] At the end *Kol nidre* is heard twice: once in its by then standard cinematic cello presentation, and afterwards in the high violins from whence it deliquesces via a Steineresque harp into the implicit heavens along with Solomon's soul (an impression established by camera angle).[38] Once again the film revisits the theme of Jewish patriarchal obligation: Rabinowitz, Klauber, and Solomon are Jewish fathers who, for the sake of their families, and especially their sons, must stand as representatives of the life well lived. And once again the Jewish character's ethics along with his end are defined, melodramatically, by reference to the Yom Kippur chant.

I would think that Schoenberg's dissatisfaction with the state of *Kol nidre* in the 1930s derived as much from its apparent trivialization for sentimental, commercial purposes as from the harmonic environment that allowed such readings to flourish. *Kol nidre* had found nonliturgical niches before the advent of sound film. It was already circulating, especially in lower Manhattan and Brooklyn, as a popular standard in a variety of contexts. However many times its diegetic presentation in films was linked to synagogue visuals, *Kol nidre* was not really—in the circles that mattered for the creation and consumption of movies—a liturgical hothouse flower. There it was already common currency.

Symphony of Six Million, Steiner's first experiment in leitmotivic continuity scoring deserves a bit more attention, particularly since it (and not the more familiar *King Kong,* with its rampant and specific Wagnerianism) is the node on the music-historical timeline that prefigures the next several decades of film-music practice. Not that Steiner's score in any way reflects the modernist tendencies in the literate art music of its own time. Yet as one strand in a multimedia fabric it is remarkably innovative and thoughtful, although not quite as revolutionary as Steiner made it sound in retrospect (or—maybe more precisely—as revolutionary as we have made his claim appear in our still rudimentary film-music histories). We have already seen that the notion of musical continuity over a wide expanse of time in multimedia was on Silvers's mind when he presented the *Romeo and Juliet* theme first in a truncated and deflected statement and only later as a complete utterance, thereby lending the second more meaningful weight. Steiner's score for *Symphony,* like Silvers's score, is made up of more than a little unoriginal material. Silvers had, after all, made his own arrangements of Chaikovsky as well as the Chasidic dances and Yiddish tunes that lend the score its ethnographic flavor. And so it was with Steiner.

Not only those "Jewish Classics" but other familiar tunes, too, find their way onto the mise-en-bande; the crucial difference here is simply Steiner's emphasis on continuity and musical development over time within all, not just one, of his strands. His choice for the opening of the picture, after the Elgarian processional that sets a somewhat academic tone as title music, signals his long-range intentions, especially with respect to the themes of domestic ethics I have touched on above, which he must have deemed particularly significant in Hurst's tale or at least in Selznick's "picturization." This attests to his understanding of the ethical substance of Yiddish-oriented drama in general, for Hurst's ethical message will be privileged by the composer's long-range formal plan for the score above the more specific elements of, for example, the plotline's presentation of the problematized love between the hero and heroine or that of Felix's psychological turmoil. In the end the scoring will emphasize the characters' roles as emblems in the melodrama's social commentary.

GASLIGHT SONATAS

For all the altruistic posturing on the part of Hollywood spokesmen during the first wave of sound film production in the late 1920s, their bottom line was business and the sale of tickets to audiences of higher tone and deeper pockets than those traditionally associated with the movie house. This accounts for the emphasis on symphony and opera as the centerpiece of the new sound aesthetic, and for the publicizing of Hollywood's marvelous capacity to bring "good" music to "the town halls of [America's] hamlets."[39] While this emphasis drove the proliferation of specially equipped theaters (e.g., those that could handle the Vitaphone projection system) and thus increased the potential size of the audience, we should keep in mind who the principal consumers of film were in New York and other cities of the East Coast. Who were these viewers and why did film moguls feel compelled to replace them with a new demographic?

The Jews in Hollywood were quickly to form their own sort of elite in a place with no defined aristocracy, no defined institutions, and a social structure that was "primitive and permeable."[40] Memories of the low-end movie houses of the ghettoes likely fed the self-loathing of that sector of moguldom (like Columbia Pictures' Harry Cohn) who defiantly rejected their heritage, especially the notion that Judaism comprised an inexorable social bond. By the midteens approximately twenty-five percent of Manhattan's 123 movie theaters were located in the Lower East Side ghetto, while the Bowery (a landscape that included Yiddish saloons of the sort depicted in the early segment of *The Jazz Singer*) housed thirteen more; there were seven in Union Square.[41] Ben Singer has demonstrated and mapped the extent of Jewish management from the time of the earliest theaters (Nickelodeons), pointing out that while in 1910 Jews constituted only about a quarter of the Manhattan population, they owned sixty percent of its movie houses.[42] The second decade of the century witnessed a substantial conversion of Yiddish theaters into movie exhibition venues. Even the stage upon which Jacob Adler, "the Jewish King Lear," had established his formidable reputation was by 1913 showing "the latest photoplays with eight acts of Yiddish vaudeville."[43]

Following upon the transformation of legitimate Yiddish theaters into movie houses was an influx of Yiddish actors to the screen. Filming with orthochromatic stock—especially its deep focus that emphasized the "real" view of the staged mise-en-scène associated with theatrical productions—provided a suitable visual environment for the histrionic code associated with Yiddish melodramatic acting, but the transition was by no means an easy or natural one. The intimacy of screen space rendered exaggerated gestures, especially those of the face in close-ups, more over-the-top than ever. (The close-up was a technique of long standing: it had been introduced by Edison in the 1890s.) *Moving Picture World* critiqued "a well-known Jewish actor . . . said to have been very successful on the so-called Yiddish stage" for having been "hampered by a lack of camera experience. He talks too much and too vehemently. . . . Emphatic elocution before the camera is worse than wasted" (especially, of course, when the words go unheard).[44] Hollywood moguls would not soon forget that the roots of the silver screen were embedded in the soils of Jassy and Leopoldstadt and the asphalt of the New York tenement districts. David O. Selznick had throughout his career been quick with verbal stingers others deemed inappropriate, as when he turned his attention to the 1940 picturization, directed by Alfred Hitchcock, of Daphne du Maurier's "celebrated novel" *Rebecca* (so the title shot reads). Selznick remarked that the book's title was terrible for a film that wasn't aimed at "the Palestine market." Yet, more seriously, he "asked Hitchcock to make [Joan] Fontaine's emotional moments more Yiddish art theatre and less English repertory theatre," resulting, according to Leonard Leff, in odd moments like the actress's exaggerated double-take upon her first sight of the big house, Manderley.[45]

Prior to cinema the Yiddish stage had served as an important model for the histrionic code. Franz Kafka was so taken with Adler's own mentor, Jacob Gordin (who was a prime mover in the "elevation" of Yiddish theater), that he incorporated gestural Yiddishims in his written work.[46] A comparison of scenic details shared by *Symphony of Six Million* with the 1920 silent production of *Dr. Jekyll and Mr. Hyde* clarifies the extent to which certain forms of melodramatic expressionism survived the transition from silent to sound film. Both screenplays represent medical doctors who have lost their way in the topography of social ethics (with social ethics, in the case of *Symphony*, explicitly represented as derivable from certain ethnographic and religious frames). In each film we are confronted by a quintessentially melodramatic mise-en-scène: long shots frame the hordes of poor, suffering from want and illness, seeking the help of a wise and kind doctor. Jekyll's clinic served the "white" occidental poor, Felix Klauber's those of the New York Jewish ghetto. Each aggregation, though, is simply an emblem of melodrama's representation of the anxiety, in Brooks's words, "brought by a frightening new world in which the traditional patterns of moral order no longer provide the necessary social glue."[47] Both Jekyll and Klauber will, in the course of their lives, become *un*glued, turning their backs upon the huddled masses that constitute the full extent of the society around them. The theatrical mise-en-scène of Klauber's waiting room (a staircase leading upwards to the doctor's small office and his panoramic, ethical worldview) revisits melodrama's reliance upon clear and accessible signals of the social machinery and niveaus that define ethical norms, and within which such norms will operate, barring injustice or imbalance.[48] A photograph of this crucial shot would be featured prominently in the book that "novelized" the story shortly after the film's release. Klauber's literal and figural elevation at this point reflects both his fundamental goodness and the Jewish community's specific evaluation of the intertwined social practices of education and medicine.

Felix Klauber will abandon the clinic for a life as a renowned and wealthy workaholic (and a lofty perch in a skyscraper accessible only by elevator); he even fails to show up on time for an important family ceremony for his nephew: the "redemption of the first born." His ethical detour is—in terms of plot—represented by his failure to participate in the change of generations. This is a serious misstep; his father, Meyer, knows better. When Felix eventually appears on the scene, Meyer—to Steiner's accompaniment of the most famous of all Yiddish folk songs, "Oyfn Pripetshok" (the "Alef-Beyz")—is relieved, and tearfully expresses his overwhelming contentment with his family and the happiness of his children. At the end of the monologue, Meyer collapses and is quickly diagnosed with a brain tumor, the set-up for the death scene mentioned above. *Kol nidre* sounds as Meyer is wheeled into the operating room, leaving no doubt as to the eventual outcome. About a decade earlier, in 1920, Dr. Jekyll and his evil alter ego were portrayed by John Barrymore, who, as a film actor, was known at the time primarily for his success in lightweight farces.[49] His portrayal of Jekyll served as a testing ground for the deformative gestures he would eventually bring to his role of Richard III. The film's famous transformation sequence employs no special effects: Barrymore's monstrosity is composed of facial and hand gestures, and I think we might extract from his performance the influence of the Jewish Lear's histrionic expressionism. Barrymore had gone to see Jacob Adler in a Yiddish production of Tolstoy's *The Living Corpse* in 1916, and he very much admired Adler's technique.[50]

In 1920, the same year as Barrymore's *Jekyll*, one of the most famous of Fannie Hurst's stories depicting the "Every Man's Land" surrounding New York's Bowery, "Humoresque," was released as a successful film.

A sound version of the story was made a quarter of a century later, with an impressive score by Franz Waxman—marked testimony to the longevity of Hurst's mode of drama as a vehicle for mainstream expressionism. Hurst's success as an author was paralleled throughout her career by the popularity of films based upon her writing. Her stories were already being made into movies by 1918, and between *Humoresque* in 1920 and *Symphony of Six Million* in 1932, Hollywood produced twelve Fannie Hurst feature films. Hurst's role in bringing to cinema and popular media in general a Yiddish theatrical sensibility, alongside her familiarity with and commitment to concert music, calls for greater consideration. Indeed, her work—not surprisingly, given that it was instantly successful, instantly commercial, and slanted especially toward women protagonists and women consumers—has been consigned to the corners of academic literary study.[51] Among several historically revelatory passages in her fiction is one that crystallizes the problematic class issues of the cinema demographic prior to the advent of sound.

One of Hurst's most celebrated short stories, "Sob Sister" (1916), represents the main character Mae Munroe and her "maid-of-all-work," Loo, who share an appreciation of popular song and movies. Loo (presumably an African-American woman, as in Hurst's famous *Imitation of Life*), even suggests that they attend the movies together to lift Mae's spirits, a notion that might have suggested to any American rural Christian of the period the level of social abandon promoted by the movie house environment. But Hurst's authorial eye was equally trained upon the world of the concert hall. (For Hurst, this *Zwiespalt* would mark her authorial dilemma throughout her career.)[52] I would suggest, in fact, that the proliferation of "women's films" during the World War II era and immediately following (those formerly assigned the sobriquet "soap operas") whose titles or plots revolve around musical concepts (including the sound version of Hurst's own "Humoresque") descend from her particular style and arsenal of vocabulary employed a generation earlier in print media. Married to a student and former companion of Raphael Joseffy (who even makes a brief appearance in her novel *Anitra's Dance*), Fannie viewed the world of her characters from a perspective markedly influenced by the musical threads of her own life.

For the history of early twentieth-century media, the most fascinating element of Fannie Hurst's own story is its revelation that style and gesture in media passed during this period in two directions at once. We are accustomed to thinking of films as picturizations of stories, but Hurst's oeuvre was marked by an inverse approach: she was among the first authors to create literature with a cinematic sensibility. On the one hand, her access to melodramatic presentation clearly derives from the principles of stage melodrama, as in this vignette from "Sob Sister": "On her knees before the piano . . . Mae Munroe listened to his retreating steps. . . . You who recede before the sight of raw emotions with every delicacy shamed, do not turn from the spectacle of Mae Munroe prone there on the floor, her bosom upheaved and her mouth too loose . . . for the sobs that bubbled too frankly to her lips [she] had no concern."[53] At the same time, we may sense in this 1916 text a capacity for literary visualization that could be transferred without effort to the filmic close-up. Such effects became part of the author's stock-in-trade.[54] It rendered the expressionism of her writing even more accessible and immediate, and it rendered her works more attractive to filmmakers. Both consequences were undeniably commercial, but the style—especially in its link to the ethical facets of melodrama—was not fundamentally or intentionally so. Hurst felt her own work was inspired by and responded largely to a commitment to an experimental, modernist aesthetic with socially progressive undertones.

The frontispiece and the title page of *Symphony of Six Million* as released in book form in 1932 reveal a new aspect of multimedia, one we tend to associate with much later practice: the circulation of a film as a novelized adaptation after or nearly simultaneous with its movie-theatrical release. (We are now familiar with such crossovers from books based on film and television series favorites like *Star Trek* and *Murder, She Wrote*).[55] Indeed, how can we assign *Symphony of Six Million* as a title or a concept to a single genre or medium? According to this apparently studio-authorized text, the title represents a novel (or "novelization"), a "screen story," and a "picture," the last underscored by the inclusion of one of the most melodramatic tableaux presented in the movie (a scene embodying its sense of class-related ethics) in a photo on the facing page.[56] Snapshots from film circulating as popular literature, then, well predate the full-blown Hollywood products of the technicolor and television eras. Quaint as "picturization"—that cliché of Hollywood studios in the early sound period—now sounds, its complement in the process of "novelization" of pictures demonstrates the potential range of media that might now be generated by or (in the case of traditional or popular songs) subsumed within a single title. This new eye (belonging to commercial interests, to be sure, but also to a new class of media consumer) toward the constituent parts of what we now call multimedia will eventually extend to the independent circulation of film score material in the form of theme recordings and sheet music. The speedy release of a texted version of Raksin's well-received title music for *Laura* is perhaps the most familiar historical example.

A very short item among the *Gaslight Stories* (1918), "Russia Free: Most Rigid Autocracy in the World Overthrown," reads almost like a sketch and dialogue for a cinema scene, including close-ups (of newspaper headlines, facial reaction shots) and the background music of an unseen orchestra (conveniently hidden behind some foliage). Music as a topic, and music of an especially cinematic sort as a literary ploy, makes its most effective and unprecedented appearance in one of Hurst's lesser-known large-scale efforts, the novel *Anitra's Dance*, published in 1934, two years after *Symphony of Six Million* and Steiner's score for it made their way to movie theaters. On the dust jacket of the first edition Hurst is called "one of America's most important writers," and this was certainly less hyperbolic at the time than it might appear to those who recall her now—following her rapid eclipse in fame after the 1930s—as nothing more than an evocative name linked to a particular era and milieu. *Anitra's Dance* is frankly experimental. Contributing to its relatively obscure stature even among students of Hurst's work has to be the book's off-putting graphic elements, notably the intrusion of musical notation throughout and the reliance of the book's climax on the acoustical content of a musical example that will be unrealizable by any nonmusical reader.

Hurst's protagonist Rudolph Bruno is a composer, attempting to complete the final movement of his "Span of Life" Symphony. His first two movements were, we learn, already in circulation (they had been completed in the Old World, in Vienna and Saalburg [*sic*]) and had met with great critical success. Within a short nine-page introductory chapter of the novel, the same four-measure unfinished theme appears (in piano score) five times, beginning with the first page. On the second page, two statements of the theme frame a graphic sketch for the span-of-life concept that Bruno obsessively reinscribes on every "telephone pad," "tablecloth," and "menu." An arc marked SPAN OF LIFE joins two tall and narrow rectangular pillars (BIRTH and DEATH, respectively). The drawing resembles nothing so much as one of the numerous steel bridges that link Manhattan to its outposts over and within its complex of rivers. Hurst vividly portrays the composer's artistic isolation against the backdrop of the island city in her description of what Bruno and his family term "the last house," perched at the end of Riverside Drive and 163rd Street, prior to the building of the drive's aqueduct, its landscape falling "in a rocky cascade to the Hudson River." The house, "solitary as a lighthouse . . . stood in a semblance of isolation." Hurst's topography stands as an effective literary device, but also as a sketch for what might have served as an effectively scenic film montage (one that was, of course, never realized).

Bruno's four measures reappear throughout the novel in those episodes in which he is installed as the primary figure. At the end of the novel his daughter Anitra (nothing like Grieg's, the character once remarked) expires of a chronic respiratory affliction familiar to readers of other Hurst tales. Heroines who press forward in spite of disease are hallmarks of Hurstian melodrama (in this she sits squarely within the parameters of the genre). Hurst's Jessica, reminding Felix toward the end of *Symphony of Six Million* of his medical obligations to the poor and of the domestic ethical system that imbued his and her youth with its special aura, is likewise situated within the expressionistic ethical register of melodrama (which Steiner, as I will explain, underscores appropriately). She is—from the perspective of character typing—above all a "cripple." The film's scenario introduces the theme in its earliest moments: young Jessica limps and is depicted as an object of playground ridicule.

At the moment of Anitra's passing, Bruno "goes through," his compositional efforts finally shattering the wall of musical and creative stasis as he effects a modulation from B Minor (a choice related perhaps to its popular association with "the unfinished" in music) to E Minor by way of a mode shift in the sixth measure (Example 3). Musical antecedent and consequent, the symmetry of Hugo Riemann's *Vierhebigkeit,* recall by their stacked appearance on the page the architectural, graphical effect of heavy symmetry that had marked Bruno's drawing of the span, the process taking us from birth to death, the signposts of the generations.[57] Beneath the notation, the last cinematographic sentences of the novel seem predestined for a series of camera close-ups (sentence two) in response to the off-screen music of Bruno's piano:

> Bruno had gone through!
> The house, along with everybody in it, had jumped forward like a hop-toad. All except Anitra, whose face on the pillow beside the splotch of red poppy was too calm.
> The sun, at its noonday zenith, practiced its trick of reaching into the very core of the Last House.
> It found out the recesses of the staircase, it reached into the niches which had originally been designed for the handles of the coffins, in order to facilitate maneuvering them down the stairs.
> THE END

Example 3. *Anitra's Dance:* "Symphony of Life"

Were we to take Bruno's portrayal as a serious composer at face
value, we might be tempted to seek models for his musical utterance in
repertoires associated with the concert music that was certainly familiar to Fannie and her friends. Her husband, Jacob Danielson, was supposed to have enjoyed a stellar career as a concert pianist but, because
of debilitating stage nerves, diverted his piano career in the direction of
pedagogy; he was likely Bruno's ghostwriter. The excerpt resembles in
some ways Schumann's simplest character pieces long anthologized in
teaching collections, in others the parlor pieces of the late nineteenth
century (a berceuse or barcarolle). But the form and style of *Anitra's
Dance* is primarily that of melodrama, especially Jewish melodrama. If
we listen to Bruno's symphony with those ears, we are likely to hear a
very marked similarity between this theme and the minor-mode "arias"
in 6/8 composed by Abraham Goldfaden in the late nineteenth century
for Eastern European "operatic" productions like *Shulamis* (source of
the very famous "Raisin and Almonds") and *Die Zauberin* (compare,
for example, "Elend bin ich," from the latter), although it has been com-
positionally bumped up from the perspective of harmony, perhaps by
Danielson.[58] Goldfaden's role in musical theater was similar to that of
Gordin for the more "classical" stage; his intention was to unite Yiddish
expressionism with a more elevated musical style (as Gordin had infused the elevated repertoire, including Shakespeare, with Yiddish expressionism).[59]

Cinematically the model for Hurst's gimmick here is twofold. A truncated presentation of a theme, eventually finished in a climactically melodramatic moment, was precisely the technique Silvers had brought to his treatment of Chaikovsky's *Romeo and Juliet* in *The Jazz Singer,* and I think it reasonable to assume that Hurst had this cinematic notion in her ear (particularly since she was at the time most familiar with silent film strategies, and since Silver's background score was attached to the silent portions of the Jolson film).[60] However, Steiner's score for her *Symphony* interceded between Jolson and Anitra, being the score in which he brought the notion of "continuous" hearing (i.e., a mode of musicodramaturgical understanding based on musical memory and interpretation) to a considerably more sophisticated level. As a novelistic device, Bruno's theme is an Ariadne's thread that leads the reader through a complex of episodes, locations, and characters (some of whom, like Raphael Joseffy, are quite peripheral). In this it functions less as a melodramatic effect (the Silvers model, the melodramatic *feu*) than as a leitmotif, precisely the model Steiner drew upon for his innovative (but, conventional film historiography notwithstanding, hardly epoch-making) scoring procedure. From the perspective I am advocating here, the gap between silent and sound film scoring yawns less impressively, and it might be supplanted by an understanding of surface innovations against the backdrop of generic continuity such as we regularly attribute to other genres—say operas or symphonies—that have been measured against chronological rulers of much greater magnitude.

Symphony of Six Million stands at the head of the history of sound film scoring as it came to be practiced through most of the first two-thirds of the twentieth century (and as in all but its surface aspects is still practiced today). Its operatic elements draw upon what Goldfaden (an untrained musician) had called, within the context of Yiddish musical theater, "the big world," to him the classical repertoire—including, he said, Meyerbeer and Verdi. Goldfaden's project in late nineteenth-century Romania was not very much different from Steiner's, whose description of *Symphony* resonates distinctly with the former's represented intention to "elevate" the musical elements of Yiddish theater above the primitive and the makeshift, and to link them to drama in a way that went beyond caricature. Hurst's literary Yiddishkeit has largely been expunged from the academic canon of significant topoi. Steiner's music is a looming presence in academic music studies, but here again its frame in Yiddishkeit has remained virtually ignored, aside from a few brief remarks, often no more than quips.[61]

Selznick's production opens with a shot of children on the streets of the ghetto, and Steiner responds with the tune generally associated with the children's game "Ring Around the Rosy." That tune is also employed (not only in America) as a conventional childhood taunt *(nyah-nyah-nyah-nyaaaah-nyah)*, rendering it appropriate for setting a juvenile scene as well as for setting up the children's cruel mockery of the crippled heroine, Felix's friend Jessica: their singsong taunt sung to the same tune is "Felix loves a goy-ul! Felix loves a crip-ple!" Steiner's treatment of the simple motive—which today can only be heard as quaint—was for the time a manifestation of virtuosity and, for media of the period, acoustical overload. First heard in the mouths of the children, it passes out of the realm of the diegesis to the background sector of the mise-en-bande. There it undergoes some modal deflections and eventually morphs into a Yiddish dance, whence it returns to underscore a dejected Jessica as a minor-mode transformation of another nursery rhyme, "London Bridge." (This material will be recycled later in leitmotivic fashion attached to the grown children at a critical, ethical juncture in the story.) Within the space of less than a minute of real time, at the very start of his first continuity score, Steiner inscribed the blueprint not just for the fundamental process and range of continuity scoring but for the zone of ambiguity between on- and off-screen sound so cherished by writers today.

As commentary, the multimedia matrix reinforces the understanding that Felix, his siblings, and their friends are not, even as children, inherently ethical creatures. Some of the children in the neighborhood are cruel and brutish. The particularly admirable moral compass of Felix, who is kind to Jessica, derives from Meyer, the father (this being the fundamental lesson concerning socialization transmitted in scripture). Returning home from work, Meyer Klauber engages in a semicomical interaction with his children that stresses throughout his emphasis on education. Chiding his older son for neglecting bar mitzvah lessons in favor of baseball, he raises his hand and waves it as a threat, but the threat is clearly not real. He is no Rabinowitz; the specter of corporal punishment is nothing more than a communicative trope within the family's practices of affectionate intergenerational banter. Even though it is his own birthday, he brings gifts for the children.

Significantly, the first of the gifts is a book for his daughter, a book "from classical piano pieces:" "I don't want my child to grow up and be ignorant that there was a man like Mozart, 'Beh-to-wen,' Rubinstein." The scene presents in microcosm the Jewish system of musical ethics conjoined to the immigrant aspiration to something better and more noble.

Whether these are linked to problematic sociological readings (posing, whiteface, bourgeois assimilation) or to systems of professional aesthetics (Goldin, Goldfaden)—and cinema sits somewhere between—the theme of music as part of a tradition of education within the family structure is significant. Music is the zone wherein the practice of the synagogue intersects with the registers of domestic human expression.[62] Hurst set the scene for "Humoresque" the same way. Even a work as raw as Michael Gold's 1930 novel and social critique *Jews Without Money* includes passages that espouse or imply the same principles of family and community ownership of music and its effects.[63] Meyer Klauber, shortly before his death, explicitly links the twin themes of music and education to an ethical position (i.e., one situated in the life well lived): "When the children were all young and lived 'way downtown, I used to say to them, 'Children, each one of you must know how to play a musical instrument.' Why? I'll tell you why! . . . Because I wanted them to grow up to be educated. Not only for themselves, but to give others happiness."[64]

Linking his own happiness to the successful education and full lives of his three children within the community (they have become doctor, businessman, mother), he declares himself fully satisfied with his time on earth "if the Lord should want to take my life away." It is a Yiddish digest of Aristotle's exposition concerning happiness, goodness, and political science in book 1 of his *Ethics*. When Meyer dies, he dies an Aristotelian, but more specifically he dies a father and a Jew. Steiner's cue, "Father's Death," reiterates the cinematically standard reading of *Kol nidre* as a familial lament linked to the patriarchal succession. But there is more. Steiner makes a seamless transition to another melody, presented in an extraordinarily funereal, lugubrious manner on the organ (not a grand organ, but the small sound associated with poor synagogues and domestic parlors). The tune again is that of "Oyfn Pripetshok." It is not a song of death, per se, but of children (hence its original presentation in the film during the "redemption of the first born" scene). Its lyrics describe the warmth of the hearth, linked to the ever important theme of education: the rabbi is teaching the children the aleph bet, linking it to "the tears and weeping of our people." In Steiner's score, "Oyfn Pripetshok" represents the primary ethical thread that binds the generations, and (as a vehicle for performance) it does so specifically through the act of song. It is the popular foil to *Kol nidre:* not a song of the synagogue but a composed popular song (one that, though often called a folk song, was written in the late nineteenth century by Mark Warshawsky).

Meyer Klauber, in his last moments, cannot speak for himself, but Steiner's cue—consisting of the dovetailing of two Jewish classics linked in vernacular entertainments to paternal heritage and the patriarchally defined system of domestic ethics—sings of his status as a father and an ethical Jew. His ethical sensibility, as we learned at the outset, is revealed in his commitment to the elevation of his children to the better life, one in which the expressive potential of art finds a place. To situate this element of the score in a broader historical context, I should point out that Steiner's resort to popular song lyrics (unheard, but familiar to a substantial segment of the audience for this decidedly Yiddish-oriented film) foreshadows the superabundant reliance upon pop song lyrics as tracking glosses that informs so much of recent pastiche scoring, from the innovations of *The Graduate* to the tiresome bathos of pop song commentaries that constitute much of contemporary television scoring. Indeed, Steiner seems to have been just what he represented himself to be, a verifiable original.

Felix Klauber, the surgeon of Hurst's *Symphony*, is a stand-in for the musicians she frequently draws upon from her own set of expressive registers. Notable here is Leon Kantor, the violinist of "Humoresque"; that story began with the depiction of children in affectionate confrontation with their father over matters of lessons (spelling and music). Rehearsing but inflating a standard trope of Yiddish musical theater regarding the expressive violin, Hurst describes Leon's virtuosity in melodramatic terms: "To Leon . . . life was a chromatic scale, yielding up to him, through throbbing, living nerves of sheep-gut, the sheerest semitones of man's emotions." For most Jews of the early twentieth century, the doctor was "a community idol," as Gold wrote in 1930. "In every pauper Jewish family the mother's dream was to have one of her sons a Doctor, as in every Irish family she dreamed of a Priest."[65] Felix's "million dollar hands" are part of the mise-en-scène depicting his emotional breakdown after Meyer's death and scored with a minor-mode version of the title's "education" processional. As horrifyingly severed as those encountered elsewhere in this book, the body parts that have secured his fortune and reputation (the illustration for a *Vanity Fair* magazine cover story) are framed and hung on the wall.

My suggestion that Felix is essentially a replacement for Hurst's musicians is based upon the resemblance between that image and those found in musical publications that proliferated in the early part of the century, driven by what Slobin has called "piano fever," particularly in Jewish cultural aggregations in America. Many editions of early- to mid-twentieth-century classical or semiclassical music that was geared toward consumption by household amateurs portray on their covers drawings or photos of hands divorced from bodies. T. B. Harms Company's series *Jerome Kern's Popular Favorites in Classical Style* in the 1930s featured monochrome covers depicting a woman's perfectly manicured and bejeweled wrists and hands pressing on a keyboard, likewise severed from its host piano and displayed at a dynamic angle. Covers of music produced by Jewish presses in New York and reproduced in Slobin's *Tenement Songs* show how the same trope extended to the violin, an image effectively cinematized in the 1946 version of *Humoresque* during the "demonic" sequence of the protagonist's concert scene (featuring "real" concert music composed by Waxman). Sheet music for a piano arrangement of "Play Fiddle Play" published by E. B. Marks in 1932 represents a dizzying hybrid. It features eight negative-silhouette images of hands at piano keyboards skewed at several different angles. They appear to be engaged in a process of exponential generation and suggest a multiplanar depth despite their monochromatic environment. A signature of Marks's "Modern Standard Piano Series," the image, linked in this specific case to the title's anthropomorphized violin, participates in a visual conflation hinting at the near-Orphic impossibility of musical virtuosity in general. Nothing more than sheet music for a sentimental gypsy standard (missing its crooner lyrics), the object is emblematic of the communicative potency residing in all fragmentary representations of classical music, an expressive power located in this case within the visual register of the musical classic.

WHOSE CLASSIC?

Film music's debt to Jewish modes of expression—whether liturgical or commercial—are clear especially when the films under consideration possess unambiguously Jewish content. But to satisfy our academic lust for originary models, might we locate in Jewish musical practice a model in general for conventional "Golden Age" film scoring that fits its parameters better than the ultimately unsatisfying examples of European opera and European melodrama? Both are part of the mix, but neither—as genres—really reflect the essential components of film scoring, especially its marked discontinuity of utterance and affect (even in the case of a score that "sounds" continuously) and its reliance upon familiar material drawn from a wide range of registers, including liturgical song, popular song and dance, and national or ethnographic musical emblems.

When we speak of Yiddish theater what are we talking about? Yiddish theater is an umbrella term that covers a lot of stylistic ground from vaudevilles and revues to would-be dramatic classics. Within the surviving repertoire there are certain musicodramatic types that offer illuminating backdrops to any understanding of how the language of film music beyond the realm of the film musical (the Broadway or Tin Pan Alley film), and especially music for film dramas, coalesced in the way it did. Steiner said that he treated the Jewish classics "as if" in an opera. How, then, might such items be more regularly presented, that is, not in an opera? I refer not exclusively to *Kol nidre,* "Oyfn Pripetshok," or his Jewish dance tunes but to the full range of musical dialects presented in melodramatic (i.e., dramatically punctuating) fashion from 1932 onward.

We can begin with the spotty remnants of what Yiddish musical theater looked like with respect to its musical components. Mark Slobin has reconstructed one such four-act drama, *David's Violin (Dowids Fidele),* premiered in New York in 1897 and alive for decades thereafter (Slobin cites a 1911 Prague performance mentioned in Kafka's *Tagebücher*).[66] I would suggest—judging by Slobin's description of the materials for the musical content of the play—that they resemble nothing so much as twentieth-century film scores and cue sheets. These in many cases do not survive, since they were consistently cannibalized, with fragments removed and inserted into other productions. Film-music cue sheets merely identify by name and source the music to be applied to a certain segment of the film. As in film music of the 1930s to the present, arrangers in Yiddish musical theater were often responsible for more of the finished product than were the "composers." As Slobin described the extant material for Yiddish music drama: "No contemporary scores exist for these works, nor for any others. Full scores were rarely used in this tradition; conductors worked from sets of scrawled instrumental parts, using a 'lead sheet' marked *Direction.* These were expected to be durable; one such set for the all-time favorite musical drama Goldfaden's *Shulamis,* was copied in 1903 in Odessa, Russia, reached Lodz, Poland, by 1904, and was signed out for use in Vilna, Lithuania, in 1940. . . . Also clear is the impact of arrangers."[67]

Yiddish music drama's content is equally interesting to consider as a model for film practices. Original dramas will regularly call for the presentation of already familiar musical items within their librettos. *David's Violin* is about music, about musicianship, and it concludes with an intergenerational celebration of the value of music and musical education.

Slobin's reconstruction incorporates "Auf'n pripetchok" as the second big song, and he reproduces a 1916 sheet-music cover of the song, featuring the caption "Sung by Cantor J. Rosenblatt," whose concert performance was a highlight in the film of *The Jazz Singer*. It sits atop a photo of the cantor mounted on an easel drawn in the stylized shape of an Orphic lyre. At the top of the page the blurb reads: "The Success of the Season," signaling the mixture of commerce and religion that characterized New York theatrical venues.

But of even greater historical significance are the marginal indications—like "here the violin enters as *melodram*,"—that appear in librettos and direction sheets for Yiddish dramas and likely point to the use of musical fragments as background scoring for dialogue or action. The earliest surviving scores, from Jassy in Romania (where Goldfaden had established his theater), date from 1881. They include many international tunes, including most notably "*Janke dudil* in C Major," an early example of the integration into Yiddish melodramatic scoring conventions of the very emblem that would throughout his career serve Steiner so well in such dramatic scores as his award-winning films *The Informer* and *Now, Voyager*.[68] In Gordin's *Got, mentsch, un tayvl*, a musical setting of Psalm 23 (see *Sons of Liberty*) is treated as a leitmotif, being sung and also played on the violin.[69] Any tendency on the part of Steiner and his contemporaries (like Forbstein) to rely upon national and ethnographic musical icons in dramatic scoring possibly derives not only from their familiarity with that gambit from Yiddish theater but also from the subject matter of those productions.

An unusually specific genre within Yiddish musical theater (specific with respect to its formal parameters) was the *melo-deklamatsye*, discussed by David Mazower.[70] The *melo-deklamatsyes* of Joseph Markovitsh, dramatic poems with musical settings that were suitable for concert performance, were for the most part written before the end of the 1920s. Among the most popular was *Kol nidre;* it circulated throughout the 1920s and into the 1930s. It opens upon the cantor singing the prayer when, suddenly, to the accompaniment of march music, German and Russian armies approach the *shtetl*. The liturgical melody, then, is woven into a musical fabric in which it stands as a marker of the Jews' ethical position maintained against the forces of oppression. Subjugating groups are marked by musical fragments that represent not so much their heritage as some sense of their political, aggressive, or antiethical positions. Even if they are not national anthems, one cannot fail to hear in this musical exchange a foreshadowing of the scoring that Steiner will eventually apply to *Casablanca* (juxtaposing the "natural" music of the North African "gypsy song" to the catalogue of anthems in Rick's place) and Forbstein to *Sons of Liberty*. Like other Yiddish theater items, the *melo-deklamatsye* consisted of a dazzling array of stylistic and genre references.

Markovitsh's *Kol nidre,* according to Mazower, is about five minutes long but includes "four languages (Yiddish, Hebrew, German, and Russian), as well as frequent changes of tempo and musical style (including khazons, recitative, march, military songs, and unaccompanied declamation)."[71] Its nod to Jewish melodrama is located in its conclusion: Moyshe the coachman offers himself to the soldiers for execution in order to save the rest of the community. He is shot, and the piece concludes with a return to *Kol nidre.* Both that plotline and the role of *Kol nidre* as a sign of noble death and sacrifice (one of the themes Peter Brooks positioned at the core of true melodrama) resonate in the prison scene of MGM's *Sons of Liberty.* The extensive range of musical types proliferating within the opening segment of Steiner's *Casablanca,* linked to one of the most overt conflations of ethics and political positioning within the library of Hollywood's Golden Age, likewise seem to reflect precisely this aesthetic, inherited from Yiddish musicodramatic forms.[72]

Steiner was perhaps not a Yiddishist, but he had plenty of appropriate exposure to the norms of Yiddish entertainments. His father, Gabor, was an impresario of musical theater and an entertainment entrepreneur. Gabor Steiner had purchased the Prater in Vienna in the 1890s and, as part of his program to expand the park's audience to the humbler classes—"maids and sailors"—commissioned the construction of Vienna's now iconic Riesenrad. Praterstrasse, leading up to the park, was one of the principal thoroughfares of Leopoldstadt, the Jewish district, and the site of a significant number of vaudevillian Jewish entertainment venues whose presence increased throughout the first years of the twentieth century and especially after the beginning of World War I. (The district's Budapester Orpheum was known as "the home of Jewish humor.")[73] Max Steiner, after graduating from the Vienna Academy with distinction, obtained a position as a conductor at the London opera but was in 1914 declared an enemy alien and emigrated to New York. His musical occupations in the period prior to his 1928 move to the West Coast were confined primarily to vaudeville, where he earned a living as a pianist, and then to higher-toned musical theater, where he served as musical director for important revues like the "Ziegfeld Follies" and shows by Gershwin, Kern, and others.[74] Steiner, true to the model for film-music composers, emerged from a highly diversified background, but it was one that was substantially infused with Jewish musical traditions, and those same traditions have already been linked historically— through the transformation of theater venues into movie houses—to the development of cinema conventions.

By allowing that the high-toned musical soundscape of big-budget Hollywood may have derived from similar models, we might get past one of the thorniest questions facing academics working with film music, whether as scholars or as teachers. Does film music constitute a genre? The assumption that it might—indeed, that it does—lies behind the quest for a simple generic model that has occupied scholarly attention for some time. Attempts to fix it specifically, to align film music with some model category that it reflects in toto, have depended mainly upon the perspective of whoever is doing the fixing.[75] I would argue that it is as much a genre, and as much bound to a system of genre parameters, as was Yiddish theater. This is to say not a genre but a tradition. Styles, forms, genres, and even institutions are prone to disposal or radical rethinking by successive generations. Societies tend to take better care of their traditions, however homely or even embarrassing to their intellectual aspirations, particularly when they seem to be linked in some unexpressed way to community ethics (of family, faith, village). Every household will cling tenaciously to its recipe for turkey dressing or potato latkes, to its position on whether or not the tree should be tinseled. Small wonder that despite the extent to which its invocation often offends cutting-edge sensibilities, the expressionistic potential of the classic register and the register of the classic has remained viable from the Yiddish stage through Hollywood's golden age and beyond, to the virtual mise-en-scène associated with pop, rock, and rap.

PART TWO

Envisioning the Classic

CHAPTER 4

Hearing Monsters

In 1967, shortly after the now classic "Strawberry Fields Forever" made its way out of the studio and onto the British record charts, pop radio listeners with an ear for progressive content celebrated the release of Procol Harum's debut single "A Whiter Shade of Pale."[1] "Strawberry Fields" (the Beatles' tone poem *d'après* Debussy, according to producer George Martin) never reached the number one spot occupied a few months later in the United Kingdom by "A Whiter Shade of Pale."[2] Procol Harum's effort achieved greater and more immediate success in the United States as well. For those hearing "A Whiter Shade of Pale" for the first time, Gary Brooker's vocal—marked by an earthy and familiar soul timbre wrapped around Keith Reid's disjointed fantasy lyric—was effective and alluring, but when it appeared at the foreground of the musical texture it could only briefly upstage the song's principal draw: a sinuous organ ritornello in the style of J. S. Bach performed by the group's keyboard player, Matthew Fisher. Throughout the spring and summer of 1967 the British pop trade paper *Melody Maker* hyped "A Whiter Shade of Pale" in stories and interviews; by June, Decca announced with considerable satisfaction that it had been the company's fastest-selling record ever for a new group and was, according to their representative speaking through the publication's pages, "some feat because not even the Monkees or Rolling Stones sold that quickly with their first records."[3] Journalistic encomia inevitably highlighted the unusual soundscape of the number, which combined, in the words of one of *Melody Maker*'s writers, "Bach-inspired

organ chords and modern soul vocal."[4] More recently, as musicologists
have constructed methodological frames for the analysis and criticism of
popular music, the song's structural and acoustic elements have been addressed in the same terms, and with a similar lack of precision.[5]

Within a few years after the arrival of "A Whiter Shade of Pale,"
rock's acoustical territory had been transformed by the unchecked proliferation of concert hall affectations and a glib reliance on ham-fisted
symphonism. *Melody Maker* unwittingly recorded the rapid decline of
the previously experimental "classical" mode into a commercial staple
(normally indicative of stylistic decadence in rock repertoires) in its review of King Crimson's acoustically muscular but aesthetically disap-
pointing offering *In the Wake of Poseidon*. Within the perimeters of the
popular imagination as it was inscribed in commercial rock journalism,
the musical resources and practices of the past had become a form of musical steroid linked above all to aural mass as encapsulated in the review's
laudatory headline: "If Wagner were alive today he'd work with King
Crimson."[6]

But any story of what I will term "fantastic" rock's predisposition for
the musical discourses of the past calls for contextual enrichment, especially as it represented a cultural position bounded by the arts, commerce,
technology, and society that was only superficially new. Reid's lyrics offer
a useful vantage point from which we might begin to look back. These
were, according to his own account, suggested by a moment observed at
what he euphemistically termed a "gathering." Interviewed at the height
of the song's popularity by *Melody Maker,* Reid recalled: "Some guy
looked at a chick and said to her 'You've gone a whiter shade of pale.'
That phrase stuck in my mind. It was a beautiful thing for someone to
say. . . . I wrote down more ideas later. They tend to come out in an abstract way instead of a literal way, though. If you read meaning into things
it loses its abstract sense."[7] The room portrayed in Reid's lyrics was
"humming harder," amplified by the electric buzz of drug intoxication
and fed by the ambient noise of musical playback.[8] Gatherings and hap-
penings in which background music and recreational drugs came together
were by the late 1960s standard arenas for a particular mode of public listening. Considered as ethnographic events, they combined the traditional
ritual of the straight, adult cocktail party (the song's lyrics portray, in fact,
a waiter with a tray) with the diluted remnants of the recent hallucinogenic age of exploration.[9] Marked by a largely sincere if inflated opti-
mism, the investigation of consciousness, fueled not only by drugs but
also by music, was central to the lives and works of earlier poets of

abstraction, especially the Beats, whose fractured rhetoric provided the model for much of the psychedelic poetry of the subsequent generation.[10]

WAGNER ELECTRIFIED

In 1959 the Beats' bard Allen Ginsberg penned a contemplative lyric, "Lysergic Acid," in response to a controlled experiment with LSD that he undertook at the Mental Research Institute in Palo Alto, California, another stage in his long-standing exploration of the implications of a 1948 vision in which he had heard the voice of William Blake:[11]

> It is a multiple million eyed monster
> it is hidden in all its elephants and selves
> it hummeth in the electric typewriter
> it is electricity connected to itself, if it hath wires
> it is a vast Spiderweb
> and I am on the last millionth infinite tentacle of the spiderweb,
>   a worrier
> lost, separated, a worm, a thought, a self . . .
> . . . .
> But at the far end of the universe the million-eyed Spyder that hath no
>   name
> spinneth of itself endlessly . . .

Ginsberg's monster, the absent "spyder" ("the Nameless . . . the Hidden-from-me") in his altered state of consciousness was God, he thought, or maybe the Devil. It was the recognition of unquantifiables more than theology that concerned him: this monster expands to the "billion-eyed," yet at the same time "thrills in its minutest particulars."

In preparation for the experiment, the poet had been offered his choice of musical accompaniment for the journey; he had selected Wagner's *Tristan und Isolde.* Wagner's rich web of motivic threads issuing from an unremarkable electrical source (the phonograph) must have functioned as an acoustical metaphor and inspiration for Ginsberg's hallucinogenic epiphany of life, body, and mind, particularly as he expressed it in the image of a monster inhabiting an electric spider's web suspended across the infinite. If as metaphor its obviousness renders it trivial, it is nevertheless suggestive of the extent to which hallucinogens encouraged the reconsideration and reinvention of historical modes of aesthetic production and reception.[12] By combining the potential of LSD with what he understood as the potential aural experience of *Tristan,* Ginsberg initiated a new poetics of listening that was specific to his aesthetic and ethical positions, and his sensual and analytical impressions during the session were captured as written (typed) text. Within the lab, the acoustical *Tristan* metamorphosed from an experienced localized phenomenon (i.e., the music emanating from the player) into something else during the course of the experiment. Wagner's sound crossed an experiential line and entered the realm of the noumenal, conforming to a mode of backgrounding that rendered the poet's experience perhaps more cinematic than operatic.[13]

But even more significantly it served, as Ginsberg had hoped it might, as an indicator of the numinous—of revelation concealed just beyond its sensual acoustical content: "I cry out where I am in the music, to the room, to whomever near, you, Are you God?" Ginsberg employed the mundane pronouns "it" and "I," thus normalizing his description of experiential space and, however unintentionally, cinematizing the topography of the poem through the introduction of antagonistic characters. In this the poet's strategy was reflective of his general tendency to domesticate spiritual ecstasis—and hence to diminish the force of its eventual and inescapable deflation—by poetical means, even while other features of language explode his image out to unfathomable and incongruent dimensions.[14] Locating himself as a speck upon an intangible web of electricity (the unseen force), he is enveloped by its acoustic double: the sound of a ubiquitous and equally insubstantial hum. He concretized that impression in another telling image: a tangible network of visible wires, reminders of the presence of those hard-science laboratory accoutrements that were feeding with electrical energy both the musical numen and the typewriter receiving and fixing the poet's sensations as text. Even though Ginsberg's *Tristan* was a monaural recording, and the numen within humbly described in the poem as "the radio of the future," his construction of distance in the poetic mise-en-scène (the poet as tiny being located at the tip of the last tentacle) invokes an explicitly stereoscopic and implicitly stereophonic perspective: "This image of energy which reproduces itself at the depths of space from the very Beginning."

A century and a half earlier, in a pre-electrical world, Keats had described social and artistic intercourse in a remarkably similar way, each man's web (his "airy Citadel") intersecting and overlapping with countless others.[15] His webs, like Ginsberg's, had something to do with the notion of soul and the way we might put it together, soul being as much an aesthetic as a theological immanence. Engulfed in the musical wash that helped to inspire "Lysergic Acid," Ginsberg wrote expressively of radiating "aethereal lightwaves," resonating with "whatever drug, or aire, they breathed to make them think so deep or simply hear what passed" from its similarly themed contemporary, "Aether."[16] Keats's spider, too, created an ethereal music: she "fills the Air with a beautiful circuiting." In the end, each point of intersection on his spider's web embraces a sameness of souls: "Minds would leave each other in contrary directions, traverse each other in Numberless points, and at last greet each other at the Journey's end." The significance of these congruent points was familiar to Ginsberg, updated from one of his principal sources of inspiration: Huxley's (Bergsonian) notion of the Mind-at-Large. In midcentury Palo Alto, three souls—Ginsberg, Blake, and Wagner—came together after a metaphorical journey (or "trip"), and the point of arrival lay in a sounding realm that bridged any number of contraries, including the distance between "art" and "something else," measured in this peculiar instance between Wagner and a range of mediating technologies embracing the electrical, the acoustical, and the medical.

Ginsberg's undertaking was based on an additional Romantic conceit, the notion that the artist's muse should inhabit a space even more extensive and unimaginable than those described and inscribed in the Judeo-Christian construction of the supernatural. Romantic poetics located both inspiration and practice in something that was, as Wordsworth painted in the lines of his *Prelude,* greater than Jehovah, the shouting angels, the noise of chaos, heaven, and hell. Its power was unleashed only "when we look Into our Minds, into the Mind of Man."[17] Even if his poem's invocation of immeasurable number recalls Kant's mathematical sublime, Ginsberg's numen—the unnamable "who" encrypted by his arachnid tetragrammaton and literally "sensed" as a presence behind and within the music—encompassed a dimension not merely of apprehension but of experience that exceeded both it and the "dynamical" thunderbolts of Enlightenment aesthetics.[18] The reconfigured Romantic position, by which I intend something considerably more specific than a bloat of hyper-Romantic excess, matched well the particular extremes of imagination and action that characterized the marginal lives and artistic productions associated with a range of midcentury drug subcultures.

Conjoined to scientific positivism it points toward an antitranscendent present approaching, as Allen Weiss has argued, something like an aesthetic "counter-sublime."[19] Weiss locates the "oxymoron of an innate apocalyptic sublime" in a temporality that "is constituted by a closed, reflexive circuit of physiological rhythms and thresholds; where consciousness, subsumed by pure presence, eschews all transcendence;

where the imagination exists in direct proportion to somatization." Circuiting bears a literal relation to the electrical network in Ginsberg's revelations, but in highlighting the reflexivity of the aesthetic circuit Weiss (who was concerned with early modernism) was thinking particularly of Mallarmé's metaphorical fold *(pli)*. David Code has associated the metaphor with Debussy; Weiss follows Ginsberg in his description of the poetic convolutions of Mallarmé as "not unrelated to Wagnerian chromaticism and the evanescence of the infinite melodic line" (echoes of the poet's "indefinite unfolding" and "syntactic convolutions," within the frame of a highly stylized discursive system, may be heard throughout Ginsberg's own work, of course).[20] However we might theorize the details of Ginsberg's bizarre setting—one that brought the machinery of high technology (including stroboscopes and electroencephalographs) to bear upon measuring the dimensions of the human spirit—his turn to classical music, *generaliter dictum,* was apparently not that far out of line with other more mainstream musical imaginations.[21]

AETHERNETS

About a year after the Palo Alto experiment, on the other side of the country, another Wagnerian explorer was at work. In his one-room New York apartment above the main office of Philles Records, Phil Spector (then producer for the girl groups the Crystals and the Ronettes) conjured Wagner from his sound system, according to the songwriter Ellie Greenwich, who recalled that "he would be upstairs in his one room listening with the speakers blasting, conducting. Wagner was his idol and Wagner was power and bigness and heavy and all that and I think he was going after that in his records."[22] Greenwich's report is corroborated by the words of Spector himself, who termed his perfected sound environment—what came to be known as the wall of sound—"a Wagnerian approach to rock and roll."[23] His model, originally manifested as an essentially opaque acoustic projection, achieved greater dimensionality in the hands of other producers (e.g., George Martin) in the stereophonic era, at which point the sound box, as Allan Moore has characterized the aural dimensions of pop production, began to take on the acoustic architecture and implicit sonic perspective of a virtual concert hall.[24]

Spector's Wagnerism obviously yielded results different from Ginsberg's, since the two worked in different media and for different audiences. Both, however, sought through Wagner—technologically mediated—a path to the future, even if few musicians hearing the Ronettes' "Be My

Baby" or the Crystals' "Then He Kissed Me," two of Philles' hits in 1963, will recognize Wagner's presence as *"acousmaître"* in the mix.[25] "Bigness" and "heaviness," the terms invoked by Greenwich, appear to argue against Spector's musical and cultural stance as a particularly nuanced one. Even in the 1960s his wall was critiqued by rock insiders for having launched a trend in recording projects that diverted authentic rock in the direction of Muzak by way of what one critic wryly characterized as "eclectic silence denial."[26]

And yet the sound of the acoustical environment Spector achieved in the girl-group records for Philles, its density notwithstanding, has also been described as "almost ethereal," positioning the end result of Spector's experiment in the same experiential dimension—and recalling the music of self mapped by Keats—as the one I suggested was discovered by Ginsberg in the MRI's *Tristan*-drenched lab space.[27] A member of Spector's first band (the Teddy Bears) insinuated the same, remarking that the sound production that Spector called for from the players was perceived by his musicians as being "played in" and "moved through" "the air."[28] Crucial to the ethereal presence in Spector's recordings was his use of ambience effects (i.e., reverberation) which characteristically serve as powerful expressive agents in prompting imaginative reception processes within a wide range of recorded media and multimedia. For example, an explicitly dimensional and almost pointillistic mix of percussion effects (*Klangfarben* distinguished by timbre and prominence) map nodal points in the airy acoustico-spatial sound web of Crystals numbers like "He Hit Me (It Felt Like a Kiss)" and "No One Ever Tells You." In their reliance upon the aural construction of imaginary empty space, both serve as effective counters to the "silence-denial" critique—even if the former contains some rather lush string parts—and underscore the relevance of Albin Zak's description of the power of ambience effects, especially their noumenal implications: "Because we associate ambience with space, it provides the illusion that the recording exists in some unique place, the true world of the disembodied voice."[29]

Spector's use of reverberating percussion to open up the sound space has more recently been acoustically referenced and reenvisioned by the Danish band the Raveonettes. Their "Red Tan," for example, features Spector's trademark sleigh bells.[30] Even more striking with respect to Spectorian ambience is "Ode to L.A." The group's output has been for the most part purposefully and imaginatively "retro," drawing in the past on classic rock sources like Buddy Holly. (Perhaps we should consider a happier descriptor than "retro"—perhaps *stile antico*?—for such reinventions.) Songs of this type serve alongside other alternative twenty-first century media as reminders that musical retrospect is not and has never been retrogressive—in any century or generation—except to the ears of modernists.

Ginsberg's electrical web (literally an *ethernet* before the fact) was co-incidentally an apt metaphor for the rich relational matrix of all twentieth-century media culture. As poetry the text embodied its own time yet looked back to the future (in its juxtaposition of the quaint—*hummeth*—with the technological—*the electric typewriter*). Wagner's acousmatic presence in the lab, electrically conjured, was another element of that network. Twentieth-century cultural critics and their heirs in late twentieth-century media theory have consigned by means of what is now a flaccid critical trope virtually all twentieth-century reinventions (Procol Harum's Bach) or relocations away from "the hall" (Ginsberg's or Spector's Wagner) of earlier art music, so called, to categories of cultural regression. This remains a fundamental position even when such reinventions are understood to possess some potential to function in a culturally anticipatory manner. The first wave of such critiques was directed most pointedly toward anything linked to the "hyper-Romantic" models of Wagner and Richard Strauss, whose dramatic constructions already looked back—problematically—to imagined mythical or quasi-historical pasts.[31] At the acoustical surface, the lushness of mass-mediated instrumental sound was, it has been suggested, a new kind of trap for the consuming herd. Worse, though, was the leitmotif. Adorno's descriptions of the Wagnerian leitmotif highlighted its communicative obviousness, its need to "hammer its message home," a criticism that has been regularly directed at leitmotivic film scores (and also the subject of Adorno's own critique, written in collaboration with composer Hanns Eisler, *Composing for the Films*).[32]

A more fundamental problem than motivic transparency, at least for Adorno, was the formal irresponsibility of leitmotivic procedures, especially their evasion of "the necessity to create musical time," something that makes them useful for the discontinuous scoring requirements of most narrative films, and—in the more abstract sense in which Adorno intended it—the very quality that likely attracted Ginsberg to *Tristan*. Musical invocations of the psychedelic (more broadly, the fantastic) that followed in the decade after Ginsberg's experiment often mined the musical potential of Baroque music which, with its tendency to emphasize the division of time units into fixed and regular subsets, may seem an odd choice.[33] But it is the process by which the sense of Baroque melody coalesced through gestural reiteration and gestural expansion, carrying within it the implication of its own possibly uncontainable potential to spin out to an immeasurable brink (like the *unendliche Melodie* of Ginsberg's Wagnerian spider) that clearly drew the attention of twentieth-century ears accustomed to pop introductions built from staid and predictable four-bar units; hence the appropriateness of Fisher's Bachian prelude to Reid's fantastic verse in "A Whiter Shade of Pale."[34] The loosening up of time—a central concern of the Beats—found a new realization here, in a realm that (as I will argue in the next chapter) featured acoustical markers linked to specific historical modes of aesthetic production and reception that included the fantastic, the picturesque, and the nostalgic.

Those so-called regressive, Romantic, and sentimental excesses of twentieth-century mass media—with the third adjective usually invoked in its most general sense as part of a presumptive critique of the sentimental as a category of aesthetic negation—have recurrently been consigned to a critical no-place, the *utopia.* Utopia is lately a term of cultural-critical derision; it has been in some instances superseded by the notion of the *dystopia,* a construction doubling its critical potency and decoupling it from any troublesome historical associations with Thomas More's original, a no-place that was hardly a happy *eutopia.* But if we dismiss Spector (Wagner's acousmatic projection as a bubble-gum wall) and Ginsberg (Wagner's acousmatic projection as psychedelic wallpaper), if we reduce them to historically contemporaneous instantiations of the century's collective and regressive desire to flee toward meaningless, homogenous, and irrelevant utopias, we will not likely arrive at a very interesting position of historical or critical insight.

Theory reveals itself in such formulations as a praxis of taxonomic entomology in which beautiful and idiosyncratic webs are shattered for the sake of grabbing, naming, and classifying their "spyders." Adorno, interestingly enough, also found the spider's web a useful simile. His interest lay neither in the process of its spinning nor in the uncertain timeline governing its creation or the point at which it might—if ever—reach its conclusion. To Adorno, the web (a site of critique rather than a form of artistic discourse) was a fixed and hard structure, a sort of radioactive peephole into the real world. "Properly written texts are like spiders' webs: tight, concentric, transparent, well-spun and firm." The writer's web "proves its relation to the object as soon as other objects crystallize around it. In the light that it casts on its chosen substance, others begin to glow." Always ready to confront the shamefulness of reality, rather

than hiding behind ornament and the surface beauty of expressive artifice, these inhospitable webs of critique negatively mirror, by Adorno's
standard dialectical inversion, those others I have described. Their construction depends not on the power of invention and its source in a diffuse yet lively collective memory but on an individual craft that, however
beautiful in its "purity of expression," must remain harsh and predatory.
The textual webs of social critique do not undulate or breathe with the
air; they are black holes of entrapment: "They draw into themselves all
the creatures of the air. Metaphors flitting hastily through them become
their nourishing prey. Subject matter comes winging towards them."[35]

By contrast to critical theory we might, for example, bring a critical
focus to bear not upon Wagner's inauthentic position with respect to an
understanding of the historical reality of mid-twentieth-century America
but upon other features of these reports. The solitary nature of these two
historical moments is striking, even if both were linked to broader societies by implication or effect. To hear Wagner in such a specific and unusual way, in solitude rather than in the company of others, represents
a radical experiential transformation of the music's original reception
and, considered from this perspective, might suggest frames more flexible or open to further interpretation than those based on an understanding of the social, economic, and historical contexts for its musical
surface. On one hand either of these isolated acts of creative listening,
Ginsberg's or Spector's, might be relegated to the same intensively personal, deliberately self-indulgent modes of aural immersion celebrated in
recent "critical neo-Lyric" texts produced by some academic writers on
opera, or to the sort of musical narcosis targeted by Marxist theory.[36]

On the other hand, it can be argued that Ginsberg's mind-bending
musical experience embraced by the isolated laboratory conditions of a
marginal scientificism, and Spector's megalomaniacal Wagner fantasy
(apparently a private restaging of the *Dirigent-als-Übermensch* fantasy deeply inscribed in the multimediated imagination by the opening Bach sequence of Disney's *Fantasia*) situate each rather specifically
within the tradition of mad science.[37] Mad science (revisited in subsequent chapters), the cornerstone of science fiction, finds its roots not in
Romanticism, per se, but at the Romantic edge of Enlightenment
thought, especially Mary Wollstonecraft Shelley's *Frankenstein: A Modern Prometheus*.[38] Spector and Ginsberg were not "fans" of Wagner but
aesthetic Prometheans seeking in the technologies of electricity or chemistry a way of gaining individualistic mastery over the perception and
recreation of natural phenomena. In fact, Spector's Wagnerian sound

creature, one that existed in his mind well before it was realized in his own laboratory at Gold Star Studios, continues to be characterized as not just a wall of sound but a *monster* sound, revealing an inclination (particularly in journalistic writing about popular music) to invoke specific metaphorical registers when addressing acoustical technology and acoustical content.[39]

One of our most beloved madmen, Norman Bates, constructed the elaborate web of his own consciousness (more poetically, his soul) by endlessly reinventing through his own voice the sound of his mother—no accident that Hitchcock lands a fly upon that last extraordinary image of the mother and child reunion, Norman / Mother.[40] Earlier in the film, responding to Marion Crane's polite hint that Mother might belong in an institution, Norman—in a claustrophobic room surrounded by the products of his own peculiar aesthetics (large stuffed birds)—offered a prescient critique of those who, by their failure to comprehend his absent Mother as a source of in-spiration (i.e., as the numinous breath that awakens an artistic life) undermined the beauty and authenticity of the monstrous web he had so laboriously crafted: "They cluck their thick tongues and suggest—oh so delicately—why don't you put her *someplace?*" With a critical someplace (i.e., no-place) in place to imprison them, creative reinventions (effected by acts of production and of reception) in new bodies, forms, and spaces are inevitably reduced to a sort of regressive, meaningless—and sick—reenactment. The eccentric angles, arcs, and projections of historical and conceptual links between artists, products, and consumers are thereby expunged from the critical-historical enterprise, replaced by rectilinear traces of the grid constituted by machineries of production and consumption.

Not only those committed to an aesthetic life but the rest of us, too, might be inspired by the sound of Mrs. Bates. Some acoustical content, if we are to take Ginsberg at his poetic word, might even trigger or mimic sensations akin to ecstasis, the experiential leap from real to imagined fields of perception, and offer hints of its spiritual ramifications.[41] Disney's projection of Leopold Stokowki's silhouetted image in *Fantasia*, summoning from Bach's music fluid and dizzying representations of the ineffable in shape and color within the unprecedented and unnatural acoustical environment provided by his "Fantasound" theaters, was part of an audacious and notoriously problematical mad-scientific experiment to define, control, and reproduce that variety of experience. Along the way he encouraged American media audiences to embrace the viability of historical aesthetic positions in new mass media environments.[42]

Bach, Disney believed, could be Virgil to America's Dante. For in the liminal zone between the real and imagined, it has often been the dead who have served as caretakers and guides: this thread runs through the material presented in subsequent chapters. When Edison invented sound recording technology, it was to preserve "the sayings, the voices, and the last words of the dying member of the family."[43] In the vernacular imagination of the next century Edison's family would be extended, unconstrained by genealogical limits, as the cacophonous disembodied voices of its absent members were welcomed home.

CHAPTER 5

The Fantastic, the Picturesque, and the Dimensions of Nostalgia

. . . sie spielte auf ihrem Klavier, mannigfaltige Melodieen,
und all den Ausdruck! All!—All! . . . Ich neigte mich und, und
ihr Trauring fiel mir ins Gesicht—meine Tränen flossen—und
auf einmal fiel sie in die alte, himmelsüße Melodie ein, so auf
einmal, und mir durch die Seele gehn ein Trostgefühl und eine
Erinnerung des Vergangen, der Zeiten, da ich das Lied gehört,
der düstern Zwischenräume des Verdrusses, der fehlgeschla-
genen Hoffnungen.

Goethe, Die Leiden des jungen Werther

I have left the passage from *Werther* in its original German partly because the text includes nuances that require further exposition below (see
chapter notes for a standard translation), but also as a reminder that
some sounds—even if uninterpretable or unrealized—demand our attention in special ways. T. S. Eliot made a similar case over a half century ago in his remarks concerning Norwegian poetry, as I discussed in
chapter 1. Eliot, however, was interested in the nature of implications,
whereas I am more interested in the process by which we sense them. An
English reader with no knowledge of German who takes the time to scan
the epigraph will doubtless alight upon the cognate, imaginatively hearing something meaningful in *"All!—All!"* for example, and forming a
vague impression (correct or not) of what topic or issues might be treated
in a chapter announced by such a noisy reiteration. Whether those imaginative exclamations lead elsewhere or nowhere is beside the point for
now. On the other hand, if the passage were a reading—that is, a
performance—English monolingual auditors might overlook the cognate
(since it would be vocalized *"ahl, ahl"*) yet would likely derive implications

from the register of expressive intonation that any sensible declamation would begin to draw upon after the second comma, within the first exclamatory clause. Both cases are suggestive analogies for the reception of sounds described here and in the following chapters.

Gestural or timbral matter drawn from the musical museum—often skewed or unexpected—formed part of the collection of fantastic elements that imbued much of rock music in the late 1960s with a particular spirit. In early psychedelia and progressive rock, traditional literary associations between the fantastic and moments of apprehensive hesitation, the zone of uncanny in-betweenness, was given an aural dimension.[1] Psychedelic rock embraced the fantastic by a range of means. Many songs and longer yet arguably coherent forms like that of the semicontinuous concept album regularly introduced moments of narrative—and musical—reversal of expectations, invoking the "quality of astonishment" that marks recognition of the fantastic.[2] Others (like "A Whiter Shade of Pale," my primary concern in this chapter) constructed a more stable environment, but one whose elements were understood to be fundamentally incommensurable ("Bach-inspired organ chords" as opposed to "modern soul"). Reid's text for the song is particularly telling in its subversion of normal words, logic, and syntax in the manner of the "secret language" trope that has conventionally informed fantastic literature, twisting "tripped the light fantastic" (from the 1890s favorite, "East Side, West Side") into the authentically fantastic utterance "skipped the light fandango."[3]

SENSING THE FANTASTIC MOMENT

Jefferson Airplane's "White Rabbit" was the anthem for rock's fantastic tendency on several levels, not the least of which was that of the text that drew upon some of the most accomplished fantastic writing in the literary canon, Lewis Carroll's "Alice" books.[4] Largely because of Charles Dodgson's (Carroll's) command of mathematical and scientific logic, his "use of the fantastic" has been taken as "the most complete and rigorous rejection of logic in English," his antilogical stance one that is fundamental to the fantastic environment.[5] Even while maintaining an apparently coherent musical surface, "White Rabbit" successfully explored Carroll's tendency to hinge the fantastic moment on the experience of reversals of expectation, invoking in its lyrics not only the imagery of Wonderland and Looking-Glass Land but also, more specifically, the failure of logic. Alice moved through Looking-Glass Land with a set of rules (bound to the chess game) upon a landscape grid that was mathematically regular. Each of her moves, however, revealed such regularity to be an illusion. With each brook she crosses "she fantastically arrives in a totally different landscape."[6] In "White Rabbit" an introductory trio (bass, guitar, and snare drum) installs a metrical grid at the back of the soundscape that is not merely regular but as musically constraining as Alice's chessboard or its extension, the mechanistic Victorian science that Dodgson's Carroll sought to escape.[7] However exotic the sensual contours of the guitar solo that has been overlaid upon the snare's ostinato— a reference back to that familiar classic, Ravel's *Bolero*—the rhythm and the effect here is essentially military, particularly to a listener uninterested in or unfamiliar with the song's historicist association with the European musical museum. Historicity was an effect in the drum's original conception, but it was further underscored in the stereo version of the hit single produced for the album *Surrealistic Pillow* (1967), in which the reverberation (of a type discussed further below) further enhanced the sensation of physical and temporal distance.[8]

From its first moments, the instrumental prelude to "White Rabbit" emphasized the first beat of a mechanical four-beat bar; indeed, it feels like a regular pulse in the physiological sense. The music commences on a downbeat (played by the bass, which unambiguously marks each beat of four), the drum enters on the downbeat two bars later, and the guitar enters similarly two bars after that. Jorma Kaukonen's eight-bar solo begins to free itself from the repetitive engine of the bar, but he takes care to land solidly on the downbeat in the seventh and eighth bars, preparing for Grace Slick's vocal entry. When Slick embarks upon the fantastic journey constituted by her lyrics, however, that moment is marked by a concatenation of fantastic effects: she enters on the second beat of the measure (specifically, a microsecond before) and begins her narrative with a metrically elongated and portentous enunciation of the word "one," repeating precisely the same play with the beat structure when she reiterates the word two bars later.[9] If the casual listener experiences a momentary hesitation as the tale unexpectedly coalesces from the mesmerizing prelude in a strange position and with a note of not precisely measurable duration, the attentive musical listener will be further dislocated by the dislocation's insistence on its identity with a musical place it is not and cannot be. Only when the narrative shifts from the fantastic capacity of Wonderland's apothecary to the ineffective pills tiresomely served up by "Mother" is the text's "one" reintegrated with its normative musical embodiment, the downbeat, within the regular grid of the musical chessboard.

In "White Rabbit," fantasy is lodged in the song's structure; the Ravel-style prelude is just icing on the cake. But for other rock fantasts, the act of looking back was crucial to the fantastic effect. Before King Crimson was linked to a one-dimensional Wagner, the Doors had nodded in his direction with "Light My Fire," released a few months prior to Procol Harum's "A Whiter Shade of Pale." As that song, too, would do, "Light My Fire" began with a solo organ prelude that situated its musical turf within what at the time was becoming a familiar territory of the unfamiliar.[10] Suggestive of the same connections between music, altered states, and adolescent sexuality as is its contemporary, "Light My Fire" suggested an explicitly and especially morbid end to carnal passion by invoking love's "funeral pyre," a hyperbolic word gimmick (arguably Wagnerian, like the song's portrayal of cosmic conflagration: "set the night on fire") that positions the lyrics within broader literary and dramaturgical traditions wherein death and sexuality are equated.[11] This, along with features of the song's musical surface—in particular the music's tendency to move fluidly and without special preparation among a variety of stylistic regions—draws it into the realm of the fantastic.

The historicist implications of the Doors' Baroque-style organ prelude (the emblem of their song's musical antiquarianism) ignited no particular critical response, suggesting that the appreciation of "A Whiter Shade of Pale" derived not specifically from its prelude's historical exoticism, its stylistic alterity, but from something that resided in the full collection of auditory stimuli that the song projected, among which the organ part may have taken pride of place. Even if Procol Harum's organist, Matthew Fisher, was not an experimenter at the edge or an intermediary between the forces of chaos and commerce, I will argue in this chapter that the song and its reception vibrated with the proto-Romantic spirit embraced and explored by the Wagnerians (Ginsberg and Spector) discussed previously, although here Wagner's music is not part of the story.

PICTURESQUE ROCK

Ray Manzarek's prelude to "Light My Fire" employs an organ timbre (essentially *quasi cembalo*) that is markedly distinct from that of Fisher's melancholic Hammond, but it draws in its figuration upon models only slightly less obviously Bachian. The tempo is allegro and the melodic profile less serpentine than the one we encounter in Fisher's introduction. Manzarek's melody and rhythms resemble those of a right-hand part in an early eighteenth-century keyboard invention or prelude. Such figures are generic, and Manzarek may have had them in his fingers from any number of J. S. Bach keyboard classics that were well known to piano pedagogues and students (classics like some of the two-part inventions, preludes from the first book of *The Well-Tempered Clavier*, the *Musette* in the *Anna Magdalena Bach Büchlein,* or even Wilhelm Friedemann Bach's *Frühling,* which was circulating at the time in a jazz-pop arrangement by the Swingle Singers). Fisher integrated his introductory keyboard material into the body of "Whiter Shade" as a parallel presence alongside the soul-ballad vocals; I shall address this more fully below. The material of Manzarek's introduction was likewise redeployed throughout "Light My Fire," but there are fundamental differences at the formal level.

Most significantly, in "Light My Fire" the prelude's musical presence has not been confined to the reiterative procedure associated with a Baroque ritornello, but has been subjected to significant and extravagant improvisatory processes of melodic, rhythmic, and metrical dilation or transformation in its appearances. (Surprisingly, it will be partly the formal constraint of Fisher's ritornello that provides the frame for the powerful affective features of the work outlined below.) Manzarek's first extended solo within the body of the song translates the decorative elements of Baroque keyboard style into exotic cadential turns within a predominantly monotone environment reminiscent of Semitic cantillation. Manzarek addressed the range of musical discourses that flavored the Doors' music in 1967, when he said that the group's "primary concern is to blend different styles into uniform sound and still retain our individual identities."[12] For Jim Morrison and Ray Manzarek, as well as Gary Brooker, Matthew Fisher and other representatives of the epoch, music of the past or of ethnic others—however vaguely conceived—constituted a viable and manipulable sound collection, an acoustic register within current musical language as vital and relevant as any other (particularly when it could be linked to political or ethical positions).

Coherent pastiche structures like those promoted by the Doors have much in common with late eighteenth-century notions of the picturesque and its associated aesthetic system, as described by Annette Richards, and particularly as it was manifested in the art of landscaping. Components of "instability and surprise, rough textures and partial concealments, as well as the invitation to spectatorship and aestheticised viewing" permeate the music of psychedelia and early progressive rock.[13] Relevant picturesque musical elements include the noncontemporary (i.e., the ornamental out-of-place), the dimensionality of engineered sound (with its ability to conceal, highlight, and cause the ear to wander, especially in a stereophonic environment), and the abrupt shifts of style, meter, and timbre.[14] Stereophonic effects have a rather precise analogue in the split-vision cognitive practices associated with nineteenth-century stereoscopy, itself a product whose success was driven by photography's claim to picturesque representation.[15] Picturesque landscapes encouraged, and indeed required, contemplative, meandering trajectories on the part of viewers whose paths were guided by successively revealed and occasionally astonishing landmarks ranging from the wild to the serene to the monumental (including the Egyptian).

Musical psychedelia and early progressive rock were also linked to a specific mode of aural reception: a contemplative acoustical spectatorship in this case attached to the awareness-heightening effects of drugs. The picturesque aesthetic provides meaningful analogues for the elements that make up the aesthetic system of this rock genre and the mental journeys with which it was associated. A tendency of academic and journalistic rock critics to trivialize certain components of the musical mix of the time resembles a similar failure to comprehend the implications of the late eighteenth-century picturesque. Annette Richards has argued that "taken in its technical sense the picturesque is a complex aesthetic category which encompasses and encourages fragmentation and disruption, contrast and variety, and problematises the limits of form and conventional expectation; in modern music criticism, however, the term has generally been taken colloquially to describe quaint or pastoral associations or obvious pictorialism."[16]

One of the most familiar songs of the next decade, Led Zeppelin's "Stairway to Heaven" (1971), might serve as a model for the transition from one understanding of picturesque to another, a transition in the direction of the decadent phase that typically follows hard upon the commercial institutionalization of new styles and devices in rock (a shift, one might say, from style gesture to style gimmick). In its opening, "Stairway"—by means of a recorder consort and a reiterated modal cadence gesture (VII–i in A Minor)—calls for something other than reflective engagement with its historical elements. Instead, the song impels the listener's imagination toward a predigested cinematic envisioning of historical "pastness," one whose reception was likely prefigured by the gorgeous and wildly popular teen-oriented Zeffirelli production of *Romeo and Juliet* (1968). Nino Rota's title music (in particular the airy flutes hovering within the modal environment that wrapped Zeffirelli's foggy Verona in an acoustic haze) and updated Elizabethan lute song provide a context for the way in which the recorders and arpeggiated acoustic guitar of "Stairway to Heaven"'s first section would likely have been heard in its own time. The love song ("What is a Youth?") featured similar VII/i cadences and served—after its on-screen presentation by "historical" instruments—as the orchestral background score's "big love theme." Rota's style relied predominantly on the model of Respighi, who was, if not cinematic in the literal sense, largely pictorial in his modal-timbral, snapshot approach to "ancient" music, most pointedly so in the *Trittico Botticelliano*.[17] At the formal level, and characteristic of the new megasong aesthetic of the 1970s, "Stairway" maintains the sharp contrasts of the earlier progressive era, but blown out now to grander dimensions. By its insistence upon undeveloped acoustical indexes of musical and textual historicity, however, the song's antiquarianism and picturesque aspects can only be understood as quaint ("bustle"), and its landscape as domesticated and pastoral ("hedgerow," "Spring clean," "May Queen").

At the extreme end of the more innovative turn to the picturesque aesthetic lie moments of disruption, reversed expectations, and, potentially, horror, which describe the points of intersection between the picturesque and the fantastic. The Doors' song "The End" (on the same 1967 album as "Light My Fire") approaches this sort of mix, with its unexpected invocation of literally pastoral elements within a highly processed mix of electronic sounds and distance effects. Wilderness and insanity are themes of the text, and the song's aural landscape comprises elements of the garden (chirping birds) and a more dangerous, fantastic wilderness; visual contrasts between the tamed and the wild characterized the garden aesthetics of the historical picturesque. An unnerving collection of animal sounds piled upon the gentle birds leads ultimately to a mad vocal-electronic cacophonous conclusion. "The End" perhaps lacks elegance or economy, but it is no less interesting an experiment for that.

Richards suggests that in music the moment of hesitation required for fantastic experience in Todorov's terms may only be manifested in the "performative here-and-now," above all in the improvisatory environment of the free fantasy. Indeed, the new emphasis on solo keyboards in music of the late 1960s underscores the relevance of earlier picturesque and fantastic styles. The extravagance of Ray Manzarek's solos in "Light My Fire" has more in common with the clavichord cult of the late eighteenth century than with the more mechanical, if virtuosic, figuration of the Baroque practices his (and Fisher's) music drew upon.[18] I would not characterize "A Whiter Shade of Pale" as primarily an essay in the picturesque in light of its tendency not to wander with respect to time.[19] Yet the throbbing timbre of the Hammond organ that lends Fisher's solo its

melancholic edge may be heard and characterized in this instance as a
new technology for conjuring the affective power of *Bebung* at the heart
of the eighteenth-century clavichord's voice of intimate expression.[20] Indeed, the long prelude's failure to signal in advance the musical content
of the strophic song to follow recalls Christian Michael Wolff's setting
of "Erleichtre meine Sorgen" (1777), in which the clavichord's introduction "immediately establishes the unusual primacy of the keyboard
over the voice, for this is indeed a piece about keyboard playing."[21] Behind the picturesque lay the models of the earlier *stylus phantasticus,*
with (according to Mattheson) its "unusual passages, obscure ornaments, ingenious turns and embellishments."[22] Late Baroque musical
works like some of Buxtehude's Preludes and Fugues were full of abrupt
and unexpected turns and even—as in the case of the rock picturesque
I have described here—references to learned styles that in the fantastic
mode need not be addressed with rigor or completeness, existing as "undeveloped iterations" (pace Julian Johnson) imbued with special resonances of past practice.[23]

As acoustic objects these "different styles" seemed for consumers to
be drawn from someplace other than the rational or the corporeal, implications that were encouraged by the increasing focus in recording
technology on acoustic dimensionality and by the increasing popularity
of drugs as aids to meaningful listening.[24] Interestingly, while we associate these special effects with the edge of progressive rock, even the
pablum of classical contrafacts of the sort that so irked Adorno provided
an important testing ground for new acoustic versions of stereoscopy
(for example, the "natural echo" and "ghost choirs" of Ray Conniff's
arrangements of Chaikovsky, Schubert, and Rachmaninov).[25] In psychedelia, cross-temporal and cross-generic items (acoustically manipulated) became icons of a fundamentally Romantic aesthetic and served
for artist and listener alike as—to borrow Romantic language—restoratives
for sensitive spirits in a world of "unbelief," spirits that others might
deem mad.

That this madness might represent, in Charles Rosen's words, "a way
of life that could be chosen with all its terrors" was as fundamental to
the psychedelic enterprise as to those of Blake or Cowper.[26] And if madness in this sense is constituted by "any extravagant form of alienation
either of behavior or of perception," the Doors, above all—from their
choice of name (from Huxley's drug odyssey, *The Doors of Perception*)
to their nihilistic social and political positions ("When you make peace
with authority, you're dead without knowing it," as Morrison put it)—

illustrate the extent to which rock's invocation of any sort of "classical" music (in the general sense) was linked to the Romantic perspective as has been, so often, its reception.[27] And while some may fault Morrison and Manzarek for the apparent artifice of their adopting perspectives, actions, and positions encountered in the course of a university education in theater arts and literature, their "imperfect" understanding of past practices, filtered through a commitment to re-creative acts in life and in art, is, as we have seen, fundamental to the viability of the classic register.

For Morrison and contemporaries the terror lay not in death itself; indeed, to fashion one's own larger-than-life end, and to really know it or sell it (richly, fully, and with acoustic decoration), was a Romantic end.[28] It was also already, prior to the advent of music videos, implicitly mediated by a visual, theatrical sensibility. Manzarek and Morrison had found each other in college, studying drama and film. A principal project for musicians and technicians in the mid-1960s was to infuse the imaginary (invisible) dimensions of sound with the dislocative power inherent to visual experiences of the sort described by nineteenth-century opium eaters and their descendants, among whom must be counted the purveyors of cinematic illusion considered in chapter 6. In the case of Procol Harum and "A Whiter Shade of Pale," that same Romantic mode somehow found its way past the boundaries of the song's creative concept to both apprehension and actualization within the domain of its pattern of reception, a circumstance that deserves particular consideration in light of what seems to be, by all accounts, Fisher's straightforward and apolitical appropriation of his Baroque musicohistorical model.

IN THE ROCK MORTUARY

Melody Maker's anonymous reporter who first pointed to the song's mix of "Bach-inspired organ chords and modern soul vocal" characterized "A Whiter Shade of Pale" as *"a beautiful monster,"* a verbal turn to the aesthetic that was for its time surprisingly elegant and unintentionally revelatory. We have in the intervening decades grown accustomed to describing hugely successful musical products as "monsters," but in this early instance the phrase was likely intended as something more than a lip-smacking reflection upon the magnitude of the creature's likely financial payoff or trajectory of consumption. *Melody Maker*'s staffer obviously meant to suggest something fundamental about the song, and about some special quality that resided in this evocative conjunction of musical voices from the recent and distant pasts, a position that within the space of only a few years was to lose much of its magic, as embodied in King Crimson's claim upon Wagner as absent member.

From the beginning, "A Whiter Shade of Pale" as promoted in the press was understood to bear with it some implication that by purely musical means the song had set in motion a special power or force, one that was dark or perhaps even pathological, and even more impressive (or oppressive) than that suggested by the physiognomical blood drain evoked in the song's title and refrain. I emphasize "purely" musical because the lyrics, with their implicitly sexual combination of cocktail party and pills, of Chaucer, sea myth, and scripture, appear not to have made their way into the imagination of mainstream consumers as a particularly significant element in the song's reception, aside perhaps from the quotable incipit, "We skipped the light fandango." By August 1967 the musical substance of the group's debut essay was being addressed in terms that were specifically monumental: the song's dimensions, it was suggested, were derived from its implicitly ecclesiastical musical architecture and invocation of monumentalized memory, which is to say: the tomb. In the words of one writer, Procol Harum had "made a *majestic and reverent* entrance into the pop world with a record that sounded more like a *funeral march* than a pop single."[29]

Further reinforcing the notion of the music's existence on a plane of reception that was essentially divorced from its esoteric and at times silly and playful lyrics was an unreleased film version of the song that had been shot in conjunction with a projected U.S. tour by the group. Set in a derelict mansion, the visuals contained interpolated war clips; in the end the film was deemed too sickly morbid for public consumption.[30] Yet the film's imagery—adding a realistic, mundane dimension to the purely literary morbid-fantasy implications of the song—was very much in keeping with the tone that was being set in the new rock journalism of the time, especially the early volumes produced in 1967 and 1968 of the future bellwethers of American rock journalism, *Rolling Stone* and *Crawdaddy*. Both publications are shot through in these years with intentionally edgy evocations of the physiology of death: references to morbidity, corpses, and even necrophilia are commonplace.

Both sickness and mortality had been items in the expressive registers of rock since its earliest commercial phase, a function perhaps of rock's tendency to dwell upon the significance of its own novelty. Rock's claim to cultural legitimacy lay in its commitment to an aesthetic program in which the ambition to supersede by innovation was paramount. Its fundamental stance was enabled by expectations regarding the inevitable decay of precedent (granted both political and ethical status by practitioners and audience), combined with a faith in the natural authenticity of rock music's own artifice.[31] In "Roll Over Beethoven," Chuck Berry, even as he announced his "news," located the source of his inspiration in a pathological condition ("a rockin' pneumonia"), thereby literalizing rock music's infectious capacity and celebrating the Romantic union of disease and creative power. At the same time he conjured forth and reanimated ("roll over!") the lifeless body of mass market midcentury variety radio, as Beethoven and Chaikovsky were reminded of their inevitable submission to the new order.[32]

Also falling among the topoi of morbidity in early rock were invocations of the beloved and inspiring dead, whether in absurd, elegiac, deadgirlfriend narratives like "Teen Angel" or more covertly: one of Spector's first experiments in studio production, the treacly ballad "To Know Him Is To Love Him," transformed the epitaph on his father's grave marker into an adolescent swoon.[33] The clavichordists who haunt the background of "A Whiter Shade of Pale" and other keyboard fantasies of the late 1960s were likewise moved by what was then termed a "secret sickness," and they too communed with the memorialized dead and their tombs "over an unbridgeable gap," one that in the European past was, in Richards's formulation, the site for "the typical *empfindsamer* exchange."[34]

By the time Keith Reid invoked the Romantic pallor of a mysterious Lady in "A Whiter Shade of Pale" (a shade whose beauty was inscribed within the inventory of beautiful monsters populating nineteenth-century literature, from victims like the somnambulant brides of Dracula and the singer-prisoners of E. T. A. Hoffmann to murderous aesthetes like Dorian Gray) the contemporaneous pop rhetoric of death and corporality was growing more naturalistically morbid, and was beginning to bleed outside the borders of song lyrics. *Rolling Stone* in November 1967 issued a journalistic polemic little different from that implicit in Berry's song, although the entombed items it described were not the popularized light classics but rather—according to the standard parlance of the day—the golden oldies, here darkened and rendered organic as "moldy oldies." Pop radio is baldly described as "a rotting corpse."[35] Procol Harum's filmed adjunct to "A Whiter Shade of Pale" was intended to generate interest in the group's upcoming appearance in the states. Its artificial conflation of disturbing war photos with the song's unrelated lyrics reveals the extent to which the increasingly dark tone of packaging and published discourse surrounding rock products in 1967 and 1968 was fed by popular reception of the innovative—if disturbing—new wave of daily televised reportage of the Vietnam War, with its gruesome multimedia emphasis on videographed body bags and superimposed audio body counts. Rock journalism's commitment to promoting a sense of identity between vernacular musical expression and the casualties of war was rendered explicit in the first "cover" of *Rolling Stone*. No rock group appeared on the front page, which featured instead a close-up shot of a grubby John Lennon in battle gear, taken from Richard Lester's dark comedy *How I Won the War*.

Traditional adolescent and Romantic fascinations with aestheticized morbidity (whether of the *Werther* or "Teen Angel" variety) historically had constituted a safe space in the imagination remote from the physiology of daily life. Popular music participated in the transformation of that conventional aesthetic into an expressionistic mode in which death was subject to corporealization, monumentalization, and formalization. In this, music responded to and defused the imaginative grip of those new and unsettling reminders of death's potential facelessness, namelessness, and proximity—especially for young male Americans of the Vietnam era—that were represented in daily media, and projected it all back into the realm of the aesthetic by invocations of formal monuments and monumental musical forms. Even crossover folk artists who had experimented with esoteric material explored this expressive ground. John Fahey was a pioneer, beginning with *The Transfiguration of Blind Joe Death* (1959; revised 1964); it and *Death Chants, Breakdowns & Military Two-Steps* (1968) featured cadaverous skeletons in the cover art. His personal aesthetic was easily translatable to the revisionist morbid aesthetic (i.e., the imaginatively formalized, monumental, historicist), most notably with respect to *Requia* (1967), a collection containing the four-part "Requiem for Molly," Fahey's spatiotextural experiment in sampling, looping, and musique concrète. Its advertising art depicts a cemetery monument and funerary decorations. No hint of this grim cultural context figured in Fisher's own descriptions of his music for "A Whiter Shade of Pale," but the song encouraged listeners to construct their own meaningful readings in intersection with its discourse; these continued to haunt many years after the song's first flourishing.

Example 4. "A Whiter Shade of Pale," mm. 3–6

BACHIANA

Fisher told *Melody Maker* that his inspiration for "A Whiter Shade of Pale" was Bach's so-called Air on the G String, that is, the Aria movement from the D-Major Suite BWV 1068.[36] That model is readily apparent in the form taken by the bass line and the way Fisher's cantabile melody spins out from a long held note at the outset.[37] Other Bachian models are clearly at work, though. In combination, the song's Baroque and soul elements produce a polyphony of musical discourses; each strand is invoked through stylistic conventions associated with one of the relevant generic categories, a procedure reminiscent of Bach's own two-tiered architecture realized in the second chorale stanza of BWV 140 (the cantata *Wachet auf*), in which the old chorale emerges from and defines an acoustic position superimposed upon the introductory string ritornello.[38] The same Bach material (as the "Schübler Chorale," BWV 645) was a standard item for organists and one likely familiar to Fisher through his music school training; it even enjoyed some commercial presence during the 1960s in recordings by the crossover classical artist E. Power Biggs.[39] In its original form, the second chorale stanza of *Wachet auf,* especially its alternation of instrumental ritornello with the vocal material of the chorale tune and in certain turns within the string melody (Examples 4 and 5) provided some of the details that Fisher incorporated into the frame of the song's fundamental musical source, the "Air."

But identifying any Bach originals as a source for Fisher's solo may be in the end the least interesting and revealing way of making sense of Procol Harum's unusual success with the number, or of the way in which it was rendered meaningful in the imaginations of such twentieth-century listeners as the *Melody Maker* reporter. Even though there was much about "A Whiter Shade of Pale" that marked it as special, most of the acoustical components of the Bach-style introduction had been commercially mainstreamed well prior to this song's release by the Swingle Singers' Grammy-winning Bach releases beginning in 1964, launching

Example 5. J. S. Bach, *Wachet auf,* 4th movement, mm. 7–8

their extraordinary reception by consumers of all generations. The Swingles' version of the Air on the G-String, perhaps the best-loved track on their internationally acclaimed debut Bach album, provides an important link between Bach and Procol Harum. If Fisher's prelude combines the suite with elements drawn from BWV140, the Singers' chart-busting *Jazz Sebastian Bach* album may have provided the impetus, for the Swingle version of the Air ("Aria") is preceded on the album by a vocal cover of the "Schüblersche" organ version of the chorale. The Swingle Singers' jazz-inflected bass in their "Aria" projects much the same heavy-footed quality as the similar bass in "Whiter Shade" (a sense of heaviness that was expunged in the re-recording of the number by a later configuration of Swingle Singers personnel).

More significant in terms of the overall mix, though, is the added percussion, particularly the reiterative ride and hi-hat cymbals. Indeed, the ride cymbal, a jazz staple, figured prominently in most of the slower-tempo cuts on the Swingle Singers' early releases. Percussionist B. J. Wilson's appropriation of the sound for the organ solo sections in "A Whiter Shade of Pale" lent them, despite their insistent musical alterity, a hint of acoustical familiarity.[40] The Swingles' cantabile tracks highlighted the unusual voice of Christiane Legrand, whose tone could approach that of instrumental pipes, well outside the norm for "classical" soprano vocalization, and a standout within the spectrum of instrumental-style scatting practiced by the ensemble.[41] Procol Harum's Brooker had been a fan of the Swingle recordings (his primary source for his knowledge of Bach), and Christiane eventually participated in the recording of "Fires Which Burnt Brightly" for the group's *Grand Hotel* album (1973). In short, both the acoustical and stylistic elements laid out at the opening of "A Whiter Shade of Pale" were, with the exception of the replacement of a quasi-instrumental voice by Fisher's quasi-vocal Hammond organ, familiar well beyond the walls of classic-oriented music schools (like Guildhall, where Fisher had studied) and already in place within the normative range of popular musical experience and vocabulary; only the admixture of soul via Brooker's vocal represented a marked innovation. If the musical inspiration for the song was

Bach, it was a Bach already flavored by contemporary practice and mass-market listening. To fix a contextual frame that might account for the extent to which the song took hold of the imagination of a generation of listeners, then, we will have to look beyond its appropriation of historical material.

A comparison of the Swingle Singers' "Aria" and the preceding album track, "Choral Nr. 1" *[sic]*, with "A Whiter Shade of Pale" reveals (beyond their sharing the same general stylistic space, i.e., the Baroque) some critical intersections at the level of acoustical detail, and also significant divergences beyond those expected in different pop genres. Indeed, the genre distinction is probably the least significant among these points of comparison. I referred above to the imaginary space between two musical discourses in the original Bach chorale movement and in the soundscape of "Whiter Shade." "Choral Nr. 1" draws the distance implicit in Bach's music onto the imaginary three-dimensional field of sound space. One of the most crucial features of these recorded environments is their engagement with the construction of a sense of space—a landscape for aural exploration—by acoustic means. Even prior to the period in which binaural recordings became the norm, and certainly within the aural dimensions of monaural 45-rpm singles that coexisted with early stereo albums, recording mixes encouraged the illusion of acoustic depth, especially by manipulation of what Albin Zak has called "prominence," essentially the engineering (and one might argue, hearing reception) of a sound's dynamic level.[42]

I would suggest that any understanding or perception of such depth was not—even by analogy—straightforwardly optical, however, for there was rarely a sufficiently complete or consistent field laid out for the total simultaneous mapping of a full, multidimensional acoustical view (even left-right stereo effects were more often transitory than continuous). Instead the illusion was haptic (engaging a virtual sensation of touch) and essentially planar. It was not, thus, two-dimensional but manifested as the suggestion of a series of receding two-dimensional imaginary sound surfaces. Each required sufficient clarity and level of detail to be acoustically "tangible," along with sufficient perspectival differentiation to produce at some calculable degree of acoustic recession, resembling the deep focus effects of some black-and-white cinema. In film the recession effect is provided by the visual, and so, even in deep-focus photography, the sound track generally disregards prominence as an acoustic contrivance.[43] To think of a quality of "deep-focus sound" in this case serves, then, as just a useful conceptual analogy for the deliberately visual implications of aural prominence and ambience effects, since (with only rare exceptions) deep-focus sequences in cinema were generally attached to antirealistic sound environments.[44] By contrast, music recordings of the 1960s, especially binaural recordings, extended the clarity and overall potential of audiospatial analogy, and their effects were, as Zak has argued, often bound to implicit narrative strategies.

Early attempts at three-dimensionality in popular recorded music might best be understood to operate along the lines of the photographic stereoscopy developed around the turn of the twentieth century, when illusions of depth were created primarily by means of overlapping planes whose closeness to the viewer, that is, the physical span required for the planes to be "touched"—the haptic aspect of stereoscopy—was defined primarily by the degree of perceptible detail in each (analogous to Zak's notion of the auditory reception of prominence).[45] Through the suggestion of nearly tangible aural planes mapped by the illusion of sound in place or motion, stereophony (in this analogous sense, whether it was monaurally or binaurally recorded) similarly constructed acoustic distances that could be "measured" from front to back, closer and farther away, and, eventually in the binaurally recorded environment, left to right. If the pop sound box constituted a three-dimensional imaginary space, that space was defined by a few clearly outlined objects and positions, with the remainder left to the constructive enterprise of the listener.[46]

A comparison of the implicit stereophony in the Swingle Singers' recording of the *Wachet auf* chorale with "A Whiter Shade of Pale" demonstrates the extent to which these effects may best be interpreted with respect to other materials in the work, not always purely acoustical. In the former instance, when the chorale tune enters as an overlay (a stereoscopic effect already present in Bach's original) it is recorded at a lower level (it sounds, in fact, as if the singers are remotely placed with respect to the mike) and blurred by the addition of reverberation; that effect is reminiscent of Conniff's stairwell experiments in echo effects.[47] For a listener of any experience there is no mistaking the sensation of an empty distance separating two acoustic planes: one is occupied by the sharply etched vocals of the scat "orchestra" in the foreground, the other by the almost ghostly resonance of the chorale in the background. In Bach's cantata that distance was constructed not by means of the physical characteristics of sound but through an act of intellected reception, a recognition of the historical distance separating Bach's new decorative material from the old and familiar tune. Fans of the Swingle Singers, unless they were familiar with Bach's music in its historical context, could not feel the distance in this way. The stereoscopic or stereophonic space Swingle brought to the recording of this work is in a sense a substitute for the original's special historical dimensionality.

"A Whiter Shade of Pale" lays out a similar path and a similar space, and yet the effect offered the pop listener a zone within which might be constructed something rather more significant. Gary Brooker's vocals occupy by their prominence (literally, their up-frontness) one of two planes separated by some distance, with the other constituted of the Baroque material presented in the song's prelude, which (as in the case of the Bach cantata model mentioned earlier) serves throughout as a punctuating ritornello. It recedes from prominence to "back" the vocal when the lyrics are present. Whatever studio disposition, mixing, or miking may have been employed in the song's production, the nuances of amplitude and, especially, waveform (the special timbres) that mark the organ material are themselves sufficient to inscribe the dimensions of the song's imaginary depth.

That space has been defined and negotiated most precisely by Fisher's exuberant glissando, which occupies the boundary between Bach and soul, for it marks quite literally the organ's forward trajectory from a distant evocation to a fully present partner engaged with the voice during the text refrain sections ("And so it was a lady"). At these points Brooker's vocal quality shifts from its narrative mode to something throatier and more expressive, without entirely abandoning the retrospective perspective ("it *was*") with which the lyrics have been imbued since Brooker's first utterance.[48] Reid's fantastic verbal construction "skipped the light fandango" fixed several layers of past temporality at once: the gilded age (with its lopsided reference to "tripped the light fantastic"), a hazy and deliberately exotic past and place ("fandango"), and a temporal location for the narrative of reminiscence (established by the tense of the verbs).

Crucially, it is in precisely the moment at which the past skids to the foregrounded present (rather like a wheeling bird) that the Hammond's Leslie speakers really kick in and give the instrumental part (which now abandons the walking bass and cantabile melody for straightforward chords) a brighter edginess that is lacking in its lyrical and aloof solos. With the instrumental sound opened up in timbral quality (while still backgrounded in prominence), the organ moves into the realm of soul convention as embodied most proximately in Percy Sledge's performance of "When a Man Loves a Woman," another song that looked to the Baroque (if more discreetly) in its Pachelbelian harmonic ostinato.[49] Fisher's glissando functions not merely as a component within an overall crescendo but as a literal slide from the shadows to the foreground, from a dark space to the light, and from then to now. When after the first refrain the ritornello again takes center stage (to expand upon a theatrical analogy that Zak employs in one of his analyses), alone beneath the acoustic spotlight, the organ's return to its original timbre minus the intense speaker "wah," that is, the unconstricted and more naturally quasi-vocal sound, its proto-Romantic *Bebung*, encourages the ear still to place it in the distance, even though it is now afforded acoustic prominence by its high amplitude value, or volume.

In sum, "A Whiter Shade of Pale" manipulates timbre—of the voice, and especially of the featured instrument—to create a sense of dimensionality that contravenes the basics of prominence-defined space and allows for the construction of other meaningful forms of distance. The ear of the listener is taken along on the ride from one temporal node to the other, confronted by and compelled to "measure" the distance between through an instinctive mental process that lies beyond the norms of monaural listening. This process resembles the dimensional projection in stereoscopy that subverts ("splits") the monocular perspective associated with pictorial viewing, occurring "not via the retina and in the eye but as a computational process in the brain . . . [three-dimensional viewing] is a cognitive effect, in other words, rather than a perceptual fact."[50]

In all of its aural details the song exceeds the invocation of historicity and lays claim to the musical expression of pastness in a way, it may be argued, that nonrecorded music will always fail to accomplish.[51] In stationary art forms, including film (in which even as the camera moves it defines stationary environments like rooms and landscapes), the spatial component of what Bakhtin called the narrative chronotope (time space) is laid out and remains in front of us.[52] In the case of a song, however cinematically its effects may be interpreted, however intense its implications of space, time, and narrative trajectory, the auditor must assemble the sound image based on the kind of information discussed above. When an engineered sound object is reproduced in a live performance, chronotopic hearing is likely to be diverted by the anti-imaginary aspects of the real. "A Whiter Shade of Pale" proves that point.

Procol Harum, a month after the peak of the song's popularity, had still only once appeared in a live concert.[53] When they ultimately elected to tour in the United States rather than England, the response was discouraging. *Rolling Stone*'s report is revealing: "The Beatles do not attempt to reproduce their electronic music in dance halls and on the concert stage. Procol Harum does. . . . It will not work. . . . Procol Harum is neither diversified enough *nor able to make the sounds faithfully enough to retain the image.*"[54] I would suggest that among the parts of the beautiful monster problematizing its live, anti-imaginary version some were in fact visual (related to the implicitly cinematic aspects of its reception) rather than acoustic. Chief among them was that the obviousness and modesty of the mundane corporealized electric keyboard was no longer hidden like some emoting Pythagoras behind a veil of knowing monumentality. Stuck in place, no longer attached to hidden revelation or a wheeling bird soul of expressivity, the organ's voice lost dimensionality in both time and space, and the constituents of the chronotopic construction evaporated. It could no longer lay claim to special power over the gap that keeps us from the dead and their places of rest. Thus, even if all the elements of the studio sound could have been reproduced on stage, the "image" would almost certainly have been difficult, if not impossible, to "retain."

PRE-RAPHAELITE KITSCH?

In 1891 William Morris presented a retrospective lecture on the achievements and program of pre-Raphaelite art, in the course of which he invoked the model of the "Great Gothic Art" and specifically its "epic" and "ornamental" qualities. Eric Rabkin argues that by ornamental, "Morris meant that the whole effect should be such that one would be pleased to have the work hang at home, in church, or in some other architectural environment that was regularly inhabited for reasons other than the viewing of paintings."[55] Combining the ornamental with the domestic is often taken as the textbook (or cookbook) recipe for kitsch, and many critics of the nineteenth century treated it as such, even if they did not use the word. Domesticity (of topic, setting, or display) pushes art into the realm of the sentimental, as it has typically been defined. Richard Taruskin, in an essay on musical kitsch and Weimar opera, called attention to the late nineteenth-century physician Max Nordau's quack attack on artistic degeneracy, which included among its targets the pathological, "eroticized mysticism" of the pre-Raphaelites.[56] Taruskin never revisits pre-Raphaelitism in his essay, but the ingredients Nordau drew together in his formula for "pure kitsch"—ersatz religiosity, crass voyeurism, and the dynamics of domestic sexuality—might seem to sum up much of pre-Raphaelite art. Paintings like Dante Gabriel Rossetti's

Bocca Bacciata adapted sixteenth-century liturgical models to sensual portraiture often based on the real women who engaged in intercourse (domestic or extramarital) with their painters.[57] Such renderings of both faith and sex as artistic topoi are, as even many rational thinkers might argue, "inauthentic."

I would like to use the linkage to visual art as a device to call attention to the ways we traditionally address musicodramatic works (e.g., operas, sound films) by focusing on the stylistic surface (including melody, harmony, orchestration) in conjunction with elements of narrative (themes, characters, cultural topoi). In addressing other media with similarly dramatic implications (like the narratives abbreviated in the momentary visions captured by pre-Raphaelite painting—Morris's "epic" dimension—or the implicit cinematic narratives of recorded and engineered rock and pop), we might extend critical analysis to additional factors. At the end we may find ourselves in a rather different position with respect to the aesthetic evaluation of a work or its cultural significance, and in possession of another viable model for multimedia analysis in general.

Aside from the sensualized pseudo-medieval, antiquarian Christianity that marks the thematic content of many of the best-known pre-Raphaelite paintings, their most familiar aspect will be the level of obsessive, fetishistic realism that informs the characters, landscapes, and especially the draping of individuals and rooms. Read as the technical expression of an artistic idea (of idealized naturalism, or fanatical perspectivism), these works appear as pale imitations of the museum pieces produced in fifteenth- and sixteenth-century Europe, paintings whose medieval Christian aspects (if not their own epic pretensions) were inarguably "authentic."[58] But as expressions of the painter's technical hand, they offer something else. Pre-Raphaelite art combines its level of detail with a peculiarly antinatural color saturation, the feature that lends it its enchanted aspect and makes it so hard to reproduce in color plates. In this technical stylistic element as applied to the medium, pre-Raphaelite art conjoins the domain of the fantastic—the real and yet not real. The impossible effect was achieved by the use of a new "wet white ground" technique, involving the application of white pigment that was then carefully dry-brushed and painted over, with each area of the painting addressed individually and slowly; it yielded a capacity to achieve an unprecedented "brilliance of color and minuteness of detail."[59]

Some critics of twentieth-century recorded repertoire might deem the original Swingle Singers recordings (prior to the group's attaining modernist legitimacy in collaborations with Berio et al.) as nothing more than aural kitsch of the pre-Raphaelite sort, bringing Bach and other church and concert hall contemporaries into the unnatural, domesticated display spaces of the basement rec-room or college dormitory. Particularly in those sensual, breathy adagios sung by Christiane Legrand, the buttoned-down Baroque keyboard was transformed into something more explicitly sexy than it could ever have been and, thus, ersatz. And yet the combination of recording technology that allowed for the acoustic application of foreground and background layers, and above all the minute attention to detail (the choice of syllables, shaping the sound, microphone technique) turned the Swingle Bach tracks into something that was no longer Bach (just as Rossetti's portraits no longer merely imitated those of Giovanni Bellini), or even much about Bach.[60] Constructing another poetics of listening, these recordings insisted upon attention to individual sound objects, sounds in series, and details of vocalization and backgrounding: therein lay the music's new and different power to engage or enchant. Multimedia today is engaged with the same poetics, especially in the tendency to skew supposedly natural sounds (creaking hinges, footsteps, mechanical clicks) toward a kind of hyperrealism.[61] Its aesthetic, however, is to render sound objects as digital fetishes that stand in for a fully dimensional field, suggesting it by means of their isolated, individual acoustic dimensionalism.

Of course, not all pre-Raphaelite art was painted with the same strokes. By the end of pre-Raphaelitism, British politics—and, at the last, the Boer War—positioned the vestiges of the style against a new backdrop, in which government interests promoted a "spectacular rise in imperial sentiment" and an imperialization of artistic topoi, as the unified British empire "took on the quality of a religious ideal."[62] It remains to consider the ways in which the recording and performance practices addressed here inform the aesthetics of death that I believe flavored the reception of "A Whiter Shade of Pale." Here Werther's tears come into play at last, drawing me into a consideration of the effects related to the depiction and promotion of nostalgia in media contexts. Bringing nostalgia to the foreground of an understanding of the temporal and psychosomatic experience of "distance rock" will call upon not just literary nostalgia but also visual analogies drawn from other periods of political strain and collective memorialization. Ultimately I hope to suggest that nostalgia might follow more than one path, and that not all paths empty into the cisterns of sentiment, kitsch, or the purely decorative. Even within the domain of accessible art, nostalgia may function as a specific formalistic mode of expression and reception, worthy of critical and historical attention.

NOSTALGIC SPACE

An assertion frequently encountered in cultural criticism is that when academics and cultural critics say "nostalgia" we do not mean *nostalgia*. Frederic Jameson's reflections upon what he called nostalgia films triggered a terminological anxiety, a self-conscious need for dispensatory footnotes that might free the term for service with no embarrassment to the scholarly author as a slightly gentler stand-in for its critical cousins, utopia and dystopia. In the first pages of *Postmodernism, or The Cultural Logic of Late Capitalism,* Jameson took care to distinguish the expression "nostalgia film" and its characteristically decorative historicism from "that older longing once called nostalgia."[63] Caryl Flinn, in her study of the "classical" Hollywood film score, painstakingly rehearses the history and etymology of the term, but locates her discussion finally in the most recent, "demedicalized" sense, linking it specifically to "utopia" (although her argument actually takes the terms in reverse order).[64] Following the example of Richard Dyer's tendency to personalize utopia ("what utopia would *feel* like, rather than how it would be organized"), Flinn's discussions of individual film scores emphasize utopia or utopian nostalgia as a flight toward an idealized sanctuary, based either in the past or the future.[65] Many other scholars have invoked nostalgia handily to fill a syntactical and conceptual hole in a widespread critical stance: if utopia is a place name, a topographical frame for the enactment of artistic or media discourse, and sentiment is an intentional (if aesthetically unacceptable) attitude lending its adjectival form to objects so informed, nostalgia provides a substantive box. Adjectivally, nostalgic usefully permeates and envelops work, creator, and moment as a state of mind, an effect, and an affect.[66] Its currency is recall skewed by sentiment, its content a simple juxtaposition of then and now, "the abdication of memory."[67] When the list of standard equations is extended to kitsch, the envelope of nostalgia possesses the scent of cheap perfume.

One element of the confusion surrounding nostalgia, utopias, and their function as critical staples has been the tendency to conflate the experience of nostalgia (its psychosomatic dimension) with literary constructions of utopias (in the generalized sense of golden-age topoi) that have been located in literarily constructed pasts and revisited in literarily constructed presents.[68] Even as astute a writer on the topic as Linda Hutcheon has implied that the process or characteristic of "historical inversion" applied by Bakhtin to certain mythic and folkloric traditions reveals something fundamental about the "operation" of nostalgia. Hutcheon in fact takes her argument to the conclusion that "the aesthetics of nostalgia might, therefore, be less a matter of simple memory than of complex projection" (a position with which I concur); but she continues with the gloss that "the invocation of a partial, idealized history merges with a dissatisfaction with the present" (an extension of Bakhtin's analysis of myth) and in conclusion writes, "You can think of your own experience—or, if need be . . . think of the power of the taste of Proust's madeleine or the scent of violets in Tennyson's "A dream of fair women," or of a geranium leaf in *David Copperfield*." That is, the "aesthetics" of nostalgia are simultaneously an authorial construct and a highly individual "feeling" (compare here Dyer's approach to utopia). However, to draw nostalgia into the region of aesthetic intellection, in other words to render it a useful aesthetic category—in the sense of a way of seeing or hearing an object—requires, I would suggest, a somewhat different perspective.[69]

From the time of its inception in the mid-nineteenth century, the art of the pre-Raphaelite brotherhood was nostalgic in the generalized sense, looking back to idealized pasts (like Morris's Great Gothic). Some have suggested that its level of detail was precisely the feature that rendered it incapable of conveying nostalgia in an aesthetic manner, since the way in which it aped the reality of faces, clothing, textures, and the like drew the viewer's attention away from the contemplation of distance that marks the nostalgic experience.[70] I will argue that this position proceeds from a reading of the painting's surface, analogous to musical "style" analysis, and that it fails to take into account the dimensional possibilities of nostalgic representations. Physiological or psychosomatic nostalgia in its historical and often most intense manifestations has been associated with death, the fear of imminent death, the view toward death; this is why nostalgia flourishes—as experience or topic—in times of war (or in war's cinematic and musical reflections). Closely related to the sense of nostalgic displacement experienced by young soldiers abroad is the more universal category of exile, an important topic for nostalgic visual art in the nineteenth century. One of the most celebrated pre-Raphaelite paintings, Ford Madox Brown's *The Last of England,* demonstrates that the extension of narrative or literary nostalgia to other media occurred well before the advent of cinema or recording studios.

Brown's painting, which is linked topically to contemporaneous nostalgia imagery, depicts a husband and wife in the stern of a ship with the white cliffs of Dover in the background.[71]

Ann Colley quotes Brown's own description of his technique for the painting—"the minuteness of detail which would be visible under such conditions of broad day-light, I have thought necessary to imitate, as bringing the pathos of the subject more home to the beholder"—and points to the lack of any nostalgic distance in the picture (the pair gaze out in a direction opposite to England's shore, barely visible in the back of the scene). Their strangely fixed eyes might hold the clue to the painting's nostalgic understanding. But, she explains, "Reflecting his century's interest in physiological optics, he painted the husband's and wife's eyes as if depicting the isolated images composing the two sides of the stereoscopic slide. One expects them—these images, these eyes—as through a stereoscope, to converge and compose a single picture; however, in Brown's painting each one stares out, sees independently of the other, and waits in vain for the integrated image."[72]

The Last of England, in its "failed binocular vision," abandoned the stereoscopic elements of depth and distance expected from a visual snapshot of aesthetic nostalgia (e.g., expansive landscapes, chiaroscuro effects, emphasis upon perspective and visual recession) for the sake of a montage consecrated to the evocation of the pathetic. Brown's painting reveals the metamorphosis of the topos of exile (from the past or from the homeland) into a prompt for immediate sympathetic response from the viewer. His representational sleight-of-hand, involving pathos switched for nostalgia, is a gimmick hardly unfamiliar to modern film audiences.

Items produced by artists now associated primarily with the arts and crafts style (like William Morris and the lesser-known John Byam Shaw [1872–1919]) had found their voices within the societies and techniques of pre-Raphaelite art, but the movement was fading by the final decades of the century. By 1900, art as a social practice now out of step with the times had by necessity retreated from its intersections with the domestic and had grown specialized, increasingly confined to the domains of the aesthete and the academician. A rare instance in which the pre-Raphaelite eye was turned toward the mood of the day was John Byam Shaw's *The Boer War* (Figure 1), attached in its original 1901 exhibition to lines of Christina Rossetti: "Last summer green things were greener / Brambles fewer, the blue sky bluer." Whether or not the intention was, as has been suggested, to mourn the passing of the beautiful age

Figure 1. John Byam Shaw, *The Boer War* (Courtesy of
Birmingham Museums & Art Gallery)

and its associated artistic practice, the painting's success as a vehicle of
aesthetic nostalgia is revealed by its most striking formal element: the visual alienation of foreground elements from background elements. The
pensive woman appears suspended in front of the backdrop she con-
templates, with—from the viewer's perspective—each plane in full
focus.[73] The entire vision is in the end not realistic but stereoscopic, constructed at a time when the imagery of war had grown increasingly naturalistic and unsettling, courtesy of new media. For example, photographs of dead soldiers taken on location in Africa were now available
to the public. Shaw's aesthetic stereoscopy embodies the nostalgia
chronotope, and it is a startlingly apt analogue for the relationship of "A
Whiter Shade of Pale"—which I have suggested was informed by an

acoustic interpretation of a stereoscopic model—to the historical environment of its reception in the United States during the Vietnam era. In the film *The Big Chill* (treated in detail below), Vietnam's psychosocial aftermath was layered upon this original association, testimony to the power of the song's intimations of space and time, real and imagined.

TAKING MEASURE

Among the earliest proto-Romantics it may have been Goethe's *Werther* who opened the door for the easy conflation of the nostalgic and sentimental domains. Werther's tears have been problematic for the reception of the character and the text, but Goethe actually captured within his protagonist's effusive words that essential feature of nostalgia that separates it from sentimentality, providing an abstract core that extends nostalgia's utility beyond its original application (related to what was perceived in the seventeenth century as a physical pathology of homesickness confined to a young, displaced military), and its later, more generalized and demedicalized, variants. Nostalgia's pain *(algos),* as Werther melodramatically enacts through his dash-laden syntax, resides not in the return home *(nostos),* or in an act of sweet recall, but in the recognition and analysis of the entire space in between. Indeed, Werther's nostalgia revisits in a flash more than an idealized glittering past; it does not (as Hutcheon has it) "sanitize as it selects." In more literal translations than the one provided at the beginning of this chapter, his *"Erinnerung der düstern Zwischenräume"* has been rendered variously as "dejected gloom" and, even more precisely, "dark intervals."[74] Taken together, all of Werther's envisioned moments add up to another, greater, and more horrible (because unbridgeable) *Zwischenraum.* To feel nostalgia requires the simultaneous experience of two places and times as an impossible present, accompanied by an instantaneous taking measure of the distance between them.[75] It is for this reason that cultural theory has abandoned, at least with respect to the evocation of historical musical material in pop or film scoring, nostalgia *specialiter dictum.* For how could mass listening take such a measurement when the pastness of the sound of the past is usually little more than a manufactured chimera spun from the elements of purely decorative historicity?

Jameson's discussion of the mutual "wrapping" of texts included a photograph of the filmmaker Andrei Tarkovsky's extraordinary cinematographic superimposition of a Russian house wrapped in an Italian cathedral, taken from Tarkovsky's *Nostalghia* (1983). Jameson was not concerned with the relationship between the film and the concept of nostalgia, per se. But it is worth revisiting the scene that leads up to this unforgettable image, since it is a rather precise exemplar of the formal elements of aesthetic nostalgia expressed as musical multimedia. Before that image appears, Tarkovsky's poet Gorchakov walks a straight line, footstep by footstep, measuring the length of the empty, monumental stone architectural space in which he finds himself; he holds a burning candle, shielded by his cupped hand or his coat. Tarkovsky has indicated time and space by their millenia-old universal measures, candle and foot.[76] Touching the wall at one end to mark the starting point, he embarks upon his journey.

For Gorchakov, taking measure is a haptic enterprise: the hand's touch, the foot's step. His only ocular concern is the candle's flame. Twice the candle goes out, and he performs a retrograde action at the same deliberate pace, beginning over from his original position. After seven minutes, the off-screen sound of a dog barking (which will gradually increase in prominence) enters the sound track. Viewers will recognize the sound: since the beginning of the film it and the dog serve as icons for his Russian childhood. Eventually the sound track comes into focus and we come to understand that the point of arrival is the moment of the poet's death. In the culminating visual montage of the house in the cathedral, a sense of distance and time are again emphasized, now in static form, by the regular, proportional disposition of the church's pillars (flanking each side of the symmetrical image) and its empty windows (at the back). As the camera's eye recedes, the perspectival element of length is enhanced. Ultimately, the entire sequence makes explicit a notion that lies beneath much of the film, an unexpected extension of Bakhtin's notion of narrative chronotope, of time space, to the realm of human experience beyond the pages of a novel or the confines of a standard novelistic film.[77] Our experience of nostalgia—its odd mix of spatial and temporal calculation with intense somatic involvement—is our real-life time space, no doubt the only example of what might be thought of as a natural chronotope. Tarkovsky concretizes its parts through a complex revelation of real time, real space, and meaningful visual metaphors.

Within the domains of media criticism, of course, nostalgia has come to serve instead as a kind of chrono*trope*, a figure of critical rhetoric related to nothing more than a sense of temporality superimposed upon a sense (or sensibility) of feeling. I am arguing that aesthetic nostalgia—if it is to form more than a trivial subset of style or mood effects—must somehow intersect with or represent the experiential mode of nostalgia, one that is grounded in (and necessitates) a panoptic (or panhaptic) perspective on some timeline; that line, envisioned (or embodied) marks the spatial topography of nostalgic experience. Most often it measures an individual life, although the nostalgic may extend that perspective to longer-lived social aggregations in which the individual locates himself as a metonymic cell.[78] While the experience of nostalgia transforms recall and sensation into adjacencies in an enriched present, the nostalgic must at the same time acknowledge the illusory nature of his experience and, above all, take measure of the distance between then and now. For a poet, musician, or filmmaker authentically to represent nostalgia will be far more difficult and require more components than the simple setting of a trigger (for example, a radio playing in a 1962 Chevy) or an on-screen imitation of nostalgic reception (as occurs in The Big Chill). The measured distance must figure as the primary topos of any such textual, aural, or visual unit; it will define the chronotopic dimensions of the nostalgic work. And for the critic or analyst to infer nostalgia as a category for judgment, attention must focus upon that dimension, not upon the simple comparison of its temporal nodes (the now and the past) and their associated affects. Here, of course, is where the critical resort to nostalgia as an aesthetic negative linked to the generic utopian has fallen short, eliminating nostalgia's aesthetic range and potential textures in the interest of phrasal expediency.

A significant aspect of Tarkovsky's representation of nostalgia involves its acoustic projection by means of aural stereoscopy of the kind I have discussed above. The film's entire timeline is wrapped by the title sequence (at one end) and the house-in-the-cathedral at the other. In each, the off-screen music consists of two planes: on one is positioned the thin, natural voice of a woman's folk song; on the other the rich sound of a church choir with orchestra, performing Verdi's Requiem, with the latter at first distant and then increasing in prominence until it blends with and eventually replaces the former.[79] The left and right sides of the imaginary stereoscope (or stereophone), then, are constituted of material distinguished by performing forces, texture, and sociological or ethnographic status. One might also add cinematic status, since for Tarkovsky, instrumental music (like the orchestra here, and unlike the natural sounds of the Russian village) "is artistically so autonomous that it is far harder for it to dissolve into the film to the point where it becomes an organic part of it."[80] The two sound images are brought together briefly in a stereoscopic (that is, stereophonic) moment. A multiplicity of subsidiary planes is suggested by other sounds (voices, the dog's bark). In this imaginary acoustical space the dimensions of Tarkovsky's visuals are constructed in sound.

Like so many items in the fantastic rock repertoire, "A Whiter Shade of Pale" intersected with a number of potentially revealing aesthetic models. If the disembodied organ points to the secretive clavichordist, its acoustical distance (based on prominence relative to the voice and to the volume of the non-Bachian sections of the song) is a reminder of the impetus for Werther's nostalgic moment, Lotte's keyboard melody from the past. The song's acoustical emphasis on the construction of distance may have lain behind the capacity of "A Whiter Shade of Pale" to elicit a nuanced form of aural reception, something beyond that inspired by the Doors' figurational model or the Swingle Singers' less multidimensional, albeit attractive and (for the time) aurally esoteric, Bach revisions. I suggested that the Swingle Singers did not promulgate kitsch, but what about Procol Harum? Does the song, whose acoustic content I hear as conforming to the category of nostalgic aesthetic expression based on technical and formal details, merely add up to a different flavor of nostalgia kitsch? In the nineteenth century, nostalgia in its original sense—the literal homesickness of soldiers abroad—certainly made its way out of medical discourse and into the mainstream in mass-market literature and mass-market objets d'art.

Thomas Campbell's poem "The Soldier's Dream," written earlier in that century, enjoyed a second life during the Crimean War. Immensely popular as British troops were dispatched to Istanbul and the Black Sea, the poem survived long after as a sentimental staple in such domestic literary volumes as Palgrave's *Golden Treasury* of 1875.[81] Campbell's sentimental depiction of here and there, of now and then, a young soldier's "sweet Vision" of home, wife, and children, had by 1860 been embalmed in the form of a charming and best-selling Staffordshire ceramic mantel figure portraying a young Scottish soldier asleep by his cannon, with his head supported by his hand and his arm propped up on a drum (Figure 2). A reader can at least identify the temporal and topographical nodes of the nostalgic in Campbell's poem, even if they are not conjured into aesthetic being by any technique of poetic nuance. The ceramic, though, cannot retain even that much of the image. The history of *The Soldier's Dream* illustrates a pattern of production and reproduction in which the attempt to render the experience of nostalgia satisfies its critics, resulting in sentimental domestic art: first in the form of Campbell's poem ensconced in a parlor treasury, and afterward as an item of

Figure 2. *The Soldier's Dream* (photo courtesy of Arnold Berlin)

mainstream decor. *The Soldier's Dream,* the household ceramic, is a lovely avatar of domestic kitsch. Still, it represents an interesting object within the nuanced history of nostalgic representation, for its subject matter—nostalgia in its "medicalized" form and as the experience of soldiers abroad—makes it authentic nostalgia kitsch.

By contrast, "A Whiter Shade of Pale" is not "about" then from the perspective of now, although those temporal poles are part of its "image." Its special quality resides neither in its invocation of Bach nor in its mixing Baroque models and soul. The distinction of the song lies in its uncanny ability to project a sense of the dimensions of nostalgia without calling upon its reenactment. Like many of the scenes in Tarkovsky's *Nostalghia,* the song constructs a more abstract structural chronotope that may be apprehended without resort to novelistic glossing. Its acoustic dimensions, as described earlier in this chapter, provided a physical basis upon which the temporal and spatial distance from there to here, and from the past to the present and back, could be heard, mapped, and felt. The acoustical format of "A Whiter Shade of Pale" lays out a particular form of spatial trajectory through the presentation and manipulation of temporal markers. Space between the markers—the invocation of space, its apprehension by the ear, and its intellection as a physical image—is, aurally, what the song is about. As an object for critical engagement on the part of a musicologist, it does not idealize its pastness or problematize its present. Both musical elements are celebrated for what they are, and for their imagined cultural resonances.

In the imaginary *Zwischenraum* the aesthetic heart of the work may be found; the ways in which it has been set in place, the power it possessed in its time to effect a subjective response, the imaginative understandings listeners and critics projected upon it—all these lend interest to the song as a historical item. And beyond its acoustical boundaries, those perceived intimations of a nostalgic time space have been encouraged and lent greater potency and affective value from the time of the song's release by the details of its promotion and reception history. According to that reception history, Procol Harum's beautiful monster, once set free, moved before us reverently in a monumental space as a harbinger or emissary of the dead. It may be that Tarkovsky's poet is not manifested in the song's cathedral of sound (we might sense his presence, though, in the aesthetic morbidity of Keith Reid's lyrics); his careful journey of time and measure is evoked nonetheless. The Swingle Singers' productions of Bach were pre-Raphaelite in certain technical dimensions, particularly those associated with the application of detail to the aural canvas. My assigning "A Whiter Shade of Pale" to the category of aesthetic nostalgia derives again from technical acoustic features, in this case as they relate to the formal aspects of nostalgia aesthetics and style. Distance, or its measure, is at the heart and soul of it. But beyond even this, the imaginary stage on which Procol Harum's sound played involved yet another rather specific dimensional analogy, that of the stereoscopic. This technique enriched both media tracks (visual and aural) in Tarkovsky's remarkable representation of the true nostalgic mode.

POSTLUDE I: DEATH WARMED OVER

Lawrence Kasdan's *The Big Chill* (1983) was for tail-end baby-boomers a
nostalgia film in the generalized Jamesonian way, at least with respect to
its musical "score," a collection of pop "classics" that circulate in and out
of the film's diegetic and nondiegetic sound fields. The screenplay's protagonists formed a social clique in their college days, and the items chosen
for the pastiche sound track—including "A Whiter Shade of Pale"—are
presumed to resonate in the memories of audiences likely to identify with
the experience of the characters.[82] And yet, despite the commercial nostalgia kitsch aspects of the film, when "A Whiter Shade of Pale" emerges
in the mise-en-bande it participates in a two-tiered manifestation of nostalgia. One tier is comprised of the materials of the original song that I have
categorized above as nostalgic in a particular sense, even if viewers from
its time recall its content nostalgically (the Jamesonian nostalgia-trigger
operation). Beyond this, the song occupies a planar position with respect
to the mise-en-bande of the film in general, materializing within the scope
of the sound track in such a way as to realize its potential as not merely a
musical but a multimedia construction of stereoscopic nostalgia effect. In
The Big Chill, "A Whiter Shade of Pale," through elements of prominence
combined with visual and narrative cues, is heard as doubly distant, a
stereoscopic object wrapped in a stereophone.

 Melissa Carey and Michael Hannan recently examined *The Big Chill*
in an effort to bring composite sound tracks of the type encountered in
the film into line with what the authors (and many musicologists writing about film) take as the principal analytical region pertinent to discussions of film scoring: meaning and narrative.[83] Again, the influence
of Claudia Gorbman's sophisticated and original formulations is paramount in such assumptions. Carey and Hannan cite, for example,
Gorbman's assessment of the implication of scoring in the full cinematic
experience: "Image, sound effects, dialogue, and music track are virtually inseparable during the viewing experience; they form a *combina-
toire* of expression . . . it is the narrative context, the interrelations between music and the rest of the film's system, that determines the
effectiveness of film music."[84]

 For Carey and Hannan, "A Whiter Shade of Pale" is just another
cog in the machinery of narrative as they lay out their intention to
"provide a particular and substantive case study of the manner in
which they [popular songs in *The Big Chill*] effectively fulfill the general and theoretical functions of music in film," which, following the

Gorbman quote, they elaborate as music's "role in the process of interpretation and the attribution of meaning." Whereas Carey and Hannan characterize most of the songs as underscorings of "pacing and mood," they link "A Whiter Shade of Pale"—relevantly it would seem—to "spatialisation." The space to which they refer, however, is the setting constructed (literally) to house the narrative, and nothing more: "Songs playing on the hi-fi system in the house provide an ideal opportunity for the viewer to understand the spatial interconnections of the rooms. As 'A Whiter Shade of Pale' is playing, the song bridges scenes in different parts of the house. Changes of volume (as a door to an upstairs room opens) give sonic reality and help create a sense of spatial orientation."[85]

But the film's re-invention of the song as acoustic epitaph—by its placement in the narrative, on the first night following the funeral of the protagonists' first deceased contemporary—in fact cinematized for thirty-something audiences in the Reagan era an understanding they had already formulated fifteen years earlier: that the song somehow encapsulated a melancholia of distance and possessed the mesmerizing allure of a death mask. Death, in the film's diegesis, is—for both the dead and the living—a thread running through life's tapestry; its dye for the protagonists was recreational or anaesthetic drug use (the latter linked in the story to Vietnam and its associated post-traumatic stress). This perspective is reinforced, of course, by the lyrics, which, while owing much to antiquarian sources like the Gospels and *Canterbury Tales,* begins with the suggestion of an unexpected drug reaction.

Words, as in other psychedelia, were insufficient to project those altered states (whether of the dead or the drugged); the acoustic dimension was fundamental to such effects (consider Whiteley's hearing of the song as reminiscent of hallucinogenic experience). Procol Harum's producer, Denny Cordell, had made this connection at the time of the song's release in an unabashedly naive and telling set of remarks: "Their music is stimulating intellectually as well as emotionally. It's pretty introvert music and definitely not for leaping about. They are real mood makers and should be listened to whilst stoned out of your mind at 3 A.M."[86] His perspective recalls the mode of listening invoked in the publicity for King Crimson's "Cat Food", and both point to an aesthetic of reception that figured prominently in the "aestheticized viewing" of the historical picturesque and was effectively reinvented for psychedelia and progressive rock. Cordell's association of the song with solitary listening (the frame for both intellection and emotion) within a particularly liminal segment of clock time (the predawn hours) recalls the secretive musical practice depicted in so many *empfindsame* clavichord songs:

> Return my laments
> To the silent nights;
> Sing, until dawn appears,
> And until I can cry no more.[87]

Rock's musical landscapes, however, were located not outdoors but in enclosed spaces containing electrical sound devices. These were the secret spaces of rock's fantastic-picturesque clavichord cult, a matrix of musical, literary, and reception practice that was, we have seen, frequently morbid or even funerary long before most of its aficionados were facing adult responsibilities of family, profession, and ceremonial burial. Musical introspection and the clarity of aesthetic insight that might proceed from solitude and madness (natural or induced) were inscribed in Friedrich Rochlitz's 1804 account of the lunatic clavichordist "Karl."[88] Revisited in numerous Hollywood film scenarios, especially in the 1930s and 1940s, and relocated to Hammond organs and synthesizers, such states were reproduced on personal audio equipment in the private chambers within virtual madhouses of late twentieth-century listening.

In Kasdan's film, characters reenact as adults—in the hours following the funeral of their college friend—that characteristic ritual of late 1960s dormitory living: the conversation with no beginning and no end positioned within the only zone of clock time that is felt as profoundly liminal, located somewhere between midnight and dawn. Musically backgrounded, such exchanges were unintentionally staged throughout the period (and no doubt still are) in artificial listening environments comprised of institutional housing units. They manifested a cinema of the real, one relying upon the same willing suspension of disbelief that characterizes the modes of cinematic reception that I will consider in the chapters that follow. Such conversations were encouraged by the cultivation of a frame of consciousness untied from the quantitative marks of mundane time and space that restrict normal waking hours. Loosening the bonds that constrained ordinary perception was, of course, a fundamental impetus to drug use in the 1960s, and to the growth of a specialized musical repertoire to background it. Both were encouraged by reiterations of the same perspective (even if not always as clumsily expressed) as that of Cordell's recommended conceptual mélange of music, intellect, body, clock time, and drug haze.

"A Whiter Shade of Pale" enters *The Big Chill* as off-scene music for the late-night conversation in which the characters assess the present against the past; they look back and take measure of the distance traveled. Located in the same temporal and atemporal spaces of consciousness that it had in the characters' college days, the song is positioned metonymically with respect to the mise-en-scène of the whole, just as was Matthew Fisher's organ prelude to Procol Harum's original song, which projected to listeners its own quasi-cinematic mise-en-scène. In both instances the organ's sound constitutes an invocation by synecdoche of certain emotionally charged processes of aural reception that are understood to reside more typically in musical experiences of greater temporal extension. They include intimations or understandings that such sound is generated by an agent that resides, in the end, not merely off scene but in a room of unfathomable dimension, that is, the realm not of the phenomenal but of the noumenal. The noumenon is attached to special categories of perception or experience, in this case relating to those grandly liminal zones of passage from life to death and from present to past. The latter may be effectively achieved by the instantaneous triggering of temporally dislocative experiences of nostalgia that, in the case of Procol Harum, is contrived and abstract (that is, aesthetic).

In *The Big Chill,* nostalgia has been visually reinforced and multiplied by the diegetic enactment of acts of listening that are shared by the actors and the target audience; both groups are consequently positioned simultaneously in the now and in the past. Prior to this moment in the film the pop sound track had been acoustically prominent (whether positioned within or behind the diegesis). Despite the presentation of "A Whiter Shade of Pale" within the film's "real" narrative space, however, the low volume (its lack of prominence) renders it effectively out of the scene, so far out with respect to even the subdued dialogue level as to suggest its source in some other place. Notably, the audio equipment is not shown on screen; the music, even if diegetic, is not "source" music. The actors' voices add a third plane to the stereophony of the original mix and another measurable line between the past and the present moment constituted at the edge of mortality, a trace of what I have suggested may have marked the particularity of the song's original reception. Here we encounter in sharp relief and side-by-side the two forms of nostalgia. One is generic, constituted by the script's emphasis on reminiscence and the simple historical juxtaposition of then and now—and especially "A Whiter Shade of Pale" as a representational object. Beyond that, the other is the scene's very effective rendering—by the manipulation of specific media effects—of the chronotopic dimensions of human nostalgic experience.

POSTLUDE 2: MEDUSA

Annie Lennox's version of "A Whiter Shade of Pale" reveals the extent
to which rock covers (as opposed to tributes) so often miss the conceptual boat. The tasteful arrangement featured on Lennox's *Medusa* (1995)
spotlights only the historicity of Fisher's prelude, exaggerating its
Baroque element by replacing his throbbing semivocal organ with the inescapably quaint sound of a synthesized harpsichord. It ramps up the
Baroque mannerisms of J. S. Bach while timbrally damping the languid,
throbbing voice of C. P. E.'s *empfindsames* keyboard that had been reinvented in the original's Hammond sound, and decorates the prelude
with additional, extraneous Baroque mordents and other embellishments. No surprise, perhaps, that I found a journey through a local su-
permarket backgrounded, courtesy of the Muzak corporation or one of
its competitors, by Lennox's version. In its restricted commitment to the
power of pastness, the song inspired reflection upon nothing more
weighty than the inevitable passing of the week's produce.[89]

CHAPTER 6

Listening in Dark Places

From the mid-1960s through the mid-1970s fantastic rock grew increasingly cinematic in its insistence upon imaginary visualization as an adjunct to and, indeed, a goal of listening. At first abstract and undefined even when referential—in line with the consciousness-expanding programs of psychedelic experimentation—the unseen visual dimensions of pre-video rock were later inscribed and prescribed through the multiplication of special effects, often bearing skewed resemblances to identifiable natural or mechanical sources. Increasingly opaque lyrics and, most significantly, the expansion of the time frame for individual songs, drew much of rock's musical content into the realm of "scoring" rather than "setting" the text (if there was one). Rock's fantasts and their immediate parents, like the Beats, invented their visions and audiations from a vocabulary of imaginary sound and time spaces (thus, perhaps, "audiochronotopes"). These were originally absorbed and compiled through the mental operations of a previous generation's audiences who had first listened in the dark, thanks to the enterprise of imaginative filmmakers, composers, and technicians.

In the early sound film, stereoscope and stereophone were presented in tandem; by the latter half of the century, music alone—if sufficiently cinematic in its implications—came also to be heard in an implicitly multimediated way. A particularly apt expression of the historical continuity embodied in this bleed-through is the film composer Max Steiner's reductive declaration (which foreshadowed *Melody Maker*'s uncannily similar assessment of King Crimson): "If Wagner had lived in this century, he would have been the number one film composer."[1] Steiner, however, had something in mind other than the landscapes through which I wandered in the last chapter. And Wagner—Allen Ginsberg notwithstanding—will hold no more sway in the classical mix than do Strauss, Stravinsky, Schubert, or Mendelssohn when it comes to the construction of the fantastic (from the intimate to the monumental) in twentieth-century cinema.

TRIGGERS

One of the most perfect representations of fantastic hesitation in film is the "apparition" of Laura Hunt halfway through *Laura*. As a moment in a narrative trajectory that has already been destabilized by voice-overs, it embodies the impossible—an astonishing one-eighty—and forces the viewer to hesitate between reality and phantasm, conscious and subconscious.[2] On screen, Dana Andrews's detective, Mark McPherson, supports the expected audience reaction by enacting fantastic confusion (he rubs his eyes and shakes his head). Meanwhile David Raksin's background music has suddenly and discomfitingly dropped from the scene, on the heels of that long and famous sequence densely scored in the style of early Schoenberg, leaving behind only a suffocating silence punctuated by the ticking of a diegetic clock and the thumping hearts of the astonished audience.[3] But Raksin had already signaled the fantastic moment by luring viewers into a receptive place with the "len-a-toned" piano chord that accompanies the shot of Mark's drifting off to sleep in an armchair.[4] Such special acoustical effects have distinguished the liminal zones of film, including especially that of the fantastic, in Hollywood cinema for much of its history.

Most familiar among them is the sound of the theremin, which began its association with abnormal states in the mid-1940s in Miklós Rózsa's scores for *Spellbound* and *The Lost Weekend*. If the ondes martenot had been more readily available in the United States in the decade preceding, it may well have staked out the same territory as Theremin's more domesticated electronic instrument. Franz Waxman failed to procure one for *Bride of Frankenstein* (he had used it in *Liliom*), and Rósza's plan to use an electronic instrument for *The Thief of Baghdad* in 1939 was frustrated by Martenot.[5] In both of Rósza's fully realized productions from the 1940s, theremin timbre functioned as an acoustic trigger for the audience to mark the transition from diegetic reality to diegetic psychosis.

The Hammond organ, crucial to Procol Harum's suggestion of a different sort of psychoacoustic space, and its sibling the Novachord were frequently called upon to mark the fantastic border, as for example by Waxman in Hitchcock's *Rebecca* (1940), where a Novachord and amplified violin wind around Mrs. Danvers's invocations of the title character, a presence acoustically conjured if not corporealized.[6] Her weird imaginings of Rebecca constitute a fairly explicit sexual fantasy, and their consummation is manifested ultimately in another grand act of self-immolation (cf. *Bride of Frankenstein*'s finale).

Timbre is usually an even more effective signal than contour in conveying information regarding the intended register or its genre associations, especially to the nonmusical auditor. Beyond the more restricted capacity of the theremin, electric organs and their descendants have often been employed as timbral triggers for other strains of fantastic experience, including those associated with zones outside the individual psyche. Bernard Herrmann featured the electrified organ sound as an effect in *Vertigo* (1954), wherein a quick stinger locates the fantastic in the otherwise purely quotidian moment at which James Stewart's Scotty gets out of his car and then, as signaled by the organ chord, enters what will function structurally as a liminal zone of insecurity: an empty church, in which the oscillating organ is replaced by a Bachian pipe organ sound. That sound is aurally positioned on a plane closer to the "natural" diegetic environment, but its solitary player (whose solitude is imaginatively denoted by the hollow emptiness of the church and an engineered sense of spatial acoustics) remains disconcertingly invisible. Herrmann's reinvention of Bach inside the church consists of an impossibly extended harmonic sequence, an expression of the circular forms that permeate Herrmann's score and Hitchcock's visuals. David Raksin jokingly referred to the church as "Our Lady of Perpetual Sequences."[7] Exiting the church from the other side, Scotty will encounter the tombstone of Carlotta Valdez; it will serve as the impetus for his imminent conundrum, a forced confrontation with irreconcilable manifestations of the living and the dead. It is here that imbalance, associated from the start of the film with Scotty's medical condition (vertigo), begins palpably to weigh upon the audience's narrative expectations. For the moment at which Scotty looks at the stone, and to mark the end of the sequence, Herrmann provided another cue: a single chime. Filtered through its other uses—especially in Ennio Morricone's scores for Sergio Leone's westerns, including *The Good, the Bad, and the Ugly*—the chime, often electric or digital, became an acoustical marker of implicit monumentality in the morbid cinematic topographies of late twentieth-century rap music.[8]

In Herrmann's score for Robert Wise's *The Day the Earth Stood Still* (1951) an organ stinger again denoted a critical moment of fantastic astonishment, enacted on the screen and felt again—courtesy of Herrmann's effect—by the audience. The scene takes place in the claustrophobic box of an American-style elevator. Moving among numbered floors with no visible point of reference outward for those in motion within, the elevator is another sort of electric machine that enforces an experience of liminality, an unnerving in-between that plays with the characteristic physicality of human locomotion. In this special space within the imaginative regions of the film, an oscillating sound interjected by the electric organ stops normative time dead.[9] Such special effects timbres moved freely between the supernatural and the scientific marvelous, testimony to the features the two genres had shared for more than a century.

The category of experience specifically assigned to that of the subconscious, neurotic, or psychotic is often rendered by a classically inscribed signature effect for expressionistic madness: the sudden manifestation of unprepared, nonfunctional chromaticism. Access to electric sounds could intensify the weirdness of these moments (as in Rózsa's chromatic theremin music in *Spellbound*), but simpler sources could make the point. Cinema audiences were trained in the hearing of chromatic melodies or oddly juxtaposed chromatic harmonies from the earliest years of the fantastic sound film. The musical component of Tod Browning's *Freaks* (1932) is for the most part characteristic of many nonmusical sound productions of the transition-to-sound period, consisting simply of prerecorded bits, economically scattered throughout the film for scenic continuity and atmospheric definition (most consist of "circus" music, reinforcing the screenplay's setting in a traveling sideshow). Among all the monster features of the early 1930s, *Freaks* stands out by forcing the audience into a harrowing, long-term confrontation with fantastic hesitation, as they must repeatedly negotiate—scene by scene—the film's unprecedented marriage of the real to the cinematic.

Freaks has always been a site of controversy, since the horrifyingly effective trigger for its uniquely visceral projection of the fantastic to the audience was Browning's decision to cast the human monsters of the title with players whose physical and mental challenges were real (those with backgrounds in show business were primarily from circus or sideshow environments, and none were trained actors). At the moment most removed from the grubby reality of the sideshow, when the "freaks" turn on the beautiful Cleopatra, whom they will chase down and mutilate (effecting her metamorphosis by a gimmick of Ovidian retribution into a duck-woman), each strange player becomes an abstract face of murderous intention defined by expressionistic camera shots and lighting. As they confront her, one of the little people (with no obvious rationale) begins to play a chromatic, mad tune on an impossible ocarina: there is no synchronization of the character's finger movements to the number of notes in the melody. Chromatic psychosis has never been abandoned as a topos, and continues to circulate, most often these days in electronically synthesized melodic gestures in which pitches are continuous rather than discrete, à la the old theremin.

FREAKING OUT

I have called attention to the case of *Freaks* as an indication of the "historical authority" that the chromatic fantastic enjoys as one of the essential musical effects of sound cinema. When rock became fantastic it predictably followed suit. Chromatic effects in psychedelia were numerous and have been addressed by other writers who note the characteristic associations between nonfunctional chromaticism and the hallucinogenic perspective on matters of time, gravity, etc. But meaningful intersections between the psychedelic fantastic in music and in film could work both ways. Strawberry Alarm Clock's 1967 hit "Incense and Peppermints" is particularly relevant. The song's weird chromatic juxtapositions, especially bold in the refrain sections, were featured in the sound track of Richard Rush's rather interesting (and interestingly cast) film *Psych-Out* in 1968 as an acoustical emblem of the states of mind explored in the story. *Psych-Out*, though a period piece, explored artificial psychosis as it was cultivated in and expressed through the lives of its spaced-out protagonists, concretizing as physical multimedia the implicit connection of psychedelic music with the cinematic mode of imaginative representation. At a time when pop pastiche was not yet a standard for film scoring, *Psych-Out*'s reliance on a quintessentially psychedelic musical object was marked by the naive cleverness typical of first-generation multimedia discourses; its newness was rapidly eclipsed as the psychedelic aesthetic grew increasingly trivialized by patterns of consumption, until it—like other media tools before it—became a target of critique and counterpractice.

For Paul Morrisey's *Heat* (1972), third in the Joe D'Alessandro trilogy emanating from the drug-saturated circles surrounding Andy Warhol, John Cale (an original member of the Velvet Underground) composed original title music. As a "theme song" it marked a radical departure from the casual and exclusively diegetic appearances of any extended music in the earlier Morrisey productions released under Warhol's name, for example in the dance sequence of *Trash* (1970). *Heat*'s signature music (presented at the beginning and end of the film, and bearing no obvious "expressive" relationship to it) is as Hollywoodian in its artificiality with respect to score form as the story's amusing transformation of *Sunset Boulevard* was to conventional film narrative. Cale's theme music, assigned to a solo trumpet, is marked by simplistic and repetitive scalar chromatic motion. Ascending and descending to suggest a particular kind of circularity, that of the circus and its associated musics (an identification reinforced by highlighting the preeminent circus band instrument), the meaningless tune represents, as an isolated and stylized gesture, the meandering topography of psychedelia, rejecting it as inauthentic and—it might be argued—essentially cinematic. Appearing at a time when "freak" served as standard argot for a drug user, *Heat*'s minimal and seemingly meaningless original scoring encapsulated and commented upon a significant stylistic and expressive timeline.

The Velvet Underground (and Warhol's Exploding Plastic Inevitable) rejected not only the Romantic cinematicism of most musical psychedelia but also the pretensions of mass-mediated modernism. "Progressive" art had been finding its way into the video mainstream for years: Jack Kerouac (for whom drugs and alcohol were integrated with Beat Romanticism) was featured on *The Steve Allen Show* in 1959; and the young Frank Zappa (an outspoken critic of drugs throughout his career) performed a "work" that included a prerecorded tape component on the same program in 1963.[10] Through mimicry, fragmentation, and distension of detail, Warhol's cohorts denied the inevitability of formal and temporal continuity that had informed both conventional cinematic practice and conventional artistic historiography. Approaching the psychotic and somatic aspects of drug experience from this perspective in, for example, the classic song "Heroin," they might explore the same poles of saint and sinner (God and Devil) encountered in the most effusive renderings of psychedelic Romanticism, but the music's topography is neither picturesque nor fantastic. If the song's single-minded viola drone and incessant percussion thump realize a stylistic perspective, it was one that was not merely antipop but antiaesthetic. Directing the listener toward a literally anaesthetic perspective on the subjective implications of the text by techniques of stasis and single-mindedness, "Heroin" underscored the irrelevance of picturesque viewing practices to other spheres of midcentury drug culture and drug experience.[11]

Chromaticism had been linked specifically to addiction in Rózsa's first theremin score, completed just before *Spellbound,* for Billy Wilder's *The Lost Weekend,* in which Ray Milland played a writer struggling with alcoholism. Its theremin material, like that Rózsa composed for the Hitchcock film, is chromatic in a sort of Debussyan way; in fact at times it emerges from a chromatic orchestral wash (reminiscent of *Prélude à l'après-midi d'un faune*). While intended as a musical representation of a sort of psychosis, the theremin quite specifically fills out the expressive space of Milland's enactment of physical and psychological craving. Paul Morrisey, commenting on his own filmic essay in which a couple was recorded using heroin (included on the DVD release of *Heat*) suggested that if this short film were to be fitted with music, it would not be composed (i.e., cinematic) but would, rather, consist of the sound of a radio playing in the room. Here, whatever their polemical intentions, his and the Underground's perspectives reveal themselves in fact as more anti-Romantic than anticinematic in any original sense, for Morrisey's notion is another cinematic trope. It exists, however, among the conventions of a different expressive register in cinema.

Morrisey's insistence on a detached, diegetic sound environment is prefigured in a fundamentally cinematic (yet anti-Romantic) effect: the diegetic radio background to the first cold-blooded murders in the noir mini-classic *Born to Kill* (1947). All characters in this Robert Wise production are amoral, greedy, or sociopathic.[12] Sam Wild (who kills whenever the mood strikes him) carries out his first pair of on-screen murders in a dark, tiny kitchen. Bludgeoning his victims to the inexorable accompaniment of a radio playing swing music in the next room, the mechanistic quality of his actions and the radio's indifference, and the spatial constraints of the room, render these deaths "smaller than life," nonoperatic, nonmelodramatic, expressively anaesthetic. The presentation is perhaps more "authentic" than, for instance, Waldo Lydecker's overblown death throes in *Laura,* but it is still cinematic artifice. *Born to Kill* has borrowed from a register containing those utterances that might express the difficulty of remaining human in an age of machinery and money-madness, indeed, the same expressive register that had been explored within different genre and style parameters in *Now, Voyager*'s stuffy parlor. A cinematic model might even be suggested for the musical single-mindedness of "Heroin." Its implicit constriction of experiential drug space, one markedly different from the "spacey" breadth projected by psychedelia, had been in some sense foreshadowed and cinematized in the raunchily insistent ostinato triggered by Frank Sinatra's on-screen representations of Frankie Machine's heroin use throughout Elmer Bernstein's jazz-inflected score for Otto Preminger's naturalistic and visually claustrophobic *The Man With the Golden Arm* (1954).

SQUARING THE CIRCLE: SCREEN, IMAGE, MOVEMENT

Max Steiner was the first composer to fit a full-blown, original orchestral score to a fantastic film in *King Kong* (1933). Steiner's contribution to the development of film-scoring procedures is formidable and original, but when it came to matters of dimension, Steiner counted two: up and down. For Max Steiner, most acoustic representations of screen space proceeded from the analogy of pitch space as it has been constructed in the European tradition, in which "high" and "low" are the terms associated with both physical space and acoustical frequency. Franz Waxman, on the other hand, recognized around the same time the potential of cinema to divert normal perception onto additional planes, and in his scores for *Liliom* (1934) and *Bride of Frankenstein* (1935) he accomplished something Steiner had not. The nature of that contribution has been insufficiently emphasized by writers on film music committed primarily to the hunting down and cataloguing of motives and leitmotivic manipulation in early film scoring. Throughout *Liliom* (directed by Fritz Lang) the fantastic aspect of the story (which wanders between earth and heaven) is emphasized through suggestive multimedia effects that play with flat, foursquare "screenic" expectations well before the narrative reveals its intersection with the impossible and with the registers of the fairy-tale marvelous.

From the outset, in the title sequence and first scene, the soundscape is directed toward the border of the fantastic by Waxman's emphasis on the mechanical organ of the carnivalesque hippo-palace, an unusual space that will be represented throughout the first portion of the film as one that is both fixed in place and in constant motion. *Liliom*'s title sequence is striking for its time. Each title "card" is transparent (i.e., the names and words appear to float on the screen's surface, but they are framed by a rectangle graphic). As one proceeds to the next, it appears to pivot on a vertical axis, objectively realizing the text as part of a glass window. This introduces an important motif in the film's construction of stereoscopic perspective that has been achieved even more stunningly in the scenes playing behind those cards of glass. Lang, in his choice of images and lighting effects, presents the audience with a suggestive series that will range from the conventionally uncanny (eerie circus automatons) to the realistically volumic; spherical objects—components of the circus games—are perceived as three-dimensional abstractions.

In a move that on one hand foreshadows the "cinerama" effects discovered by Hollywood in the 1950s and on the other acknowledges the seminal Lumière *cinematographes* of trains in motion, a clattering roller coaster threatens to leap from the screen in a remarkable head-on shot. Lang's mise-en-scène reveals the hippo-palace as a sort of perpetual motion machine that defines its own multiplane environment and dislocates the world around it. The back of the screen image (tents, walls, crowds) is blurred, but the carousel has—from front to back with respect to the spectator's view—a remarkable depth of focus. Lang has taken care to provide devices that will encourage a stereoscopic view. These include the poles on which are positioned the animal seats and an additional bit of visual artifice: an intoxicated sailor, who will wander through the dynamic volume of the mise-en-scène, carries a group of balloons onto the carousel platform, further glossing the spherical topos in Lang's multidimensional image system.

Within the wheeling space of the hippo-palace carousel, we soon understand, adult sexuality coexists with both childish play and the superficial social constraints of dancing and dance tunes (a theme that will be elevated to a code by Herrmann and Hitchcock in the waltz- and arabesque-infused soundscapes of *Vertigo, Psycho,* and *The Birds*). Liliom (Charles Boyer), the carousel barker, charms us along with the young (and not always innocent) women on the carousel by launching into a waltz song that will serve as a signature tune throughout the film. Swinging his arm in a circle, he entreats the audience ("Come, child's child") to *faire le tour*.[13] In Liliom's spinning song, real time has been halted. His round-and-round is the time zone of childhood and its infinite perspective. The waltz song—more Parisian dance hall than Chaikovsky or Strauss—captures the heart of young Julie, but her romantic understanding of love will eventually be dashed as their relationship grows increasingly strained as a result of Liliom's drunken amorality. Lang captures the inherent sexuality of the waltz in the first shot of Liliom in song: directly behind him, set in what appears to be a niche in the pivot machine at the middle of the carousel, is a three-dimensional carving of Adam and Eve.

Moments after the death of the title character, Lang and Waxman set up what will be the film's narrative diversion into purer fantasy by a (fantastic) rejection of the motif of circularity that was—for all of its mad qualities—decidedly earthbound; from this point, the dimensions of the fantastic space will be measured along a vertical axis. This is achieved first by invoking real time (i.e., clock time) and thus "stopping" the marvelous diegetic time associated with the circus ride. The moment is in fact remarkably similar to the fantastic turnabout in *Laura*. The carousel's organ music stops, accompanied by the winding down of those spooky mechanical circus toys and automata inherited from nineteenth-century literature, again shot by Lang in expressionistically lit close-ups. All that remains of the formerly rich sound environment is the ticking of a clock, shown operating normally on screen. That machine had enjoyed its own fantastic debut earlier in the film, when Lang marked the impossible passing of diegetic time by a special effect, sending the hands spinning around the clock's face in a mad circle.

From the time that the first Lumière products were shown in 1895, the quadrangular photographs that constitute film's material substance and the rectangular plane of its projection space have intersected with intimations of circularity (eventually realized in the film reel, and on screen through the 1920s in the circular frames of so-called iris shots) and the evocations of cyclical forms and trajectories. In film's first experimental phase, looping—in the form of immediate replay or playing the film forward and then in retrograde—was an action of display rather than an element of filmic content, and was carried out at the time of projection.[14] In these early, primarily scientific demonstrations of the new medium's capacity for the analysis of movement in time and space lie perhaps the first inkling of what would be celebrated a generation later as avant-gardism (notably the loops and inversions in Léger's *Ballet mécanique* of 1924, most comically in the washerwoman sequence). Reinvented in sound by musicians of the later twentieth century, looping would eventually constitute a conventional operation applied to bits and samples, especially in rap and techno. Along the way, loops and retrogrades would make it into the arsenal of progressive electronic effects in musical works by artists as diverse as John Fahey and the Beatles (for example, "Revolution No. 9" on the *White Album*).[15]

To draw connections across this broad an expanse of time and genre is not an exercise in historical legerdemain. The experimental filmmaker

John Whitney's autobiographical treatise, *Digital Harmony*, made much the same case in formidably theoretical terms a quarter of a century ago. Whitney, who devoted his career to what he termed "aural/visual complementarity," inscribed lines (I might say spun webs, were he not a graphic artist) from Léger to Riley, Glass, and Reich, and to his own mathematical and computer algorithms for audiovisual loops.[16] The long line of machines and, eventually, computer programs he developed for the production of abstract images to embody his theoretical aesthetics (formulated beginning in the late 1930s) have intersected with Hollywood cinema since 1957, when Saul Bass, who would eventually design the edgy titles for *Psycho,* was creating the title sequence for *Vertigo.* Bass used one of Whitney's mechanical drawing machines to create the animated portions—those spirals, circles, and arabesques—that emerge from and dance to the music of Bernard Herrmann.

Herrmann's predilection for the waltz has not gone unnoticed, but it has been underemphasized in discussions of the Hitchcock scores and of the cinematic fantastic in general.[17] One of Herrmann's most ingenious (and early) essays in the nondiegetic waltz was attached to an invocation of the scientific marvelous, Robert Wise's science-fiction film *The Day the Earth Stood Still.* A waltz for theremin is featured in the title music, and another during the sequence in which Klaatu walks through his space ship. He treads the hallway's circle prior to entering the round interior chamber that houses a multiplane collection of circular and spherical forms and volumes. His almost tender interaction with his space machinery, which functions by touchless on and off switching like that developed by Leon Theremin in the 1920s in a number of his nonmusical technologies, is backgrounded by a music-box waltz featuring harp, glockenspiel, vibraphone, celesta, and piano; its melody (Example 6) is provided by a high theremin, one of two, distinguished by range, that Herrmann used in the score.[18]

Even in the nineteenth century, waltzing possessed twin connotations of circularity (not merely in its choreography but in its etymological derivation from the Latin *volvere*) and sexuality, provoking criticism for its tendency to encourage forms of socially unacceptable bodily contact between dancers.[19] It could be argued that the waltz, again by its etymology, was fundamentally sexual in its suggestion of the female "parts" (Latin *volva = vulva*) and thus, it would seem, especially appropriate to Hitchcock's fetish motifs, beginning with the disturbing title sequence in *Vertigo,* where the camera engages in the disassembling of Kim Novak into the alluring features that only when taken together might form the

Example 6. Klaatu's Waltz ("Space Control" cue)

whole of normative, non-neurotic sexual attraction. Or so Hitchcock's auteur-voyeur theorists might put it. Precisely the same act was performed by Léger's camera upon the beautiful young woman in *Ballet mécanique*. The resemblance of her lips and eyes to Novak's as photographed in *Vertigo*'s title sequence is extraordinary, and so the analytical story is complicated (or enriched) by the imagery's historical referentiality. Herrmann's score for the title (the "prelude") includes a quick-tempo ("Viennese") waltz that emerges from the folds of the broader, purposefully dizzying 6/8 waltz that kicks off and permeates the sequence.[20]

One wonders whether, had Herrmann been available to score *Spellbound* as Hitchcock desired, something less square than Rósza's chromatic theremin music (the dark flip side of the film's 4/4 love theme) might have accompanied the obviously representational sexual impressions made with the tines of Ingrid Bergman's fork on the commissary napkin. In *Spellbound* that image triggered Gregory Peck's first psychotic episode; it reappears in more abstract form among the figures produced by Whitney's animation machinery in Bass's title for *Vertigo*. Herrmann's waltzes in *Vertigo* are big and obvious, metrically reinforcing the film's network of circular and spiraling motifs (to which the impossibly long Baroque harmonic sequence heard in the church scene is also related). They will culminate in the projection of the concept to the camera's eye and the cinematic machinery in *Vertigo*'s famous "roundy-round" scene.

Hitchcock's commitment to what he considered "pure cinema" drew him into regular conversation with film's brief history, and particularly with those moments at which cinema had addressed its own previously unrecognized potential to manipulate perception and its representation. (By the 1960s the earliest repertoires—of Lumière and Edison—were to become more generally recognized for their avant-garde potential by film "progressives.")[21] Perhaps the best known of all those looks backward to the antique cinema was the Dalí-designed, theremin-accompanied dream sequence in *Spellbound,* homage to Dalí's 1928 collaboration with Buñuel, *Un chien andalou* (at least to its famous eye-slicing sequence).[22] *The Birds* (1963) stands at the end of a long series of well-developed images derived from Hitchcock's understanding of the cinematic eye and its invention, and so it is noteworthy that as multimedia this film is peculiarly "flat." Its entire acoustic landscape, its mise-en-bande, exists on the same plane as the mise-en-scène. As multimedia, it subverts the standard film-narrative practice that underscored a distinction between "real" and "background" sounds, and especially the background score. The two instances of audible music in the ordinary sense heard during the film are perceived by the audience as issuing from on-screen sources (Melanie's piano performance of Debussy's imagistic *Arabesque* and the play song of the schoolchildren). In this it represents an inversion of *Psycho*'s sound world, in which *no* music is heard emanating from within the "real" acoustical world of the characters. A score prepared by Oskar Sala and Remi Gassmann on the trautonium fills the remainder of the musical strand of the mise-en-bande, effecting an acoustical masquerade: the score is perceived as diegetic noise—bird screeches, calls, and wing flaps—linked to the images on the screen.

While it is hardly apparent to the audience or even to analysts of the film (most of whom will be unaware of the composed nature of the bird sounds, unless they pay attention to the dynamic, timbral, and textural shifts synchronized to specific moments within the title sequence, most obvious in the quite musical response to Hitchcock's title credit), the film's scoring is in fact tightly arranged, perhaps the result of Herrmann's input as "sound consultant." An aspect of the film that has been neglected by writers, it is through sound that *The Birds* is brought in line with the specific vocabulary of visual-musical complements encountered in the other classic Herrmann-Hitchcock collaborations. For example, the refrain of the round-and-round children's song, of special interest to Hitchcock, reproduces the rhythms of the first part of the *Arabesque*. The notion of arabesque, of course, ties into Hitchcock's image palette from the graphical perspective. Aside from its specific choreographic or balletic implications, the first *Arabesque* of Debussy differs little in its metrical and rhythmical profile from Herrmann's 6/8 waltzes. The children's song, like many other play songs, is repetitive and circular. An incremental lengthening of the text, sung to the same melodic phrase in each repetition of the refrain, reinforces the round-and-round impression. This feature corresponds to the gradual aggregation of (wheeling) birds in the playground during the scene. Hitchcock had audiovisual complementarity in mind for this scene from its inception. His notes contain what was for him an unusually specific instruction: "MUSIC DEPARTMENT: Practice children singing song, at certain point possibly double the tempo."[23] Also remarkable in this sound-image structure is the *Arabesque* rhythm's reappearance, marvelously realized (marvelous in both its technical and fantastic senses) by the trautonium wing flaps in the climactic attic scene.[24]

But there is no multimedia stereoscopy, no apparent depth to the integration of sound and image. Hitchcock's mise-en-scène alone is the locus for stereoscopic effect, and Hitchcock took care to build the image (rather like a pre-Raphaelite painting) from layers.[25] Superimposing the flying birds in the most dramatic sequences in the film upon the recessive plane of the protagonists and background, Hitchcock appears to be recreating the haptic stereoscopy of one of Thomas Edison's first and most striking loops, *Feeding the doves,* in which a woman and child scatter food from the back plane of the cinematic zone (against the geometric vertical of a barn wall). A flock of wheeling birds swoop unpredictably (and rather eerily, at least for any Hitchcock fan) in the front of the zone, on a plane that requires the viewer to gauge the view as stereoscopic. Edison's short film in its effect, objects, and representation of motion is virtually identical to the big bird sequences constructed by Hitchcock in *The Birds.* I have referred here to Edison's "cinematic zone" rather than to "the screen," since his kinetoscopes (some of which predate the *cinematographes* of the Lumières) were intended not for projection but for viewing through the individual peephole of the kinetoscope booth (this encouraged repeated viewing—looping—at a nickel a shot). Which brings us to Norman Bates.

As pure cinema, *Psycho* is one of the most frequently analyzed of Hitchcock's productions. Montage sequences like the shower scene and the death of Arbogast are indicators of the director's indebtedness to the structuralist model of Eisenstein and, more generally, of avant-garde modernism in general. Norman's peephole voyeurism, however, confronts us with the classic—and for cinema, originary—intimate viewing practices of Edison's kinetoscope. Herrmann's score for *Psycho* is his most unrelentingly modernist. With respect to the image track the score creates an especially pure form of multimedia stereoscopic structure, for it admits no interplay between diegetic and nondiegetic functions (a play that had been entrenched in the structures of sound film from its inception).[26] With the exception of a few transitional sequences (e.g., the descent over Phoenix at the beginning of the film), all of the music must be taken as representative of states of mind; it is never linked to visual events.[27] Its confinement to a single imaginary space is underlined by the economy of timbral resources: the scoring is for strings only. Herrmann's exceptional ability to translate the unspoken anxieties and psychoses of the characters into sound allows "meaning" to, as Nicholas Cook has put it, "jump the diegetic gap" (that is, the space between the music and the story).[28]

Five musical themes circulate throughout the film. Two are associated with Marion Crane. The first is the famous bit of material heard at the outset of the title sequence that will be attached in the film to all of Marion's most anxiously reflective moments, as her mind turns over and over. We recall it most often as the music that, like the simultaneous noise of the rain, suffocatingly drenches the mise-en-bande during her car trip in the desert. A second is related to her specific ruminations upon the money as a concrete material object in her line of sight (and in her mind).

Two cues belong to Norman: the first is the peephole cue (a recomposition of the voyeuristic tracking music Herrmann had assigned to Scotty as he followed Madeleine in *Vertigo*). Norman's other music is related to his memories or imagining of "the madhouse." Anthony Perkins enacts quite brilliantly the detachment of his ocular vision from its agent, the eyes, suggesting to us that he is in fact "seeing back" to something that is quite real and likely a part of his experience. Here Herrmann is most explicit in his intention to invoke the language of musical modernism, since he cites in the chromatically atonal madhouse cue the opening of the fourth movement (Interlude) from his own *Sinfonietta* for string orchestra, published in 1936 in Henry Cowell's New Music Orchestra Series. How modern, precisely, is the obviously twentieth-century musical vocabulary of the title music (and of Marion's mental loop)? Most will hear the three-tiered layering of syncopated chords, nervous ostinato, and simple, lyrical tune as having been modeled upon Stravinsky's *Danses des adolescentes* from *Le Sacre du Printemps,* and this is no doubt generally true. But if the string score for *Psycho* represents the classically "new" according to Herrmann's own understanding of modern music, some sort of indicator of that perspective might be found in his opening salvo. And, particularly in the layering of the lyrical tune over the semitone ostinato and the effect of pizzicato strings in the *Psycho* prelude, Herrmann seemingly offers homage not to Stravinsky himself but to a stylistic disciple, George Antheil, specifically the second portion of the second movement of Antheil's Fourth Symphony ("1942").[29] (Indeed, Antheil's motor rhythms in the Fourth Symphony's third movement may have inspired Herrmann's title music for Hitchcock's *North by Northwest*.) Antheil was one of the first "real" composers to befriend the young Herrmann, and elements of his *Ballet mécanique*—originally intended to be heard alongside Léger's film, a notion eventually abandoned because of the impossibility of successfully synchronizing the sound to the image—may also resonate in Herrmann's *Psycho* prelude, including especially its nervous triplets and the shape of the violin ostinato, recalling a motive presented at the beginning of the *Ballet* and explored throughout most of the last section. Antheil's own balletic waltzes (for Balanchine's surrealistic *Dreams* in the mid-1930s, and *The Spectre of the Rose*) could also have been an influence on Herrmann's approach to meaningful scoring.

In that context it is important to note that not all of *Psycho* looks in a new direction for Herrmann. There remains the most familiar and iconic music in the film: the murder cue heard first during the famous shower montage sequence. It consists, as we all remember even if we have never seen the film, of prominently recorded dissonant string chords approached by glissandi. At the time of the film's release they were mistakenly taken for the sound of birds (the treasures with which Norman had decorated his rooms) or as some kind of electronic effect. Still misheard as a mickey-mousing of Norman's knife strokes despite the number of writers who have pointed to the obvious lack of synchronization between the chords and the movements of his arm, the imaginative misunderstanding of Herrmann's "shower scene" music is testimony to cinema's power as a teacher of perception and cognition; this is the way we expect the music to act.[30] It is the only theme in Herrmann's psychological score that is Mother's own (since the madhouse cue that accompanies Norman's response to Marion's suggestion that he stash Mother "someplace" is attached not to Mother herself but to Norman's act of rumination).

Viewers of the film, distracted by the mayhem and by the angularity of Hitchcock's Russian-style collision montage and its overwhelming profusion of individual shots, may not recognize that Norman's music of sexual release in *Psycho* is nothing other than a mad waltz. Herrmann's choice of the waltz was appropriate not only for its sexual connotations but for its "old-fashioned" aspect (Mother, armed with her knife, literally "trips the light fantastic"), a motif implanted visually at the same time by the decades-old Sunday-best fashion and coiffure partially glimpsed by the audience. Not the typical *valse triste* with which Herrmann is regularly associated, this one is a *valse macabre* that seems to possess only meter, no melody. Scholars who have discussed the scene invariably describe the music as a series of chords. But within the cue's overwhelming sense of verticality (overwhelming in its extreme features

Example 7. Mother's Waltz ("The Murder" cue)

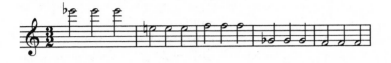

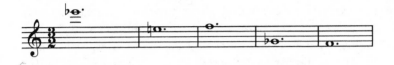

of tessitura and attack) may be discerned Mother's tune, generated by the incremental addition of new pitches. What emerges out of the noise is a neoclassical chromatic waltz—similar to the one he had written for Klaatu's operations on his machinery—deformed by rigor mortis and registral displacements into a petrified sway. The sensation is rendered more evident if the strident, beat-by-beat (1–2–3) half-note divisions of each pitch in the original cue are expunged, as in Example 7, which shows the melody in both forms.

Hitchcock's bathroom montage was formed by shots in virtual collision (suggested by such techniques as image angles and direction of motion within individual juxtaposed shots), modeled upon the Russian mode of montage that he had come to admire after seeing Eisenstein's *Battleship Potemkin* in England in the late 1920s. (Indeed, some of the very angles that filled Eisenstein's shots of the ship and sailors below deck seem to be recapitulated in Hitchcock's sequence.) Background scoring of the standard variety (even Herrmann's) was likely to interfere with this pure-cinematic experiment, and the director's eventual willingness to go along with Herrmann's music for the montage suggests that the music's regularity and genre markers were in the end congenial not to his narrative but to his multimedia vision. In this case the disjunction between the actors' motions (especially as captured in individual shots) and the motion suggested by the music's relentlessly regular temporal and metrical units resembles the confrontation of Eisenstein's montage with the sectional forms and consistent metrical phraseology (related to stylized dance types) that Prokofiev wrote to accompany the grand battle sequence in *Alexander Nevsky*.

Gus Van Sant's "remake" of *Psycho* (1998) has been subject to a good

deal of deserved criticism not just for its ultimate aesthetic failure but for
its intention to reperform a film in the first place. Many critics will insist
that classic film does not encourage or allow the sort of creative recreation that characterizes and enlivens the reception of such other genres as, for example, classical symphonies or operas.[31] In assessing the
problems in Van Sant's *Psycho,* little attention has been paid to the manner in which Van Sant and the music crew (headed by the rocker-turned-
Hollywood-fixture Danny Elfman) trampled over Bernard Herrmann's
highly nuanced and precise scoring procedures, which made sense in
(and made sense of) Hitchcock's original production. Van Sant seems to
have misunderstood the role of the score's non-narrative aspect in Hitchcock's and Herrmann's special vision for *Psycho*'s biplanar multimedia
edifice. For instance, the madhouse cue, triggered by Norman's uttering
the word, enters the original at such a low level of prominence that the
ear is forced into a cognitive act of identification with Norman's barely
acknowledged and obviously unwelcome moment of recall. It has been
transformed in Van Sant's film into a bit of garish musical illustration
painting the word "madhouse" in the acoustical colors it has conjured
forth and flaunted in conventional filmic and televisual representations.

Not only has Van Sant bumped the volume level up appreciably but
the music has also been "sweetened" by the application of digital wails
and swoops (apparently voices). Herrmann's "Madhouse" has been
acoustically materialized as a cheap special effect in the narrative dimension, thus linking the new version of the scene to the old language
of indiscrete pitch events that had characterized theremin madness fifteen
years before Hitchcock's *Psycho.* The updated Elfmanized score invokes
a model of digitized natural sound that is cheaply televisual. For the past
two decades anyone with need for a bit of musical aberration has been
able to resort to the kinds of pitch-bending timbres now available in digital sound libraries. As an across-the-board media convention, the electric sound of the theremin has been replaced in most of these contexts by
the electronic manipulation of the naturalistic sound of ethnic flutes, especially those of Japan and the Andes.[32] Martenot might have been
pleased that the new music of the psychic edge is timbrally linked more
to the discreet and discrete aspects of his instrument and its pipe-like
timbres (as in Messiaen's fourth *Feuillet inédit* or the second movement
of Bernard Wisson's *Kyriades*) than to the aggressively electric wobble of
the aetherophone. Musical weirdness has come full circle, at least in multimedia. Hitchcock's visual emblems and Herrmann's musical gestures
form a very special sort of two-directional expressive register of com-

munication. But without specificity of nuance and vision, the register of the weird has very little to express.

A more egregious violation still was Van Sant's addition of Norman's on-screen masturbation in the peephole sequence. His understanding and reinterpretation of that scene is located firmly within the conventional film-theoretical frame for Hitchcock, one that is especially concerned with conversations pertaining to aesthetic representations of the voyeuristic gaze as it is linked to topoi of sexuality.[33] The scene's historical dimension, its reenactment of the kinetoscopic birth of cinema itself, has been largely irrelevant to such theoretical conversations.[34] Herrmann's enormously constrained music for the sequence—forming the audience's lifeline to Norman's mental condition—was the only thing moving on his side of the peephole in Hitchcock's film. Again turning implication into straight-out, nonaesthetic narration, Van Sant's Norman not only distracts us visually but, more to the point, he distracts us aurally, as the noise he produces while masturbating is irrelevantly layered upon the originally formalist design of the 1960 mise-en-bande.

That he masturbates to climax puts an abrupt on-screen end to the natural trajectory of Herrmann's specific handling of pitch and register that in the original was not yet finished. Our sense of the explosive inevitability associated with Norman's mind (and not his phallus, the Freudian knives of conventional film theory notwithstanding) was insured by Herrmann's careful tightening of the sound throughout the peephole cue, with the violin timbre growing tauter and thinner as Norman gets "wound up." While that trajectory was briefly deflected by his good-son's conscience, as he returns to the house and the register relaxes back down, its predestined point of arrival still hangs unresolved: it will be the first stratospheric sforzatissimo note of the murder cue, Mother's (and Norman's) rigidly morbid dance of ecstatic release.[35]

Hitchcock's Norman has been something of a prize for film theory. He has embodied and disembodied many of film's central issues for many writers, issues ranging from sex to sound. Michel Chion located in Norman's voice the frame and emblem for his discussion of what he called the "impossible" *anacousmêtre* (an entity in which filmic voice, corporeality, and character expressed as a name might be integrated).[36] Chion emphasized the power of sound to produce imaginary populated topographies, wherein he generally located the human voice on a special plane with respect to audience perception. The impossibility in Norman's case is related to the instability of the corporealized (materialized) voice of Mother in the figure of Norman/Mother, particularly at the very end of *Psycho*. Chion extended this phenomenon backwards through historical time to "the first talking film." To position *The Jazz Singer* with respect to its imaginary acoustical space is a worthwhile project. To position it in the especially problematic way Chion did calls for some consideration of the potential for acoustical bewilderment in early sound cinema from a general perspective. His misrepresentation of Jolson's *Kol nidre* as lip-synching to a real (unseen) cantor's voice implied that the monstrous potential of the voice-image mismatch was lodged in sound cinema from its inception (see chapter 3).

OTHER SPACES: THE IMPLAUSIBILITY OF THE IMPOSSIBLE ANACOUSMÊTRE

Early sound cinema's exploration of the fantastic as a genre took its characteristic elements of confusion and hesitation to additional levels. One was the purely theatrical, in the cinematic projection of the stage playbill. Title credits for *King Kong* (1933), *Frankenstein* (1931), and *Bride of Frankenstein* (1935) playfully yet pointedly blur the distinction between the real and the imagined, suggesting their extension beyond the scope of the filmic zone. In *Frankenstein,* the actor's credit for the monster (played by Boris Karloff) reads "?"—as does that for Elsa Lanchester, the "Monster's Mate" (as the creature is identified in the titles) in *Bride of Frankenstein*. King Kong is billed as a part of the cast.[37] These gimmicks underscored the identification of the genre at play in the films, and of the fantastic cinema as a special environment, remote and liminal, in which all bets are off with respect to logic and expectation. By this time, the last phase of the occasionally bumpy transition to sound cinema, spectators were no longer confused and astonished simply by the motion of photographic images (as they reportedly were when confronted by the approaching train in Lumière's *cinematographe* at the end of the nineteenth century). Sensory ambiguity continued to be nourished within the dimensions of cinematic visual and acoustical space, however, with deliberateness.

Chion introduced his treatise on the cinematic voice with a historical overview in which he appropriately pointed to the "calmness" with which press and public responded to the advent of sound films.[38] His project, however, ultimately entails magnifying sound cinema's apparent dualism in order to highlight the "stitch at the seam" that splits body from voice.[39] And so, armed with the contemporaneous critical rhetoric of Alexandre Arnoux, who in 1929 had cited the ventriloquistic aspects of the cinematic voice, of its seeming to have been "glued on" to the image, Chion projects his multimedia perception of Norman Bates—poster boy for the impossible *anacousmêtre*—back to *The Jazz Singer*.[40] It would seem that for Chion some demonstration that the union of sound track and image track was from its inception problematic and fraught with unease was a theoretical requisite: "We *must* return to *The Jazz Singer*, officially the first talking film."[41] Along the way Chion misses the implications of his own earlier points. Before I attempt to frame the special qualities of uncanniness and impossibility that were eventually cultivated by some producers of cinema sound, it will be useful to clarify Chion's misunderstanding and misrepresentation of *The Jazz Singer* and its acoustical environment.

His position in this case was weakened by his post-Schaefferian perspective on acousmatic listening, for the level of discrimination that allowed him to frame disparities between sound and visual so effectively were not operative in the late 1920s. Reports that characterize vocal timbre in sound film of the time were limited to aesthetic matters, that is, to judgments of the quality of the "real" voice or of the grain of the mechanical sound. Only in the first instance was the link between singer and song relevant. In the case of *The Jazz Singer*, all of the adult Jack's renditions, including his "jazzy" performance of *Kol nidre*—which Chion inexplicably and incorrectly assigned to an invisible professional cantor—feature the voice of Jolson himself and were taken by listeners, simply, as Jolson numbers, as if in a stage show.[42]

For the rest of the music, sung or instrumental, there was little understanding of or concern for where the sound was coming from, other than that it was in the vicinity of the screen. In 1927, when *The Jazz Singer* premiered in a Broadway movie house (on the day before Yom Kippur, a theatrical gesture on the part of the Warners that forced the association of the melodramatic crux of the film's story with the "real" calendrical topography of the Manhattan audience), many Americans still associated electronic sound production with the "space between two worlds" commonly termed the "ether."[43] An invisible repository of infinite noise that, even while recognized for the most part as—in the words of a *New York Times* report of 1920—a "polite fiction," the ether was regularly invoked in descriptions of musical hearing that extended from radio broadcasts to the sounds produced by Leon Theremin's new instrument, which arrived with Theremin in New York in the same year as the Warners' talkie. Concert publicity for Theremin's demonstrations often emphasized the "ethereal" aspects of the process ("Music from the

Ether" was the headline on the poster for Theremin's first demonstration at the Metropolitan Opera in January 1928), and Joseph Schillinger's work composed for the instrument in 1929 was titled *Airphonic Suite*.[44] Even though the spiritualism associated with the first wave of radio listening had largely waned by the end of the 1920s, listeners were still unaccustomed to the emanation of sounds from man-made objects that possessed, it seemed, the power to pull them from the air.[45] When synchronized sound was introduced to movie audiences in the late 1920s, there was still considerable confusion on the part of the public regarding the source of electric sounds.

The Vitaphone recording technology developed by Western Electric and Bell Labs in the second half of the decade was intended to serve the radio industry, and especially the expanding network structure (CBS and NBC were founded in 1927 and 1926, respectively) that would provide nationwide broadcasts from a single recorded source. A 1928 *New York Times* review of Theremin's massive outdoor concert in Lewisohn stadium reveals the extent to which all of the new electronic sound resources—the acousmatic nuances of which are easily differentiated today—were at this early phase heard as essentially identical by the nonspecialist listener. The writer describes the theremin's "loud, full tones, with a *radio* sound similar to a *movie theatre vitaphone*."[46]

Vitaphone is now familiar primarily to historians of film, and it is associated above all with the synchronized portions of *The Jazz Singer*, but even though it is a sound-silent hybrid, the entire music and voice track is synchronized to the film via the new process. Contrary to popular myth, by the time of the film's release most within the film community, and many filmgoers nationwide, were familiar with the synchronized sound presentations that Vitaphone made possible.[47] The most favorable responses to the early Vitaphone experiments (all of which, aside from Warners' *Don Juan*, had been shorter than "feature" length) addressed their contents as if they were real: critical response was to the speakers and singers, and reviews of the technology itself were ambivalent.[48] Indeed, there was some confusion regarding whether or not on-screen individuals were to be applauded. The studio, which depended upon demonstrable popular response to synchronized sound in order to sell, often to small theater proprietors, the expensive notion (which required a substantial investment in equipment), encouraged the public to participate in the illusion; often the performers in the film would bow after a short space to allow applauding to begin in the theater.[49]

In *The Jazz Singer*, each of the "jazz" numbers in the first portions of the film (prior to Jack Robin's return for his Broadway debut) are followed by diegetic applause that may have served to reduce shyness on the part of theater spectators and encourage them to join in the applause. Audience and critics responded to the film as they had the other Vitaphone features: Jolson's musical performance was lauded as the best aspect of the film; the remainder of the soundscape was considered less successful. As one reviewer put it, the film consisted of "Al Jolson with Vitaphone noise," underlining once again the assignment of all sounds other than the voice of Jolson to the same acoustic dimension, characterized by "radio sound."[50]

While moviemakers on the West Coast were beginning to process the financial and artistic implications of a new medium, New York theater patrons were contemplating a different sort of relocation of the actor's voice in Eugene O'Neill's 1928 play *Strange Interlude*. It was an experiment that would soon find its way to the screen. O'Neill's drama was compared by some to classical tragedy, a cultural recall effected through the technique of asides in which the characters reveal to the audience their thoughts extradiegetically, each envoicing—in tragic terms—both the actor's solo dialogue and the classic choral stasima (updated by O'Neill along Freudian lines).[51] The work of O'Neill and other dramatists found its way to Hollywood at the end of the 1920s, a time at which the direction in which sound might be driving the film industry was still contested. Musical revue movies were waning in popularity, and many in the film community looked to theater as a source of potential properties and name-brand directors of high tone. By the time *Strange Interlude* was transformed into a "photoplay" for MGM in 1932 (like *Freaks,* an Irving Thalberg experiment), the sound of spoken dialogue perfectly synchronized to the actor's image was no longer new to the movie audience; it had found a secure place within an apparently naturalistic mise-en-bande.

With much of the responsibility for cinematic continuity now assigned to the voice track, the auditor could not help but perceive in film a sense of reality that had been impossible in the silent era, when pantomime was interrupted by dialogue and additional information relating to place, time, and character, all of which had to be read off the screen, most of it backgrounded by a steady stream of—often distractingly familiar—musical bits. The illusion of realism (of incarnation) that sound provided was further enhanced by a new mode of dramatic exposition on film, in which reminders of the gap between the audience and the story were expunged, notably those on-screen credits or epigraphs that had often appeared in silent films—and that are still vestigially present in *The Jazz Singer*—when an actor or a character first appears on the screen, a practice that intruded upon diegetic or dramatic continuity. Visual elements, too, participated in the illusion. After the switch from orthochromatic to panchromatic film stock in the late 1920s, the early deep-focus photography, which had lent a degree of perspectival realism to the full-screen image but simultaneously drew attention to the staged aspect of the set, yielded to a more intimate dimensionality of individual forms. A previously unimaginable range of grey shades made people and objects more substantial in close-up, and, since panchromatic black-and-white film could record the red and pink tones of Caucasian skin without darkening them, actors could be seen as they (apparently) were, without the white make-up that had dehumanized players in the silents.

We might even locate in this technical alteration a primary impetus behind the wholesale shift in the reception of cinema and its affective elements from the dramaturgical to narrative. In the orthochromatic period, film's apparent reality owed much to the naturalness of the perspective. Panchromatic film brought the characters to life in a different, more naturalistic, and less theatrical way. All of these changes forced, virtually immediately, a wholesale reevaluation of music's previous ubiquity in cinematic presentations of the silent era. Once thought an essential (if at times annoying) aid in the realization of cinematic drama, the technology of sound had consigned music to the territory of the unreal, and during the transitional period it was often relegated to positions outside the story, unless associated with an on-screen source.[52]

It would seem that O'Neill's play was especially well suited to such an environment, since characters' thoughts could be expressed in sound without necessarily requiring the director to relocate them outside the diegetic frame. This should, after all, constitute a more realistic representation of what we imagine mind-reading to be like. Such acoustic voyeurism falls well outside of O'Neill's dramatic concept, in which the actors were understood to be playing two roles and to be invoking a specific tradition of classic dramaturgical structure and theatrical spectacle. In the stage production, director Philip Moeller froze the action while the actors delivered their soliloquies, creating an unusual mise-en-scène and calling attention to the acoustical soundscape's placement upon the unnatural field of the theater stage. The asides, therefore, blended smoothly with the dialogue yet emerged from another dimension of "physical quiet" as Moeller expressed it. The effect achieved was one "of eddying moments in time, small pools of feeling set out of the main current of narrative in an extraordinary counterpoint of movement and stasis, of time and timelessness, of sound and silence."[53]

Hollywood's new acoustic realism made of *Strange Interlude* something even stranger. The shade of acoustic variation in the two imaginary voice tracks underscores the acousmatic nature of cinematic hearing.[54] In order to split the actors into two functional locations without the benefit of the full stage, the film's director Robert Z. Leonard and recording director Douglas Shearer resorted to what the *New York Times* film critic at the time, Mordaunt Hall, generally termed the "sound close-up."[55] More important, it revealed Hollywood's capacity to construct, even if unwittingly, multiple regions of the mise-en-bande that might serve a range of purposes extending beyond the purely narrative or the purely dramaturgical. *Strange Interlude* offered listeners a set of superimposed sound planes, one of Hollywood's first experiments in true aural stereoscopy. The effect is in the end nonsensical, since the visual is absolutely realistic and continuous, and the actors (including a young Clark Gable) must pause and look profound during the moments when their own voice-over runs on the sound track, distinguished from regular dialogue only by its engineered effect of prominence, seeming to have been recorded with the actors' mouths close to the mikes.

These sound close-ups are almost invariably attached to visual close-ups, thus forcing an uncomfortable amalgam of the fantastic (the imaginary voice) and the hyperreal (the new, natural look of actors in panchromatic close-up). At times the actors themselves seem confused regarding whether or not they are intended to be "hearing" the thoughts of other cast members. As a result of these techniques, the classic and formal elements of O'Neill's vision are effectively stifled. The film ultimately fails because the image undermines any stereoscopic perception of the sound; it is, like Procol Harum live on stage, anti-imaginary.

In the midst of the characters' vocalizing there are some odd musical intrusions. As in the case of *Freaks, Strange Interlude*'s "score" is a pastiche including "Happy Birthday to You," J. L. Molloy's "Love's Old Sweet Song," Mendelssohn's *A Midsummer Night's Dream*, and Chaikovsky's op. 64. There is little about these frail and dislocated prerecorded musical backgrounds that might recall the dramaturgically expressive scoring that accompanied melodramatic silent films or that looks ahead to the weighty presence of the later, classic original film score. Put in place by practitioners credited as anything ranging from "sound recording" to "music director," these musical backings originally grounded their films in an imagined realistic present, imitating prominence—to the best of their ability—as it would occur naturally. By the time of *Strange Interlude*, the volume level of the music was nearly always adjusted so that it and the dialogue amounted to an invariable sum throughout the film, a "psychoacoustic" rather than naturalistic approach, as Rick Altman described it.[56] In the long birthday party scene, music is first heard unrealistically but presumably diegetically ("Happy Birthday To You" is featured on the sound track). After the scene shifts to the confrontation between Nina and Ned outside the dining room, the mise-en-bande grows exceedingly complicated. Music is heard more or less continuously throughout the scene as Nina, Ned, and their biological son, Gordon, engage in dialogue and voice-over communication with the audience.

At times fading to accommodate dialogue intelligibility, music is just as often edited to suggest swells and caesurae in the emotional morphology of the characters' interactions: sound engineering is employed in these few instances (confined to confrontations between the two "lovers" at the center of the narrative) to achieve the effects that composers will eventually prescribe in original film scores for the rest of the century. The birthday scene, and the mise-en-bande of *Strange Interlude* as a whole, are worthy of more detailed analysis than I can provide here. What matters most is that the film, in its eccentricity of vision and its experimental approach to the possibilities offered by the new field of sound construction, is a significant indicator that acoustical stereoscopy was a phenomenon ensconced in the earliest phase of the transition to full sound-drenched productions. If it confused its audience, their confusion derived not from the multiplanar effect of the mise-en-bande, or from the dislocation of voice from the pseudo-realistic image, but from inconsistent and ineffective planning and realization, and from the inability of actors to keep up with the conflicting demands of an unusual hybrid.

Critics probably objected to most aural artifice more than did audiences, which perhaps provided additional motivation to constrain the medium's potential visual and acoustic range and to reproduce the structure and the one-dimensional dialogue voices of more straightforward stage productions. Even then there were criticisms, mainly about the increasing "talkiness" of the talkies.[57] Studios, however, continued to support explorations of recording technology in the interest of a particular and new version of acousmatic, rather than natural, reality, in which not the simulation of a single realistic soundscape but rather a range of technical priorities was brought under control, including intelligibility of dialogue, vocal personality (e.g., foreign or regional accents, if they were not off-putting), and design of spectacular sound effects. But if some films hinted at an awareness of the possibilities surrounding the integration of sound recording into the conceptual architecture of filmic visual perspective, any significant exploration of this aspect of complementarity in Hollywood cinema would not be undertaken for some time.[58]

James Whale's *The Old Dark House*, a contemporary of *Strange Interlude* and no less theatrical in concept, has never figured in discussions of musical scoring in early sound film. This is hardly surprising, since there is, after all, no music beyond the bit stuck onto the title. What there is, however, is an almost continuous aural background beyond the dialogue, comprised of sound effects, specifically the sound of howling wind. Especially interesting and, arguably, significant about the mise-en-bande of *The Old Dark House* is that the wind effects, engineered by William Hedgcock, were made to conform with the new principles of psychoacoustic soundtracking. At moments of high emotion throughout the film (when, for instance, the young lovers kiss in their car, or in the terrifying confrontation between Karloff and the ingenue), Hedgcock gives the wind effects increased prominence, whereby they are projected toward the foreground of audience perception. This was rather a bold and unusual experiment in sound-image complementarity, even if it seems now trite from the perspective of later Hollywood practice, which would link prominence effects to orchestrated musical nuance.

Yet it might be argued that Whale's 1932 film provides a significant and unappreciated model for the apparently innovative multimedia structure encountered in Hitchcock's production thirty years later of *The Birds,* in which—most clearly and conventionally in the Hollywood-style title sequence that includes appropriate dynamic shifts in the "bird noise" to accompany certain on-screen credits—nonmusical sound was engineered or synthesized in conformity with the accepted understanding of the emotional and perceptual morphology of expressive hearing. More broadly, it also suggests that Altman's construction of the role of music per se in the mise-en-bande might be applied to a level of greater abstraction (i.e., to include the role of all "controlled" or "composed" sound, even if it does not consist of music in the ordinary sense). As early as 1932 it was recognized that not "music" but any organized sound would form with respect to dialogue and diegetic noise another and independent strand of the mise-en-bande and thus be subject to particular modes of recording, engineering, and listening practice.

EGYPTOGRAPHY

Among the horror products of the early 1930s, *The Old Dark House* and its eccentric inhabitants stand out as odd ducks indeed. But monsters of all shapes and sizes—along with fields for contemplation of imminent death at their hands or of a mysterious afterlife in the numinous realms that spawned them—filled the spaces within the vernacular imagination framed, built, and decorated by the wizards of cinematic machinery. In these rooms were often found points of intersection between music of the concert hall and the American media mainstream. They were often quite large, innovative reconstructions and explorations of death or the dead, monumentalized according to a particular slate of established aesthetic traditions. Chronologically the origins of Hollywood's multimedia machine coincided with the world's aesthetic revision of Egyptian culture that followed upon the excavation of Tutankhamen's tomb. As Paul de Man noted, it was the Egyptians who—according to Hegelian aesthetics—first made of death a monumental art form.[59]

Along the path of monumentalization they found time and space to create a vocabulary of aesthetic decoration appropriate to the invocation of the world that lies just beyond the contrivances of the phenomenal; this space was revisited and reinvented in the first wave of fantastic sound cinema. Like many title sequences in Universal's classic horror films, that of *The Mummy* (1932) incongruously rehearses Chaikovsky's *Swan Lake* in the background, perhaps as a signature for the director Karl Freund's "brand name."[60] "The Mummy" is drawn as if carved in stone on the face of a pyramid. Pyramidical form was one of the trappings of art deco style, and it appeared often in Hollywood graphics (e.g., the next year as an abstract form, inverted, in the titles for RKO's *King Kong*). A bit of track music with a recognizably "exotic" melody transitions away from the titles, and the first bit of visual is an interpolated piece of documentary footage of contemporary Egyptian excavation sites.

For much of the first part of the film, there is no scoring. After the reincarnated mummy Im-Ho-Tep begins his quest in the twentieth-century world, several cues taken from the Universal inventory and some newly composed by James Dietrich enrich the multimedia environment.[61] Most significant is a scene in which Im-Ho-Tep reveals to the beautiful descendant of his beloved the story of his mummification. Dietrich's music for the scene invokes a whole-tone environment (with chromatic admixtures recalling the opening of Debussy's "Pour l'Egyptienne" from

Six épigraphes antiques); the sound had been associated with fantasy and enchantment, especially in the Russian tradition, since the nineteenth century. By sorcery, Im-Ho-Tep constructs on the screen a fantastic space, a go-between. His magic pool allows him to see beyond normative constraints of time and space.

When Im-Ho-Tep looks into the immeasurable dimensions of his pool, the audience does as well. Freund's gimmick for these fantastic moments was to leave the carved pool edge as a graphic, framing the scene viewed within it. Not surprisingly, the effect is stereoscopic, with the marvelous perceived as receding in imaginary space from the foregrounded frame. As a cinematic device, this fulfilled two functions. On one hand it enhanced the film's topography of spatial monumentality and the association of physical space with temporal dimensions, as most perfectly represented by the ancient pyramids foregrounded in the vernacular imagination of the day. On the other it deflected any critique of background music for those who objected to its presence as potentially "confusing" by confining it to moments in which the reality value of the newer naturalistic style of film visual is not in play. Music only accompanies the moments that launch receptive vision into the zone of the fantastic.

Dietrich's music must be taken as having been conjured, like the images before the viewer, out of the dark. In this case the darkness embraces the audience in a physical sense, but it also hides the source of unimaginable power of the Egyptian sorcerer. It is the sound of the noumenal realm beyond the doors of the tombs, the sound of a past we cannot hear. The creature's supernatural powers emanate—we come to understand by music's noumenal presence—not merely from his ancient origins but from the ethical force behind his actions, a supernatural payback for the fad of grave looting that had followed upon the opening of Egyptian tombs in previous decades. What we do not hear are the terrible noises of Im-Ho-Tep's live mummification that will be seen in the marvelous depths of the pool. The orchestra must stand in for them. There is no melodrama in the musical environment, no attempt to match visual with acoustic gesture, and no acoustic stereoscopy. The music is repetitive and brooding, and it suggests among other things the passing of time, as measured by the narrative process (of the mummy's tale, not of the filmic whole) and by the great historical span between ancient Egypt and the United States of 1932.

A theater audience watching the scene is likely to stop noticing the presence of the frame. The illusory reality of the principal narrative and its multimedia space is replaced by the illusory reality of the embedded tale; negotiating the trip back requires passage through the zone of fantastic hesitation once removed (i.e., the hesitation is located not between real and unreal but between filmic illusion in the service of implicit reality and filmic sorcery in the service of implicit fantasy).

Already by the time of *The Mummy* the monumental fantastic was a staple in silent cinema. In 1920, outside of Hollywood and prior to the advent of synchronized sound, the Golem—a legendary giant fashioned of clay and brought to life by a Jewish sorcerer in the German film artist Paul Wegener's film of the same name—silently roamed the streetscape of an expressionistic reconstruction of sixteenth-century Prague.[62] With no recorded voice track, but surrounded by special visual effects, Wegener's creation—film's first beautiful monster—was mute; resolutely so, in fact, for its physiognomy emphasized the long horizontal of tightly closed lips. A helmet of hair enhanced the Golem's resemblance to familiar images of the Egyptian sphinx, one of the oldest of the monsters who have loomed as acknowledged, if not entirely understood, presences among the treasured features of earth's civilizations. Greeks attributed to the sphinxes enigmatic knowledge, but the Egyptian sphinxes, wingless, were grounded: they provided a dwelling place for the numinous entities who might resemble the gigantic hybrid creature. Such creatures lived in our presence as guides while guarding the dead in their funerary bellies. The resemblance between Wegener's Golem and these creatures extended to his size and his role as a protector.

Many beautiful monsters have been engineered in scientific experiments arising from something regularly called "faith." The Golem's creation, for example, was based on a faith in a certain form of righteousness; other monsters (e.g., most commercial rock and roll hits) emerge from unsanctioned systems of belief, but have always been grounded at the same spiritual poles of experimentation and commitment. From the beginning of Wegener's film, as we learn how the Golem came into the world, the scientific marvelous is conjoined to a supernatural fantastic by means of effective imagery. An impressive expressionist graphic of the night sky yields to a shot of Rabbi Loew looking through his telescopic apparatus. The rabbi cuts a fantastic figure, as he appears to be floating in a stone trough amid the stars. When it is eventually revealed by the camera that he is in fact at work in the highest point of his own laboratory—a large and weirdly contrived space made of stone wherein his young disciple watches over some steaming beakers—the union of the two strains of fantastic discourse is fully accomplished. All of these motifs, and the expressionist visual elements will reemerge in a more familiar form more than a decade later in Hollywood.

In 1931 the director James Whale brought to the screen in *Franken-stein* the Promethean creation of the novelist Mary Wollstonecraft Shelley. This monster was played by Boris Karloff, whose now iconic make-up emphasized the flat lip-line and geometric head of Wegener's Golem. Karloff based his own performance on that of Wegener.[63] Unlike the Golem, though, Karloff's creature had a voice; by 1935, in Whale's sequel *Bride of Frankenstein,* it could even speak, albeit only in fits and starts. In this, Whale's monster was unlike Wollstonecraft's original—whose moral education and language acquisition made for good literature but a potentially tedious screenplay—and more like Wegener's Golem. When he was angry the monster preferred to growl, a sound that Franz Waxman matched in his musical score with an effective timbral and gestural reflection: the monster's principal leitmotif in the score consists of a throaty, dissonant, and grotesque brass fanfare.[64]

The monsters realized by Wegener and Karloff had another side, however. Fearsome as they were, both monsters possessed a beautiful core projected in each film's dramaturgical space through the realization and invocation of pathos. Had the Golem not been endowed with human emotions by his creator, the monster's mission in the world (the protection of the Jews) could never have been waylaid, specifically by his emotional overreaction to the misappropriation of his powers by the forces of evil. The Golem's potential for existence as an embodied ethical abstraction was compromised by his intersection with the subjective field of the human condition, and the Frankenstein creature of Whale's and Karloff's imagining found himself in a similar fix. Mary Wollstonecraft's monster—which a century earlier embodied her Romantic ethics and aesthetics—evolved in the American cinema of the first half of the 1930s from a terrible apparition to a figure of Romantic alienation. The monster's consistent attempts to find his way in the world of unbelief with his naive and plaintive interrogative "friend?" and his contemplative recitation of the circumstances of his own creation in James Hurlbut's script for *Bride of Frankenstein* culminated in a memorable tag line: "I love dead, hate living."

Waxman's score is leitmotivic in the way that was, by 1935, Hollywood convention. Unlike Steiner's (1935 was the year of his score for *The Informer*), which contained very few full quotations of the concert hall classics, the music for *Bride of Frankenstein* was marked by the intrusion of two quotations (from Schubert's *Ave Maria* and Mendelssohn's *Spring Song*). Often, however, the scenes to which classical music has been attached, or that have been set in a style outside the general discourse of the film's leitmotivic matrix, are visual set pieces. There is, for example, the Ravel- and Debussy-style interlude heard during one scene in which, surrounded by sheep abandoned by a terrified shepherdess, Frankenstein's monster sees his image reflected in the water, a Narcissus inversion as moving as it is quaint. The reflection scene and the famous sequence involving the blind fiddler in his cottage invoked, weirdly inflected, the *locus amoenus* that had since Theocritus formed the topical soul of European pastoral. In their wry artificiality these scenes—each a pastoral inset— called for precisely this heavy-handed yet accomplished kind of referential scoring. As for their having been rendered weird, that is of course a result of the monster's on-screen presence. Acoustic oppositions, then, support the thematic friction of the visuals, allowing pathos via multimedia noncomplementarity to transcend the unfolding of the storyline and the enactment of the melodrama.

In these portions of the film (and others, like the crucifixion of the monster, another pathetic inset), Waxman's score is more like a tone poem running parallel with the film than a musical response to its visual or dramaturgical cues. This sharply differentiates his approach to scoring at this time from that of Steiner, particularly Steiner's early essays in the fantastic genre, *King Kong* and *Son of Kong,* and is perhaps related to Waxman's having only just left the orbit of European filmmaking practices (Steiner by contrast had been in the United States since 1914). Waxman's set pieces reflect perhaps a European aesthetic, originating in silent film scoring, that was especially valued in early twentieth-century French cinema and represented by Saint-Saëns's score for *L'Assassinat du duc de Guise* (1908).[65]

Another feature of Waxman's scoring procedures that creates a palpably different effect is his concern for matching the pacing of the music to that of the dialogue (as opposed to pacing the music on the basis of visual events).[66] Nowhere in the film, perhaps, is this as apparent as in the introductory "Menuetto and Scherzo" that emerges (in a clever audiovisual bait-and-switch) from the thunderstorm and dark castle shown in the opening shot, and which viewers will assume is the setting for the thriller to come. Whale's camera, in its approach to the warm, cozy room, and the engineering of the music's entry "from within" create a very effective sense of cinematic depth. Even as the music imitates very convincingly the formal features and formality of late eighteenth- or early nineteenth-century chamber music, the long cue tracks with finesse (by means of tempo, dynamics, and even harmony) the expressive speech patterns of the actors portraying the Shelleys and Lord Byron throughout their "historical" conversation.

The monster's own horrific theme, a musical echo of its "real" voice that we imagine we hear emanating from the screen, is rendered more profound and meaningful through its opposition to the remainder of the acoustic universe in which it is located in the film and to which it refers outside the cinema sound track. The monster's fanfare motive is grotesque not primarily because it is dissonant (this merely tags it as scary or threatening) but because it represents the pathetic collapse of the larger intervals (the major third, the fourth, or the fifth) that marked European conventional practice: heroic orchestral hornblowers of nineteenth-century operas and tone poems are deformed by the motive into the dissonant interval of a major second and the sounding of a minor third. Indeed, Waxman inserted just this sort of recognizable acoustical foil to the monster's music into the score in the horsemen's fanfare proceeding the funereal "Processional March."[67] This was a nice touch on Waxman's part, since Karloff, like Wegener before him, played the creature as a pathetic antihero.

"Danse macabre," another of the film's cues, reproduces not the music of Saint-Saëns's famous original but only some of the markers of its supernatural and grotesque spirit, a spirit closely allied to one of the principal leitmotifs in Waxman's score and attached to the mad Dr. Pretorius. This role was played by Whale's friend Ernest Thesiger, who was more flamboyantly gay than Whale (as an aficionado of needlepoint he referred to himself on the set as "the stitchin' bitch") and plays the part with "arch effeminacy."[68] He is the prime mover of the plot and the cabbalistic guardian of all scientific and demonic secrets—and likely some sexual ones as well. As Frankenstein and Pretorius hunker down in the lab to create life without the participation of a woman for the second time—they had done it a few years earlier in the original *Frankenstein,* in which Henry was still known by what was for Universal a problematically foreign name, Victor—Henry's bride is taken away and imprisoned against her will. Pretorius's machinations are responsible for Henry's failure to consummate his marriage to Elizabeth and to engage in heterosexual procreation. Both his eager assistant and the monster pay the price for his prideful and deviant experimentation.

Whale's direction and Waxman's scoring playfully reflect the mad doctor's tweaking of heteronormative conventions, as the new monster-bride rises from the table to take her first tentative steps. Pretorius strikes a proud, affected pose, majestically announcing with much rolling of the "r" in "bride," "The *bride* of Frankenstein!" (followed by the sound of wedding bells in the score). Since the original (male) monster was never called by the name, Pretorius can only be referring to Henry, toward whom the new bride now (literally) sways. Henry takes her hand in a courtly gesture that resembles the prelude to a dance. A few moments later, to the accompaniment of a brief bit of music that Waxman has given a clearly Latin and dramatic flair, the pair continue what Whale must have intended as their wedding dance, ending with an extravagant dip as Henry guides her into a chair.

Pretorius is the linchpin for the film's propulsion into realms of the truly fantastic, for he (like *The Golem*'s Rabbi Loew) is a scientific sorcerer, and Henry Frankenstein his apprentice. Perhaps it is not surprising that the orchestration and rhythmic features of Pretorius's motive recall the familiar theme of Dukas's *The Sorcerer's Apprentice* (when Pretorius's music was added to the title music in revision, Waxman indicated bassoon and bass clarinet in the orchestration notes).[69] Specifically, it would appear that Waxman ingeniously derived the motive's rhythm from the line just uttered by the comic housemaid, Minnie, who calls attention to the strangeness of the doctor's name (Example 8). Pretorius's cue was important enough to Whale's vision of the film that it was eventually added to the title sequence, replacing a few measures of melodramatically dark mood music unrelated to the rest of the score. Universal, who like other studios regularly cannibalized film scores once they were in the can, attached some of Waxman's *Bride of Frankenstein* music to later fantasy films. His cue for Dr. Pretorius, the sorcerer with a scientific edge, was attached to the figure of the "mad scientist" in the studio's 1936 Flash Gordon offering *Rocket Ship*.[70]

If the story's representation of the battle between good and evil lies largely outside the social dimension of true melodrama (with the exception perhaps of the pastoral scenes), the score's musical effects do not. A dissonant brass chord marked *fffffff* in Waxman's short score, heard behind the main title, recalls a specifically melodramatic form of musical interjection.[71] Whenever I hear it, I can't help but think of Hanns Eisler's analysis of his own *Hangmen Also Die* (directed by Fritz Lang, 1943) in *Composing for the Films:* "For example, *Hangmen Also Die,* after the preliminary music, begins by showing a large portrait of Hitler in a banquet hall of the Hradshin Castle. As the portrait appears, the music stops on a penetrating widespread chord containing ten different tones. Hardly

Example 8. "Pretorius" cue, underlaid with dialogue prompt

[Pre - to - ri - us   ]

any traditional chord has the expressive power of this extremely advanced sonority."[72] Eisler's chord is truly a melodramatic stinger, working in context in the same stop-the-presses way as does Waxman's scary
explosion; indeed, its seriousness of purpose does nothing to stifle the
chuckles it usually elicits from student audiences. Eisler's promotion of
its greater expressionistic potential was, it seems, a function of its greater
generosity in providing dissonant notes, recalling the aesthetic position
taken by Julian Johnson with respect to post-tonal music. (Ten is not
quite twelve, though, and so in facing up to Berg's chord for Lulu's operatic death in the next sentence, Eisler does so reductively, suggesting
that "it produces an effect very much like that of a motion picture.")[73]

But we need listen no farther than the title music to locate Waxman's
score in a particular domain of the classically supernatural. Harps,
tremolo flutes, melodramatic dynamics, and most of all the exuberant
whole-tone chords at the opening recall Stravinsky's music of enchantment in *The Firebird*, a work that wanders through another world of
monsters and, like *Bride*, reaches a cataclysmic yet happy conclusion. In
part because of budget constraints, Waxman was unable to reproduce
the distinctive timbral features (except those of the celesta and vibraphone) of his score for Lang's *Liliom*, the work that had attracted Whale
to him in the first place. Waxman had not only defamiliarized that score's
acoustic environment by using the ondes martenot but established a
sense of musical stereoscopic perspective reflecting the film's fantastic
verticality: music accompanying the road leading from earth to heaven
was rendered "marvelous" by sound engineering, with mikes placed high
above the recording stage. It was this effect of realizing an otherwise
unimaginable cinematic dimension through music that inspired Whale to
approach him for *Bride of Frankenstein*.[74]

The sequence leading up to the monster's soulful confession, his love-
death credo, was marked by overtly sexual content. Evil Dr. Pretorius
has identified a female corpse to use as the monster's mate and comments
on the body's potential, while the monster, having shared food and a

good cigar with the doctor, muses in suggestive close-up over the possible advantages of a "woman-friend-wife." Elsa Lanchester portrayed both the lovely Mary Shelley in the film's prologue and the monster's mate (who was, as evidenced by the response of Karloff's monster, just as beautiful in her own way) within the main story. She had found the model for her voice in the honking of swans, realized in the series of gagging squeaks she emits after being released from her mummy-like bandages. The "Creation" sequence preceding that unforgettable moment is the best-known portion of the film. Here the monster's mate is brought to life amid an electrical storm and its associated mad-scientific sizzles, pops, and buzzes, an enchanting and overwhelming sound barrage that advertised the potential of a new, seemingly limitless playland for the cinematic ear. Like the patchwork creature herself, diegetic sound has been stitched all over the musical track to create an impressively deep and thick acoustical environment.

In Whale's version of creation, nature's life force is drawn from the air by a scientific instrument that in its art deco design reflects the creature's own deco elegance. The mechanism consists of linearly arranged spheres and rings with terminal points; her gown is form fitting but flowing. Most notable in terms of deco sensibility is the inverted triangle of her pyramidical Nefertiti coiffure and her exaggeratedly angular eyebrows. Part of a poetics of monumentalized death, these visual, decorative gestures recall Hegel's placement of that form of reminiscent excess in the particular historical moment associated with the construction of the pyramids and sphinx. Decorative elements of the fantastic environments of the early 1930s are linked to similar decorations employed in the staging of Theremin's aether music of a few years earlier, especially his planar-geometric decorative speaker designs.[75]

Waxman's music for the creation is a fascinating treatise on acoustic stereoscopy in the most literal sense. Drawing together several functionally differentiated planes of the mise-en-bande, Waxman leads the ear from one space of reception to another, propelling us into a zone of constant uncertainty and liminality. His hook is the sound of the tympani, heard (with some small exceptions) throughout the full scene of approximately ten minutes' length. Film histories, even those written by musicologists, invariably associate the tympani with the beat of the creature's heart.[76] True up to a point, such an association is embedded within the screenplay, since the tympani enters the sound track as Frankenstein and Pretorius stare at and talk over the irregularly beating heart on the lab table. But this is only the beginning. The tympani will follow a labyrinthine path through the elements of audiovisual complements, beginning, to be sure, as an imaginary "representation" of the irregular beat of that first, failed, heart. But a bit into that portion of the sequence, the heart meter is shown on screen, at which point the sound functions as an audio response to a visual cue: the motion of the indicator hand on the heart meter with which the beat is synchronized (a moment of so-called mickey-mousing).

As the gnomic Carl leaves to fetch fresh body parts, a string tremolo launches a bit of atmospheric nondiegetic scoring, which culminates as he murders a young woman; this is signaled—since we don't witness the full act—by a tympani roll (now recessively located in the "nondiegetic" realm). Afterward, the inexorable beat of the tympani is reinstated. For the remainder of the creation sequence it will remain absolutely regular, a reflection (narratively) of the health of the new heart. From this point on, its regular pulse—even if understood partly as a diegetic sound associated with the new heart—will inevitably register simultaneously and subliminally in the reactive pulse of the film audience; it forms the electric pulse emanating from the hearts of anxious viewers. (Waxman went back to the tympani to induce a similarly psychosomatic effect during Max's confession to "I" in Hitchcock's *Rebecca*.)

With the consistent beat in place, Waxman was free to layer the rich nondiegetic score and all of its accumulated leitmotifs on top of it. Even today one cannot help being enthralled and mesmerized by the unrelenting noise that fills the remainder of *Bride of Frankenstein*. Maintaining a constant presence on one plane of the sound track, the drum's affective implication shifts throughout, depending upon which theme is attached to it. For example, the monster's grotesque horn calls transmit their military aura to the drum strokes, which momentarily become reinterpreted (i.e., they are heard within the context of the military register). At times the sound follows motions on screen, for example those of the monster's footsteps as he climbs the stairs in the lab; the sound underscores the monster's pace, not his feet. Indeed, "pace" (as might be expected of Waxman) is the critical issue, the multimedia topos of the entire sequence. As the monster drinks with Pretorius, the drum engages in a bit of interlocking hocket with the orchestra, an unusual and interesting spatial effect within the scoring, abstracted from the melodramatic trajectory. In that brief moment the drum leaves one multimedia plane and enters another of "pure sound." Any careful musical listener will feel the difference.

In the whole last part of the sequence, only twice will the ear be released from the tension produced by the insistent pounding. At one point the camera shifts to Elizabeth, who is being held captive outside. The drum misses one beat at the time of the transition, marking the change to a new mise-en-scène, then reenters the new scene.[77] Here, since the scene is outside the lab, the drum beat loses its diegetic rationale and serves merely to keep the audience on track (or in the track). It is also inaudible during a long panoramic shot of the castle exterior; what might be an acoustic void there is filled by the wind and storm sound effects. William Hedgcock, who was also responsible for engineering the mise-en-bande of *The Old Dark House,* turns at this moment to the kind of effect he had used then, borrowing naturalistic (engineered) sound as a stand-in for musical content. With the return to the lab's interior, the score will feature the "Bride" theme extensively. On one of its iterations its tempo has actually been adjusted so that each note of the tune coincides with the regular stroke of the drum.

Once the sorcerer-scientists call for the electrical kites, both mise-en-bande and mise-en-scène begin to draw upon additional arsenals of sound and light objects. Expressionist lighting and camera angles emphasize depth, line, and vertical space, bringing the features and dimensions of the lightning storm raging outside into the formerly stifling, confining darkness of the lab. Waxman had already called upon the tympani as a special melodramatic element in Lang's *Liliom,* but more relevant here is that Gottfried Huppertz had used a similarly exposed tympani gesture to close out the "Metropolis" theme music at the end of the title sequence he had composed for the presentation of Lang's ("silent") *Metropolis* (1927), a work that stands as a visual and musical link between *The Golem* and *Bride of Frankenstein.*[78] In Lang's film, Rotwang's laboratory houses the machinery to produce a hybrid between the woman, Mary, and a robotic machine; the set was an important model for the lab of Frankenstein designed by Herman Rosse and Danny Hall, to which Whale himself added details.[79] Rotwang is part scientist (like Henry) and part sorcerer (like Rabbi Loew). (Lang had originally intended more medievalia than survived in the final version of the film, a notion that resonates in Huppertz's drawing upon the *Dies irae* as a leitmotif throughout his score.) Modern audiences will typically find the lyricism of Waxman's theme for the Bride herself a bit odd as it emerges against the background of sci-fi crackling and popping. But its musical model is clearly the machine woman's music in Huppertz's score for *Metropolis,* a work that Waxman must have known especially well given his association both with Lang and with the fantastic edge of expressionist cinema in Germany (an arena in which he produced his first scores). Huppertz had attached to the creation of Robot/Maria the same type of expansive, lyrical, gently chromatic utterance, employing similar iterations and "arrival" climaxes as those Waxman subsequently brought to Whale's creation scene.

A new noise emerges from the darkness as the moment of the creature's "birth" draws near: bells and triangles jingle (seemingly "in the night sky"). The effect has been termed "religious," but such a naive reading misses the specifically Straussian timbral associations of pitched percussion instruments and musical climaxes.[80] Lest there be any doubt, the final buzzing, popping moments that bring to life Whale's marvelous *Überweib* are marked by the tympani's relinquishing its beat-by-beat single drum strokes to quote the double-drum moment of arrival from *Also Sprach Zarathustra*. The music finds its culmination in a big major chord, and—to seal the deal—the chord lingers while much of the orchestra drops out beneath it.

Whale, when he originally approached Waxman to do the score, asked for something "unresolved," and we might hear in this moment Waxman's deepest interpretation of the director's imperative.[81] The chord is the culminating arrival; it releases tension after ten minutes of relentless musical preparation, but even as it arrives, it quickly dissolves, not into silence but into something diaphanous, a shadow of its monumental self. In 1935 not many audience members were likely to hear past the great, extended chord to its roots in the sublime moment ("und es ward Licht") from Haydn's *Creation,* or in Strauss's rehearsal of that moment in his own Nietzschean sunrise. They were fixed in the realm of the fantastic, blinded by the extraordinary flashes of light that the special effects department and the cinematographer John Mescall (a master of chiaroscuro) had brought to life. But as Johann Georg Sulzer told us in his famous analysis of Haydn's music, the sublime is apprehended not in a moment of simple grandiosity but in one of "astonishment."[82] Perhaps we may locate his remark at one of many historic intersections between the fantastic and the sublime realms of aesthetic experience charted by Whale and Waxman in *Bride of Frankenstein* by means of a multimedia construction without precedent.

CHAPTER 7

Concertos, Symphonies, Rhapsodies (and an Opera)

The Summer of Love was on the horizon, but its musical, political, and social elements had not yet come into sharp focus in the second half of 1965, when consumer reception propelled two new girl-group numbers to positions among the top twenty on American (and, in the months to follow, the UK's) pop music charts.[1] "A Lover's Concerto" was for the Toys their only substantial hit. For the Supremes, "I Hear a Symphony" was just the latest in a chain of successes (intended originally for the Isley Brothers, the song was expected to ride the wave set in motion by "A Lover's Concerto"). Both numbers seemed to occupy what was for the time unusual cultural ground in their titles, which invoked the European musical museum through reference to genre. Before considering either in detail, however, a detour is in order: to three decades later, in what should have been—but as it turns out, was really not—another and very different time. In the waning years of the twentieth century "A Lover's Concerto" reentered the universe of high-consumption American media objects as an acoustic shadow briefly materialized to serve a purpose related to but not entirely congruent with the song's original cultural dynamic. The difference can remind us of the extent to which pedagogues have often co-opted and diverted musical expression into other categories of rhetoric, and of their (i.e., our) commitment to reenacting the dilemma of Hermes, weaving veils of darkness only in order to prepare the ears of the faithful for the thrill of revelation.

THE CONCERTO PRINCIPLE

Mr. Holland's classroom was not as big, dark, or wet as the laboratory of Frankenstein's castle that the director James Whale and composer Franz Waxman had embedded in the American imagination in *Bride of Frankenstein*. Hollywood's first monumental sound space was extraordinarily spooky, but not much more so than the one that confronts us in the director Stephen Herek's 1995 reconstruction of a 1965 high school "music appreciation" class. Among the film industry's most cringeworthy misrepresentations of the potential of music to support or determine identity, *Mr. Holland's Opus* reminded teary-eyed, feel-good audiences of something beyond the simple-minded parable of its storyline. *Holland* underscored the threatening allure that has resided generally in exotic music words, but especially so in twentieth-century media, reinstructing moviegoers about the relationship between sanctioned words and certain forms of power and authority, both secular and spiritual. Less obviously, and more significantly, the film contained an unspoken lesson that hinted at the consequences—aural and psychological—that might follow upon the release of *musica reservata* into the environment of the everyday. From the strange Latinism of the film's title to the home-grown bombast of the protagonist's diegetic masterwork, "An American Symphony," *Mr. Holland's Opus* looked back to a magical dictionary that had achieved prominence within the full spectrum of American media decades earlier. In this chapter I will examine some of the ways in which twentieth-century media built imaginative places to house special expressive techniques associated with the music of the concert hall—transplanting them effectively, without diminishing their power to be expressive—and the role musical terminology has played in these mediated fields of understanding.

In the period between the two world wars, short story, novel, and movie titles were frequently based on words drawn from a generic collection associated with the realm of classical concert music. Some of the stories and their picturizations——a term current in Hollywood during the first decades of sound films—featured scenarios and characters related to the world of concert practices (e.g., *Humoresque, Intermezzo*), but others contained less in the way of specifically musical subject matter (e.g., *Symphony of Six Million*). Some pictures distorted or rendered nonsensical the musical implications of their titles. In *The Cat Concerto*, a Tom and Jerry cartoon that won an Oscar in 1946 for MGM Studios, there isn't a concerto in sight (or hearing). The cartoon featured as its title music an arrangement for piano and orchestra of Chopin's D-Minor Prelude, a work that in a number of arrangements was an item in MGM's musical pantry, having been featured as the signature tune for Oscar Wilde's amoral protagonist in the studio's adaptation of *The Picture of Dorian Gray,* released the previous year. After the titles, MGM's cartoon featured a performance by Tom (the popular animated cat) of not a concerto, or even Chopin, for that matter, but Liszt's C♯-Minor Hungarian Rhapsody.

However effective Tom's cartoon parody might be as a generalizing take on midcentury American concert repertoire and concert life, *The Cat Concerto* was most directly a lampoon of Paderewski's on-screen performance of Liszt's Hungarian Rhapsody ten years earlier in the Hollywood production *Moonlight Sonata,* as well as being a slightly sedate twin to Warner Brothers' more appositely named *Rhapsody Rabbit,* which featured Bugs Bunny performing the same composition.[2] All of the films I have mentioned here form part of a subgenre within a broader network of works from the 1930s and 1940s in which music was represented as a zone of conflict, and I will return to them in that context. Alliteration aside, the Tom and Jerry feature capitalized on a special linguistic vibe: few music words share all of the compelling features of "concerto" as a trigger for the receptive imagination. Its register can be recognized as that of the exotic or foreign (unlike "sím-fuh-nee" or "ráp-suh-dee" for example) by its phonemic details, including the stressed penultimate syllable, and the deep, final "o" sound that lends the word acoustic weight even though it is a nonstressed syllable. At the same time the word is situated within the aural—even if not the writing or reading—experience of most English speakers. Most Americans, if they don't know exactly what it means, will at least intuit something about it and its implications from concerto's acoustic resemblance to the English "concert." (That resemblance allows even a nonliterate speaker to understand that the "chair" sound in the middle of concerto is a foreign variant of the "ser" sound in concert.)

By contrast, the symphony had been appropriated as a red-blooded American cultural icon long before Mr. Holland's essay. It was planted in the vernacular imagination in that particular form by machinery housed in the factories and offices of corporate America during the period in which uniformity as a positive value grew in direct proportion to corporate size. In Thomas Watson's vision for International Business Machines Corporation (IBM), conformity was elevated to the status of an ethical component in a unique value system attached to something that resembled an eternal church of the corporate faithful. As he put it, "The IBM is not merely an organization of men; it is an institution that will go on forever."[3]

Eventually his church patronized an aesthetic offering that they hoped might serve as balm for the world's unrest, confusion, and weariness in a time of political anxiety. The year 1938 witnessed the premiere and radio broadcast of Vittorio Giannini's *IBM Symphony,* a one-movement multisectional orchestral work that in its second section (Sostenuto), as explained in the corporate publicity, "uses the first six bars of the IBM song, 'Ever Onward,' thus identifying the spirit of IBM with the world movement for international understanding." "Ever Onward" was the centerpiece of Watson's brainchild, the notorious *IBM Songbook.* The tune returns, not unexpectedly, in broader tempo and stated in its entirety at the end of the symphony, as its grand culmination. Giannini's treatment of "Ever Onward" belongs to a classic tradition of hymnal quotations in the symphonic repertoire.[4]

More original, but no less indicative of the symphony as an icon of corporate unity, efficiency, and nobility of intention, was Ford Motors' 1940 audiovisual *Symphony in F,* an eerily inverted multimedia *Vordoppelgänger* of Godfrey Reggio's technology sequences for 1983's *Koyaanisqatsi.* Ford's *Symphony in F* did make a quick stop in the more esoteric musical world of the concerto in its enthusiastic and optimistic "V-8" finale, which features a piano-concerto-style chordal passage of a sort I discuss below; the rationale behind its appearance during the culminating moments of the company's propaganda-art product will emerge in the course of that discussion. *Symphony in F* depicted Ford's machines, products, and workers—or parts thereof—as abstracted, looped, and otherwise manipulated montage units, moving in time to the orchestral score (credited to Audio Productions, Inc.). In its resemblances, material and polemical, to portions of the contemporaneous *Fantasia* of Disney Studios, Ford's audiovisual *Symphony*—which includes an unusual stop-action animation sequence—reflected the dark side of corporate aspirations while providing an index of the extent to which animated and abstract musical film was promoted midcentury as a ground for the practice of scientific-utopian avant-gardism.[5] *Symphony in F* emphasized once again the potential value of the symphony as a genre concept to the economic health of the American heartland. In short, American symphonies promoted and embodied good citizenship.

Mr. Holland's Opus reinscribed and celebrated the powers of the much less cooperative concerto to oppress, evoke, and be outrageously

oracular. For Mr. Holland, in the schoolroom setting of the film, concerto was above all a badge that identified the alterity of the trained musician, and by extension that of all the music he presumably controls.
Holland (portrayed by the actor Richard Dreyfuss, himself an amateur
classical pianist) plays *magister* in his classroom, as he derides a male student for having responded with an incorrect answer on a written exam.
Confronting the hapless *discipulus* with an oral reincantation of one of
the exam's unfathomable questions, one that Holland had inexplicably
inflected toward genre specificity, he asks "How do you tell what key a
concerto is in?" His formulation of the question does not betray its loop-
iness to musical outsiders (who presumably constituted most of the film's
audience). After all, the teacher has been represented in the screenplay
not merely as a musical insider but as an artist, a composer.

Holland approaches his classroom, though, less as an artist's studio
than as a laboratory of mad science. His project is in a sense familiar
to all teachers of "music appreciation." The goal, shared by all mad
scientists, is to infuse dead matter with life (or at least, as Colin Clive
dispiritedly suggested in *Bride of Frankenstein*, its simulacrum). Lacking the know-how or materials to achieve his end using standard mad-
scientific methods (generators, body parts, smoking beakers, or a degree in musicology), Holland followed the example of the Golem's
rabbinical magus and did it the old-fashioned way, by conjury. Unexpectedly, and to the delight of his formerly disaffected pupils, the
teacher pulls from his hat the Toys, as he performs the girl group's "A
Lover's Concerto" on the piano from memory, *sans* text. Holland has
undertaken here another kind of work—the opus known only to al-
chemical theory—effecting the transmutation of Motown into a new
musical substance.

Although virtually all of the students, denizens of the film's version of
1960s American suburbia, correctly identify the title of the piece and
name the artists, they mistakenly think that the Toys are not just the
singers but also the original creators of the song (the song is "by" them),
an error that the teacher makes no attempt to correct. At this point the
screenplay reveals its entrenchment in the established Hollywood discourse of musical necromancy. Triumphantly revealing the tune's source
in, as he puts it, "*The* Minuet in G" by Bach, Holland feels compelled to
withhold from the bedazzled students any generic or historical amplifi-
cation. Why tell them, for instance, what a concerto might be, or why
the Bach minuet doesn't have the same "beat" as the song, or what (forget about who) Bach might have been, aside from being another corpse

drawn from among the dour ancestral busts and portraits that ornament the classroom walls framing the film's sepulchral mise-en-scène of mad pedagogical practice?

But the master has saved the best for last. In a moment of revelation that reinforces the disorienting power of his glossolalia he pronounces with wild satisfaction that both the original Bach minuet and "A Lover's Concerto" are "examples of the Ionian scale," changing Motown steel to philosopher's gold and confining the music's sound to the other side of the veil of obfuscatory terminology behind which he hides. Had we wished to determine what to make of the 1965 pop "Concerto" that served as touchstone for the master's facile wizardry, *Mr. Holland's Opus* would have provided no guidance. Generous filmgoers will read warmth into the scene for its apparent suggestion that music encourages community and promotes bonding between unlikely partners.[6] That bond, however, is really a hermetic snare. Holland's invocation of the classic tells us, in all good faith it seems, that real music and its discursive unveilings—located within the praxis of allegory and parable—will always lie beyond the grasp of the uninitiated. In this the 1995 screenplay portrayed as a trivial miniature the inexorable and alienating force that musical knowledge and its associated vocabulary continue to exercise upon the mainstream vernacular imagination.

In American film, *The Picture of Dorian Gray* had staked out similar ground in a rather more effete cinematic rendering fifty years earlier. Embarking upon the sensual investigations that will eventually lead to his disintegration, Oscar Wilde's eternally beautiful monster, Dorian (played by the pallid Hurd Hatfield), effects the musical seduction of a beautiful low-caste music hall singer (Sybil Vane, played by Angela Lansbury). Mesmerized by Dorian's semidemonic performance of the Chopin D-Minor Prelude from opus 28, she asks him tremulously whether the piece has a title. He replies with a feint: "a sort of title; it's called Prelude," at which point her virtual enslavement and destruction have been rendered inevitable not just by the word's sexual tease but by its alluring unintelligibility within the limited range of her Cockney experience, one in which titles make sense (like that of her own signature tune, "The Little Yellow Bird"). Dorian understands the power of putting his hands to the keyboard and claiming its terminological space, as he claims Sybil's passionate kiss immediately afterward. As Lady Wotton put it in Wilde's original novel, even Englishmen, if they are pianists, will eventually recede from the zone of the normative and become "foreigners." "It is," she muses, "so clever of them. And such a compliment to art."

Dreyfuss's performance of the Toys' song in *Mr. Holland's Opus* retained nothing of the original beyond an abstracted reminiscence of its musical materials, that is, its classical Bachian melodic and harmonic architecture ornamented only by his impenetrable reference to its classification as "Ionian." His presentation did not include the words that in the original had engaged in a not entirely predictable relationship with the instrumental environment and revealed another side to the concerto concept as an imaginative construction in popular media. More to the point, Mr. Holland's rendition left out the song's signal concerto element. In its original form "A Lover's Concerto" (and its 1965 contemporary, "I Hear a Symphony") included a presence that was alien to the generic soundscape of pop, yet stereotypical enough to render it comprehensible to listeners. Both featured fanfare flourishes of piano chords, imitating the annunciatory ejaculations at the head of many late nineteenth-century piano concertos—fragments of oratorical power associated, particularly in filmic environments, with the music of highbrow musical venues, real or imagined (Example 9). As we will see, nothing else in the Supremes song in fact manifests any obvious link to the title's talismanic emblem-word "Symphony," one that (were it not for the piano's presence) might be taken in a less literally musical sense. No wonder that Joseph Kerman's 1997–98 Norton Lectures (published as *Concerto Conversations*) begin with an illuminating gloss on the "marvelous sonority" that Chaikovsky's crashing chords brought to his Bb-Major Piano Concerto in its revised and most familiar version.[7] That sound, along the lines of the word (concerto) it has come to represent as synecdoche, is familiar to most American audiences regardless of their musical training, and thus for Kerman's lectures was a useful hook with which to draw a mostly nonspecialist audience into his conversation.

In the 1960s, pop consumers—even those who had never attended a highbrow concert—could digest a series of big piano chords as a cultural trope on the basis of its constant multimedia iteration in straight and parodic contexts in movies and on television. Differences between the texting, musical structure, and performance of our two songs reveal, however, positions with respect to this avatar of musical pastness (and some components of the musical present) that are not in full alignment with one another. Moreover, even as both songs explore and play with the acoustic dimension of music words and music sounds drawn from outside of R & B or Motown praxis, they perforate the fabric of Mr. Holland's shroud of secrecy by insisting on the familiarity of the unfamiliar to realize a "vernacular" understanding of the final work. While the sur-

Example 9. "A Lover's Concerto," introduction (piano part)

face of each work seems to be Frankensteinian, stitched together as pastiche, I would argue that each possesses coherence as musical discourse: neither rhetoric nor poetry requires absolute continuity of tone.

Categorized as pure rhetoric, the piano chords fall within the domain of metonymic effects. Like other severed hands encountered more than once in this study, they provide a synecdoche that is easily grasped on first hearing, the goal of all rhetorical decorum. As in verbal substitutions, the object of representation may be taken literally. That is, the piano chords are meant to initiate, by reference to a part, some comprehension of the sound of a whole concerto. But, particularly in the case of "I Hear a Symphony," in which the word "concerto" never figures as title or text, the piano concerto sound, once perceived, stands in another broader synecdochic relationship to a range of potential representations and interpretations: for example, the world of the concert hall (as opposed to that of the music studio, site of creation; or the car radio and record player, sites of reception), the acoustical magnitude of concert hall sound (reproduced here in the pop sound box), or the powers incorporated within the imagined body of the absent pianist. All have played some role in the reception of concerto tropes throughout the twentieth century, but the last was particularly implicated in the media-inspired frames of reference that dominated the American imagination in the middle of the century. The nationalistic heroism of Chopin (as represented in Hollywood's *A Song to Remember*) and the Polish aviator of Britain's *Dangerous Moonlight* (renamed *Suicide Squadron* for its American release) coexisted alongside the dark powers insinuated in Dorian Gray's keyboard prowess and in the purest multimedia representation of the severed-hand topos, MGM's 1945 production *The Beast with Five Fingers*.

Musical frames of reference for the piano chord sequences in "A Lover's Concerto" and "I Hear a Symphony" are easily located among the most-consumed popular classics of the mid-twentieth century: the standard versions of the openings of Chaikovsky's Bb-Major Concerto,

Grieg's A-Minor Concerto, and Addinsell's *Warsaw Concerto,* the last composed specifically for diegetic presentation by the hero pianist of *Dangerous Moonlight.* Each of them opens with a characteristic series of pianistic "power chords." In contrast to other gambits that commandeer the keyboard—for instance the toccata model, in which a player lays claim to the instrument's topography by a form of contact with the keys that emphasizes their number and ordinal relationships, mapping distance incrementally—the concerto flourish stakes out the same ground by way of an athletic flyover. Heavy metal musicians were to absorb this lesson; their power chords similarly mark the territory of their dominion, the guitar fretboard. Significantly, like the concerto chord introits that are often the least challenging portions of the works they introduce, movable power chords yield big effects accessible to rockers of limited technical proficiency, even if expert players (like expert pianists) can invest such chords with tonal nuance.[8]

There is more to the severed hand's business in "A Lover's Concerto" than the flourish chords struck in the second measure. At least as important is the opening gesture on the pitch *d.* Its functional purpose is to open up the bass for the repeating ii7/V progression that will prepare the tune's arrival in C (the key to which the Bach minuet, reformed or deformed as a duple meter structure, has been transposed for the song). More to the point, it cleverly invokes by acoustic resonance Liszt's identical iteration of *c♯'* at the opening of the Hungarian Rhapsody No. 2 (Example 10).

Approached linguistically rather than rhetorically, the gesture is too fleeting to bear meaning in the syntactic sense, but it immediately marks a register, or collection, of associations and thereby locates the rhetorical zone of the song quite specifically. American media audiences knew precisely what that sound indicated. Certainly most teenagers of the 1960s would have been exposed on numerous occasions to the popular Tom and Jerry and Bugs Bunny offerings discussed above, whether as short subjects in movie theaters or—more effective as an *aide-memoire*—the repetitious children's programming of daytime and Saturday morning television.

I am hardly equipped to consider the cognitive processes attached to children's perception or memorizing of multimedia musical images, but it may not be entirely irrelevant to note that an especially striking feature of the Tom and Jerry version of the Liszt Rhapsody is the fetishistic accuracy with which the opening portion of the performance has been drawn. Any pianist might be surprised at Tom's adherence to the notes of the score in such an absurd context. When he begins to play, the film

Example 10. Liszt, Hungarian Rhapsody No. 2, opening

moves in for a virtual close-up of his fingers and the keyboard; we can see that Tom is hitting the right keys. Liszt's single-pitch reiterations (two on *c♯'* and three on *g♯*) have been visually reinforced each time by Tom's exaggerated arm lift and finger attack; on the third occasion the collision of his hand with the key causes a see-saw effect as he gently bounces off of his seat.

Bugs's performance of the same music is impossible with respect to the keys on which he lands. He is not quite as extreme in his initiatory pianistic gesture as Tom, but he reinforces the musical and muscular associations of the two-note units by playfully improvising additional statements octaves higher, à la Chico Marx; these will eventually be appropriated by a mouse who serves as comic foil. Liszt's gesture is a focus in the film for memorable musical comedy on several occasions, which received some notice at the time of the film's release. Daniel Goldmark has argued that "no cartoon, spoofing the classics or not, could expect more coverage than a blurb in a film exhibitor's daily," citing a review in *Film Daily* of award-winning *The Cat Concerto* as evidence for such products' "lack of prestige." His position is contradicted, though, by James Agee's detailed, insightful, and enthusiastic review of *Rhapsody Rabbit* in *The Nation* (September 12, 1946). Goldmark's insistence that reviewers were unlikely to address the musical content of satirical cartoons is not borne out by Agee's review, especially its culmination in a perspicacious reconsideration of Liszt's original Rhapsody: "After seeing its guts torn out in this movie short I knew more about it, and liked it better, than ever."[9]

No question, then, that "A Lover's Concerto" is a concerto of sorts.

Certainly the song reproduces the most familiar of concerto gestures in its chords. With respect not to concerto as a musical genre but *concerto* as an imaginative construction, the song significantly revisits and encourages reenvisioning multimedia representations of the exaggerated expressive concertizing mode of the concert stage. Room was made for expressionistic elements in the narrative spaces of many girl-group songs. Often they even included spoken—that is, quasi-cinematic or theatrical— passages. Considered from that perspective, the initial Lisztian bass figure effects a transfer of the song to an unexpected register without subverting the primarily expressive rhetoric of girl-group music.

To make sense of the rhetorical aspects of this song and of "I Hear a Symphony" requires further exploration of their structural surfaces. Each poetical (and musicopoetical) design reveals a different context for its aberrant elements. A marked disparity between the two is evident in the style of the vocals, the vehicle of poetic delivery. For anyone looking past the novel aspects of the titular stereotypes, this would have served as the acoustic magnet. In "A Lover's Concerto" vocalizing is constrained perhaps somewhat by the technique of the singers but more significantly by its melodic straitjacket, the familiar G-Major Minuet from the *Anna Magdalena Bach Büchlein,* metrically reconfigured.[10] The song's piano introduction lasts four measures, but this is followed by a standard four-bar Motown intro, thus highlighting several features of the work's poetics, particularly if the encoding of genre conventions is understood as a primary function of introductions (consider Leonard Meyer's "internalized probability system"). The piano's failure to "develop" or lead into the musical material of the song proper leaves it outside the world of the text, although neatly so, since its material is precisely as long as the conventional intro that follows.[11] At the same time, the eight-bar introduction that results from the need for a sensible segue to the artificial and classical musical environment of the verse expands the work's dimensions. For a musical miniature, a two-and-a-half minute pop song from a repertoire marked by conventionality and formulaic structures, the effect is not insignificant.

When the piano gestures toward the virtuosic masculine presence of European pianism, it pushes the girl singers aside before they have even been heard by means of three oxymorons: maleness, whiteness, and sophistication, all of which are lacking in the Toys and in the rest of the song which is based not on a big concert number but a woman's practice piece. If, in terms of the song's poetics, it fashions a moment of disorientation by emphasizing for four bars an acoustic, sexual, and cultural absence, it also sets a dynamic process in motion by forcing the remainder of the song to be perceived as something "more" than another expression of the standard girl-group romantic position. By cinematizing the song's register up front, the lyrics that follow call for visualization; the second strophe even begins with the verb "see" employed as an imperative. And it calls from its first hyperpoetical interrogative ("How gentle is the rain?") upon European traditions, in this case Shakespeare's *Merchant of Venice.*

What we do "see" is maybe more painterly than filmic, constituting a mise-en-scène devoid of any particular drama, but we have encountered that elsewhere in "antiquarian" pop. Descriptive images eventually include a meadow, singing birds, trees, and flowers, thus recreating the classic pastoral's *locus amoenus;* even that trope's requisite flowing water has been provided by the song incipit's gentle rain.[12] "A Lover's Concerto" drew upon an image that was geographically and culturally far removed from the candy stores, hops, beaches, and convertibles that had informed the virtual scripts created for most 1960s pop musical romances. For moral resonance the song relied upon the common misconception that the gentle rain (textually linked to the "quality of mercy" in Shakespeare's play) derives from scripture. This placed the song within a landscape of domestic moralizing sentimentality not far removed from the rhetoric of middle-American sermonizing, a tone encountered in other works of the period as well (including "Silence is Golden" by the boy group Frankie Valli and the Four Seasons).[13]

By domesticating the sexual heat of adolescent affairs through a poetry flavored with tropes borrowed from the register of what the medieval world knew as *ars praedicandi* (the rhetoric of preaching), the propensity of old-school rock and roll to alienate adult guardians might in some of these instances have been deproblematized. But whatever the intention, such songs emerge from a creative operation that had also figured in historical European pastoral, a text type that required not only the imitation of other languages and registers than those of formal art but, frequently, the appropriation of aphorism and proverb. Any student of early pastoral will understand that structural poetics (that is, form and words "cognate to the subject") govern poetic pastoralism quite strictly. Systematic poetics at the same time offer creative advantages, even if they constrain generic discourse, by providing a background field on which subversive poetical acts may be carried out and framed for the apprehension of readers or listeners.[14]

Pastoralism in "A Lover's Concerto" is generated primarily by its text: the Elizabethan-Jacobean reference is quaintly pastoral (and by its reference to landscape, quaintly picturesque) in the same way as those featured in "Stairway to Heaven." The pastoral mode might be extended to the song's Bach quotation, since it belongs to the category of "beginner's" music. Thus Bach's simple melody invokes childishness and the tabula rasa of elementary education—for a learner of any age—which in classical and medieval poetry permitted the same Latinate word families, related to our modern English "rustic" and "rude," to represent the beginning student as well as the country rube. Medieval pastoral, like pop, was encoded at the beginning of poems and songs, most often by a catchphrase associated with temporality. Chief among them were *l'autre jour* (the other day, effectively "once upon a time") and "when" words *(Quan, Quando,* or in the pastoral prologue to Chaucer's *Canterbury Tales, Whan)*. A cursory perusal of the catalog of all thirteenth- and fourteenth-century European pastoral songs would uncover a lot of formula and not much depth or innovation, at least of an obvious sort.[15] To assess objects generated by a re-creative energy calls for a fairly sophisticated comprehension of possible syntactical and registral variants: details embedded within or behind the surface of conventional genres. In the case of "A Lover's Concerto," the sore thumb with respect to its pastoralism is the power-concerto incipit, based on a widespread cultural understanding that resonated throughout midcentury American media by virtue of its constant and apparently conventional reiterations. It appears in this song to encode a conventional system entirely inappropriate to the ones called upon in the lyric that follows.

In early pastoral we have a model for something like this (specifically, its inversion) in Johannes Ockeghem's famous fifteenth-century rondeau "L'autre d'antan." Ockeghem's contemporary, the musical encyclopedist, composer, and curmudgeon Johannes Tinctoris, refers with no explanation to the song (in the *Proportionale musices*) as *carmen bucolicum,* one of the standard Latin designations for pastoral lyric. In fact, once the text gets past its code-phrase pastoral incipit, most of the song draws upon images of military formations and weaponry. To extend this to the concerto incipit of "A Lover's Concerto" would be to suggest that, like "L'autre d'antan," the song as a whole represents an interesting subversion of the expressive implications of initiatory musical encoding. Any characterization of the song as an aesthetic misfire purely by virtue of its incongruent parts is insupportable from the standpoint of historical poetics, and it is inappropriately prejudicial to an item

·within a repertoire that operated in its time primarily as an agent of conventional expressive discourse.

The conversation between the opening flourish and the rest of the song, specifically with its simple tune and quaint lyrics drawn (for listeners) from a nonspecific past, "A Lover's Concerto" stands within the systematic parameters of musicopoetic practice usually assigned to a very different evaluative slot than Motown love songs. Its poetical play with historicist tone and its construction of temporal distance was prefigured in the songs of Virgil's bucolic pseudo-Doric shepherds, that is, in the field of real pastoral. In this sense the song's pastoralism is more authentic, I would say, than that projected by the idyllic landscapes of twentieth-century program music (Grofé, Copland, Respighi, and their imitators among later Hollywood film scorers) or by Berlioz's gimmick of joining physical topography to aural perception through the on- and off-stage players in the *Ranz des Vaches* of his *Symphonie fantastique*.

Ockeghem's military pastoral had inverted the conventional implications of gender roles in its text. Typically in medieval pastoral the armed knight has ridden out (the other day), encountering a beautiful young woman (usually a shepherdess). The two will often engage in verbal sparring, with not always predictable results. In some cases the knight eventually takes what he wants by force.[16] It is, however, the woman in "L'autre d'antan" whose countenance has been "forged in Milan," a reference to the city's central role in medieval military technology. Medieval pastoral was inherently sexual, and its dynamical narrative operation was one of conflict. If concerto flourishes, by their claims to acoustical power and territory, were, as they clearly were, fundamentally masculine signifiers in the vernacular imagination, "A Lover's Concerto" constructs, beyond the conflict of its musical poetics, a palpable tension between the "me" and the "him" of girl-group relational utopias. Those utopias were not usually realized in song narratives; they are located in a hoped-for future (in this sense they are not unlike the love lyrics of the Middle Ages). Via its weight and image content the concerto opening perhaps suggests—rather like the rapist knight—a potential threat, a capacity to stifle or constrain the "girl" whose voice carries the simple and straightforward delivery of the song's less spectacular registers. After all, 1962's "He Hit Me (It Felt Like a Kiss)" by Phil Spector, Gerry Goffin, and Carole King—a popular number for the Crystals—called attention to precisely such a double-edged dynamic.

DO I HEAR A SYMPHONY?

"I Hear a Symphony" only gradually fashions a soundscape that in any way conforms with the song's title. By the time its classical-style concerto chords emerge we have already heard a standard R & B saxophone solo and have been treated to multiple iterations of the text phrase "I hear a symphony." Its first utterance prompts a familiar musical interjection, a quick upward glissando, from the (symphonic) violins. They respond to the word throughout the song. If the piano material also communicates a symphony's rhetorical or expressionistic range, to what specifically does it point? In this respect the sophistication of the musical arrangement is apparent. The chords are not static registral icons but generators of a broader musicopoetical process that tilts the interpretation of the song's lyrics in a particular direction. Their manipulation and their participation in purely musical structures is more to the point than the imaginary acoustic context from which they have been excavated; this marks the song's point of separation from the poetics of "A Lover's Concerto." Each invocation of the piano in "I Hear a Symphony" corresponds to what the listener perceives as an open-ended upward chromatic spiral of harmonic center. Transpositions upward by a semitone are familiar expressionistic elements in pop music, typical especially of "standard" vocals. (Barry Manilow, for instance, has built a career on chromatically jacking up a song's last strophe.)

Such transpositions can, by musical shorthand, lend emotional presence and vocal power even to singers who on their own lack the equipment to invest a song with much expressive content, as witnessed by the use of the gimmick by almost every singer on amateur televised talent contests like *Star Search* and *American Idol.* But the Supremes were hardly amateurs and didn't require gimmicking-up, and the technique is extended beyond any conventional expectations. The song remains in C Major for one minute and nine seconds, after which we are propelled through a modulatory "development" section consisting of three swift upward transpositions. In this passage the piano functions as a harmonic trigger each time, with its acoustic potential *(ff)* only realized with finality as the harmony settles into its eventual location in E♭ Major. Exceptional here is not just the proliferation of transpositions but the short-form landscape (two minutes and forty-two seconds) on which they are projected. The string of modulations invokes, by musical artifice, a sense of symphonic proportions in an incredibly compressed space. The result is—in the song's accompaniment—an unacknowledged concerto environment for piano and orchestra, squeezed into the time space of a conventional lyric form.

The modulatory process and the "grand" acoustical environment will be familiar to viewers of standard filmic narratives. Cinematicism also links the musical structure to Diana Ross's delivery of the text. What the singer-protagonist "hears" is not, piano chords notwithstanding, a masculine power construct; it is instead "a tender melody." Melody embodies the morphology of sexual response as taught by cinema; it is set in motion in film—and in this song—by physical closeness ("Whenever you're near me"). We are invited by the text imaginatively to construct both a mise-en-scène and a mise-en-bande (a rather interesting multiplanar effect for a small item) as the lover draws closer. Throughout, the listener's expectations are configured by multimedia (that is, cinematic in a sense that exceeds its "story line") rather than simple pop convention. In most of the song Diana Ross's declamation retains its adherence to conventional R & B style, above all in its rhythmic flexibility, that is, her placement of syllables with respect to the musical pulse. But the vocals turn toward the purely cinematic—toward the privileging of the diegesis over the projection of metrical nuance—at the moment of the diegetic kiss: "suddenly . . . your lips are touching mine." At this point Ross's delivery edges towards a naturalistic—or filmic—speech rhythm.

Sentiments like those expressed in the lyrics might be contextualized by long-standing poetical metaphors, but Ross's and the background vocals direct us toward another, more immediately relevant model. The Supremes remind us that love in a mass-mediated world is—or must be characterized as—a synaesthetic sensory experience, an understanding that the symphony is not a musical alien but a familiar acoustical presence in our soundscape. The song's construction of "symphony" is clearly derived from the cinema sound track and rendered effective through the group's performance. How else can we decipher Ross's confession that she is "*lost* in a world *made* for you and me," except as a reference to the manufacture of cinematic experience? But such a notion takes us no further toward making sense of the piano and its chordal punctuations.

I would suggest that the sound box of "I Hear a Symphony" has admitted an additional presence, one that might be categorized as metafilmic. It reproduces not the sloppy and rudimentary performance of the opening moments of "A Lover's Concerto" (filmic as that was) but, in shorthand, the sharper, more glittery sound and style of the contemporaneous popular duo-pianists Arthur Ferrante and Louis Teicher.

The pair, now considered more easy-listening than pop, were trained at Juilliard (where they were "avant-garde hellions") and upon graduation embarked on a series of experiments in "new music" composition and recording that involved, in some cases, prepared pianos à la Cage.[17] Their first hit was an arrangement of the title theme from the film *The Apartment*, which hit the charts in the late summer of 1960. By the end of that year their second film-music release, the theme from *Exodus*, was more formidable in its commercial success (it skyrocketed to a position high on the pop charts) and especially in its rhetorical tone. The music of *Exodus* was already much on the American public's mind, particularly on both coasts, whose consumption patterns determined the shape and scale of movie ticket and recording income, and where Zionism (the movie's message) was a cause of particular interest and immediacy. Released earlier that year, *Exodus* was a blockbuster with all requisite elements: a star-studded cast (including Paul Newman and Eva-Marie Saint), a top-tier director (Otto Preminger), and an Oscar-winning score by Ernest Gold that matched in its self-importance the oratory of the film's bloated script, which was based on Leon Uris's popular novel of the same name.

In the Supremes' number, the rhythmic content of the "I Hear a Symphony" phrase follows the natural declamation of the words. But the combination of a dotted value ("sym") with a descending fourth leap to "pho-ny" is revealingly oratorical and—if we recall the musical implications of our concertizing cat paw—decidedly concerto-like as it foreshadows the rhythmic content of the piano interjections that will appear later in the song. Within the repertoire of film music with which practicing musicians might have been expected to have been familiar, other examples of romanticized versions of such figures may be found (for example in "Laura," the pop and jazz standard generated by David Raksin's "symphonic" title music for Otto Preminger's film *Laura*). But Ferrante's and Teicher's hit take on the *Exodus* theme is the more proximate to "I Hear a Symphony," more allied in its grandiosity, and virtually identical in its performing forces. Cultural encodings of gesture, and the passage of such gestures from one medium to another, are not at issue in this particular case; what matters is that the concerto content of the song only "makes sense" within the context of the notion that romanticized love requires or launches an extradiegetic sound track. Encouraging young listeners to cinematize their own lives, "I Hear a Symphony" simultaneously enacted an invisible cinema and reinforced the decades-old relationship between cinematic scoring conventions and the imagined shape of human emotion, which suggests that the audio-emotional conformance represents a natural manifestation of the human condition. What Holland didn't get, but Motown did, was that the "classics" by 1965 were hardly the protected autonomous acoustic landscapes he wished they were, even if he couldn't confess his position.

Analyzing the melodies of these two girl-group songs takes us only so far but we might, like the music teacher, note that both explore in their opening phrases the pentachord *c'-d'-e'- f'-g'*; "A Lover's Concerto" arrives at its first caesura, optimistically, on *g*, whereas "I Hear a Symphony" releases its ascendant melodic energy with the (cinematic) dotted descending fourth figure *(g'-d')*. The contrast in melodic conception is emphasized by harmony. "A Lover's Concerto" relies on a more conventional harmonic motion from I to iii, whereas "I Hear a Symphony" moves from I to V to v.

More powerful contexts emerge, however, by considering the extent to which each plays out a different model of the cinematic representations of women and women's voices. In "A Lover's Concerto" the Toys (and Anna Magdalena, perhaps) are domesticated, framed by a house built of a masculine pianistic voice and—significantly with respect to these and other African-American woman singers and listeners—one that is fundamentally European, bleached, and desexed. Ross's vocals, on the other hand, are more overtly sexual, particularly in the quasi-recitative unpitched passages. Any symphony we hear is hers; the woman's voice establishes and explores the musical terrain of the entire number, a dramaturgical structure that characterizes the so-called women's movies of the late 1930s and 1940s (young male bodies were in short supply then as potential filmgoers), when soap-operatic scoring took on especially gendered inflections.[18] Both of these relatively slight productions, as they would likely be judged in any history of pop (a lightweight one-hit wonder and a noniconic Supremes tune), are in fact strong and valuable indicators of a much broader historical field of media reception.

DO I HEAR A CONCERTO?

The concerto remains incantatory in places more congenial than Holland's secret chamber of pedagogical horrors. Carlos Santana, an artist who emerged in San Francisco in the late 1960s, while psychedelia was still in flower, hit the pop charts again at the turn of the millennium with his hugely successful album *Supernatural*. The collection contained two monster hits: "Smooth," created by Rob Thomas who—in his vocals for the song—explored the sound of "radio miking"—and "Love of My Life," cowritten and performed with Dave Matthews. In the opening moments of the video for "Smooth," the most widely transmitted and promoted cut on the album, "Love of My Life" makes a brief appearance on the sound track, linking the two songs as multimedia and perhaps underscoring the nostalgic features, in the common sense of the word, they shared. For "Smooth," that feature was its "radio sound" that pointed back to the first half of the century now drawing to a close; in "Love of My Life," the melody quotes the third movement of Brahms's Third Symphony, transposed in the song from C Minor to G Minor and, as in "A Lover's Concerto," recast in a new metrical environment (to make it "swing," according to Santana). Yet Brahms is not the hook on which my nostalgia comment hangs.

The symphony tune, first heard as a prelude performed by Santana on guitar, grounds the whole song and eventually moves to the vocal. Santana's original, rather contemplative, lyrics, which inform the first part of the song, were given a more overtly sexual tone by Matthews, who wrote the remainder of the text. Those unfamiliar with the symphony or with publicity surrounding the work's genesis are unlikely to hear anything out of the ordinary in the music. Many of Santana's songs (including early tracks like "Oye como va," "Samba pa ti," and the later "Bella") explore in their opening hooks the lower third and lower fifth of minor-mode scale structures (often in A Minor, his "home" key). From the beginning, in marked contrast to most rockers, he has been particularly identified with sensuously lyrical, legato, slow-tempo solo material. Santana, an intelligent and trained musician, must have heard in the Brahms theme at some level a reflection of his own well-developed melodic aesthetic.

Be that as it may, it was a different story that made the rounds after the song's release. In an interview with *Guitar Player* magazine, Santana—like the Doors' Manzarek—staked pop's claim to all musics in what he calls "rainbow" or "diamond" music.[19] Carlos Santana has consistently reiterated this position formed a generation ago. Santana hoped that *Supernatural* would be like the content of a free television channel dedicated to excellence and beauty: "This would accelerate the world to a place beyond the corruption of politics and the corruption of religion."[20] In a phrase that recalls Keith Reid's commitment to textual abstraction in the 1960s, he noted that "sometimes words get in the way" and suggested—diverging here from the psychedelic notion of the universality of all musics—that his own trademark sound embraces a synthetic universality: "Palestinian, Hebrew, or Aborigine or Mexican or Chinese, this speaks really clearly."[21]

When asked about the genesis of "Love of My Life" and about its special musical material he responded that "a story" lay behind it. The story Santana told wasn't in fact much of a narrative: he had turned on the radio as he was picking his son up from school, heard the music on a classical station, and gone to Tower Records to ask about the source. At the core of his story lie some matters of interest for the present study. He began his reply to the interviewer: "When my father passed away two or three years ago, I didn't listen to the radio for four days—that's a long time for me. I turned on a classical station, and the first thing I heard was this melody [he gently sings a slow, six-note theme]. The melody just stayed with me. They didn't say who the composer was, but I thought it was Strauss. I wanted to find out what this was, so I went to the classical music section at Tower Records and said, 'All I have is this melody.'"[22]

A counter to the song's sensuality was the phantom of death, a stand-in for the absent father (already encountered in one of Phil Spector's earliest productions) and perhaps also for a century past. There is, then, a note of nostalgia that Santana has brought to the story, although it is nothing more than the nostalgia of sweet reminiscence relating to his father; Santana does not admit Brahms (or, as he thought it, Strauss) as a presence in his own past in any way. Comparing "Love of My Life" with what I argued was the more literally and aesthetically nostalgic "A Whiter Shade of Pale" reveals that the Santana song shares with the earlier work aspects of musical citation (in that work an even more precise quotation), morbid associations, and a classical-soul mix (in the style of Matthews's characteristic vocals). But the anecdotal details located within the trail of reception skew the song more in the direction of the mediated concerto principle, whereby aesthetic weight (and in this case, perhaps, morbid monumentality) may be conjured by talismanic utterances. Note that the real source of the music (the Third Symphony) is transformed by Santana, who continued his story of the visit to Tower Records: "I sang it, and the guy goes, 'Oh yeah. Brahms Concerto No. 2.' They get me the CD, and that's the song! I said, 'Damn, you guys are good!'"

In the Spring of 2000, Dave Matthews gave his version of the same tale to *Rolling Stone*. He told the interviewer that Santana was (he thought) writing about his father and that he (Matthews) was writing about his lover. Matthews identified the source of the music as "Brahms's Piano Concerto No. 3."[23] Taking into account Santana's aesthetic position with respect to musical diversity—according to which Brahms would likely be a single facet of the musical diamond—any critique of their misnomers on the basis of inaccuracy would be meaningless and irrelevant. That both Santana and Matthews ascribed the musical inspiration for "Love of My Life" to the realm of the (piano) concerto, ornamented appropriately by an esoteric numerical nametag that was meaningless aside from its evocative force, constitutes important testimony to the weight of the concerto principle as popularly imagined, that is, as a general repository for the expressive voices of the hall and of the collective past.

DORIAN'S PRELUDE FANTASTIQUE

Works representing a range of musical genres might usurp the concerto's role in the vernacular imagination by an operation of transference or masquerade. One of the more interesting of these cases is represented in the film *The Picture of Dorian Gray*. The director, Albert E. Lewin, who also wrote the screenplay, was regarded as "bookish" by most in the Hollywood community. His undergraduate training had been at New York University (NYU), after which he received a Master's degree in literature from Harvard and went on, though without finishing, to the English doctoral program at Columbia. It is therefore not surprising that he found a place early in his Hollywood career in the circle of Irving Thalberg. Thalberg's dedication to elevating (in his mind) the tone of cinema led him to his famous attempt to hire Arnold Schoenberg to score a production of Pearl Buck's *The Good Earth* in the late 1930s. That deal fell through when the composer made it clear that the actors would need to master *Sprechstimme* (reportedly, he suggested that the effect would be "similar to *Pierrot Lunaire*, but of course less difficult").[24] Lewin was a part of that project, and Thalberg called upon his expertise in all book-related projects.[25]

As a director, Lewin was unusually concerned with detail, and his literary background insured that his cinematic rendering of Wilde's original story would be a careful one. Wilde's text had in Lewin an interpreter of unusual erudition, who could transfer the preciosity of synaesthetic detail, which Dorian had learned from Huysmans's Des Esseintes, to both the Hollywood mise-en-scène and, in collaboration with the composer Herbert Stothart, the mise-en-bande. When elements of the original made for impossible cinema, Lewin introduced changes that might retain and express Wilde's spirit and intention, as he saw it, more practicably. There is no telling now (nor is it particularly important) which musical decisions stemmed from Lewin and which from Stothart. The score of *Dorian Gray*, although a blend of leitmotivic and borrowed quotations of the sort frequently encountered in mid-1940s "serious" films, is remarkably coherent in its formal aspects, notably those pertaining to meaningful key relationships. Lewin came by his understanding of operatic principles as an early aficionado. According to his autobiographical note, his parents were relatively poor, and his mother essentially illiterate. Still, they loved music and often took him to the Metropolitan Opera. Herbert Stothart's score for MGM's 1937 adaptation of Sigmund Romberg's *Maytime* reveals his familiarity with the music of opera and operatic conventions, including, most significantly, the narrative function of tonal areas.[26]

Music, generally, and Dorian's pianism, specifically, are fundamental images throughout Wilde's narrative. Lewin's version includes many of the specific musical details of Wilde's text, particularly once Dorian begins—according to the euphemistic voice-over—his "visits to the abyss" (houses of ill repute near Bluegate Field). However, he swapped out Dorian's signature music, as imagined by Wilde, for something more cinematically expressive, Chopin's D-Minor Prelude, op. 28, no. 24. Ordinarily one would not expect directorial intervention in such choices. That Lewin's intentions, or at least his close collaboration, lay behind the choice and treatment of most of the preexistent items—that is, those derived from the classical repertoire—woven into Herbert Stothart's score for *Dorian Gray* seems evident. As readers, we get a sense of Dorian's childlike essence when Wilde has him express particular interest in Schumann's *Waldszenen*. He thinks the pieces are "charming." Like all truly picturesque art, *Waldszenen*, however, lead the composer's absent musical viewer to some nasty turnabouts, and Wilde must have seen in "Verrufene Stelle" an emblem for Dorian's cold emptiness and statuesque beauty, ornamented as it is by striking contrasts of (perhaps pre-Raphaelite) color fields: fine skin surrounded by "rebellious curls," and the vital red of his lips and flushed cheeks. Wilde's image of Dorian was well served by the Hebbel poem attached to Schumann's piece.[27] The book's Dorian—unlike the film's preternaturally white protagonist—has a "romantic, olive-coloured face," but Wilde ingeniously wove the morbid pallor of Schumann's *blasse Blumen* into the description of the boy's hands: "His cool, white, flower-like hands, even, had a curious charm.

They moved, as he spoke, like music"; this was Lewin's cue for shooting Dorian's hands on the piano keyboard to suggest power and presence.[28]

While I am speculating on the circumstances that brought Chopin's D-Minor Prelude to Dorian's fingers in the film, certain features are clearly relevant. Lewin needed to convince the audience of the effete Dorian's monstrosity and potentially demonic power. "Verrufene Stelle" did not provide the visual impact of the Chopin, which falls nicely within the required multimedia components linked to the concerto principle: the prelude regularly requires the hands to negotiate a lot of keyboard space at once or in a short time span, often in remarkably disjunct fashion (especially in the uncomfortable left hand part), and thus makes for clear and meaningful piano cinematography. Both the Schumann and the Chopin are in D Minor, but the Chopin is, at least for the first statement of the principal material (mm. 1–15) suffused with church-mode dorianism, studiously avoiding $c\sharp$, and shifting freely between $b\natural$ and $b\flat$ (that is, exploiting the modal *mi–fa* ambiguity of many D-mode plainchants). Chopin's disease—and its associated palette of pale skin and red blood—perhaps underscored the appropriateness of the substitution.

In the score the prelude will eventually appear in its normal pitch position when it is played by a strange old man in one of the dives Dorian has been haunting, but its diegetic debut is Dorian's performance for Sybil Vane. The piece had been recorded in full by Lela Simone but was then edited for the scene.[29] Each cut has been made to emphasize the concertizing elements of the piece and to lend its pitch content a more fantastic tone. Dorian performs the prelude's measures 21–24, 34–56, 59–65, and 72–77. By beginning with the A-Minor statement of the theme, Stothart and Lewin establish a pitch relationship to Sybil's own signature, "The Little Yellow Bird" in A♭ Major, which was heard immediately prior. That tonal relationship will reach its resolution in the last moments of the film, when some of Stothart's original music in the nondiegetic score turns (for the first time since that crucial scene in Sybil's music hall) to A♭, backing Dorian's prayer that God might forgive his sins. His abuse of Sybil was of course the first item in his treasury of demerit. These particular regions, defined by the semitonal relationship of innocent Sybil's A♭—or, enharmonically, G♯—to Dorian's A, is one of the more familiar in the mainstream opera repertoire (specifically in Wagner, where, for instance, it joined Elsa to Lohengrin), but in this case it was probably derived from the melodic $g\sharp$ (of the longing motive) and the central *a* of Tristan's *Prelude* and *Liebestod*. Sybil,

Example 11. Chopin, D-Minor Prelude, op. 28, no. 24, mm. 21–24, 33–34

in Wilde's book, bestowed upon the unattainable object of her pathetic desire a code name: "Prince Charming." Lewin has substituted "Sir Tristan" (an identification graphically emphasized by a Beardsley-style poster bearing the name displayed on the wall behind Dorian and Sybil).[30]

Concerto powers are invested in Dorian by his visual control of keyboard space; aurally the cuts and other features of the score emphasize the fantastic regions of the music and the story. In leaping from the end of the A-Minor statement (mm. 21–24) to the dominant preparation (for the move to E Minor) in measure 34 (Example 11), even the hearing practice of an untrained ear will likely sense logical discontinuity, a fantastic trait. Melodically, measure 34 emphasizes the tritone C–f♯ in the left hand figuration, marking it as especially *disfig*-ured. The dissonance of both the C and the e in the left hand with respect to the melodic f♯' of the right is also rendered more notice-able than in the original, since the C and e of measure 34 appear without the preparation of measure 33 that lent coherence to the pas-sage. Other cuts from measure 56 to measure 59, and from measure 65 to measure 72 highlight another tritone, *d–g♯*, in several registers on the way to D Minor. Each of those gestures resemble Schumann's similar move to D Minor in the final two measures of "Verrufene Stelle."

Chopin ("Chopin's beautiful sorrows") comes into Wilde's text in passing, and rather late in the story, in the company of Beethoven and Schubert. All three composers are invoked here as contrasts to the musical content of Dorian's Des Esseintes-inspired explorations of synaesthesia. Huysmans's exoticism infuses the passage. At times, Wilde tells us, Dorian played impresario, giving "curious concerts" of mad gypsy music, of "grave yellow-shawled Tunisians" playing "monstrous lutes," and of Indian snake charmers. Eventually he undertakes the study of exotic music himself, learning to play instruments that—like any good fantast—he collected "from the tombs of dead nations." In Lewin's and Stothart's sound track we are treated to an example of Dorian's musical New Hedonism: a Balinese-style cue is heard while the camera focuses on one of its visual leitmotifs, Dorian's Egyptian cat. The cat statuette, emblematic of the monumental tombs of that dead nation, was a prop Lewin was particularly concerned to feature (it was based on an original in the Louvre), and it links Dorian and the repertorially multidimensional score with cinema's conventional fantastic discourse through what I have suggested was the cinematic practice of Egyptography.

Beethoven, although invoked briefly by Wilde (for his "mighty harmonies"), plays a more significant diegetic role in Lewin's adaptation. Toward the end of the film the strange old man at the keyboard plays the Chopin prelude (his second rendering), whereupon Sybil's brother—who had been witness to her original conversation with "Sir Tristan"—reenacts that scene, asking the name of the piece.[31] The old man responds with Dorian's line (beginning with "a kind of a title"). When the brother angrily orders him to play something else, the old man launches into Beethoven's "Moonlight Sonata," which haunts the background during the sequence that follows, where Dorian's undoing is set in motion. Beethoven and the impossibly wise old pianist take up residence in the mise-en-bande as ethical foils to the doomed sensualist. Lewin's decision to use Beethoven in this way—to locate him on a fantastic plane removed from the action as a moralistic overseer—was carefully taken. Through multiplanar multimedia Lewin was able to represent Dorian's rejection of respectability and humane behavior, and Wilde's depiction of Schubert, Chopin, and Beethoven as the music that "fell unheeded on his ear."

In *The Picture of Dorian Gray*, Chopin's D-Minor Prelude engages in two modes of cinematic discourse invoking both the musical effects of the fantastic and the grand oratory of the concerto and its associated powers. Both had been reiterated throughout the century in a range of mediated forms. That the media public learned to hear these musical codes as expressive gestures was a function not only of their extensive circulation but of their early attachment to image systems sufficiently coherent to support the mnemonic enterprise.

ENCOUNTERS WITH RHAPSODES

Other implications permeate mid-1940s representations of keyboard virtuosity. One strain imbues the prowess of the musician with a capacity for expressionism that appears demonic or at the least morally suspect. We have sensed it in Dorian's Chopin, but Hollywood wove the theme into on-screen presentations of Liszt and Brahms, too. Both of the animated animalian performances of Liszt's rhapsody were hijacked midway by a jazz interruption. The anonymous Warner Brothers mouse and MGM's mouse Jerry lure the virtuosos Bugs and Tom into abandoning the printed score for jazz improvisation, and after initial confusion and hesitation each of them seems to enjoy it. Implications that the mice are "natural" musicians unbound by the straitjacket of musical institutions (represented most comically and perfectly when Bugs's fingers turn into a tangle of knots) are obvious, and these implications—followed to all their conclusions—would raise issues related to the musical representation and reception of race and musical typing.[32] Jazz as a musical environment is also rendered explicitly sexual, indeed salacious, in the Warner Brothers production, as Bugs's face contorts demonically and his drooling tongue protrudes, a bestial extension of Groucho Marx's leer (Groucho was a source for many of the rabbit's mannerisms, including his carrot "cigar").

In one of the Marx Brothers' least successful films, *A Night in Casablanca* (1946), Harpo comes across a harp and launches his own performance of the same Liszt rhapsody. Here again the middle section of the performance turns into jazz. Although Harpo's demeanor remains serious, we see a lot more body English. We can only assume that his jazz digression has been inspired by the sexy pinup he had taped over a dour ancestral portrait just before he started playing. A more strictly demonic, Dorian-style possession afflicts Al, the pianist protagonist of the low-budget noir cult classic *Detour* (1945). Al's musical detour is taken in the middle of a Brahms waltz and marked at first by exaggerated dynamics and virtuosity, but he, too, will transgress by layering the Brahms melody over a jazz bass like those encountered in the cartoons.[33]

All of these instances suggested to audiences that spontaneous musicality was at odds with concert hall etiquette and style. More to the point, they underscored the notion that the natural musician was an inspired rhapsode, in the general sense in which the terms rhapsody or rhapsodic are taken today. In classical antiquity the rhapsode was more specifically one who "stitched" material together, and his product was often decidedly pretentious (think of Plato's Ion). No more apt description could be invoked for one of the best-known and most cherished of multimedia rhapsodies, Queen's 1975 monster hit "Bohemian Rhapsody." In stitching that together Freddie Mercury, the composer and soloist, acted the rhapsode in the purest sense, and his rhapsody was—in line with those of the Homeric bards—primarily a vocal manifestation. His rhapsodic frame extended to his presentational mode. As Socrates put it in Plato's dialogue: "I often envy the profession of a rhapsode, Ion; for you have always to wear fine clothes, and to look as beautiful as you can is a part of your art."[34] The rhapsode's appearance will play a role in the sense of the song transmitted in its filmed version (intended for television) as well. (This "Bohemian Rhapsody" is often credited with founding the genre of MTV-style music videos.) Rhapsodic vocalization is emphasized in the rudimentary special effects of the introduction, in which only the group's heads are shown, a tableau vivant reproduction of the previous year's album cover for *Queen II*. They overlap, forming a single virtual head, and, with Mercury's face at the bottom of the screen, his face constitutes the group's mouth. Within the wide-open, dark vocalizing cave of his mouth, we see his image again (Mercury as rhapsode *en abyme*).

When the song was represented within the diegetic frame of Penelope Spheeris's 1992 comedy *Wayne's World,* its introduction as talisman (a cassette inserted into an automobile tape player) yields to a representation of its supernatural vocality: Wayne and his friends perform along with the song in Wayne's "mirthmobile" (a performance that lies somewhere between lip-synch and karaoke), as it gradually replaces the "partied-out" shell of the weak and nauseated headbanger Phil with its own body, constructed of sheer vocal force.[35] In Fuzzbox's cover of the song, all of the original instrumental material is replaced by the women's voices. Their version is something of a goof and yet manages to transmit a sense of appreciation for some of the expressive elements of the original. (By contrast, the London Symphony Orchestra's inflated concert version rolls over those elements and flattens them.) But even within the song's near-fetishistic framing of voice as a power extending beyond and emanating from beyond the body (an *acousmêtre*, perhaps, in Chion's terms), the "classical" piano will function as a significant presence, marking music's capacity to engage in acts of transgression and subverting the conventional contexts in which such acts are imbedded (in this case, the zone of rock, and even—not unusual for its time—that of symphonic rock).

After an extraordinary amount of studio work—roughly eighty hours for the middle chorus section alone—and constant tweaking by the composer and lead singer, Freddie Mercury, Queen came up with a final version of their classic "Bohemian Rhapsody" that lasted for roughly six minutes. Industry insiders warned that no radio station would ever play it all the way through and that it could never be a hit (although it's actually about two minutes shorter than "Stairway to Heaven" and ten minutes shorter than Iron Butterfly's 1968 "In-A-Gadda-Da-Vida" that had launched the phenomenon of the rock megasong).[36] Queen resisted all pressure to cut material, and the single took England by storm, after receiving its first exposure from the DJ Kenny Everett, who played a pre-release version fourteen times in two days. Within two weeks of its official release in October 1975, "Bo Rhap" (as it is often abbreviated) had sold more than 150,000 copies, and by January 1976 it had occupied the number one position in the UK charts longer than any record since Slim Whitman's "Rose Marie" nearly two decades earlier. For two decades following the song's release it remained (along with "Stairway to Heaven") one of the most frequent plays on FM radio. Its status as a cult object was compromised for some by the song's presentation in the comic film *Wayne's World* and, more seriously, by the glossed version of the *Wayne's World* sequence on VH1's *Pop-up Videos,* which took specific aim at Freddie's homosexuality, information the singer had disclosed only one day before his death from AIDS.

Even though fans received the song with enthusiasm, rock pundits were less generous at the time of its release, expounding positions based on the now familiar parameters constituting rock's purportedly authentic discourse. From that perspective, it was argued, "Bohemian Rhapsody" relied excessively upon studio effects. Indeed, excess often was invoked as a tag for Mercury himself, even in his *Rolling Stone* obituary.[37] As a target for critical derision, "Bohemian Rhapsody" has now entered the academic mainstream of sociologically inflected rock scholarship.[38] Authenticity in the context of rock, however, may serve as a handy bludgeon for those committed to the construction of a single uninflected register of conventional practice. Objects outside the register signal—for those invested in this form of discursive orthodoxy—uncomfortably dangerous blendings or impurities. Rock's freedom to engage in its discourse on a grand public and commercial scale has been seen as an incidental reward for an intransigently revolutionary progressive stance. At the same time, practices drawn from so-called regressive musical institutions and commercial structures have typically been viewed as anathematic, a view that remained tenacious through the latter half of the twentieth century.[39]

In maintaining the flavor of rock's essential narrative, critics have not often considered rock products against the background of those generic and stylistic particulars that resonate within them. For example, "excess" (for most cultural critics) might suggest a useful model for critical analysis in the realm of melodrama, and that linkage might reveal that megasongs project something beyond the narcotic inducements of oversaturated and problematically rich acoustical surfaces. In any event, all listeners, regardless of metaphysical or political position, will recognize in "Bohemian Rhapsody" a high-calorie acoustical project. The song was the centerpiece of Queen's fourth album and their first to go platinum. Bearing a doubly referential title, A Night at the Opera, the production was at the time advertised as "the most expensive album ever made."[40] The range of acoustical effects produced by layering of just the essential ensemble is impressive; perhaps most so in the predominantly vocal track entitled "The Prophet's Song." However, despite the obvious and significant intervention of studio technicians in the final version of the album, the liner—representing Queen's own staking of the territory of mid-1970s authenticity as performers—proudly announces "no synthesizers"; the keyboard is identified, pointedly and impressively, as a Bechstein. That position was reiterated in their exclusion of the studio-enabled passages during live performances of the album's repertoire. The group may also have understood from earlier models, like Procol Harum's, that nothing at all might be preferable to a pale reflection.

Even in the face of its accumulation of text and music references (its most literally rhapsodic element), "Bohemian Rhapsody" hardly makes a significant case for the specific influence of opera on rock music in the mid-1970s. The distinction for meaningful influence belongs to Wagner, as channeled by Phil Spector over a decade earlier. Nor does the collection of sound objects in either "Bohemian Rhapsody" or the album add up to a "postmodern" bricolage, unless the Marx Brothers' translation of vaudeville to cinema are to be tagged with the same label.[41] Before considering the more familiar and celebrated vocal elements of the work, I would like to focus on that Bechstein, especially its presence as a member of the ensemble in the video presentation of the song, one of the first instances of rock multimedia and visual special effects brought to bear upon the representation of rock performance. In the video, solo and ensemble portions (in terms of vocal content) are visually separated into "naturalistic" concert scenes (that is, full body view with instruments visible) and abstracted representations of the group (the disembodied singing heads). These visual disjunctions don't really reflect structural discontinuity in the song (it is despite its sectional form a conceptually coherent opera scena); rather, they stem from the work's problematization of its own performance. Because there were some 180 overdubs in the middle ensemble section (usually called the "opera section"), "Bohemian Rhapsody" could never be performed live in its entirety. In concert—and Queen was one of the most successful arena bands in history—the overdubbed ensemble prologue was often omitted; during the studio-created middle section, the group, rather than engage in a lip-synch exercise, physically exited the stage while it played, returning to the live performance only when the musical focus shifts from the chorus to the guitar. The primary motivation for producing the video was to enable presentation of the full song on television, especially on Britain's *Top of the Pops* show.[42]

Costuming in the solo sections reveals the embryonic features that eventually turned—by the addition of yards of fabric, sequins, and feathers—into the more elaborate indicators of glam rock. These include the satin, Bowie-esque clothes, Freddie's black nail polish and eye make-up, and perhaps the camera's visual interest in the piano. Robert Walser has documented the denunciation by heavy metal musicians of the piano as a "gay" instrument that, along with make-up and costumes, denotes the performing arena of "glam fags."[43] The visual excess of seventies and eighties glam for either male or female performers, an Elton John or a Suzy Quattro, offended many rockers (though, interestingly, not many mainstream audiences). Such reaction sprang from glam's camp representations and, specifically, inversions of gender conventions (feathers, sequins, and large sunglasses for John, leather and artificial bruises for Quattro).[44] According to Walser's informants, real metal musicians (and by extension, real men) play guitars. John's and Quattro's musical gender identities are thus inverted by their association with the piano and electric guitar, respectively. The piano, most of all the curvaceous grand piano, is, of course, effeminate by virtue of its being a marker of musical register, and emblematic of the rarefied (or sissified) atmosphere of the concert hall (home to—I quote a long-standing graffito in my own university music building's stairwell—"music fags"). Mercury was aware of the meaningful weight of both instruments, electric guitar and concert grand, and one of the neatest musical gambits in the song is the way in

which, by its end, "Bohemian Rhapsody" has exposed and musically reconciled the two instruments and their respective registers.

The all-vocal prelude introduces vocality as a topos, as well as several
of the thematic threads of Freddie's "mock opera," as he called it. These
include "real life" and "reality" (pointing to late nineteenth- and early
twentieth-century verismo, one of the stylistic registers the music and
text invoke), high and low, and resignation (the notion that "nothing really matters"). In the live section that follows, the camera turns to Freddie's performance at the keyboard, shot from above to emphasize his
hand and arm movements. His morbid aria (in B♭) is underscored with
an accompanimental figure in which Freddie crosses his left hand over
his right to play the high register g-f octaves. The tonal environment as
well as the left-hand crossover to g''' must have been derived from Debussy's familiar piano *Rêverie* (mm. 76–81), a suitable complement to
the introspective and retrospective elements projected by the text and his
vocal nuance. Nonmusicians will associate such moves with virtuosity,
and especially with salon showpieces in which a musician is compelled
to cross over, transgressing pianistic norms. In Freddie's case, though, the
effect is of weightlessness, a marked contrast to the power chord representations of the male keyboard monsters discussed above. Mercury
wears small wings on his sleeve, linking him visually to Hermes and to
the idea of flight; this feeds the overall perception.

Freddie seems not to fit the mold of keyboard representation encountered in other mass media products, even if the register is clearly outside
the realm of rock norms. I have encountered one fascinating instance of
a similar scenario in the fragmentary remnants of one of the first gay-
themed films in cinema, Richard Oswald's *Anders als die Andern* (1919),
in which Conrad Veidt portrayed Paul Körner, a concert violinist being
blackmailed for his relationship with an admiring student. In one of their
lessons he accompanies the young man at the piano. Veidt's long tapered
fingers are emphasized by the jewelry he wears when at home. In their
first meeting he wears a rich-looking silk kimono. Almost as soon as he
starts to "play," Veidt's hands begin crossing with the same floating quality we witness in Freddie's hand and arm motions. While not entirely impossible that Freddie could have seen this (since the 1919 film, although
unavailable in its entirety, has for some time been subject to documentary excerpting), I prefer to read this correspondence more generally.

Since Veidt was straight and Mercury was not, a sociological perspective would attribute to the first a kind of effeminate miming and to
the latter something more authentic. That reading would not really co-

incide with Mercury's own commitment to defining his persona entirely through the act of staged performance. I think both scenes are enactments of expressivity. Each represents melodrama in its most literal sense. They reveal not the exaggerations of a stylized affect but reliance upon physical gesture to transmit expressive or expressionist content. Such reliance is part of the code of stage presentation shared by this early twentieth-century expressionist actor and this late twentieth-century arena rock star. Every gesture Mercury made on stage, whatever the corresponding affect, was amplified by the physical exaggeration of its component features, from the position of his lips to motion of his body through stage space.

OPERAS, OPERAS, OPERAS

Freddie Mercury never disclosed what the song was all about, proposing that everyone should read their own meaning into it.[45] According to the authorized report, he would say only that "it was a personal song, about relationships. He was never drawn any further."[46] While disingenuously distancing himself from his passion for opera when he maintained that "I certainly wasn't saying I was an opera fanatic," he admitted that "'Bohemian Rhapsody' didn't just come out of thin air. I did a bit of research." The title calls to mind those piano works that possessed such a presence for midcentury cinematic culture, but the replacement of the Hungarian by the Bohemian was perhaps a nod to Puccini. As one extended operatic scena marked by dramatic compactness, a melodramatic libretto, and abrupt changes of emotional tone, the song stands firmly in the "Cav and Pag" tradition. That Freddie's first solo is addressed to "Mama" suggests a model in Turiddu's farewell to Mamma Lucia in *Cavalleria Rusticana,* whose title significantly embodies the characteristic high and low registers associated with word types since the Middle Ages, the chivalric and rustic. *Pagliacci* shares with Richard Strauss's *Ariadne auf Naxos* the device of a pre-opera prologue, one that distorts the expectations of operatic fantasy and calls attention to the reality of the play's actors (recall the song's first lines: "Is this the real life? Is this just fantasy?"). Both operas also include the complication of an embedded commedia dell'arte troupe.

Strauss's *Harlequinade* is the operatic source for the Scaramouche of Freddie's song (Scaramuccio in the opera), an identification that will be corroborated by the music. He is the dancing master in the troupe who argues forcefully in favor of the lighter elements of the entertainment.[47]

But Scaramouche also plays a central role in a 1921 swashbuckling novel
(and its 1952 film version) by Rafael Sabatini. Both book and movie are
fascinating in their understated intersections with the conventions of
opera (particularly those involving mistaken identity and parentage) and
the liminal zone between real life and theatrical fantasy. Sabatini's *Scaramouche* shares a special mise-en-scène with the Marx Brothers' *A Night
at the Opera*, depicting the destruction of a theater ("The Fracas at the
Théâtre Feydau"). In Sabatini's story, Scaramouche is a late eighteenth-
century French aristocrat with libertarian sympathies and a mercurial
temperament, who eludes authorities by disguising himself as a member
of a traveling comic theater ensemble. In his first stage performance he
plays the twins Scaramouche and Figaro (the latter name is also registered within the operatic components of Mercury's song).

I have no way of knowing whether Freddie knew the book or the
movie (he was a fan of old Hollywood films), but we may recall that the
song about which he would say so little was about relationships and, for
him, a personal work. At the center of his personal conflicts was his difficult relationship with his parents, a key issue in Sabatini's *Scaramouche*, which climaxes when the title character, about to shoot his
mortal enemy, learns from the mother he desires yet despises that his
enemy is his biological father. Perhaps the shooting ("just killed a man")
that sets the aria portion of "Bohemian Rhapsody" in motion was part
of Freddie's oedipal fantasy. Crucial to Sabatini's novel is the title character's inability and unwillingness to reveal his true self to others; he is
an actor always hiding behind the words, histrionics, and smile of a
clown. The novel's opening, "He was born with a gift of laughter and a
sense that the world was mad," which served as epigraph for the MGM
film version, would have been extraordinarily congenial to Freddie.
Sabatini's Scaramouche regularly alludes to himself as a "mouthpiece"
for other voices, which is particularly significant in the context of "Bohemian Rhapsody" and its vocal collage.

Within "Bohemian Rhapsody" Richard Strauss supplies the principal
voice. *Ariadne auf Naxos*, like the Marxes' *Night at the Opera*, tells the
story of a planned serious opera production on a collision course with low-
register farce.[48] (Structurally, "Bohemian Rhapsody" resembles *Ariadne*'s
division into *Vorspiel* and *Oper*, while reflecting through its sectionalism
and, in the latter half of the work, increasing reliance upon normative hard
rock elements the conventional road map of rock megasongs like "Stairway to Heaven.") Strauss's skewed gender roles were likely also attractive
to Mercury, who identifies himself in part with the "pants role" of *Ari-*

adne's beleaguered "Komponist," the male composer played in the opera by a woman. Strauss's decision to assign that role (intended for a heroic tenor) to a soprano over the objections raised by his librettist, Hugo von Hofmannsthal, has been seen as evidence of Strauss's staking out an aesthetic position wherein musical issues bear greater weight than issues pertaining to sex differences or gendered realism.[49] In a sense, this perspective is realized in Mercury's one-sided (Scaramouchian) appropriation of all possible voices in the "mock opera" of "Bohemian Rhapsody."

Significantly, from the biographical perspective, *Ariadne* and *Salome* are the operas most identified with the object of Freddie's idolatrous diva worship, Montserrat Caballé, whom he eventually met and collaborated with, almost fifteen years later, on a peculiar hybrid album titled *Barcelona*. That sublime, ego-dissolving identification of the male gay fan with the female diva and her roles, now familiar from "neo-lyrical" opera criticism and queer studies, is particularly relevant to the creative equation here.[50] In "Bohemian Rhapsody" Freddie's voice serves as the instrument for Ariadne and, briefly (in the song's reference to stoning and denunciation), the iniquitous Salome, as well as *Il Trovatore*'s Leonora.[51] Indeed, one wonders whether the impetus for the entire "Bohemian Rhapsody" undertaking might have been Caballé's London appearances, the first as Leonora at Covent Garden, in the spring of 1975 (roughly six months before the song's release), which marked her return to the stage after three years' absence.[52]

These works and characters establish a thread of continuity in the song. To the extent that the song likely narrates Mercury's relationship with his musical identity, I think that the finale of *Ariadne auf Naxos,* a love scene between Ariadne and Bacchus, the beautiful young god, lies at the heart of "Bohemian Rhapsody." The scene, which is quoted rather extensively—but distortedly—throughout the song, may have provided Freddie with a double- or even three-sided aesthetic and emotional analogue. Ariadne, like so many heroines, seems fated throughout the opera for death (it is her idée fixe). Upon dying—she sings—her soul, like all others, will be blown along on the wind by Hermes, the messenger of Death, to the place where "nothing matters that mattered here," phrases and images that figure prominently in Mercury's text. Hermes in Roman mythology is, of course, known as Mercury, the name adopted by Freddie (Farookh) Bulsara around 1970.[53]

Ariadne's foil in the opera, Zerbinetta, suggests that someone else might show up first, a "pale dark-eyed youth" (Freddie wears a white outfit and black eyeliner in the video) who will transport her not with death

but with love. The beautiful young god, mistaken by Ariadne for "the messenger" (that is, for Hermes, or Mercury), is eventually revealed to be Bacchus, another deity with whom Freddie, in the 1984 video of the song "I
Want to Break Free," identified himself. In that video a box explodes open
to reveal members of the Royal Ballet in a heap, upon which sits Freddie
playing a role that conflates the piping god Pan (Faunus in some traditions)
with the wine-god Bacchus or Dionysus (including the grapes, one of the
iconographical attributes of the deity). The character in the video wears the
costume of the early twentieth-century high-register icon who stands as the
classic embodiment of "aesthetic androgyny," Vaslav Nijinsky as Mallarmé's faun.[54] Ballet was one of the musical activities that particularly interested Mercury, and he fancied himself something of a dancer; the video
of "I Want to Break Free" was choreographed by Wayne Eagling, a friend
of Freddie's and at the time a principal dancer with the Royal Ballet. The
ballet segment of the video may reference the birth of Dionysus as portrayed in the important 1969 avant-garde theater production by The Performance Group, *Dionysus in '69*, which would testify to the generic scope
of Queen's arsenal of potential cultural references.[55] If Freddie Mercury is
present in the finale of "Bohemian Rhapsody" as a protagonist, then he
lives therein a multifaceted sexual and artistic fantasy in which fictional,
real, or figurative lovers and beloveds. The divine Mercury or Bac-
chus=Dionysus, rock music, and Freddie comprise one stream and Ariadne or Caballé and opera the other. All are conjoined to the point of identity in a love that lies, safely and securely, just this side of the death
(corporeal or commercial).

The manipulation of musical material within this tour-de-force is extraordinarily clever, and participates in the song's gambits of ambiguity
and disorientation. As examples I would cite first the infamous and
abrupt opening of the middle chorus of "Bohemian Rhapsody" that follows the confusing and morbid solo aria. Marked by the sudden appearance of reiterated piano chords, this clearly reworks the intrusive appearance of Strauss's *buffa* Harlequinade characters, include the dancer
Scaramuccio, as they attempt to lift Ariadne's spirits following her *opera
seria* death fantasy, "Es gibt ein Reich." Their chorus, like that of "Bohemian Rhapsody," is initiated by two measures of repeated staccato
piano chords, a musical contrivance as striking in an opera as in a rock
megasong. Finally there is the sexy guitar material, mainly ascending
scales, some ornamented, that appear at several points in the song, mas-
querading as an authentic rock commonplace.[56]

Permeating the music of the last five to ten minutes of *Ariadne auf*

Naxos, surging ascents encapsulate the sometimes confused passion between Ariadne and Bacchus; first as Ariadne mistakes Bacchus for The-
seus, the lover who had abandoned her on Naxos ("loved her and left her
to die," as she will lament in Freddie's voice in the song), and then for
Hermes/Mercury, the messenger (who she expects will take her "right
outta there"). But the gesture registers most in Bacchus's music of desire
and consummation, during which he ecstatically proclaims Ariadne's effect on him in a recurring line with simultaneously divine and carnal implications: "Die Glieder reg' ich in göttlicher Lust" (in Queen's language,
"ooo, yeah; ooo, yeah").[57] Exceptional in this construction is not merely
the disguising of Strauss's expressive material as standard guitar riffs but
also the multiple transformations of Ariadne effected by Freddie's last
solo. Ariadne, an artificially high-toned *seria* diva in a mixed-register
opera, is imported to a rock song as a marker of something "a little
high," but she will express her most affective *seria* narration through
Freddie's voice in the guttural hard rock style he employs for the last section of the song, peppered with the lower-register interjections ("oh,
baby") characteristic of the genre. At the end of the song, just before the
final choral utterance, is a remarkably nuanced moment: a descending
scalar postlude (of relief or exhaustion) that ends with a delicate and
fleeting unison between guitar and piano as the two instruments and
their registers mark their own consummation.

Queen's sense of the conjunction of their work with cinema (in spirit
and through the idea of filming presentations of individual songs) is acknowledged at the conclusion of the "Bohemian Rhapsody" video,
when the drummer Roger Taylor, in a state of gladiatorial undress,
strikes a large gong, reenacting the trademark of such old J. Arthur Rank
films as the Marx Brothers' classic *Duck Soup.* When the song was translated to the screen (and I use that word here in the medieval ecclesiastical sense of the transportation of meaningful relics from one place to another) in *Wayne's World,* Strauss's sexual surging as reproduced by Brian
May's guitar under Freddie's direction was rendered concrete in the accompanying image: a great phallic obelisk of piled and impaled auto-
mobiles (the shot is matched to the "ooo, yeahs"). Perhaps the appropriateness of this "location" image was suggested to Spheeris by another
song on *A Night at the Opera,* Roger Taylor's suggestive anthem for boy
racers entitled "I'm in Love with My Car."

From the perspective of rock's new readings, the resurrection of "Bohemian Rhapsody" in *Wayne's World* provided yet another multimediated instance of postmodern irony, one that "denies the form of dialectic

and refuses resolution of any kind in order to retain the doubleness that is its identity."[58] Well, okay. But let's imagine for a moment that *Wayne's World* was a movie (maybe even a smart one) and not a text. And imagine that songs are mainly about the way they sound rather than about those who listen to them or where they hear them. Then perhaps "Bohemian Rhapsody" (song, video, film score, parodistic target) might be heard in all of its manifestations—some of which are likely yet to come—as a living thing, with Strauss and the others alive within.

Conclusion

Sitting Down with Mnemosyne

Most writers addressing the subject of high and low distinctions in art, media, and reception in the twentieth century have devoted some reflective space to the Marx Brothers' classic film *A Night at the Opera*. When the film was released in 1935, such distinctions were already recognized by purveyors (like the Marxes) and critics (like Gilbert Seldes) of mainstream, nonliterate media to reside less in musical objects themselves than in the institutions that patronize or present them. Those institutions, like patronage and presentation entities throughout recorded history, depend upon and nurture the industries of commerce and finance and are therefore viewed with suspicion by most outsiders. Money, as Aristotle had already warned in his *Politics,* must be treated with great care lest it topple the ethical architecture that lends stability and justice to the communities within which it circulates (whether in the groaning sacks of the few or the threadbare change purses of the many).

Queen's "Bohemian Rhapsody" was almost never launched, because its dimensions as a radio item seemed—in the eyes of rock's business sector—to exceed its potential returns. (That position was endemic to the business as far back as the Animals' "House of the Rising Sun.") It should come as no surprise, then, that the group's big album, *A Night at the Opera,* would call attention to the tensions between artist and management that has run through the history of vernacular media. This element of the album's concept, and one that rendered the Marx Brothers linkage especially meaningful, is clearly laid out in the song "Death on

Two Legs," reportedly aimed at the Trident group, the powerful corporation that gave the group their first recording contract and, as Freddie
Mercury was to put it, "ripped them off." The song's position at the head
of the record's contents, followed by the vaudevillian "Lazing on a Sunday Afternoon" (the adjective is Mercury's), located the frame for the
album within the same zone constructed by the Marxes in their *A Night
at the Opera,* in which one of the first comic insets was the famous "contract" scene (setting the terms of artistic management for the film's heroic
tenor), stitched into the cinema production from their popular stage act.[1]
Commerce remained prominent in their 1937 follow-up, *A Day at the
Races* (whose title was borrowed for Queen's next album); that film featured a similarly incremental structure in a sketch about money (the ice
cream vendor).

In a 1977 interview later released as a recording, Freddie addressed
matters relating to the band's performances, their work as producers,
and especially their having arrived at a point where they had come to understand contracts and the rock industry, topics he treated with directness and erudition.[2] And yet, when asked about anything related to musical or artistic concepts within songs and albums, his response was,
throughout, vague and circumlocutionary (a stance that echoed his invariable unwillingness to discuss the concept behind "Bohemian Rhapsody"). At one point, asked about the group's connection to the Marx
Brothers, especially in the case of *Night at the Opera,* he said the title was
chosen only because he loved their movies. Rather than linking the title
directly and firmly to the album by way of the opera concept, he said that
the group thought the title would be "okay" since there were some opera
elements in the album. In other words, the Marx Brothers film—
according to him—directly inspired the title of the album but not by way
of how the film represented opera per se.

In that same interview Mercury linked both "Lazing on a Sunday Afternoon" and "Seaside Rendezvous" specifically to vaudeville, suggesting that the Marx Brothers' characteristic stylistic mix—realized in most
of their films either through musical content or through the insertion of
stage bits into a linear filmic plot—was perhaps part of the project's conceptual frame. Although Mercury did not address this link specifically,
his admiration for the details of their work suggests to me that it was primarily the theme of art and commerce that prompted the association in
Freddie's mind, particularly since the first two numbers on the album (the
first critiquing the business practices associated with artistic management
contracts, the second a bit of pure music hall vaudeville) are Marxian,

not operatic. The opener, "Death on Two Legs," is—even judged according to the expectations of big rock—acoustically big and, especially in its stylistic range, which encompasses sheer mass and some exoticism, "excessive." "Death" is essentially a musical melodrama (with extended "orchestral" insertions), and Freddie's eruptive "kiss my ass good-bye!" acousmatic melodramatic *feu*.

While the Marx films are pure comedy or musical comedy according to standard film-genre terminology, their spirit was fundamentally melodramatic. The fissure between high and low society, not high and low art, is at the core of the Marxes' perspective. The social distinction, however, was manifested most obviously in art's promulgation and reception, which provided an easy target for caricature, and its representation a useful vehicle for expressive communication. *A Night at the Opera* sets out an easily digested dualism between vocal numbers in the popular or musical-theater style and the supposedly rigid, score-bound music of institutionalized opera. Within the popular style there are specific gestures toward the ethnic, most famously in the Italianate steerage scene in which Chico and Harpo join in a musical and gustatory celebration with a large group of immigrants. From the knowledgeable perspective of a Groucho Marx or Gilbert Seldes, this served perhaps as a reminder of opera's status in New York: opera was, however well-heeled its patrons, an immigrant musical culture. More revealing of the film's social critique (its ethical perspective as melodrama) are the scenic and shot elements of that famous steerage sequence.

On the one hand, these elements—like most of the nonoperatic musical items in the film—seem sentimental or nostalgic (for the Old World) in the general sense of that word. But the close-up shot of the old *nonna*'s face is a melodramatic gesture in the Hurstian mode: her creases and folds reflect all the stories about her that the screenplay fails to deliver (these are left to the imagination of the audience). As a meaningful moment within a media complex she is no less a figural "type" than the similarly framed faces stitched into Sergei Eisenstein's montage in the Odessa step sequence in *Battleship Potemkin*. Made about a decade earlier, *Potemkin*, which in the late 1920s in Europe enjoyed a brief and influential circulation among cinema insiders, was similarly melodramatic. In this film Eisenstein linked the melodramatic theme of sacrifice to a message of social change by means of exaggerated gesturalism. Academic viewers analyzing the Marxes' steerage sequence will most likely find in its giddy tarantella and ethnic typing remnants of a particularly Romantic sensibility (that is, the nineteenth-century sentimental) as manifested in nineteenth-century pastoral landscape art or literary representations of Italy's intoxicating social "naturalism" in writings ranging from Berlioz and James (especially the James of *Roderick Hudson*) to Forster's *A Room With a View*. (Although James, and the proliferation of exaggerated verbal gesture that characterized his scenarios, could be melodramatic in a more specific way.)

Within the imagery of cinema, however, no two sequences share quite as many features as do Eisenstein's depiction of the bringing of food to the sailors in *Potemkin* (which precedes the massacre on the Odessa steps) and the piling on of food (to the delight of Chico and Harpo) by the Italian immigrants in steerage in *A Night at the Opera*. Both address starvation with a brightly lit procession of happy abundance. In both cases the magnitude of that abundance is exaggerated by camera work, by a linear sense of temporal progress (toward the boat, or along the buffet table), and by the crowded mise-en-scène in general. And in both, abundance and its provision arising from a communal sense of domestic ethics have been linked to a geographically, ethnically circumscribed, and—at least as they are represented on screen—essentially apolitical social aggregation. The true foil for the grand celebration in steerage (and its associated Old World resonances) was not the scene being played out in the salons above (of restaurant food and snotty posturings by the tenor Lassparri). For many of those represented in stereotype on the screen the foil would be their own disillusion and poverty (the status of the iconic immigrant, the pauper Chico, who combined the real ethnicity of the Jew with the shtick of Italianicity), a condition realized only after disgorgement in New York, the dark place beyond the borders of the comedic screen and the domain that inspired so much of Hurstian melodrama.[3]

Coincidentally, when Gregory Ulmers wrote of Roland Barthes's interest in the Marx Brothers films, especially *A Night at the Opera*, as texts whose semantic bits add up to (as Barthes had characterized them) "delirious polysemy," he called the battleship backdrop that clunks down behind Lassparri during his interrupted performance of *Il Trovatore* "the battleship Potemkin."[4] This was, of course, a nod to Barthes's analysis of meaning in the visual imagery of Eisenstein's film in *Image-Music-Text*. And yet, the offhand formulation may have been right on the mark. In fact, the image that precedes the battleship in that notorious parade of deconstructive backdrops depicts a city fruit vendor's cart, something that throughout the Marx ouevre is associated with the industry of immigrant culture and especially with Chico, the Marx with the Italian accent, the Marx with Italianicity. This overflowing barrow of fruits and vegetables, abruptly cut off from sight by the battleship, projects at the end a fleeting and lasting image of the film's commentary; the message is sent by means of a visual collision of dislocated images, an Eisensteinian device if ever there was one.

Throughout the 1977 interview with Mercury, the singer invoked the word "perfect" to refer to Queen's aspirations on stage and especially in recordings. It is a noticeable and recurrent trope. The only other context for that word in his discourse: the Marx Brothers. They are, he said, meticulous, and the details of their comic representations are "perfect." Had the interview been conducted six months later than it was, I would have guessed that he knew Barthes's understanding that the "perfect book" (a notion developed in his student days) would be one that reflected the doubleness of perfect parody and the subversiveness of the perfect gag.[5]

Pasadena "dame" Margaret Dumont is the spur for many of the best comedic insets in the Marxes' films, even when she is not visible on screen. The comedic business of Chico and Harpo often comes in response to some situational prompt that can be traced back to Groucho's insinuation into the activities of Dumont or her circle. This lent a new frame to the comic bits they had already honed in their stage act. Comedic action, once removed from the sketch aesthetic of vaudeville and placed within the continuity aesthetic of film, requires some filmic representation of inspiration or motivational source. Groucho of course doesn't often clown or laugh like Harpo; he is too busy either wooing or abusing Dumont and others, thus providing a good deal of the essential setting up. Harpo is often clownish and (unlike Chico) childish, but he is at the same time sexually driven; he is a paradoxically erotic child. This aspect—conjoined to his cherubic presentational mode, especially his crown of blond ringlets—recalls Eros himself. But his "attribute," the harp, places him, within the mythemic registers of the Marx Brothers' films, closer to the muse Erato. She (the pronoun is a small matter, since Harpo's gender is often a site of representational play, especially in *A Night at the Opera*), governs the sphere in which the penetrations of Eros intersect with the playing of the lyre. Groucho is the only figure in the films with the capacity to interact with characters in every social and conceptual stratum, set actions in motion, and engage in the pursuit of women of high degree. In these activities, and in his tendency to end up in hot water for it, he is not unlike Zeus. But where does Dumont fit into such a classical cosmology? Her money—and the institutions it represents—drives most of the brothers' actions (particularly Groucho's and Chico's). However remote from the playing field of the screen, the money ultimately serves as their inspiration, and if Harpo's representational aspects revisit the allegory of the muses, the plus-sized Dumont can only be Mnemosyne, their titan mother by way of a brief fling with Zeus.

Her money sets the mythographic plots in motion but it is her insistence on looking back (culturally and aesthetically) that marks her primarily as the guardian of memory. Her presence is fundamental since, as the stylistic melange throughout the cycle suggests, contemplation of the past is the prerequisite for real social or aesthetic progress. Mnemosyne is not postmodern, and her gifts add up to much more than a grim parade of unpleasantly spectral "revenants."[6] Unlike most academic discourse, postmodern critique, or modernist manifesto, at the heart of the Marxes' Olympian enterprise is the recognition of humanity's need to laugh. This is Groucho's sacrifice to Erato and to those of us who will watch Erato laugh. Pausanias, in the ninth book of his second-century travel guide to the regions of Greece, described a special ritual practiced in the birthplace of the muses in Boeotia:

> He [the supplicant] is taken by the priests, not at once to the oracle, but to fountains of water very near to each other. Here he must drink water called the water of Lethe (Forgetfulness), that he may forget all that he has been thinking of hitherto, and afterwards he drinks of another water, the water of Mnemosyne (Memory), which causes him to remember what he sees after his descent . . . After his ascent from [the oracle of] Trophonios the inquirer is again taken in hand by the priests, who set him upon a chair called the chair of Mnemosyne (Memory), which stands not far from the shrine, and they ask of him, when seated there, all he has seen or learned. After gaining this information they then entrust him to his relatives. These lift him, paralysed with terror and unconscious both of himself and of his surroundings, and carry him to the building where he lodged before with Tykhe (Fortune) and the Daimon Agathon (Good Spirit). Afterwards, however, he will recover all his faculties, and the power to laugh will return to him.

Freddie Mercury loved to laugh; Groucho pretended not to. Norman Bates smiled rather a lot. All of them, and their modes of expression, are reminders that programs for social change may proceed without precise artistic corollaries (like Eisler's chord of ten notes or Eisenstein's collisions). They suggest that to recall in speech, gesture, image, or song the practices of the past may be to inspire future progressive acts, and that no two acts of expression—however similar or clichéd their surfaces— are likely to be identical, particularly in the eyes and ears of those most implicated in their substance. To remember without apology was part of the creed for the mainstream vernacular media in the twentieth century. To forget that one has remembered, to render remembrance immediate, was the process that brought imagination to bear upon aesthetic recall. Viewed from the position of these works, Norman and Groucho had more than a little in common with each other. They profited by listening for that inspiring breath they felt emanate from Mnemosyne's bosom. Dumont never sang an aria on screen, and no one other than Norman ever heard Mrs. Bates speak for more than a few seconds at a time. No matter, since the classics are of limited use as hermetic, uninflected wholes. They rely for their very existence—as Aulus Gellius sensed from the start—upon their lively circulation as fragmentary mnemosynic iterations.

EPILOGUE: PLAYING THE CLASSICS

Daisuke Ishiwatari is a video game designer whose works are enlivened by cultural reference: names of characters, and their associated powers and attributes, reflect those names and works among twentieth-century media products—especially heavy metal music—that Ishiwatari most values. In the highest register of his notable sources is Queen, his favorite group. *Guilty Gear,* designed by Ishiwatari and Arc System Works, was the original offering in what has grown into a series of fighting games with anime graphics now subsumed under that name as general rubric. Released for Sony PlayStation in 1998, the diegetic background for the game's actions is a world in which mankind fights against killer machines (Gear). Among the valiant is Sol Badguy, whose "real" name is Frederick (referencing Freddie's full name); "Badguy" is drawn from one of Mercury's solo recordings. Among these powerful characters there is one who possesses a special, instant-kill move. His finishing move is named "Magnum Opera," for *A Night at the Opera.* His name is Potemkin.

No trail of logic could force this bit of present-day trivia into sensible alignment with the objects bearing the same names that I discussed in the main body of this conclusion. Unlike the webs of reference that have rendered the Marx Brothers so meaningful for so many, and the music of Queen so enriching for some, this particular relationship is nothing more than an amusing coincidence now lodged in my text as a gesture, contrived from a crossing of threads. And yet its invocation sounds potentially meaningful because we have just encountered (read, heard) those words in a different environment wherein their linkage was "legitimized" by a formal frame, the structure of an academic argument. Within the multimedia frame of *Guilty Gear,* what matters is that these characters possess elements of (literal) resonance borrowed from the sound of the words from media's past that Ishiwatari has attached to them.[7] His characters and their diegetic territories move as independent agents (at least within the rules of the games), in the vernacular style of other anime warriors of the early twenty-first century: Potemkin is not fettered by Eisenstein, Barthes, or the semic implications of the tag he bears. But cloaked in a sound track that reflects the now classic heavy metal mode of musical expressionism, these fighters might well form the substance of some future analysis. Eventually it will be time to address the newer vernacular and the next phase of Aulus Gellius's experiment in collecting, disassembling, and reimagining.

Notes

INTRODUCTION

1. Julian Johnson, *Who Needs Classical Music? Cultural Choice and Musical Value* (Oxford: Oxford University Press, 2002).

2. Ibid., 102–3, 114–30.

3. Ibid., 114. The author seems to have in mind not only simplicity and repetition within individual musical objects but also the unfortunate tendency (in his estimation) for modern media—e.g., film and television—to borrow past languages that are not their own, that are not "modern." Johnson's think piece provides no specific footnote references, but Frith considers *stupidity* as a critical category for pop consumers in *Performing Rites: On the Value of Popular Music* (Cambridge, MA: Harvard University Press, 1996), 72.

4. Methodological agendas drawn from the model of sociological research were evident from the early years of the first serious journal devoted to the then new sector of the discipline, *Popular Music*. See especially volume 2 (1982), subtitled *Theory and Method*, in which Richard Middleton distanced popular music scholarship from the musicology mainstream in no uncertain terms in his editorial introduction: "This is not a musicology journal" (p. 1). Popular music study came to constitute the whitecap on the grand wave of the "new musicology" of the mid- to late 1980s, but its disciplinary skew toward the models provided by academic sociology had been inscribed several years earlier. On the flexibility of Middleton's perspective, however, see note 9, this chapter. Compare also Adam Krims, *Rap Music and the Poetics of Identity* (Cambridge: Cambridge University Press, 2000), 18–20.

5. For example, many of the points advanced by Timothy D. Taylor regarding musical style, genre, and cultural positioning with respect to several mass-media repertoires in *Strange Sounds: Music, Technology, and Culture* (New York: Routledge, 2001) hinge on the citation of reports stemming from unidentified or

noncontextualized informants and from postings to Internet bulletin boards whose influence within the groups they appear to serve is not always apparent from the author's text.

6. Nicholas Cook, *Analysing Musical Multimedia* (Oxford: Clarendon Press, 1998).

7. The image I have employed here is associated with the first attack on Melanie in *The Birds* as it was characterized by Gilles Deleuze, *Cinema 1: The Movement-Image*, trans. Hugh Tomlinson and Barbara Habberjam (Minneapolis: University of Minnesota Press, 1986), 204. For an example of the effect of these expository interruptions on critical discourse, see Bernard Gendron, *Between Montmartre and the Mudd Club: Popular Music and the Avant-Garde* (Chicago: University of Chicago Press, 2002), 15.

8. The most influential and wide-ranging studies of the medieval representation of memory processes and their link to creative enterprises are Mary Carruthers, *The Book of Memory: A Study in Medieval Culture* (Cambridge: Cambridge University Press, 1990), and Frances A. Yates, *The Art of Memory* (London: Routledge and Kegan Paul, 1966). Anna Maria Busse Berger, *Medieval Music and the Art of Memory* (Berkeley: University of California Press, 2005), 3–4, provides a succinct overview of scholarship in this area.

9. See Richard Middleton, *Studying Popular Music* (Philadelphia: Open University Press, 1990), 103–26, and the conclusion to his introductory essay to *Popular Music* 2, cited in note 4, in which he posited a musicology in which "Beethoven and popular music will require the same analytical methods" (p. 8). See also John Covach, "Popular Music, Unpopular Musicology," in *Rethinking Music,* ed. Nicholas Cook and Mark Everist (Oxford: Oxford University Press, 1999), 452–70, esp. 460–63. In the same volume, cf. the remarks by Ralph Locke, "Musicology and/as Social Concern: Imagining the Relevant Musicologist," 499–530, esp. 500–501. Allan F. Moore, *Rock: The Primary Text: Developing a Musicology of Rock* (Buckingham, PA: Open University Press, 1993), 7–15, outlined arguments on behalf of the specificity required by a musicology of popular music. Most academic scholars of popular music and of film music have operated within the perimeters of sometimes ideologically but nearly always repertorially specialized and circumscribed domains.

10. For a classic example of this tendency, see Susan Sontag's "Notes on Camp" in *Against Interpretation and Other Essays* (New York: Picador USA, 2001), 275–92. Sontag staked out an unusual position of positive evaluation: "Jews and homosexuals are the outstanding creative minorities in contemporary urban culture . . . they are creators of sensibilities. The two pioneering forces of modern sensibility are Jewish moral seriousness and homosexual aestheticism and irony" (p. 290). But still, within the discourse of the essay, Sontag positioned each sensibility against the background of the sociological aggregation or, in the case of gays, the "class."

11. Cited in Carl Dahlhaus, *Realism in Nineteenth-Century Music*, trans. Mary Whittall (Cambridge: Cambridge University Press, 1985), 112.

I. THE EXPRESSIVE VERNACULAR

1. I first explored this point in "Is This the Real Life? Rock Classics and Other Inversions" (colloquium paper read at University of California (UC) Berkeley, UC Davis, and Stanford University, April 1998, and at Columbia University and the CUNY Graduate Center, February 1999).

2. See, for example, Paul Zumthor, *Essai de poétique médiévale* (Paris: Éditions du Seuil, 1972), 250.

3. Historical musicologists have been drawn to linguistic theory, with an emphasis on semantics, more than to the kind of linguistic criticism discussed later in this chapter, even if there are points of intersection. For an excellent example of the viability of linguistic approaches to musical gesture from the perspective of linguistic "meaning," see Mauro Calcagno, "'Imitar col canto chi parla': Monteverdi and the Creation of a Language for Musical Theater," *Journal of the American Musicological Society* 55 (2002): 383–431.

4. Lacan, for example, introduced the term *registre* as a synonym for *ordre*, the latter appearing regularly throughout the *Écrits* (Paris: Editions du Seuil, 1966). The symbolic register or order is the structure of language, whence (perhaps) originated Paul Zumthor's adoption of the term. See also Lawrence Kramer, *Classical Music and Postmodern Knowledge* (Berkeley: University of California Press, 1995), 12–13.

5. Zumthor, *Essai de poétique médiévale*, 250. *Expressive* is intended in two senses: expressive *of* some affect usually related to genre, and in the sense that such phonemic constructions *express* or reveal their intended register.

6. A meaningful theoretical correlation between text, music, and performance style is revealed in the fourteenth-century *Leys d'Amors,* discussed in Christopher Page, *Voices and Instruments of the Middle Ages: Instrumental Practice and Songs in France, 1100–1300* (London: J. M. Dent and Sons Ltd., 1987), 42–46.

7. Dante, *De vulgari eloquentia,* ed. Pier Ricci (Florence: F. Le Monnier, 1968), 228. An interesting correlation between bilabial words, memory, and preliteracy is remarked on by Christopher Collins in *Reading the Written Image: Verbal Play, Interpretation, and the Roots of Iconophobia* (University Park: Pennsylvania State University Press, 1991); he suggests (p. 8) that the connection may be traced back to pre-Christian languages.

8. There are others, of course, such as the vocalization "oo," which figures prominently in any number of songs, sometimes in combination with expressive bilabials like "oo, baby." In later rock these play interesting roles in Led Zeppelin's "Stairway to Heaven" and Queen's "Bohemian Rhapsody" in light of the rather complex prevailing registers of each.

9. Consider, for example, the multiple negatives, circular rhyme scheme, and concept terms (*de trobar sabensa:* knowledge of making poetry) in Guiraut Riquier's late thirteenth-century "La redonda," or the elaborate and bizarre wordplay of Arnaut Daniel's *trobar clus* in "Lo ferm voler," which relies on acoustically related nonpoetical word sounds ("uncle," "fingernail") that deliberately distort the expected register, a phenomenon encountered in several of the popular songs discussed in this book. By comparison, pastoral lyric was registered

by simple-sounding nominative terms (caps, cloaks, belts), and singsong nonsense syllables (*hureliva, heuva, dondon,* etc.). See, for example, the poems collected in *The Medieval Pastourelle,* ed. and trans. William D. Paden, 2 vols. (New York: Garland Publishing, 1987).

10. Queen's "Bohemian Rhapsody" (see chapter 7) includes not only an extensive catalog of polysyllables—one of Dante's criteria for elevated discourse—but also words borrowed from outside the vernacular ("Figaro," "Magnifico," "Beelzebub," etc). Freddie Mercury's use of imprecise vocalic rhyme (Magnifico / Galileo / Let him go) and reiterations of the same sound as a monosyllable (No, no, no . . .) even recall the circularity of these early European high-register lyrics.

11. Compare also the opening of their "Barbara Ann" (1962), later a hit for the Beach Boys.

12. Charles A. Ferguson, "Dialect, Register, and Genre: Working Assumptions about Conventionalization," in *Sociolinguistic Perspectives on Register,* ed. Douglas Biber and Edward Finegan (New York: Oxford University Press, 1994), 20.

13. M. A. K. Halliday's remark in *Language as Social Semiotic* (1978) is cited by Lance St. John Butler in *Registering the Difference: Reading Literature through Register* (Manchester: Manchester University Press, 1999), 46. Ferguson also considers the development of register variation in groups and the formation of dialect to be parallel operations within different linguistic spheres; see "Dialect, Register, and Genre," 20.

14. T. B. W. Reid, "Linguistics, Structuralism, and Philology," *Archivum linguisticum* 8 (1956): 28–37, esp. 32.

15. M. A. K. Halliday, A. MacIntosh, and P. Stevens, *The Linguistic Sciences and Language Teaching* (London: Longman, 1964), 93–94.

16. See, for example, Diana Knight, "Roland Barthes: An Intertextual Figure," in *Intertextuality: Theories and Practices,* ed. Michael Worton and Judith Still (Manchester: Manchester University Press, 1990), 92–107, and the introduction to the same volume, esp. 22–23. Clair Wills warns—wisely, I think—against invoking notions of Bakhtin's carnivalesque in situations with no essential link to the essential structure of societies, and this is assuredly the case for concert music of any genre, along with repertoires intended for electronic reproduction. See her "Upsetting the Public: Carnival, Hysteria, and Women's Texts," in *Bakhtin and Cultural Theory,* ed. Ken Hirschkop and David Shepherd (Manchester: Manchester University Press, 1989), 130–51.

17. Andrew Ross, *No Respect: Intellectuals and Popular Culture* (New York: Routledge, 1989), 152. Cf. Sontag, "Notes on Camp."

18. Leonard B. Meyer, *Music, the Arts, and Ideas* (1967), cited in Frank Kermode, *The Classic: Literary Images of Permanence and Change* (Cambridge, MA: Harvard University Press, 1975; repr. 1983), 119.

19. Ibid. Discussing the opening of *Wuthering Heights,* Kermode writes: "Such a system [of genre expectations triggered by encoded elements] could . . . be thought of as constituting some sort of contract between reader and writer."

20. I borrow the term contrafact in this sense from James Patrick, "Charlie Parker and Harmonic Sources of Bebop Composition: Thoughts on the Repertory of Jazz in the 1940s," *Journal of Jazz Studies* 2 (1975): 3–23.

21. See, for example, *Fernando the Flute: Analysis of Musical Meaning in an Abba Mega-hit,* 3rd ed. (New York: Mass Media Musicologists' Press, 2001), 15–17. A similar blend of semiology and sociology has been invoked to systematize the components of imaginary acoustical space in Peter Doyle, *Echo and Reverb: Fabricating Space in Popular Music Recording 1900–1960* (Middletown, CT: Wesleyan University Press, 2005), 10–37.

22. Tia DeNora, *After Adorno: Rethinking Music Sociology* (Cambridge: Cambridge University Press, 2003), 104.

23. S. Royal Brown, *Overtones and Undertones: Reading Film Music* (Berkeley: University of California Press, 1994). Brown (41), for example, follows Barthes's semiotics of multimedia (from *Image-Music-Text* of 1977), attributing "nativicity" to the Skull Island music in King Kong, invoking Barthes's famous discussion of "Italianicity" in food advertising. A semiotic approach more strictly in line with the principles of Charles S. Peirce is outlined in Juraj Lexmann, *Theory of Film Music* (Frankfurt: Peter Lang, 2006), esp. 41–45.

24. For the principal approaches to the framing of film-music criticism, see Claudia Gorbman, *Unheard Melodies: Narrative Film Music* (Bloomington: Indiana University Press, 1987), chapters 1–4, and "Film Music," in *Film Studies: Critical Approaches,* ed. John Hill and Pamela Church Gibson (Oxford: Oxford University Press, 2000), 41–48; Caryl Flinn, *Strains of Utopia: Gender, Nostalgia, and Hollywood Film Music* (Princeton, NJ: Princeton University Press, 1992), chapters 1–2; Brown, *Overtones and Undertones,* Introduction and chapter 1. All of these writers address additional matters (narratology, psychology of gender, semiotics, etc.), but the location and description of "meaning" remains the central occupation of film criticism. This is apparent most recently in the introduction to *Beyond the Soundtrack: Representing Music in Cinema,* ed. Daniel Goldmark, Lawrence Kramer, and Richard Leppert (Berkeley: University of California Press, 2007), esp. 6–7. See also Kramer's analysis of the "new vein of meaning" that emerges from the attachment of Schubert's D-Minor String Quartet to Jane Campion's 1996 film *Portrait of a Lady* in *Musical Meaning: Toward a Critical History* (Berkeley: University of California Press, 2002), 154–55.

25. See Butler, *Registering the Difference,* 30. Colin MacCabe has invoked register in considering items that blend literary and nonwritten culture (e.g., Shakespeare's plays). For MacCabe, the significance of register lies in its role in the linguistic enactment of ideological conflict. *The Eloquence of the Vulgar: Language, Cinema, and the Politics of Culture* (London: British Film Institute, 1999), 45–86. His book's title plays with Dante's *De vulgari eloquentia,* of course, subverting Dante through the specific evaluative connotations of the English cognate "vulgar."

26. More recently, Giorgio Biancorosso has explored "mundane" music in several films—trivial music defined by its social or utilitarian function—by conjoining sociological perspectives and a view of narrative ("the *experience* of narrative in general") that proceeds from a critical gloss of Barthes. He nevertheless assigns to these instances a function and "meaning" enhanced by the music's "strategic placement within a cinematic narrative." See his "Film, Music and the Redemption of the Mundane," in *Bad Music: The Music We Love to Hate,*

ed. Christopher Washburne and Maiken Derno (New York: Routledge, 2004), 190–211, esp. 192–93.

27. See, e.g., Robynn J. Stilwell, "The Fantastical Gap between Diegetic and Non-Diegetic," in *Beyond the Soundtrack*, ed. Goldmark et al., 184–202.

28. Rick Altman with McGraw Jones and Sonia Tatroe, "Inventing the Cinema Soundtrack: Hollywood's Multiplane Sound System," in *Music and Cinema*, ed. James Buhler, Caryl Flinn, and David Neumeyer (Hanover, NH: University Press of New England, 2000), 339–59.

29. From the *Riverside Press* (13 November, 1942), cited in Kate Daubney, *Max Steiner's "Now Voyager": A Film Score Guide* (Westport, CT: Greenwood Press, 2000), 83.

30. Ibid.

31. Daubney's characterization refers to the "conventions of nineteenth-century Romantic music," a generalization that is standard currency in discussions of the "narrative" film score of the period.

32. Tagg, in fact, points to this as a significant characteristic of the ways in which musemes participate in connoting meaning in individual works, but his analytical apparatus and terminology point to a more fixed understanding of works as texts.

33. On the notion of the "demark," see Gilles Deleuze, *Cinema 1: The Movement-Image*, trans. Hugh Tomlinson and Barbara Habberjam (Minneapolis: University of Minnesota Press, 1986), 203. Regarding the term "middlebrow" as applied to film music, see Gorbman, "Film Studies," 41. The concept of this *culture moyenne* and its implication for consumption of media product are treated extensively in Pierre Bourdieu, *Distinction: A Social Critique of the Judgement of Taste*, trans. Richard Nice (Cambridge, MA: Harvard University Press, 1984), esp. 323–31.

34. Steven Feld, "From Schizophonia to Schismogenesis: On the Discourses and Commodification Practices of 'World Music' and 'World Beat,'" in Charles Keil and Steven Feld, *Music Grooves: Essays and Dialogues* (Chicago: University of Chicago Press, 1994), 257.

35. Although "register" was introduced as a nominative in sociolinguistic theory, it eventually, through the common forces of language transformation, appeared as a verb of process. As a variety of transformation, the expansion of register to the "active" realm reflects particular features of the "home" register in which "register" was first introduced: the "scientific-theoretical." Reminiscent of the transmutation of the *brevis altera* in medieval modal notation theory to the *brevis alterata* (and to "alteration" as a process), such transformations appear to be a special feature of scientific registers and of the "pseudo-scientific" registers that mimic them, for example that of corporate administration in which "impact" was, during the last quarter of the twentieth century, reregistrated as an active, transitive verb with a quite specific registral flavor. The notion of "reregistration" was introduced by R. A. Carter and W. Nash, "Language and Literariness," *Prose Studies* 6 (1983): 123–41.

36. On "cinematic" music, see, e.g., Simon Frith, *Performing Rites*, 122. I employ the term "cinematic" for music that compels the listener to engage in acts of "envisioning" some accompanying diegesis or as a series of images.

37. Movie theater topography and seating imposes upon the listener the kind of straitjacket that fosters anticipation and focus familiar to denizens of the concert hall, in which the most obvious, noninterpretative acts of nonanalytical hearing, that is bodily motion and vocalizing along with the music, are discouraged or impossible. Compare Frith's useful notion of "ideologies of listening," *Performing Rites,* 142–43.

38. Adorno and Eisler had suggested that the ability for the uninitiated listener to recognize meaning-values through timbre (tone color) marked it as trivial, further testimony to the importance of a model for meaning based in scripture, with its surface-essence distinction. Theodor W. Adorno and Hanns Eisler, *Composing for the Films* (London: Athlone Press, 1994), 13, 106–7.

39. I borrow the expression from Claudia Gorbman's citation of David Neumeyer's analysis of Max Steiner's score for *Casablanca;* Gorbman, "Film Music," 47.

40. Reuven Tsur, *What Makes Sound Patterns Expressive? The Poetic Mode of Speech Reception* (Durham, NC: Duke University Press, 1992), 105–10.

41. Aaron Copland, "Second Thoughts on Hollywood," and Paul Bowles, "On the Film Front," *Modern Music* 17 (1940): 141–47, 184–87. I am grateful to Beth Levy for bringing Bowles's column to my attention.

42. Ibid., 142.

43. Ibid., 187.

44. What I am suggesting here intersects, at least in its general terms, with arguments advanced in a very different context by Carolyn Abbate in her provocative and compelling discussion of musical *tombeaux* in "Outside Ravel's Tomb," *Journal of the American Musicological Society* 52 (1999): 465–530, especially those she associates with twentieth-century modernism, that reveled in the precious combative or accommodative discourse between natural and mechanical musical objects or sources (see esp. p. 473). The situation is more complex, or perhaps merely different, in the case of most works that I have suggested operate within these aspects of the register of the classic, since these works exist only as items intended for mechanical reproduction in the first place; films and pop recordings are bloodless reanimations as they are consumed. In most cases, the reanimation of "dead" referents does not function as a "topos" within the discourse of the work itself (outside the domain of "mad science" discussed in the second part of this book), and often the issue is "reincarnation" rather than reanimation. It is not, moreover, the business of such works to comment within themselves on the nature (aesthetic, historical or thematic) of their "distance" from the referents brought into play.

45. *Literary Criticism of Sainte-Beuve,* trans. and ed. Emerson R. Marks (Lincoln: University of Nebraska Press, 1971), 97. Dante intended the same thing by the word "poet." In the fourteenth century, prior to the intervention of Dante and such literary ideological heirs as Machaut and Chaucer, it was only applied to the real "classics," that is, ancient poets like Cicero.

46. "What Is a Classic?" in *T. S. Eliot: On Poetry and Poets* (New York: Octagon Books, 1975), 52–74. Frank Kermode, *The Classic* (Cambridge, MA: Harvard University Press, 1975; repr. 1983), 16–17.

47. As Robert Ray characterizes him, drawing an analogy between Eisenstein's and Eliot's theory-practice: "T. S. Eliot—the artist-critic whose writings create the taste by which his own aesthetic practice is judged." See Robert Ray, "Impressionism, Surrealism, Film Theory," in *Film Studies: Critical Approaches*, ed. John Hill and Pamela Church Gibson (Oxford: Oxford University Press, 2000), 66.

48. *The Groucho Letters: Letters From and To Groucho Marx* (New York: Da Capo Press, 1994), 161 (emphasis added).

49. "The Social Function of Poetry," in *T. S. Eliot: On Poetry and Poets*, 14.

50. See, for example, Martin Miller Marks, *Music and the Silent Film: Contexts and Case Studies 1895–1924* (New York: Oxford University Press, 1997).

51. Hans Erdmann and Giuseppe Becce, *Allgemeines Handbuch der Film-Musik*, 2 vols. (Berlin and Leipzig: Schlesinger'sche Buch-u. Musikhandlung, 1927).

52. I refer to the systematic "database" of all extant versions of early polyphonic music, organized and indexed as a nested matrix: Friedrich Ludwig, *Repertorium organorum et motetorum vetustissimi stili* (Halle: M. Niemeyer, 1910).

53. Erdmann, *Allgemeines Handbuch*, 1:63.

54. As Martin Marks points out, with sound-synchronization just a few years away, the *Allgemeines Handbuch* "was published too late in the day to have much impact"; see his *Music and the Silent Film: Contexts and Case Studies, 1895–1924* (Oxford: Oxford University Press, 1997), 11. Roy M. Prendergast's dismissal of Erdmann's handbook as "pigeonholing" does not do justice to the theoretical scope of the undertaking. Roy M. Prendergast, *Film Music: A Neglected Art*, 2nd ed. (New York: W. W. Norton, 1992), 6–7. Prendergast's citation of Kurt London, *Film Music*, trans. Eric S. Bensinger (New York: Arno Press, 1970), suggests that he had not seen the *Handbuch* himself. Compare also Max Winkler's cynical memoir quoted in Frith, *Performing Rites*, 116–17, that kinothek collections represented the crass commercialism of music publishers, eager to sell noncopyrighted music "not by the ton but by the trainload," leading to the "dismemberment" of "the great masters.

55. Leofranc Holford-Strevens, *Aulus Gellius* (London: Duckworth, 1988), 238–39; Barry Baldwin, *Studies in Aulus Gellius* (Lawrence, KS: Coronado Press, 1975), 1. Compare Kermode, *The Classic*, 15–16.

56. Charles Rosen, *The Classical Style: Haydn, Mozart, Beethoven* (New York: W. W. Norton, 1972), 19.

57. Hereafter I use "rap" for any generic type, including hip-hop, following the model of Adam Krims, *Rap Music and the Poetics of Identity* (Cambridge: Cambridge University Press, 2000), 2–7.

58. Taylor, *Strange Sounds* (pp. 152–53) contrasts this element of rap practice with the approach taken by electronica musicians to the samples they incorporate into their compositions. A more profound exposition of the intentional aspects of rap sampling is provided by Tricia Rose, *Black Noise: Rap Music and Black Culture in Contemporary America* (Hanover, NH: Wesleyan University Press, 1994), 88–90. See also her discussion of Marley Marl and Daddy-O (p. 79).

59. Brown, *Overtones and Undertones*; Gorbman, *Unheard Melodies*. See further the discussion in chapter 2.

60. An extreme case is the "skit" enacted at the opening of "Guilty Conscience," by Eminem and Dr. Dre; cf. other "skit" tracks on rap CDs, including those of Eminem and DMX.

61. Frith discusses the relation between somatic response and African-American musics in *Performing Rites*, 141–44.

62. Richard Addinsell composed the *Warsaw Concerto* for the 1941 British film *Dangerous Moonlight* (retitled *Suicide Squadron* for the U.S. release), which tells the story of a Polish pianist-aviator. In the liner notes for the 1950 Muir Mathieson recording of the work (Columbia ML2092), *Suicide Squadron* is described as "a film which expressed the self-sacrifice and courage of servicemen during World War II, seen through the heroic exploits of a Polish Aviator." Addinsell, too, became, through this work, a hero of culture, and was awarded a Silver Cross from the Polish government in 1944. Ivan Raykoff, "Hollywood's Embattled Icon," in *Piano Roles*, ed. James Parakilas (New Haven, CT: Yale University Press, 1999), 329–57, contextualizes the "heroic" aspects of the film against the background of the depiction of Chopin as a Polish patriot in the 1945 *A Song to Remem*ber (see pp. 345–46). Raykoff's points are valid, although the article, based on his doctoral dissertation, moves rather flexibly within the diachronic field of his topic, at least for the historian reader (it appears by his text presentation, for example, that the British film reinvented the topoi of the Hollywood production, although the former predated the latter by four years).

63. On the low-sound frequencies of rap, see Rose, *Black Noise*, 75.

64. See, for example, Henri Focillon's 1934 *La vie des formes*, published as *The Life of Forms in Art* (New York: Zone Books, 1992), 184, and Abbate, "Outside Ravel's Tomb," 467. Classical citation in general within the domain of early sound films is associated largely with the horror genre. William H. Rosar, "Music for the Monsters: Universal Pictures' Horror Film Scores of the Thirties," *The Quarterly Journal of the Library of Congress* 40 (1983): 390–421.

65. Touré, "DMX Reigns as the Dark Prince of Hip Hop," *Rolling Stone* (April 13, 2000): 82–91, at 85 (emphasis added).

66. See the discussion of Tupac's "theosophical" gangsta rap register in Teresa L. Reed, *The Holy Profane: Religion in Black Popular Music* (Lexington: University of Kentucky Press, 2003), 149–60.

67. Tinney's live performance is the second track of *Peg and Al: The Al Tinney Trio with Peggy Farrell* (Border City BCCD-1000). I am grateful to James Patrick for providing me with a copy of this small-circulation recording.

68. In the 1940s such abbreviated suggestions of the concerto genre were called "Tabloid Concertos." Naturally, serious musicians raised the objection that "the mere act of combining a piano with an orchestra does not make a concerto." See John Huntley, *British Film Music* (London: Skelton Robinson, 1947), 54–55. Huntley tracks the popular success of Addinsell's piece as a "hit" in Britain and the United States.

69. Peter Brooks, *The Melodramatic Imagination: Balzac, Henry James, Melodrama, and the Mode of Excess* (New Haven, CT: Yale University Press, 1976), 21.

70. René Girard, *Violence and the Sacred*, trans. Patrick Gregory (Baltimore: Johns Hopkins University Press, 1977), 18.

71. On the apprehension of universals as a terrifying threat to self and to individual identity, see Jonathan Strauss, *Subjects of Terror: Nerval, Hegel, and the Modern Self* (Stanford: Stanford University Press, 1998), esp. 206–26.

72. Cf. the discussion of "effusive" styles in Krims, *Rap Music*, 51–52.

73. Interview archived at www.mtv.com/bands/az/rhymes_busta/artist.jhtml (accessed January 20, 2001).

74. Rose cites the arguments of Christopher Small and James Snead that the repetitions embedded in late twentieth-century hip-hop express African culture's perception of such features as reflections of "circulation" and "equilibrium," analogous to, in Snead's words, "a philosophical insight about the shape of time and history." The "cut" by which samples are amputated and reorganized is a "built-in accident" that offers a means of controlling unpredictability. Repeating phenomena of "rupture," then, will express their own aural and social cyclicities that play with and against the original substance of the sample (Rose, *Black Noise*, 67–70). Less useful still from a musical perspective is the reading of Jacques Attali, who finds in repetition in general a "totalitarian code" imposed by the machinery of mass production and expressing the technological constraints of industrial standardization (Rose, *Black Noise*, p. 75).

75. I borrow this construction from the elegant commentary on the "architectural intertextuality" of Eliot's poetry in Gregory S. Jay, *T. S. Eliot and the Poetics of Literary History* (Baton Rouge: Louisiana State University Press, 1983), 54.

76. Several writers have remarked upon the lack of diegetic music in *Psycho,* which tends to emphasize the location of the score's field of discourse as lying within the minds of the characters. See, for example, Brown, *Overtones and Undertones,* 165, and my discussion of the film in chapter 6.

77. Bakhtin's understanding of the "road" chronotope is discussed in his "Forms of Time and of the Chronotope in the Novel," in *The Dialogic Imagination: Four Essays by M. M. Bakhtin,* ed. Michael Holquist; trans. and ed. Caryl Emerson and Michael Holquist (Austin: University of Texas Press, 1981), 84–258, esp. 243–45. For an example of the term's extension to film theory, see Vivian Sobchack, "Lounge Time: Postwar Crises and the Chronotope of Film Noir," in *Refiguring American Film Genres: History and Theory,* ed. Nick Browne (Berkeley: University of California Press, 1998), 129–70.

78. Janet Leigh's report of the process leading to Hitchcock's decision to use voice-overs and the film's title music for this sequence is included in Karlin, *Listening to Movies: The Film-Lover's Guide to Film Music* (New York: Schirmer Books, 1994), 83.

79. Notions of "fields" and "zones" that inform Bakhtin's reading of Gogol's *Dead Souls,* for example, underline the complex negotiations between author, outside referents and traditions, and audience within the frame of Bakhtin's "dialogic" conversations; the terminology is useful for distinguishing the dynamic layers of multiple-author discourse of film. See "Epic and Novel: Toward a Methodology for the Study of the Novel," in *The Dialogic Imagination,* 3–40, esp. 28.

80. "Vibe" is an extension of the earlier "groove," and refers both to aspects (especially rhythmic) of the song, as well as the "group consciousness" of its

consumers, and the principal hip-hop fanzine is called *Vibe*. Taylor, *Strange Sounds*, 172–77, traces the term's intersection with several sociologically defined music-consumer aggregations, based on the earlier work of Charles Keil.

81. On Bourdieu's notion of the habitus, see, e.g., *Outline of a Theory of Practice*, trans. Richard Nice (Cambridge: Cambridge University Press, 1977), esp. 78–87.

82. *The Groucho Letters*, 145.

83. On Woolcott's relationships with the Marxes, see Heywood Hale Broun, "At Play on Neshobe Island," *Architectural Digest* (June 2002): 124–32. Woolcott was Vera Caspary's model for *Laura*'s Waldo Lydecker (see chapter 2).

84. T. S. Eliot, *On Poetry and Poets*, 119.

85. Pierre Bourdieu, *Distinction*, 340.

86. Bourdieu refers to "scholastic popularization, which overtly proclaims its pedagogic objectives" (p. 323). An example of the category would be Disney's bizarre *Fantasia* project, in which concert pieces were "explained" through images and the learned discourse of Deems Taylor. Disney intended that it be presented repeatedly, with the "syllabus" changing by one piece every time the film went through the release cycle. His vision included the creation of a more synaesthetic experience involving the introduction of aroma into specially equipped theatres (e.g., incense during the "Ave Maria" sequence). When the original version was released, some, like Cooper Holsworth of the Chicago-based *Music News* deemed it "a new art"; Holsworth reported that the question "What do you think of *Fantasia*?" had "touched off more drawing-room duels this season than any event since the first performance of Stravinsky's *Rite of Spring*." Cooper Holsworth, "Of Mice and Music," *Music News* 33, no. 5 (1941): 8–9. The history of the Fantasia project is recounted in Michael Barrier, *Hollywood Cartoons: American Animation in its Golden Age* (New York: Oxford University Press, 1999), 246–60.

87. Extracts from the author's conversation with Cukor regarding the Stravinsky party are included in Hector Arce, *Groucho* (New York: G. P. Putnam's Sons, 1979), 404–5.

2. MAKING OVERTURES

1. Kathryn Kalinak, *Settling the Score: Music and the Classical Hollywood Film* (Madison: University of Wisconsin Press, 1992), 168.

2. Mikhail Bakhtin, "Forms of Time and of the Chronotope in the Novel," in *The Dialogic Imagination: Four Essays by M. M. Bakhtin*, ed. Michael Holquist; trans. and ed. Caryl Emerson and Michael Holquist (Austin: University of Texas Press, 1981), 84–258, esp. 152–53.

3. I have in mind particularly the "historical" time element of a film like *The Sea Hawk*, or even the vague historicism of *The Adventures of Robin Hood*, both scored by Korngold, vs. the "mythological" time element established from the outset of *Star Wars* (the text, "A long time ago in a galaxy far, far away," is the first item to appear on the screen). On the generic implications of the distinction, see Bakhtin, "Forms of Time," 104. The *Star Wars* theme reproduces most of the essential features of Korngold's *Sea Hawk* title music, adding some of the timbral

elements of science fiction register ("spatial" wide intervals in the brass, "twinkling star" pitched percussion) that were put on the map by Bernard Herrmann in his title-sequence music for Robert Wise's *The Day the Earth Stood Still* (1951).

4. See James Naremore, *More Than Night: Film Noir in Its Contexts* (Berkeley: University of California Press, 1998), 13.

5. Lance St. John Butler, for example, equates his understanding of register with that of "style" set forth in Geoffrey Leech and Michael Short, *Style in Fiction: A Linguistic Introduction to English Fictional Prose* (London: Longman, 1981), 39. For an excellent argument concerning the distinction between style and register, see Roger Fowler, *Linguistic Criticism,* 2nd ed. (Oxford: Oxford University Press, 1996), 185–91. See also Ferguson, "Dialect, Register, and Genre," 28, n. 4. Concerning the distinction between register and genre, see Helen Leckie-Tarry, *Language and Context: A Functional Linguistic Theory of Register* (London: Pinter Publishers, 1995), 15.

6. Kathryn Kalinak, "The Fallen Woman and the Virtuous Wife: Musical Stereotypes in *The Informer, Gone With the Wind,* and *Laura,*" *Film Reader* 5 (1982): 76–82. See also her *Settling the Score,* 120–22.

7. Indeed, Preminger's famous argument with Raksin over the character of Laura (whether or not she was, as Preminger reportedly said, "a whore") was incited by the director's suggestions for background music. According to Roy Prendergast, Preminger's suggestion was Ellington's "Sophisticated Lady" and not, as is regularly reported, Gershwin's "Summertime" (Prendergast, *Film Music,* 67). The longevity of that myth suggests to me that it derives from recall of "Summertime" performed with characteristic hot or cool mute-brass timbre (as in Miles Davis's well-known rendering) and pitch-bends, typical markers of this register.

8. Kalinak, *Settling the Score,* 122.

9. In fact, the television soap opera "picturized" the radio serials of the previous generation. The transition to picture in the soap opera retained the radio-style interjective and transitional organ scoring of the 1930s and 1940s. Daytime serials now follow the "Dawson's Creek" model, initiated by *The Graduate* in the 1970s, in expanding the musical background through the attachment of pop songs whose lyrics gloss the unspoken thoughts of characters in the drama.

10. Ferguson, "Dialect, Register, and Genre," 20–21.

11. Miklós Rózsa incorporated the theremin into his Oscar-nominated 1945 scores for Billy Wilder's *The Lost Weekend,* in which it was linked to the alcoholic's compulsion to drink, and Alfred Hitchcock's *Spellbound,* where it was heard during Gregory Peck's "psychotic episodes."

12. Compare the discussion of Gus Van Sant's remake of Hitchcock's *Psycho* in chapter 6.

13. Erdmann, *Handbuch,* 2:30. The terms mix common language (dramatic expression, serious) and musical ones (gently moving, "appassionato" climax).

14. Richard Taruskin, *Defining Russia Musically* (Princeton, NJ: Princeton University Press, 1997), 165; *Romeo and Juliet* is discussed 182–85.

15. See, e.g., Susan McClary, *Feminine Endings: Music, Gender, and Sexuality* (Minnesota: University of Minnesota Press, 1991), 59–63. While the dynamic level is "wrong" for the cinematic model, the contour and rhythmic profile is

analogous; note especially the scalar surge to the broad *Höhepunkt* in Don José's flower song from *Carmen*, the last portion of McClary's example 2b (p. 61).

16. There is a bit more to the musical analogy between *Romeo and Juliet* and *Laura*. With the glissando attached to the front, the first two notes of Raksin's *Laura* theme are transformed into a Chaikovskian long-note arrival (half note, followed by dotted half), with a sensual chromatic melodic extension.

17. This aspect of the film has also been noted by Alan Williams, "Historical and Theoretical Issues in the Coming of Sound to the Cinema," in Rick Altman, *Sound Theory, Sound Practice* (New York: Routledge, 1992), 126–37, esp. 131. The conflict between ethnocentric and commercial cultures and between the Jewish and Gentile sectors of American media cultures woven into the film reflect the social, economic and familial tensions of the film industry (and Broadway) at the time, wherein the primary producers of commercial art were first-generation American Jews of Central or Eastern European extraction, or themselves immigrants. See, e.g., Neal Gabler, *An Empire of Their Own: How the Jews Invented Hollywood* (New York: Doubleday, 1988). Jack's character embodies autobiographical aspects of Al Jolson and of the Hollywood studio set in general.

18. The full statement of Chaikovsky's theme is cue 48 on the studio cue sheet for *The Jazz Singer*.

19. Kalinak, *Settling the Score*, 68. Williams, "Historical and Theoretical Issues," 130. Mark Slobin, *Tenement Songs: The Popular Music of the Jewish Immigrants* (Urbana: University of Illinois Press, 1982), 195. On the oedipal connotations of the film's narrative from a more general perspective, see Krin Gabbard, *Jammin' at the Margins: Jazz and the American Cinema* (Chicago: University of Chicago Press, 1996), 35–63.

20. The typewritten letter is dated November 22, 1938. The performance of *Kol nidre* is mentioned in Dorothy Lamb Crawford, "Arnold Schoenberg in Los Angeles," *Musical Quarterly* 86 (2002): 6–48 (esp. 4, 17), but the author indicates, with no documentary reference, that Alfred Newman (music director at Fox beginning only in 1939) "provided the Twentieth Century-Fox orchestra" for the performance; she does not refer to Silvers or to Schoenberg's letter, which is preserved in the archives of the Schoenberg Center, Vienna. Schoenberg addressed it to Silvers as Director of the Music Department (as he still was at the time of the premiere), expressing "how much I appreciated your great assistance to the work which Rabbi Sonderling had in mind in putting all your power behind this dignified achievement. I can tell you that I was really very satisfied with all you [placed] at my disposal."

21. Peter Brooks, *The Melodramatic Imagination*, 47 and passim. See especially p. 55, where he calls melodrama "the expressionism of the moral imagination."

22. Musical-gestural correlates of this sort are also conventional expressive devices in some opera repertoires, particularly those intersecting with melodrama in the specific sense, as convincingly demonstrated by Mary Ann Smart in *Mimomania: Music and Gesture in Nineteenth-Century Opera* (Berkeley: University of California Press, 2004), 8–13, 132–50.

23. Cf. Phil Powrie, *French Cinema in the 1980s: Nostalgia and the Crisis of Masculinity* (Oxford: Clarendon Press, 1997), 61, who declares that "melodrama's excess functions as a symptom of social change."

24. Roberta Pearson, *Eloquent Gestures: The Transformation of Performance Style in the Griffith Biograph Films* (Berkeley: University of California Press, 1992).

25. Brooks (p. 48) mentions the notion of the musical talisman as part of melodramatic structure in Adolphe Dennery's *La Grâce de Dieu*.

26. See the frontispiece in W. T. Lhamon, Jr., *Jump Jim Crow: Lost Plays, Lyrics, and Street Prose of the First Atlantic Popular Culture* (Cambridge, MA: Harvard University Press, 2003).

27. See the discussion of "variety" in Fowler, *Linguistic Criticism*, 186.

28. Tsur, *What Makes Sound Patterns Expressive?* and especially his discussion of dark vowels, 20–27. As Tsur notes (p. 42), "Vowels are uninterrupted streams of energy; the same is true, typically, of emotional mental processes," a remark we might use to frame a "phonological" approach to the rocket-glissando. See also Roman Jakobson, *Language in Literature* (Cambridge, MA: Harvard University Press: 1987).

29. By contrast, *The Black Cat* (1934), with a score by Heinz Roemheld, includes a "Cat Love Theme," introduced as a lyric section within a multisectional title-music sequence, whose imitation of *Romeo and Juliet* is more "a near miss than . . . an actual quotation." Here the theme has been neutered and domesticated by removing the surge and, starting at the arrival point, robbing it of its "impulse." The musical themes and classical citations in *The Black Cat* are identified and discussed in detail in Rosar, "Music for the Monsters," 403–5. The remark about the Chaikovsky quotation is from Brown, *Overtones and Undertones*, 60.

30. Gaston Bachelard, *The Poetics of Space*, trans. Maria Jolas (Boston: Beacon Press, 1994), 63.

31. Steiner didn't need to give the matter much thought. Erdmann "registered" the theme in his second volume as item no. 1014: *Liebeswehmut* within the dramaturgical classification of *Tiefpunkt/Resignation*.

32. Compare Gorbman's discussion of the "melodramatic" close-ups of Joan Crawford in *Mildred Pierce* (Gorbman, *Unheard Melodies*, 81, 98).

33. See, for example, Elaine Sisman, *Mozart: The "Jupiter" Symphony* (Cambridge: Cambridge University Press, 1993), 13, who cites Longinus's characterization of the sublime as "the echo of a noble mind."

34. Ibid. 19, 78–79.

35. Walter Pfann seems to link the theme to the "aesthetic moment," reading it as "Das 'ach so Schöne'" in his programmatic outline of the symphony. "'Hat er es denn beschlossen . . .': Anmerkungen zu einem neuen Verständnis der Symphonie Pathétique," *Die Musikforschung* 51 (1998): 191–209, esp. 207. Schiller, who theorized the "aesthetic moment," allowed that the pathetic became aesthetic in the realm of the sublime. Cf. Elaine Sisman, "Pathos and Pathétique: Rhetorical Stance in Beethoven's C-Minor Sonata, Op. 13," *Beethoven Forum* 3 (1994): 81–105.

36. A narrative roadmap of the leitmotivic content of Steiner's score is available in Kate Daubney, *Max Steiner's Now Voyager: A Film Score Guide* (Westport, CT: Greenwood Press, 2000).

37. Discussions of Adorno's and Eisler's *Composing for the Films* (1947) are included in many of the standard film-music studies already cited, including

Gorbman, *Unheard Melodies,* and Cook, *Analysing Musical Multimedia.* See Theodor W. Adorno, "The Radio Symphony," in Paul Lazarsfeld and Frank Stanton, *Radio Research 1941* (New York: Duell, Sloan and Pearce, 1941), 110–39. See Susan J. Douglas, *Listening In: Radio and the American Imagination* (New York: Random House, 1999), 154–55.

38. Douglas, *Listening In,* 155.

39. The music director Carl Stalling would have understood, above all, the registers of classic film scoring. Stalling's first experiences in film were as a theater organist in the silent era. See Barrier, *Hollywood Cartoons,* 52–53.

40. Even the production environment participated in the carnival: "Termite Terrace," the cartoon workshop, was an eccentric foil to the main studio lot, as documented in the 1975 production *Bugs Bunny Superstar,* narrated by Orson Welles. See also Joe Adamson, *Bugs Bunny: Fifty Years and Only One Grey Hare* (New York: Henry Holt, 1990), 35–40.

41. A frequent gambit is the use of a car radio to establish the setting or period, as in the film *Local Hero,* or a mix of diegetic sound and "dislocated" musical fragments, as in *Die Hard* and *The Matrix.*

42. See, in fact, the CD compilation *Composed By: Classic Film Themes from Hollywood's Masters* (TCM/Rhino R2 72847), where this excerpt (track 11) is imprecisely identified as "Citizen Kane: Main Title."

43. James Agee, *Agee on Film,* vol. 1 (New York: Grossett and Dunlap, 1967), 349–50; Frank Nugent, *New York Times* review (20 December 1939).

44. It seems that producer David O. Selznick may have been the first to incorporate such overture sequences into "big" films (not unlikely in light of his particular aesthetic pretensions). An overture appears as early as his *King Kong.*

45. Concerning this resemblance to *Tannhäuser,* see Peter Franklin, "*King Kong* and Film on Music: Out of the Fog," in *Film Music: Critical Approaches,* ed. K. J. Donnelly (New York: Continuum Publishing Group, 2001), 98.

46. Peter Franklin has proposed a very different interpretation of Steiner's Tara theme and its conceptual models. See his "The Boy on the Train, or Bad Symphonies and Good Movies: The Revealing Error of the 'Symphonic Score,'" in *Beyond the Soundtrack,* ed. Goldmark et al., 22.

47. For example, the edition by Edgardo Lèvi, published as *Standard Songs* no. 14 by Ascherberg, Hopwood and Crew, Ltd. (London, 1908).

48. Erdmann, *Handbuch,* 2:118. His linking the number to religious worship and meditation (lyric expression/incidental music/hymn-like peaceful/religious worship/meditation) likely reflects the extent to which the largo has been contrafacted for church and synagogue use.

49. Max Kozloff, "2001," *Film Culture* 48–49 (1970), cited in *The Making of 2001: A Space Odyssey,* selected by Stephanie Schwam (New York: The Modern Library, 2000), 180.

50. Cited in Norman Kagan, *The Cinema of Stanley Kubrick* (New York: Continuum Publishing Company, 1996), 145.

51. Kozloff, "2001," 181. This aspect of the film, and observations regarding *2001*'s "mythic" quality, has found its way into most writing on the work, including that of journalists in its day.

52. Ibid., 180.

53. Paul Griffiths describes the sound in those terms in *György Ligeti* (London: Robson Books, 1983), 32.

54. Compare Griffiths's remark that the music at times projects the feeling that it has "disappeared over the top of the pitch spectrum and reappeared at the bottom" (p. 37) with Kozloff's image of events taking place or located "outside the frame." Ligeti has described the work in terms that emphasize his intention to erase—or at least disguise—structural edges, eliminating all "dialectic" or oppositional elements of the sort that constitute structural compositional thinking. In *Atmosphères,* according to Ligeti, the different states of the musical materials are realized through unnoticeable processes of transformation or through the gradual superseding of one state by another. See the remarks quoted in Constantin Floros, *György Ligeti: Jenseits von Avantgarde und Postmoderne* (Vienna: Verlag Lafite, 1996), 95.

3. YIDDISHKEIT AND THE MUSICAL ETHICS OF CINEMA

1. Whitfield, *In Search of American Jewish Culture* (Hanover, NH: Brandeis University Press, 1999), 153.

2. Michael Rogin, *Blackface, White Noise: Jewish Immigrants in the Hollywood Melting Pot* (Berkeley: University of California Press, 1996); Mark Slobin, "Some Intersections of Jews, Music, and Theater," in *From Hester Street to Hollywood: The Jewish-American Stage and Screen,* ed. Sarah Blacher Cohen (Bloomington: Indiana University Press, 1983). For an overview of many aspects of this conversation, see Whitfield, *In Search of American Jewish Culture,* 149–67.

3. Concerning this terminology, see, for example, Amnon Shiloah and Erik Cohen, "The Dynamics of Change in Jewish Oriental Ethnic Music in Israel," *Ethnomusicology* 27 (1983): 227–52, esp. 240.

4. Compare the discussion of *Kol nidre* and external resemblances in Daniel S. Katz, "Synagogue Reform in Århus, Denmark (1825)," in *Liber amicorum Isabelle Cazeaux: Symbols, Parallels, Discoveries in Her Honor,* ed. Paul-Andre Bempechat (Hillsdale, NY: Pendragon Press, 2005), 438–39.

5. See Klára Móricz, "Sensuous Pagans and Righteous Jews: Changing Concepts of Jewish Identity in Ernest Bloch's 'Jézabel' and 'Schelomo,'" *Journal of the American Musicological Society* 54 (2001): 439–91, esp. 477–82, and Ralph P. Locke, "Constructing the Oriental 'Other': Saint-Saëns's 'Samson et Dalila,'" *Cambridge Opera Journal* 3 (1991): 261–302.

6. For example, a theater musician wishing to use item no. 2929, "Jüdischer Tanz," is directed to a collection of Slavic Folk Music.

7. In a letter to Paul Dessau (22 November 1941) in the Schoenberg Center archives, Schoenberg states that he had read that the traditional *Kol nidre* melody itself was of Spanish origin, confirming his own intuition.

8. In Bruch's version of the melody (in the cello solo that launches his referentially "Jewish" opus 47), the arrival on the minor third above the final is emphasized—it is a sob more than a wail—a feature of the work that his comment suggests was perhaps especially galling to Schoenberg, and perhaps especially

comprehensible as an expressive maneuver to mainstream, "classically" trained Jewish musicians like Silvers.

9. See, for example, Stephen Sharot's review essay "Judaism and Jewishness," in *Modern Jews and Their Musical Agendas,* ed. Ezra Mendelsohn (New York: Oxford University Press, 1993), 188–202.

10. Whitfield, *In Search of American Jewish Culture,*153.

11. Gabbard, *Jammin' at the Margins,* 35–63.

12. Ibid., 42–46.

13. Whitfield, *In Search of American Jewish Culture,*154. Gilbert Seldes— sixty years before the new musicology embraced the same position—argued for the abandonment of "high" and "low" distinctions in art. In *The Seven Lively Arts* (1924), Seldes, according to Whitfield (55), "advanced a pioneering critical case for the value and importance of mass entertainment . . . insisting upon the conscientiousness with which popular as well as 'classical' art deserved to be studied."

14. For an extensive analysis of *Hallelujah,* see Alice Maurice, "'Cinema at Its Source': Synchronizing Race and Sound in the Early Talkies," *Camera Obscura* 49 (2002): 31–71. Maurice (38) has emphasized that, hackneyed as it was by the late 1920s, blackface in cinema still "retained its ability to inspire awe," and race-change sorcery perhaps played a significant role in the particular mode of response inspired by Jolson's stage shows.

15. Michel Chion, *The Voice in Cinema,* trans. Claudia Gorbman (New York: Columbia University Press, 1999), 157.

16. Gabbard, *Jammin' at the Margins,* 40.

17. Mark Slobin, *Chosen Voices: The Story of the American Cantorate* (Urbana: University of Illinois Press, 1989), 8.

18. Slobin, *Chosen Voices,* 81. Vigoda here provides a revealing anecdote concerning the centrality of improvisation to a successful cantorial performance.

19. Joseph A. Levine, *Synagogue Song in America* (Crown Point, IN: White Cliffs Media, 1989), 50–51, 126–27.

20. Jeffrey A. Summit, *The Lord's Song in a Strange Land: Music and Identity in Contemporary Jewish Worship* (Oxford: Oxford University Press, 2000), 94.

21. Summit (*The Lord's Song,* 131–36) suggests that the minority status of Ashkenazic Jews within their own ethnographic environments led them especially to adopt bilingual expressive modes and techniques of code-switching.

22. Slobin, *Chosen Voices,* 73–74.

23. Mark Slobin, *Tenement Songs: The Popular Music of the Jewish Immigrants* (Urbana: University of Illinois Press, 1982), figs. 27, 28, 15.

24. Brown, *Overtones,* 62.

25. Quoted in J. B. Kaufman, notes to *The Max Steiner Collection: The RKO Years,* BYU Film Music Archives Soundtrack Series (Provo UT: Brigham Young University Film Music Archives, 2002).

26. For an overview, see David Neumeyer, "Melodrama as a Compositional Resource in Early Hollywood Sound Cinema," *Current Musicology* (1995): 61–94. On pastiche opera, see Prendergast, *Film Music,* 30.

27. Tony Thomas, *Music for the Movies,* cited in Brown, *Overtones,* 62.

28. Brooks, *The Melodramatic Imagination*, 14.

29. Ibid., ix, 47.

30. Neumeyer, "Melodrama," 70–84.

31. See Prendergast, *Film Music*, 42.

32. Chion, *Audio-Vision: Sound on Screen*, ed. and trans. Claudia Gorbman (New York: Columbia University Press, 1994), 50–51.

33. Kalinak, *Settling the Score*, 116–17.

34. An overview of some of the correspondences and divergences between the novel and Ford's film is provided in George Bluestone, *Novels into Film* (Baltimore, MD: Johns Hopkins Press, 1959), 65–90. Bluestone does not discuss the footstep motif.

35. Neumeyer, "Melodrama," 80–82.

36. Describing his "vernünftige Reihenfolge," the composer revealed that "eine meiner Hauptaufgaben war es, die Cello-Sentimentalität des Bruch, etc. wegzuvitriolisieren . . . Diese Takte 58–63 sind zumindest kein sentimentales Moll." For a detailed analysis of Schoenberg's setting, see Steven J. Cahn, "'Kol Nidre' in America," *Journal of the Arnold Schoenberg Center* 4 (2002): 203–18.

37. There are, of course, many historical threads that might be teased out of this very small, but well-made (i.e., relatively large-budget) production, in which major players were enlisted to produce a rather small film. But the role of Hollywood, and of Hollywood's Jewish leaders, in the dissemination of multimedia position statements lies beyond the scope of this study. Concerning Hollywood's involvement in political or patriotic films a few years later, see W. Anthony Sheppard, "An Exotic Enemy: Anti-Japanese Musical Propaganda in World War II Hollywood," *Journal of the American Musicological Society* 54 (2001): 303–57.

38. Steiner's wife was a harpist, accounting for the composer's reliance on the instrument as a signature effect in most scores throughout his career, beginning with *King Kong*. Even though *Sons of Liberty* was scored by Forbstein, she is probably present on the sound track.

39. See, for example, Donald Crafton, *The Talkies: American Cinema's Transition to Sound, 1926–1931* (Berkeley: University of California Press, 1999), 80.

40. Gabler, *An Empire of Their Own*, 105.

41. J. Hoberman, *Bridge of Light: Yiddish Film Between Two Worlds* (New York: Museum of Modern Art / Schocken Books, 1991), 26.

42. Ben Singer, "The Nickelodeon Boom in Manhattan," in *Entertaining America: Jews, Movies and Broadcasting*, ed. J. Hoberman and Jeffrey Shandler (New York: Jewish Museum / Princeton, NJ: Princeton University Press, 2003), 23–27.

43. Hoberman, *Bridge of Light*, 26.

44. Cited in ibid., 22.

45. Leonard J. Leff, commentary track for *Rebecca* (The Criterion Collection DVD, 1990).

46. Hoberman, *Bridge of Light*, 18.

47. Brooks, *The Melodramatic Imagination*, 20.

48. Compare Theodora Bosanquet's description of Henry James's melodramatic life-vision cited in Brooks, *The Melodramatic Imagination* (p. 5), which

juxtaposes the refuge of the author's workspace and the "place of torment" that lay outside, populated by the "doomed, defenseless children of light."

49. Michael A. Morrison, *John Barrymore: Shakespearean Actor* (Cambridge: Cambridge University Press, 1997), 73–74.

50. Ibid., 59.

51. A good critical introduction to Hurst's work and significance is provided by Susan Koppelman, *The Stories of Fannie Hurst* (New York: The Feminist Press at the City University of New York, 2004), ix–xxvii. Stephanie Lewis Thompson, *Influencing America's Tastes: Realism in the Works of Wharton, Cather and Hurst* (Gainesville and Tallahassee: University Press of Florida, 2002), 155–93, offers an analysis of the reasons for Hurst's negative reception by authors and academics after ca. 1930, suggesting that the writer's assignment to the category of the sentimental was related to the critical and academic construction of a (primarily male) modernist canon, along with the misconceptions regarding the content of her texts engendered by their filmic picturizations.

52. See Thompson, *Influencing America's Tastes*, 157, who quotes from Hurst's 1958 autobiography: "This mass business bothered me. Rather be a classical failure than a popular success. The phrase out of my college days stuck crosswise in my memory like a bone in the throat. Did popular success mean kiss-of-death to artistic achievement?"

53. Koppelman, *The Stories of Fannie Hurst*, 111.

54. Hurst's reliance on "cinematic visualization" prior to her entry into the world of film is discussed by Abe C. Ravitz, *Imitations of Life: Fannie Hurst's Gaslight Sonatas* (Carbondale and Edwardsville: Southern Illinois University Press, 1997), 86–91. Ravitz quotes a relevant contemporaneous remark by Rex Beach: "Literature has elevated the moving picture . . . and in return the moving picture has done a service to fiction, making authors give more attention to exact visualization. . . . American novelists visualize more clearly today than they did four or five years ago, before the moving picture had become so important. . . . This sort of realism is America's chief contribution to fiction."

55. Fritz Lang's *Metropolis* provides a nearly contemporary instance of the new phenomenon in a pre-sound environment, appearing in serialized and novelistic forms very close to the time of its production in the middle of the 1920s. Thomas Elsaesser, *Metropolis* (London: British Film Institute, 2000), 12, 76 (notes 4 and 5).

56. The complicated "multimedia" title page for the book, published by A. L. Burt Company, reads: SYMPHONY OF SIX MILLION. *A Novelization By* JOHN ADAMS *of the* FANNIE HURST *Screen Story. An* RKO RADIO *Picture.*

57. Fannie Hurst, *Anitra's Dance* (New York: Harper and Brothers, 1934), 385.

58. For a piano score of "Elend bin ich," see Mark Slobin, *Yiddish Theater in America: David's Violin (1897) and Shloyme Gorgl (189-),* (New York: Garland Publishing, Inc., 1994), 55.

59. For an early report of Goldfaden's own reminiscences, see Idelsohn, *Jewish Music in Its Historical Development* (New York: Henry Holt, 1929), 450–53.

60. Although also linked to a literature of ethnicity and assimilation, and thus conceivably one inspiration for Hurst's unusual music-text hybrid in

Anitra's Dance, the incorporation of notated spirituals into W. E. B. Du Bois's *The Souls of Black Folk* (1903) represents a very different structural concept. Du Bois uses music epigraphically, a marked contrast to Hurst's procedure of working a single musical leitmotif into a continuous, arguably cinematic narration. See the description of Du Bois's book in Lawrence Kramer, *Musical Meaning: Toward a Critical History* (Berkeley: University of California Press, 2002), 246.

61. Jack Gottlieb, *Funny, It Doesn't Sound Jewish: How Yiddish Songs and Synagogue Melodies Influenced Tin Pan Alley, Broadway, and Hollywood* (Albany: State University of New York / Library of Congress, 2004), 46–47, represents a rare instance in which the musical sources (the "Jewish Classics") in Steiner's score are identified. But even Gottlieb introduces his discussion by pointing out that Steiner "was no Yiddishist."

62. The most extensive study of the musical repertoires of Yiddish-speaking immigrants and their sociological implications is Mark Slobin, *Tenement Songs.*

63. Michael Gold, *Jews Without Money*, repr. (New York: Carroll and Graf, 1996), 22, 119–20, 134–35.

64. The text is taken from John Adams's novelization of the Hurst "screen story," *Symphony of Six Million: A Novelization by John Adams of the Fannie Hurst Screen Story. An RKO Radio Picture* (New York: A. L. Burt Company, 1932), 200.

65. Gold, *Jews Without Money*, 226.

66. Slobin, *David's Violin*, xiii.

67. Ibid., xv.

68. For evidence of the survival of Jewish "Janke dudeling" in a very modern context, see Jeffrey A. Summit, "I'm a Yankee Doodle Dandy? Identity and Melody at an American Simh at Torah Celebration," *Ethnomusicology* 37 (1993): 41–62.

69. Nahma Sandrow, "Romanticism and the Yiddish Theatre," in *Yiddish Theatre: New Approaches*, ed. Joel Berkowitz (Oxford: Littman Library of Jewish Civilization, 2003), 50.

70. David Mazower, "Stories in Song: The *Melo-deklamatsyes* of Joseph Markovitsh," in *Yiddish Theatre*, 119–37.

71. Ibid., 130.

72. While other, non-Yiddish, varieties of musical entertainment in New York during the same period (most Broadway-style revues, for instance) consisted of pastiche presentations, there seems to be little evidence that venues outside the ghetto districts regularly featured Yiddish numbers as part of a coherent, conceptually thematized musical presentation. See the repertoire lists published by Richard C. Norton, *A Chronology of American Musical Theater*, vol. 2 (New York: Oxford University Press, 2002), 334–654.

73. Hoberman, *Bridge of Light*, 62–63.

74. Steiner's relationship with Kern bears further investigation. Although I have suggested that the processional theme accompanying the title for *Symphony of Six Million* may borrow its processional aspects from Elgar (or even *Die Meistersinger*), it bears a resemblance to "Journeys end in lovers meeting" from Kern's 1922 show *The Cabaret Girl* (for which Steiner was, however, not the music director). More interesting is a reverse resemblance: Kern's famous song

"The Way You Look Tonight" is remarkably similar to Steiner's theme for *Symphony*. Steiner had scored his own Fred Astaire vehicles before being released (fired) by RKO. Kern succeeded him as head of the music department, and his first production for the studio was *Swing Time*. "The Way You Look Tonight" was the film's most memorable number. One has to wonder whether the song was intended as an insider's acknowledgment of his colleague.

75. Compare Slobin's remark (*Yiddish Theater*, xiv) on the generic diversity of Yiddish musical drama: "Whether the works of the type presented in this volume should be identified as 'operas,' 'operettas,' 'musical dramas,' 'melodramas,' or some other generic tag name is probably unanswerable as a general question. We would first have to decide whether to use the shifting perspective of the dominant American culture, the emerging aesthetic of early Jewish-American tastemakers, or the rough-and-ready entertainment categories of the immigrant masses of New York."

4. HEARING MONSTERS

1. On the specificity of "pop" as a characterization for radio broadcast repertoire, see Allan F. Moore, *The Beatles: Sgt. Pepper's Lonely Hearts Club Band* (Cambridge: Cambridge University Press, 1997), 17.

2. A report of the impressionistic frame for the production of "Strawberry Fields" is provided in James Miller, *Flowers in the Dustbin: The Rise of Rock and Roll, 1947–1977* (New York: Simon and Schuster, 1999), 255. Other "art" composers whose music influenced the group's projects at the time included Cage, Stockhausen, and Berio. See Virgil Moorefield, *The Producer as Composer: Shaping the Sounds of Popular Music* (Cambridge, MA: MIT Press, 2005), 33.

3. *Melody Maker* (June 3, 1967): 10–11.

4. The characterization is that of the anonymous reporter in *Melody Maker* (July 15, 1967): 9. The incorporation of European art music and ethnic elements into rock was even at this early stage subject to journalistic skepticism from some quarters. See Moore, *The Beatles*, 20.

5. See, for example, Richard Middleton, *Studying Popular Music* (Philadelphia: Open University Press, 1990): "The basic materials derive from a harmonic sequence (with melodic elaboration) taken from a cantata by J. S. Bach" (30). Robert Walser, *Running With the Devil: Power, Gender, and Madness in Heavy Metal Music* (Hanover, NH: Wesleyan University Press, 1993), 62, reiterates Middleton's assessment with no commentary. Sheila Whitely, *The Space Between the Notes: Rock and the Counter-Culture* (London and New York: Routledge, 1992), 70, writes that the song's "surrealism and timelessness" has been constructed in the music "through the transformation of Bach's *Sleepers Wake* chorale, with its spacious tempo and use of ritornello and ostinato."

6. *Melody Maker* (9 May, 1970). See also Paul Stump, *The Music's All That Matters: A History of Progressive Rock* (London: Quartet Books Ltd., 1997), 83. The review cites *Poseidon*'s "inner complexities" that "rival those of the great classical composers," but its emphasis on sound mass—e.g., in the reference to a "shuddering monolithic structure," borrowing from Stanley Kubrick's multimedia

exploration of borderless quantity a few years earlier—is reflected in other contemporaneous publicity. An Island Records press release (reproduced on the liner
for the 2004 digital remaster of *Poseidon*) announced the pre-album release of
the single "Cat Food," one of *Poseidon*'s less symphonic items. It suggests however that still "Cat Food" was "not the kind of record you can have burbling
away quietly while you play chess, have an orgy, read a book, or knit in the
trenches," thus promoting a mode of focused (potentially psychedelic) engagement also encountered in publicity for "A Whiter Shade of Pale"; I will discuss
this in greater length in chapter 5. Between the release of the single and the album
versions of "Cat Food," the song's piano coda was in fact modified and extended,
moving the end version within the range of the concerto style and its associated
flourishes discussed elsewhere in this book.

7. *Melody Maker* (June 3, 1967): 10–11.

8. Whitely's rather impressionistic description of the song's surface (*The
Space Between*, 70–72) likewise maintains that "the lyrics suggest . . . the hallucinogenic" (citing the lines "The room was humming harder / As the ceiling flew
away"). The analogy between musical surface and drug trip is the focus of
Whitely's selective discussion of the song's elements: "In combination with the
haunting quality of the voice and the drift of the melodic shape, they [the lyrics]
give a general impression of heightened consciousness" (p. 71). Her reading in
general reflects her position as, in Allan Moore's words, a "fan-turned-
musicologist" (see Moore, *The Beatles*, 61). To support her move in the direction of classifying the song's spirit as "religious-mystical" Whiteley suggests that
"I wandered through my playing cards" is a reference to "magic," specifically the
Tarot. More likely, though, the line was intended as an oblique reference to the
same Alice tales featured in Jefferson Airplane's fantastic and hallucinogenic
"White Rabbit," released shortly before.

9. The mixing of drugs with music as part of an aesthetic and spiritual experiment is of course prefigured in the nineteenth century, and especially the programs of late nineteenth-century synaesthetes (of the sort represented by J. K.
Huysmans's fictional protagonist, Des Esseintes, in *A Rebours*.).

10. In his 2001 novel *The Poet in Exile*, Ray Manzarek, keyboard player for
The Doors, associates Jim Morrison with the best of the "post-Beatnik generation of poets." Manzarek himself has collaborated with Michael McClure, a
member of Jack Kerouac's extended circle; their readings with music recall the
model of Kerouac.

11. Allen Ginsberg, *Collected Poems 1947–1980* (New York: Harper Peren-
nial, 1988), 231–34. For an account of the experiment, see Martin A. Lee and
Bruce Shlain, *Acid Dreams: The Complete Social History of LSD* (New York:
Grove Press, 1985), 58–60.

12. In light of Ginsberg's particular interest—following Aldous Huxley—in
Blake at the time of his hallucinogenic experiments, the watercolor representations of themes associated with Revelations and the Last Judgment (particularly
those of beasts and of multitude) that Blake produced between 1800 and 1810
may well have served as visual triggers for Ginsberg's multiple-eyed monster, as
well as for the generally quantitative aspects of his experience. On the centrality
of ecstasis in Ginsberg's poetry and life, see Justin Quinn, "Coteries, Landscape

and the Sublime in Allen Ginsberg," *Journal of Modern Literature* 27 (2003): 193–206. Quinn cites several instances of Ginsberg's use, in speaking and writing, of the notion of the top of the head opening or coming off as part of the mystical, spiritual, or ecstatic experience. The image as a commonplace finds its way into Reid's depiction of the room's ceiling in "A Whiter Shade of Pale."

13. Carolyn Abbate, in a now familiar formulation, applied Kant's distinction between the phenomenal and the noumenal to the location of music with respect to diegesis in *Unsung Voices: Opera and Musical Narrative in the Nineteenth Century* (Princeton, NJ: Princeton University Press, 1991). Her terminology figures significantly in, among others, Richard Taruskin, "The Golden Age of Kitsch," *New Republic* (March 21, 1994): 28–38, where it is extended to sound film, and Gary Tomlinson, *Metaphysical Song: An Essay on Opera* (Princeton, NJ: Princeton University Press, 1999). On the concept of the numinous in music, after Sir Michael Tippett, see Christopher Wintle, "The Numinous in *Götterdämmerung*," in *Reading Opera,* ed. Arthur Groos and Roger Parker (Princeton, NJ: Princeton University Press, 1988), 200–34.

14. See Quinn, "Coteries," on Ginsberg's efforts to treat supranormal experience, at least poetically, in such a way as to eliminate the disruptive boundary between it and the return to the mundane.

15. See J. Hillis Miller, *Ariadne's Thread: Story Lines* (New Haven, CT: Yale University Press, 1992), 145. See also M. H. Abrams, *Natural Supernaturalism: Tradition and Revolution in Romantic Literature* (New York: W. W. Norton, 1971), 13.

16. Ginsberg, *Collected Poems,* 243.

17. See Abrams, *Natural Supernaturalism,* 25.

18. On the sublime in eighteenth-century philosophy and music, see Elaine Sisman, *Mozart: The Jupiter Symphony* (Cambridge: Cambridge University Press, 1993), esp. 13–20, 74–79. See also Thomas Weiskel, *The Romantic Sublime: Studies in the Structure and Psychology of Transcendence* (Baltimore: Johns Hopkins University Press), 1976.

19. Allen S. Weiss, *Breathless: Sound Recording, Disembodiment, and the Transformation of Lyrical Nostalgia* (Middletown, CT: Wesleyan University Press, 2002), 69. It must be admitted, particularly since my project intersects with musical repertoires cultivated and consumed by adolescents and young adults, that generalized critiques of Ginsberg's sublime have characterized his position as consistently "adolescent." But his genius—as Charles Bernstein has argued—lay in his ability to render his political, social, and ethical positions, as well as his literary erudition, in a form that was palatable to "adolescents of all ages." However, whether viewed as a puerile engine of crossover kitsch or as a gifted vessel for "low culture in the best sense" (as Bernstein suggests, contrasting this with T. S. Eliot's promulgation of "high culture in the worst sense") my concern here is primarily with the details of Ginsberg's textual practice, particularly as linked to the apprehension of musical experience. See Charles Bernstein, "Unrepresentative Verse," in *My Way: Speeches and Poems* (Chicago: University of Chicago Press, 1999), 270–72.

20. Weiss, *Breathless,* 32. See David J. Code, "Hearing Debussy Reading Mallarme: Music 'après Wagner' in the *Prélude a l'après-midi d'un faune,*"

Journal of the American Musicological Society 54 (2001): 493–554. As Code points out (504–5), Mallarmé's own view of Wagner was ambivalent. Weiss's formulation, however, is—as analogy—especially apt, since he draws a specific line from early modernist poetry to psychedelic aesthetics of the mid-twentieth century. Compare also my discussion of the infinite melodic implications of psychedelic Baroqueism in chapter 5.

21. "Classical music" as a vernacular commonplace has been treated in the first portion of this book. But see also Allan F. Moore, *Rock: The Primary Text: Developing a Musicology of Rock* (Buckingham and Philadelphia: Open University Press, 1993), 9–30, for a useful overview of the distinction in musicological discourse between popular and classical. Ginsberg's choice here was clearly specific to the event; for the Beat poets, bebop offered an equally liberating metrical and melodic environment but lacked the acoustical markers of the numinous necessary to Ginsberg's aural poetics. Jack Kerouac in his poem "The Wheel of the Quivering Meat Conception" invoked—not by a web but by a cosmic wheel—some of the same unimaginable universals of large and small magnitudes as Ginsberg's poem; he recorded, late in 1959, a reading of the work to the accompaniment of Steve Allen's "cool" jazz improvised accompaniment (Rhino Records, *Jack Kerouac and Steve Allen: Poetry for the Beat Generation*).

22. David Szatmary, *A Time to Rock: A Social History of Rock and Roll* (New York: Schirmer Books, 1996), 77.

23. Ibid.

24. Moore, *Rock: The Primary Text*, 106. While Spector's work in the later 1960s, particularly for the Beatles, obviously involved the expansion of acoustic dimensional space, he maintained a celebrated commitment to the advantages of monaural recordings, as indicated by the title of his recorded collected works: *Back to Mono*, taken from a button worn by the producer. See Albin J. Zak III, *The Poetics of Rock: Cutting Tracks, Making Records* (Berkeley: University of California Press, 2001), 148. The essential flatness of the monaural construction is implicit in Brian Wilson's praise of Spector's position, as reported by Zak. Wilson used the simile "like a painting" in describing the monaural acoustical product. However, Spector's use of ambience effects mitigates the flat surface.

25. The pun (pointing to Spector's "worship" of the composer) is on *acousmêtre*, the now familiar coinage introduced by Michel Chion to describe the invisible source of an aurally perceived cinematic voice as an extension of the more familiar adjective "acousmatic." Acousmatic hearing was at the core of Pierre Schaeffer's theoretical framework for musique concrète. Schaeffer's theories proceeded from his general observation that almost every musical experience in the age of mechanical reproduction involves the confrontation with classes of sound that are no longer original to their source of production. In most cases sounds are both physically absented from their sources (except in the case, perhaps, of the miked live performance) and acoustically mediated by electronic intervention. Since my discussions move between audio and audiovisual media materials throughout I will at times employ film-theoretical terms to describe nonfilmic materials.

26. Sandy Pearlman, "Van Dyke Parks New Release," *Crawdaddy* 13 (February 1968): 43. Pearlman's objections to the acoustic weight of studio productions,

and his citation in the same review of Richard Meltzer's notion of British-influenced "academic beauty" rock, reveal the extent to which the issue of authenticity was already entrenched in rock discourse, where it has remained a zone of argument. See, for instance, *Reading Rock and Roll: Authenticity, Appropriation, Aesthetics,* ed. Kevin J. H. Dettmar and William Richey (New York: Columbia University Press, 1999), esp. 17–72. See also the discussion of Queen's "Bohemian Rhapsody" in chapter 7.

27. Szatmary, *A Time to Rock,* 77. Szatmary's use of the term reflects the totality of sound rather than any particularly airy or breathy vocalism; a hearing of either song reveals an up-front directness in the timbre produced by the lead singers.

28. See Zak, *Poetics of Rock,* 78.

29. Ibid., 77.

30. The subject is addressed in David Fricke's review of the CD *Pretty in Black* in *Rolling Stone* (May 19, 2005): 74.

31. For a summary presentation of these cultural critiques, see the discussion in Caryl Flinn, *Strains of Utopia: Gender, Nostalgia, and Hollywood Film Music* (Princeton, NJ: Princeton University Press, 1992), esp. 101–15.

32. Theodor W. Adorno and Hanns Eisler, *Composing for the Films,* 4–6, and Theodor W. Adorno, *Essays on Music,* ed. Richard Leppert (Berkeley: University of California Press, 2002), 532. See also Leppert's "Commentary," 363.

33. Middleton, *Studying Popular Music,* 30, stresses only these formulaic and regularizing aspects of the Baroque material in the "A Whiter Shade of Pale."

34. Some manifestations of another variety of mid-sixties Baroqueism ("Beatles à la Baroque") is discussed by Bernard Gendron, *Between Montmartre and the Mudd Club,* 172–73. An especially clear indication of the extent to which the term "Baroque" had been effectively lodged in the popular imagination as a code phrase linked to recreational drugs is the ad copy for a Chess Records release of songs by the European group Les Baroques that appeared in the first issue of *Rolling Stone* in 1967: "The fact is you really haven't been turned on until you've been turned on by The Baroques." See also Whiteley, *The Space Between,* 72. Baroque figuration is still employed in some popular music genres as a signal for the loosening or opening up of time, e.g., in the temporally undirected, ambient electronica style of a number like "Mike Mills" by the group Air, featuring Bachian organ material in perpetual motion. Moore's analysis of "nondirected temporality" (p. 89) is also significant in this regard and addresses other stylistic means for the encoding of "lack of direction" in psychedelic, "hippy," and progressive rocks.

35. Theodor W. Adorno, *Minima moralia: Reflections from Damaged Life,* trans. E. F. N. Jephcott (London: New Left Books, 1974), 86–87.

36. On the former see, e.g., David J. Levin, "Is There a Text in This Libido? *Diva* and the Rhetoric of Contemporary Opera Criticism," in *Between Opera and Cinema,* ed. Jeongwon Joe and Rose Theresa (New York: Routledge, 2002), 121–33.

37. Concerning my characterization of Spector's reconstruction of Wagner as an artistic persona, Zak, *Poetics of Rock,* 176, reports the description of Spector by the producer Jerry Wexler "as star, as artist, as unifying force." His Wagnerian model

extended, clearly, beyond the matter of making sound to the notion of coherent, multidimensional musical productions involving—in many cases—lyrics, music, and recording. Spector's involvement in recording production, analogous in its significance to conventional "orchestration" (since he achieved a range of acoustical effects by recording techniques, even while employing the same instrumentation), is addressed at length in Zak's rich study.

38. What I have called mad science, partly by way of linking this literary, expressive, and experiential mode with the repertoire under consideration in the next chapters, was characterized in the nineteenth century as the "scientific marvelous." See Tzvetan Todorov, *The Fantastic: A Structural Approach to a Literary Genre* trans. Richard Howard (Ithaca: Cornell University Press, 1975), 56. On the Enlightenment and Romantic elements (literary, scientific, and philosophical) in Shelley's *Frankenstein,* see Anne K. Mellor, "Making a 'Monster': An Introduction to *Frankenstein,*" in *The Cambridge Companion to Mary Shelley,* ed. Esther Schor (Cambridge: Cambridge University Press, 2003), 9–25; also Nancy Yousef, "The Monster in a Dark Room: *Frankenstein,* Feminism, and Philosophy," *Modern Language Quarterly* 63 (2002): 197–226. My rather superficial comparison is intended primarily as a poetic and conceptual device in my own text, rather than as literary-historical analysis.

39. See, for example, Tony Thewlis, "Phil Spector," in *Rock: The Rough Guide,* ed. Jonathan Buckley and Mark Ellingham (London: Rough Guides Ltd., 1996), 825.

40. I have taken some poetic license in this formulation; the fly on Mother/Norman's hand is a product not of Hitchcock's imagination but of Robert Bloch, author of the novel, *Psycho,* upon which the screenplay was based (New York: Tom Doherty Associates, 1989). Bloch's image of the fly (p. 223), however, was deemed sufficiently central to and conformant with Hitchcock's vision to be retained as the focal point of the film's concluding scene, in which Mother and Norman are visually blended on screen. In fact, Hitchcock found it so engaging that he had originally planned to use it as a visual leitmotif in the film. See Stephen Rebello, *Alfred Hitchcock and the Making of Psycho* (New York: Saint Martin's Press, 1990), 129. The famous aerial view of Phoenix, Arizona, in the film's opening moments was intended, one might argue, as a fly-eye's view, since the descending panoramic camera eventually leads us through a small opening in the window to Marion and Sam's hotel room, where the couple is observed, voyeuristically, by the camera (and audience), as by a fly on the wall.

41. See, for example, the description of *ekstasis* in Renate Schlesier, "Maenads as Tragic Models," in *Masks of Dionysus,* ed. Thomas H. Carpenter and Christopher A. Faraone (Ithaca and London: Cornell University Press, 1993), 96–97.

42. For a more literal reading of the synaesthetic program behind the *Fantasia* project, see Mark Clague, "Playing in 'Toon: Walt Disney's *Fantasia* (1940) and the Imagineering of Classical Music," *American Music* 22 (2004): 91–109, esp. 96–99. On the Fantasound recording and playback processes, see Michael Barrier, *Hollywood Cartoons: American Animation in Its Golden Age* (New York: Oxford University Press, 1999), 274. Jack Kerouac was reportedly so

"entranced" by *Fantasia* that he saw it in New York's Thalia theater fifteen times in the early 1940s; see Gerald Nicosia, *Memory Babe: A Critical Biography of Jack Kerouac* (New York: Grove Press, 1983), 112.

43. See Weiss, *Breathless,* 83.

5. THE FANTASTIC, THE PICTURESQUE, AND THE DIMENSIONS OF NOSTALGIA

Epigraph: Johann Wolfgang Goethe, *Die Leiden des jungen Werther* (Frankfurt am Main: Insel Verlag, 2001), 127. In a widely known and less than literal translation: "She was playing upon her piano a succession of delightful melodies, with such intense expression! . . . The tears came into my eyes. I leaned down, and looked intently at her wedding-ring; my tears fell—immediately she began to play that favourite, that divine air which has so often enchanted me. I felt comfort from a recollection of the past, of those bygone days when that air was familiar to me; and then I recalled all the sorrows and the disappointments which I had since endured." (Thomas Carlyle translation: Harvard Classics, 1917). Regarding details of this text and alternative translations, see below.

1. The fantastic in literature (as a marker of genre or detail) has been located in such liminal moments positioned between the logical and the unreal (i.e., the imaginary and the impossible). See Todorov, *The Fantastic.*

2. See, e.g., Eric S. Rabkin, *The Fantastic in Literature* (Princeton, NJ: Princeton University Press, 1976), 41.

3. See Todorov, *The Fantastic,* 146–47.

4. Paul McCartney suggested that the "White Rabbit" and John Lennon's "Lucy in the Sky" were "God, the big figure," reminiscent of Ginsberg's spyder. See Moore, *The Beatles,* 22.

5. Rabkin, *The Fantastic in Literature,* 109. The original expression, Richard Taruskin informs me, was Milton's: "Come and trip it as you go / On the light fantastic toe" (*L'Allegro,* lines 33–34).

6. Ibid., 111.

7. Ibid.

8. "White Rabbit" must have served as a primary model for Enigma's later historicist hit "Mea culpa," which in the 1990s mixed a military drum, the *Kyrie orbis factor,* and text fragments associated with the Marquis de Sade in a sexually charged antinarrative pastiche. It was featured on the album *MDCCCC,* a representative item within the essentially commercial genre of New Age medievalism that flavored the recording industry at the time; this topic is addressed in Paula Higgins, "From the Ivory Tower to the Marketplace," *Current Musicology* 53 (1992): 109–23. Yet it shares significant common ground with the Romantic redefinition of nonscriptural Christian material (especially music and architecture) as universally relevant mythemes. Nineteenth-century manifestations are familiar (from E. T. A. Hoffmann through Wagner and the Palestrina revival). If "creative-anachronism" fantastic medievalia first penetrated the commercial mainstream during the psychedelic period (or its decadent finale: in the Electric Prunes's Mass in F Minor of 1968, soundtracked in 1969's *Easy Rider*), it was presaged even earlier in twentieth-century popular media by the Marian architectural

images of Disney's *Fantasia* (1940) and the mystical Catholic historicism of Kerouac's *Satori in Paris* (1966).

9. Such precision was not characteristic of Slick's signature improvisatory style, thus further underscoring the atypical nature of this careful, "no-nonsense" vocal performance, as it has been described by Jeff Tamarkin in his *Got a Revolution: The Turbulent Flight of Jefferson Airplane* (New York: Atria Books, 2003), 118. On the genesis of the song, see 110–11.

10. A useful survey of art music elements in rock music of the late 1960s and early 1970s may be found in Stump, *The Music's All That Matters,* 82–91.

11. Todorov emphasized the particular relevance to the fantastic of thematic components associated with sexuality and death; the two function as thematic twins in many of the cases he considers. Immolation as a sort of sexual consummation, or its avoidance, plays a fundamental role in cinematic environments linked to similar musiconarrative structures. See my discussions of *Bride of Frankenstein* and *Rebecca* in chapter 6.

12. Cited in Scott F. Belmer, *20th Century Rock and Roll: Psychedelia* (Burlington, Ontario: Belmo, 1999), 44. Carlos Santana has expressed a similar perspective throughout his career, emphasizing the value of what he calls "rainbow music."

13. Annette Richards, *The Free Fantasia and the Musical Picturesque* (Cambridge: Cambridge University Press, 2001), 5.

14. E.g., in "Light My Fire" the metrical modulation from duple to triple is accompanied by a simultaneous shift from figurational to chordal material in the organ.

15. Thomas Elsaesser, "Le cinéma d'après Lumière: Rereading the 'Origins' of the Filmic Image," in *The Practice of Cultural Analysis: Exposing Interdisciplinary Interpretation,* ed. Mieke Bal (Stanford: Stanford University Press, 1999), 70.

16. Richards, *The Free Fantasia,* 5.

17. Surprisingly, Richard Dyer's detailed overview of Rota's extraordinary range of derivative vocabulary fails to include any mention of Respighi. Dyer, "The Talented Mr. Rota," *Sight and Sound* 14 (September, 2004): 42–45.

18. See especially Richards's discussion of the relationship between voice and keyboard in "An das Clavier," *The Free Fantasia,* 167. In this aspect of keyboard improvisation their aesthetic is markedly different from that of heavy metal's baroque classicism as represented by, for example, Jon Lord, which Robert Walser discusses in *Running With the Devil,* 64–65.

19. Nor would I characterize the song's musical and textual essentials as "surreal" or "timeless" (cf. Whitely's formulation). It is, in fact, the clarity of its time*ful*ness that renders it meaningful.

20. Richards, *The Free Fantasia,* 150, cites Arthur Loesser (*Men, Women and Pianos,* 60): "What a potent engine of feeling this little movement could be! The throbbing heart, the panting breast, the trembling lip, the quivering voice—all this physiognomy of emotion could seem to be in the *Bebung.*"

21. Richards, *The Free Fantasia,* 167.

22. Cited in Paul Collins, *The Stylus Phantasticus and Free Keyboard Music of the North German Baroque* (Aldershot, England: Ashgate, 2005), 138.

23. See the discussion of Buxtehude in Collins, *The Stylus Phantasticus,* 134–39.

24. In this I differ with the exclusively nonaesthetic emphasis that Whiteley places on the reverse process: i.e., music as a depiction or invocation of the drug experience.

25. See Joseph Lanza, *Elevator Music: A Surreal History of Muzak, Easy-Listening, and Other Moodsong* (New York: Picador, U.S.A., 1995), 104–7. On Adorno's view of contrafacting in popular musics, see Middleton, *Studying Popular Music,* chapter 2, and Walser, *Running With the Devil,* 35.

26. Charles Rosen, *Romantic Poets, Critics, and Other Madmen* (Cambridge, MA: Harvard University Press, 1998), 113.

27. The quote is from Belmer, *Psychedelia,* 44. Morrison regularly declared his commitment to "chaos." Thus the acoustical turn back (and the related turn outward, to orientalism) in psychedelia marked nothing as simple or straightforward as a "return to innocence" or "love and drugs" (cf. Moore, *The Beatles,* 13). Theodore Gracyk addressed rock's generally Romantic tendencies in *Rhythm and Noise: An Aesthetics of Rock* (Durham, NC: Duke University Press, 1996), esp. 193–97, but did not analyze specific stylistic or generic topoi. See also Robert Pattison, *The Triumph of Vulgarity: Rock Music in the Mirror of Romanticism* (New York: Oxford University Press, 1987).

28. In this, poets of the 1960s were following the model of their beat forebears. On the engagement of beat writers with the concept as a Romantic topos as early as the 1940s see, for example, Ann Charters, *Kerouac* (London: Picador, 1980), 49.

29. *Melody Maker* (August 19, 1967): 9 (emphasis added).

30. *Melody Maker* (June 24, 1967) 3.

31. Cf. Andrew Ross's comments on the inevitable obsolescence of pop culture in all media in *No Respect: Intellectuals and Popular Culture* (New York: Routledge, 1989), 149–51.

32. On the mix of genres that constituted the substance of radio programming in the pre-rock era, see Susan J. Douglas, *Listening In: Radio and the American Imagination* (New York: Random House, 1999), esp. chapter 4.

33. Thewlis, "Phil Spector."

34. Richards, *The Free Fantasia,* 157–58. It is interesting that the Wagnerian musical "folds" encountered in psychedelic expression and drug-enhanced psychedelic apprehension have been (in their original Mallarméan context) linked to a morbid aesthetic. See Weiss, *Breathless,* 32–33.

35. *Rolling Stone* (November 23, 1967), 14.

36. A 2007 lawsuit brought by Fisher against the singer Gary Brooker concerning artistic ownership of the prelude's musical material is irrelevant to my discussion concerning its acoustical nuances and reception. Indeed, the music seems to combine disparate elements linked to the musical experience of both, Brooker perhaps inspired by The Swingle Singers' vocal number discussed below; and the specific keyboardisms more likely a product of Fisher's training as an organist.

37. Middleton's comments on the bass (reiterated by Walser) suggest he had the "Air" in mind, despite referring to its source as "a cantata."

38. The reference to "sixteen vestal virgins" in the lyrics might also suggest an association with Bach's *Wachet auf*, although this would have required Reid's doing enough "research" (Freddie Mercury's characterization of his own approach to the text of Queen's monster "Bohemian Rhapsody") to be familiar with the hymn's sixth line, "Where are you, wise virgins?" The lyrics also allude to *The Canterbury Tales* and *Through the Looking Glass*. Cf. Whitely, *The Space Between*, 70.

39. For example, the CBS Masterworks recordings (including the *Biggs Bach Book*).

40. That the acoustic environment constructed by Ward Swingle was in the ears of pop musicians at the time is underscored by the nonsense-syllable "fugueing" section of Simon and Garfunkel's "59th Street Bridge Song," released shortly prior to "A Whiter Shade of Pale." While most of the number is infused with a feel-good pop-folk character, at this point the singers engage in airy scatting, and the accompaniment takes on the jazz-inspired features characteristic of the Swingle Singers.

41. Note also the environment at the opening of the violin "Adagio" track on the second volume of Jazz Sebastian Bach, and the "Largo" from the F-Minor harpsichord sonata, perhaps the source for the lower-auxiliary ornaments in Fisher's solo. For Ward Swingle, the "Largo" best defined the group's identity and aesthetic. On jazz scatting in general, see J. Bradford Robinson: "Scat Singing," *New Grove Dictionary of Music and Musicians*, ed. S. Sadie and J. Tyrrell (London: Macmillan, 2001), 22: 419–20.

42. Zak, *Poetics of Rock*, 155–60.

43. Rick Altman, "Deep-Focus Sound: *Citizen Kane* and the Radio Aesthetic," *Quarterly Review of Film and Video* 15 (1994): 1–33; see esp. 6, 20–21.

44. A well-known exception is the camera's vertical ascent in the first opera scene, in which the sound was matched, through effects of prominence and ambience, to the camera perspective. See Altman, "Deep-Focus Sound," 23, and Roy Prendergast, *Film Music*, 55.

45. See David Trotter, "Stereoscopy: Modernism and the 'Haptic,'" *Critical Quarterly* 46 (2004): 38–58.

46. "Sound box" is a term for the sound mix introduced by Allan F. Moore, *Rock: The Primary Text*. In a discussion that prefigures Zak's elaboration, Moore writes: "Most rock also attempts a sense of musical 'depth' (the illusory sense that some sounds originate at a greater distance than others), giving a sense of textural foreground, middleground and background. Much rock also has a sense of horizontal location, provided by the construction of the stereo image" (106). Moore's approach to musical space "privileges the listening, rather than the production, process." Zak's focus is on sound production (or construction) but takes into account listening as a sort of reading in his narrative approach to stereo mixes (see Zak, *Poetics of Rock*, 145–50).

47. On the stairwell echo, see Lanza, *Elevator Music*, 106.

48. Middleton, *Studying Popular Music* (31) calls Brooker's timbre "rich, open-throated, sensuous." He links the song's affect to counterculture trends that leaned toward the "sensuously spiritual," a description perhaps suggested by the pseudo-ecclesiastic monumentalism of its contemporaneous press.

49. In this, "When a Man Loves a Woman" falls within the category of contrafacting as it has been applied to jazz. Cf. James Patrick, "Charlie Parker and Harmonic Sources of Bebop Composition."

50. Elsaesser, "Le cinéma d'après Lumière," 73.

51. Cf. Carolyn Abbate's discussion of the inability of music to achieve narrative "pastness" in *Unsung Voices*, 54.

52. See chapter 1, note 77.

53. *Rolling Stone* (November 9, 1967): 6.

54. *Rolling Stone* (January 20, 1968): 10 (emphasis added). See also the discussion of Queen's "Bohemian Rhapsody" in chapter 7.

55. Rabkin, *The Fantastic*, 200.

56. Richard Taruskin, "The Golden Age of Kitsch," *New Republic* (March 21, 1994): 28–38, esp. 28.

57. On the genesis of Rossetti's *Bocca Bacciata*, and the furor with which its erotic aspect was received, see Alastair Grieve, "Rossetti and the Scandal of Art for Art's Sake in the early 1860s," in *After the Pre-Raphaelites: Art and Aestheticism in Victorian England*, ed. Elizabeth Prettejohn (New Brunswick, NJ: Rutgers University Press, 1999), 21–22.

58. Spokesmen for the Pre-Raphaelite program argued otherwise. G. E. Street renounced the notion that "we . . . medievalists" do not "wish for an instant to copy what other men have done." See Andrea Rose, *The Pre-Raphaelites* (Ann Arbor, MI: Borders Press, 1997), 20.

59. Timothy Hilton, *The Pre-Raphaelites* (London: Thames and Hudson, 1970), 56–57, cited in Rabkin, *The Fantastic*, 202.

60. Ward Swingle's concern with control of these parameters is detailed in his book *Swingle Singing* (Delaware Water Gap, PA: Shawnee Press, 1997). A more superficial variety of musical pre-Raphaelitism in the same period would be a group like Pentangle, or a soloist like John Renbourn, whose music and its associated cover art was self-consciously medieval. Here and throughout this chapter, however, my analyses are based not on topoi but on technique and form.

61. See the discussion in Annette Davison, *Hollywood Theory, Non-Hollywood Practice: Cinema Soundtracks in the 1980's and 1990's* (Aldershot, England: Ashgate, 2004), 180–83.

62. Rose, *The Pre-Raphaelites*, 48.

63. Fredric Jameson, *Postmodernism, or The Cultural Logic of Late Capitalism* (Durham, NC: Duke University Press, 1991), xvii. His treatment of "utopia," on the other hand is rather specific and maintains its historical associations with political positions. As he feared would be the case with "nostalgia" (hence the footnote), "utopia" is more often encountered, especially in works on film and music, in its generalized sense.

64. Caryl Flinn, *Strains of Utopia*, 93.

65. Richard Dyer, "Entertainment and Utopia," in *Genre: The Musical*, ed. Rick Altman (London: Routledge and Kegan Paul, 1981), cited in Flinn, *Strains of Utopia*, 101.

66. On both the "celebratory and stigmatizing" aspects of "sentimental," see June Howard, "What Is Sentimentality," *American Literary History* 11 (Spring, 1999): 71.

67. The last construction is that of Christopher Lasch, *The True and Only Heaven: Progress and Its Critics* (New York: W. W. Norton, 1991), cited in Sean Scanlan, "Nostalgia," *Iowa Journal of Cultural Studies* 5 (2005); available online at http://www.niowa.edu/~ijcs/nostalgia/nost.htm (accessed May 5, 2006).

68. See Bakhtin, *The Dialogic Imagination*, 146–47. See also Linda Hutcheon, "Irony, Nostalgia, and the Postmodern," University of Toronto English Language (UTEL) Main Collection (1998); available online at http://www.library.utoronto.ca/utel/criticism/hutchinp.html (accessed May 2, 2006).

69. Hutcheon "Irony, Nostalgia, and the Postmodern."

70. See the discussion of Brown's *The Last of England* in Ann C. Colley, *Nostalgia and Recollection in Victorian Culture* (New York: Saint Martin's Press, 1998), esp. 38.

71. The painting is partly autobiographical, inspired by friends who had left England to seek their fortune in Australia, but the figures are actually those of Brown and his wife, who were contemplating a similar move to India. Rose, *The Pre-Raphaelites*, 19.

72. Colley, *Nostalgia*, 37.

73. Rose, *The Pre-Raphaelites*, 48, characterizes the effect as being "like a photo-montage."

74. The first is from the translation by Michael Hulse (London: Penguin Books, 1989), 105; the latter from that of Catherine Hutter (New York: New American Library, 1962), 99.

75. Cf. Flinn's relevant analysis of *The Country Girl* (1954), a filmic enactment of the sort of nostalgia described by Hutcheon: "Simultaneously distancing and proximating, nostalgia exiles us from the present as it brings the imagined past near. The simple, pure, ordered, easy, beautiful, or harmonious past is constructed in conjunctions with the present." Flinn describes such a moment in the film, as an alcoholic singer hears a song from his sober, happy past on the radio: "When the song is . . . played on the radio, it reminds Frank of all that had once been his. At the same time, however, it recalls his distance from that ideal state and its ultimate remoteness to him." Flinn, *Strains of Utopia*, 113. She is correct to emphasize the distance between two times. But the film (and Flinn's interpretation) focuses only on nostalgia's then and now components, arguing again for the "idealization" of the past as a necessary component of nostalgic experience. An understanding of multimedia nostalgia more in keeping with my own and somewhat relevant to my Tarkovsky example is offered by Powrie, *French Cinema in the 1980s*, esp. 26.

76. The sound of water dripping early in the film similarly recalls another ancient time-measuring device, the water clock.

77. Tarkovsky discusses the scene briefly and in a rather self-deprecating fashion, calling the house in the cathedral "a constructed image which smacks of literariness." See Andrey Tarkovsky, *Sculpting in Time: Reflections on the Cinema*, trans. Kitty Hunter-Blair (Austin: University of Texas Press, 1996), 213–16. Tarkovsky's discussions of cinema with respect to literature appear to reflect the same preoccupations with notions of narrative and genre that inform Bakhtin's theoretical writings. A more specific link is suggested by Bakhtin's formulation of the narrative zone (*zona*), a locus within which voices of characters

are manifest. In the zone's operation as "a sphere of influence" through which characters are refracted (see Bakhtin, *The Dialogic Imagination*, passim and Glossary, 434), it intersects with Tarkovsky's construction of the revelatory zone (*zona*) in *Stalker* (1979). See *Sculpting in Time,*198. I am grateful to Caryl Emerson and Peter Schmelz for their generous assistance regarding matters related to Russian language, Bakhtin, and Tarkovsky. Neither, however, should be held accountable for my speculation in this instance.

78. For example, in the first significant synchronized sound film, *The Jazz Singer* (1927), Jack Robin's recall in the diegetic present of his father singing *Kol nidre* in the past is enacted visually in a mirror and aurally in Louis Silvers's background scoring as an extended audiovisual tableau. Jack's nostalgia event is not merely personal but embedded in the ethnic and racial memories explored throughout the film by its protagonists. I would not assign this filmic representation, however, to the category of formal-stylistic nostalgia I have been exploring in this chapter.

79. Throughout this discussion, I have employed Christian Metz's term "offscreen" music rather than the more familiar "nondiegetic," in part to deemphasize any understanding of the sound track as the attachment to any potentially narrative filmic structure. The distinction is even more crucial because the track's acoustical elements include sounds that have been produced in the course of the film by characters appearing on screen, within the filmic environment, and yet not necessarily materially present in the visual mise-en-scène at the time of their acoustical manifestation. Nostalgia explores to great effect the potential relationships between mise-en-scène and mise-en-bande.

80. Tarkovsky, *Sculpting in Time,* 163.

81. The poem's third stanza introduces the present and past nodes of the poetic narrative: "Methought from the battlefield's dreadful array / Far, far I had roam'd on a desolate track: 'Twas Autumn, and sunshine arose on the way / To the home of my fathers, that welcomed me back."

82. On the audiences for progressive rock in England and the United States see Edward Macan, *Rocking the Classics: English Progressive Rock and the Counterculture* (Oxford : Oxford University Press, 1997), esp. 144–66. Also Will Straw, "Characterizing Rock Music Culture: The Case of Heavy Metal," in *On Record: Rock, Pop, and the Written Word,* ed. Simon Frith and Andrew Goodwin (New York: Pantheon Books, 1990), 97–110.

83. Melissa Carey and Michael Hannan, "Case Study 2: *The Big Chill,*" in *Popular Music and Film,* ed. Ian Inglis (London: Wallflower Press, 2003), 162–77.

84. Claudia Gorbman, *Unheard Melodies: Narrative Film Music* (London: British Film Institute / Bloomington: Indiana University Press, 1987), 12–16, cited in Carey and Hannan, "Case Study 2," 163.

85. Carey and Hannan, "Case Study 2," 171.

86. *Melody Maker* (June 17, 1967): 5. One can only wonder how fans may have taken (or Whiteley would respond to) *Melody Maker's* later declaration (August 19, 1967), 19, apparently as part of an effort to reform their image, that the group's music represented "one big 'no' to psychedelia."

87. Richards, *The Free Fantasia,* 160.

88. See Richards, *The Free Fantasia*, 145–48.

89. Manufacturers of radio and canned "wallpaper" music have often found Baroque stylistic parameters particularly suitable for constructing seamless recorded environments that house and encourage the sorts of repetitive listening procedures Robert Fink has traced through the second half of the twentieth century. See his *Repeating Ourselves: American Minimal Music as Cultural Practice* (Berkeley: University of California Press, 2005), especially 174–75.

6. LISTENING IN DARK PLACES

1. Cited most recently by Roger Hickman, *Reel Music: Exploring 100 Years of Film Music* (New York: W. W. Norton, 2006), 3.

2. I do not assign the word "narrative" to film stories recklessly. In this case I feel comfortable invoking the term, since *Laura* is (as advertised in its on-screen title) literally novelistic (see the discussion in chapter 2). Based on the novel by Vera Caspary (who eventually withdrew her support from the film project and mounted a stage production of the story), the film *Laura* is less complicated with respect to multiple narrators than the novel. In the end, however, it has remained rather more, and famously, ambiguous.

3. On Raksin and Schoenberg, see Sabine M. Feisst, "Arnold Schoenberg and the Cinematic Art," *Musical Quarterly* 83 (1999): 93–113.

4. A still picture of the famous shot is provided in Kathryn Kalinak, *Settling the Score*, 165. Kalinak outlines the basics of the len-a-tone process on p. 178.

5. Richard H. Bush, liner notes to the CD re-recording of the full score of *Bride of Frankenstein* (Silver Screen Records, 1993), and Brown, *Overtones*, 274.

6. David Neumeyer and James Buhler identify the instrument as a harmonium in "Analytical and Interpretive Approaches to Film Music (1): Analysing the Music," in *Film Music: Critical Approaches*, ed. K. J. Donnelly (New York: Continuum Publishing Group, 2001), 30. See also Rachel Segal, "Franz Waxman: A Musical Innovator," *The Cue Sheet* 22 (2007): 11–22, 15.

7. See the interview in Brown, *Overtones*, 288.

8. For example, Eminem's "The Way I Am," in which the "cursed, cursed, cursed" rapper is "the meanest," something like a sermonizing monster. His persona is granted imaginary weight and dimension by the chime sounds that, in the minor-mode environment, register them quite effectively for nonmusical listeners.

9. For an analysis of the tonalities involved in this section of the film, see Rebecca Leydon, "Hooked on Aetherophonics: *The Day the Earth Stood Still*," in *Off the Planet: Music, Sound, and Science Fiction Cinema*, ed. Philip Hayward (London: John Libbey Publishing, 2004), 30–41, at 37.

10. On the Velvet Underground's position regarding Zappa, see Ignacio Juliá, "Feedback: The Legend of the Velvet Underground," in Albin Zak, *The Velvet Underground Companion: Four Decades of Commentary* (New York: Schirmer Books, 1997), 203, 208.

11. David E. James has discussed some of the unusual features of the group's style in "I'll Be Your Mirror Stage: Andy Warhol in the Cultural Imagery," in *Pop Out: Queer Warhol*, ed. Jennifer Doyle, Jonathan Flatley, and José Esteban Muñoz (Durham and London: 1996, Duke University Press), 41.

12. Bosley Crowther of the *New York Times* wrote of that the film's aura of depravity and corruption was "so indulgently displayed that it looks as though the aim of the producers was to include as much as possible, within the limits of the Production Code." Cited in Robert Ottoson, *A Reference Guide to the American Film Noir: 1940–1958* (Metuchen, NJ: The Scarecrow Press, Inc., 1981), 27. The remark seems almost to foreshadow Warhol's position with respect to film content.

13. Liliom's "carousel song" had been composed by Jean Lenoir, who is given billing above Waxman in the film's title credits. Within the story, the "child's child" will be Liliom's own daughter, born to the sweet Julie after his death.

14. Elsaesser, "Le cinéma d'après Lumière," 68–70.

15. Already on *Revolver*, loops had been employed for "Tomorrow Never Knows," and on the *Sgt. Pepper* album a melodic loop was built into the music for the verses of "Lucy in the Sky with Diamonds." In its waltz-like surface (written in a slow 12/8), the latter resonates with several of the themes discussed in this chapter, especially in its setting of the phrase "the man with kaleidoscope eyes," that invokes circularity through the eye and the kaleidoscope image as well as the fragmentation of vision that inheres in the latter. For a review of theories regarding the "meaning" of the song's imagery, see Moore, *The Beatles*, 33–4. Small-range cycles like these complement the larger issues of chromatic harmony and infinite melody derived from other musical sources, including Wagner. An interpretation of Wagner's chromaticism from this perspective is offered by Robert P. Morgan, "Circular Form in the Tristan Prelude," *Journal of the American Musicological Society* 53 (2000): 69–103.

16. John Whitney, *Digital Harmony: On the Complementarity of Music and Visual Art* (Peterborough, NH: Byte Books, 1980), esp. 72.

17. See Steven C. Smith, *A Heart at Fire's Center: The Life and Music of Bernard Herrmann* (Berkeley: University of California Press, 1991), 172.

18. Leydon, "Hooked on Aetherophonics," 37, suggests that Klaatu's hand movements "mirror those of a theremin player." In fact, they are more like the on-off motions associated with Theremin's electrical switching devices.

19. Andrew Lamb: "Waltz," *Grove Music Online*, ed. L. Macy, http://www .grovemusic.com (accessed August 28, 2006). Francesca Draughon summarizes late nineteenth-century views of the waltz's sexual dynamics in "Dance of Decadence: Class, Gender, and Modernity in the Scherzo of Mahler's Ninth Symphony," *Journal of Musicology* 20 (2003): 396–404.

20. On the main waltz theme of the *Vertigo* prelude, see also Brown, *Overtones*, 166.

21. Elsaesser, "Le cinéma d'après Lumière," 67.

22. If Dalí's scissors recall Buñuel, the curtain that they cut, adorned with multiple eyes, is more reminiscent of a set from Lang's *Metropolis* of a few years earlier.

23. See Dan Auiler, *Hitchcock's Notebooks* (New York: HarperCollins, 1999), 520. On the perception of Debussy as essentially circular, see Dahlhaus, *Realism*, 116.

24. The rhythmic pattern begins to be highlighted through prominence a second or two before the one-hour-and-forty-eight-minute mark of the film.

25. Camille Paglia describes the technical processes by which the birds were added in layers to the mise-en-scène in *The Birds* (London: British Film Institute, 1998), 15–16. See also Auiler, *Hitchcock's Notebooks*, 506–23. In his brief but insightful analysis of the crucial flower-shop scene in the first portion of *Vertigo*, Slavoj Žižek describes another experiment involving a partitioning of the screen, but with a perceptive split marked by a vertical gash (the black crack of the door ajar) in a single monoscopic plane; see his *Tarrying with the Negative: Kant, Hegel, and the Critique of Ideology* (Durham, NC: Duke University Press, 1993), 106–7. The sensation of magnitude and open space that Hitchcock achieves in the flower shop vis-a-vis the cramped alley from which it is viewed suggests visual "depth," but it is not biplanar with respect to that depth, nor is it strictly stereoscopic.

26. See, e.g., David Neumeyer, "Source Music, Background Music, Fantasy and Reality in Early Sound Film," *College Music Symposium* 37 (1997): 3–20.

27. See the discussion in Roy Prendergast, *Film Music*, 138–45, and Brown, *Overtones*, 162–63.

28. Cook, *Analysing Musical Multimedia*, 66.

29. There are perhaps additional resonances of Antheil's Fifth ("Tragic") Symphony, related to his years as a war correspondent.

30. Herrmann's murder cue is so culturally enmeshed by now that it is pointless to attempt a catalog of instances in which this misunderstanding has been re-iterated. Among the most recent (and problematic, since it appears in a textbook on film music) is Roger Hickman's statement to the anonymous student audience for his text: "It is better to think of the sound as the slashing of a knife." *Real Music: Exploring 100 Years of Film Music* (New York: W. W. Norton, 2006), 265. See also Brown, *Overtones*, 24, who refers to the "slash-and-chop string chords." Irving Singer, in his *Three Philosophical Filmmakers: Hitchcock, Welles, Renoir* (Cambridge, MA: MIT Press, 2004), 43–44, employs language indicative of his subliminal understanding of the connection when he refers to feeling "prodded," "jabbed," and "poked" by Herrmann's music. See also Jack Sullivan, *"Psycho:* The Music of Terror," in *Cineaste* 32 (Winter, 2006): 20–28. Sullivan's work on the music for Hitchcock's productions provides an enriched historical, largely anecdotal, context for the productions but reiterates the standard interpretations of musical events, borrowed from earlier writers, including Brown. Sullivan, who is not a musicologist, emphasizes music's role as an effective, supporting adjunct to narrative and dramatic content and to scenic atmosphere.

31. See, e.g., Singer, *Three Philosophical Filmmakers* , 17–18.

32. See Paul Théberge, *Any Sound You Can Imagine: Making Music/Consuming Technology* (Hanover, NH: Wesleyan University Press, 2005), 200–201.

33. Examples include George Toles, "'If thine eye offend thee . . .': *Psycho* and the Art of Infection," in *Alfred Hitchcock's Psycho: A Casebook*, ed. Robert Kolker (Oxford: Oxford University Press, 2004), 119–46; Raymond Durgnat, *A Long Hard Look at 'Psycho'* (London: British Film Institute, 2002), 105; Brigitte Puecker, *Incorporating Images: Film and the Rival Arts* (Princeton, NJ: Princeton University Press, 1995), 52.

34. For example Puecker, whose analysis of film focuses on representations of the body, suggests in fact that Norman's peephole is related (analogously) to

cinema, but she emphasizes its "pornographic" aspects, linking this to cinema's problematization of the human, and especially the female, body. Her historical frame of reference for the viewing aperture is limited to the "invasive spying" of characters in the early films of Fritz Lang. In the same discussion Puecker reiterates the centrality of the phallic dimension of the shower murder (*Incorporating Images*, 52).

35. Durgnat, *A Long Hard Look*, 119, assigns the ecstatic aspect of the scene to Marion, citing Eisenstein's concept of ecstasy as "some extreme mental state of horror and pathos." I think it unlikely that Durgnat's sense of ecstasis was engendered by the visual alone. In his at times insightful analysis of the film's structures Durgnat does not, however, address Herrmann's music.

36. Chion, *The Voice in Cinema*, 35, 140–51.

37. The gimmick was one of which director James Whale was especially fond. In the equally fantastic but lower budgeted *The Old Dark House* (1932), Whale, with considerable delight, assigned the role of the mysterious family patriarch to a woman, Elspeth Dudgeon (billed as "John Dudgeon"), a friend from his repertory theater days. See James Curtis, *James Whale: A New World of Gods and Monsters* (London: Faber and Faber, 1998), 180–81. *Frankenstein* opens with a presenter emerging from behind curtains to address the audience, further confusing the screen with a live theater stage.

38. Chion, *The Voice in Cinema*, 10.

39. Ibid., 125.

40. Ibid., 11, 131.

41. Ibid., 156.

42. Chion, *The Voice in Cinema*, 157 (emphasis added), writes: "When Al Jolson is supposedly performing the Kol Nidre at the synagogue, the film forgoes Jolson's own light and fluent voice, which we heard singing 'jazz.' He lip-synchs to the voice of a real cantor—but we are not supposed to know." Jolson's performance is—from the liturgical perspective—unusually "jazzy," as Krin Gabbard points out in *Jammin' at the Margins: Jazz in the American Cinema* (Chicago: University of Chicago Press, 1996), 40. Personal style notwithstanding, Jolson had been coached by the cantor Paul Lamkoff, who was interviewed on the subject in *Downbeat* magazine (December 17, 1952, 22). Cf. Robert L. Carringer, *The Jazz Singer* (Madison: University of Wisconsin Press, 1979), 140. Chion further suggests that the "ragtime" performance of young Jakie (Bobby Gordon) "appears to have been recorded by an adult voice," but it is likely that Gordon recorded the songs himself for later lip-synching. The voice is hardly that of an invisible adult, in any case.

43. Douglas, *Listening In*, 40–52.

44. See Albert Glinsky, *Theremin: Ether, Music and Espionage* (Urbana and Chicago: University of Illinois Press, 2000), 85, 89–90. The poster for the Met demonstration is reproduced in Glinsky (no figure number, no page number). Cf. also the newsreel footage in Stephen M. Martin's film *Theremin: An Electronic Odyssey* (1995).

45. Timothy Taylor's abbreviated consideration of the theremin in *Strange Sounds: Music, Technology, and Culture* (New York: Routledge, 2001), 83–92, missed several important aspects of the instrument's cultural and media contexts,

e.g., the important link between outer space (the space between the planets of which the instrument became an index in the 1940s and after) and the "space between worlds" of the ethereal mind-set associated with early radio and radio-related sound technology. In emphasizing the instrument's intersection with mid-century science and science fiction, Taylor also fails to register the means by which the instrument made its way into the pop imagination in the first place, where it had served initially as a marker of psychopathology; in the words of Miklós Rózsa, the theremin became the "official Hollywood mouthpiece of mental disorders." See *A Double Life: The Autobiography of Miklós Rózsa* (New York: 1982), 128, cited in Josef Kloppenburg, *Die dramaturgische Funktion der Musik in den Filmen Alfred Hitchcocks* (Munich: Wilhelm Fink Verlag, 1986), 90. See also Royal S. Brown, "Hitchcock's *Spellbound*: Jung vs. Freud," *Film/Psychology Review* 4 (1980): 35–58.

46. Glinsky, *Theremin*, 89 (emphasis added).

47. For a description of the Vitaphone technology in its first phase, see Carringer, *The Jazz Singer*, 175–88.

48. See, e.g., Donald Crafton, *The Talkies*, 113–18.

49. Ibid., 120–21.

50. This negative review, which appeared in *Photoplay* (December 1927), is cited in Fred Karlin, *Listening to Movies: The Film Lover's Guide to Film Music* (New York: Schirmer, 1994), 238. On particular parameters of "radio sound" see Altman, "Deep Focus Sound." Cf. also *Sound Theory/Sound Practice*, ed. Rick Altman (New York: Routledge, 1992), 118–22.

51. O'Neill's experimental play temporally invoked the monumental architecture of the classic model. The play, premiered by Greenwich Village's Theatre Guild, began at 5:15 P.M. and didn't conclude until after 11 P.M. (there was a one-hour dinner break). I use Genette's term "extradiegetic" here, even though the characters do not "narrate." They did, however, engage with the real audience, even if without dramatic intention. Gérard Genette, *Narrative Discourse: An Essay in Method*, trans. Jane E. Lewin (Ithaca, NY: Cornell University Press, 1980), 228–29.

52. Royal Brown, in his brief consideration of the transition-to-sound period (*Overtones*, 56–58), suggests that the effects of the transition to realism could still be encountered in film scores decades later. For a theoretical overview of the range of possible variants on the dichotomy between source music and background music, see Neumeyer, "Source Music."

53. Travis Bogard, *Contour in Time: The Plays of Eugene O'Neill* (New York: Oxford University Press, 1972; rev. ed., 1988).

54. Similar experiments with multiplanar soundtracks were under way in British cinema in the same period. See Jamie Sexton, "The Audio-Visual Rhythms of Modernity: *Song of Ceylon*, Sound, and Documentary Filmmaking," *Scope* (May 2004); available online at www.nottingham.ac.uk/film/journal/articles/audio-visual-ryhthms.htm (accessed October 5, 2006).

55. Crafton, *The Talkies*, 356.

56. Altman, "Inventing the Cinema Soundtrack," 352–53.

57. Crafton, 353. Some objected to dialogue films on the grounds that by imitating the stage production they replaced the imaginative field of contemplation,

which had characterized the silent film experience, with artifice and theatricality (p. 488).

58. A brief and early example is featured in *The Informer* (1935). Gypo makes his way through two sets of entrance doors at the Dunboys House pub for his meeting with Frankie. As each door opens, Max Steiner's orchestral background music swells in volume; it fades as each door swings shut. However interesting historically, the effect is purely an engineering gimmick. It is "realistic" in the abstract, since it acoustically defines the on-screen space of the pub entry as if the room inside were a "sound source." Yet it is nonsensical with respect to narrative realism, since the music of the background score is not emanating from within that diegetic space. A decrease in volume and increase in reverberation to match the camera's ascent in the first opera scene in *Citizen Kane* is a more familiar (and more refined) case. Altman, "Inventing the Cinema Soundtrack," 352, points out that even in the late 1920s certain sound engineers were committed to the notion that sound scale should be matched to image scale.

59. See de Man's introduction to Hans Robert Jauss, *Toward an Aesthetic of Reception,* trans. Timothy Bahti (Minneapolis: University of Minnesota Press, 1982), xxv.

60. See Rosar, "Music for the Monsters," 401.

61. Rosar provides an inventory of cues for the film.

62. Wegener directed the film and played the title character.

63. On the horror phenomenon in general, see David J. Skal, *Screams of Reason: Mad Science and Modern Culture* (New York: W. W. Norton, 1998). On Whale's film see, in addition to Curtis's work cited above, Alberto Manguel, *Bride of Frankenstein* (London: British Film Institute, 1997).

64. For roadmaps of the motivic and "dramatic" content of Waxman's score, see William Darby and Jack Du Bois, *American Film Music: Major Composers, Techniques, Trends, 1915–1990* (Jefferson, NC: McFarland, 1990), 118–23, and Hickman, *Reel Music,* 128–32.

65. François Jost, "The Voices of Silence," in *The Sounds of Early Cinema,* ed. Richard Abel and Rick Altman (Bloomington: Indiana University Press, 2001), 53–54.

66. One of his music editors reported that "when Franz would score a picture, he would put the dialogue in his ear and he would conduct to the dialogue just to get the nuances in the music that he needed." See Karlin, *Listening to Movies,* 308.

67. "Processional March" (cue 4) is associated with Henry Frankenstein's sudden illness, which halts the expected consummation of his marriage to his lovely bride, Elizabeth. In the title music, major third fanfares are produced by the top note in whole-tone chords in the first few measures, creating another, and more immediate, point of comparison for the dissonant monster motif that occurs (at rehearsal letter C) in Waxman's sketch score.

68. Curtis, *James Whale,* 239–40.

69. Dukas's sorcerer (i.e., Goethe's by way of Lucan) was another Egyptian magician. See Abbate, *Unsung Voices,* 30–32.

70. *Rocket Ship*'s television-style screens, which form embedded frames of internal multimedia narrative, recall the artifice of *The Mummy* and reflect once

more the conceptual link (inherited from the nineteenth century) between the supernatural and the scientific marvelous in their twentieth-century representations as multimedia. On the use of studio library tracks in low-budget serials, see Richard H. Bush, "The Music of *Flash Gordon* and *Buck Rogers*" in *Film Music*, vol. 1, ed. Clifford McCarty (New York: Garland Publishing, 1989).

71. David Neumeyer, "Melodrama as a Compositional Resource in Early Hollywood Sound Cinema," *Current Musicology* (1995): 61–94, 74–75.

72. *Composing for the Films*, 37.

73. In the same film Eisler praises the dripping effect he created for Heydrich's blood transfusion, that "makes for adequate reactions on the part of the listeners and precludes the wrong conclusions." One wonders if it may have been inspired by Steiner's musical evocation of the dripping water in Gypo's cell in *The Informer*, which is perhaps Steiner's most melodramatic score. In fact, that musical effect was among the most celebrated in the film; concerning audience reception of this scene, see Fred Karlin, *Listening to Movies*, 79.

74. Curtis, *James Whale*, 245. For another discussion of Waxman's score for *Liliom*, see Neumeyer, "Source Music," 18–20.

75. From the public perspective Theremin's music represented an acoustic manifestation of scientific principles as vague to them as the mad science of Frankenstein, but, more specifically, his "music from the air" seemed to inhabit the same liminal space as that of the film scores that backgrounded the monsters.

76. Hickman, e.g., writes that "the drumbeat, which does not coincide with the tempo of the other music, can be heard as the bride's heart, struggling for life" (129).

77. Whale was unconcerned about shot continuity and matching throughout the film. See Curtis, *James Whale*, 241.

78. In *Liliom*, as the protagonist nears the end of his journey, the tympani signals what can only be the sublime sound of the angels. Any majesty, though, is mitigated by what for Whale must have seemed a charming campiness: the sound is mimed by the on-screen image of a chubby mechanical *putto* playing a drum.

79. Curtis, *James Whale*, 140.

80. The "religious bells" is Hickman's characterization.

81. Whale indicated to Waxman that the only "resolution" in the entire film would be the last destruction scene. See Curtis, *James Whale*, 245.

82. On Sulzer and the classical sublime, see James Webster, "The *Creation*, Haydn's Late Vocal Music, and the Musical Sublime," in *Haydn and His World*, ed. Elaine Sisman (Princeton, NJ: Princeton University Press, 1997), 62–64.

7. CONCERTOS, SYMPHONIES, RHAPSODIES (AND AN OPERA)

1. The girl groups shared chart space with Barry McGuire's "Eve of Destruction," arguably a harbinger of the sea change that would take place in the next two years.

2. The cat and rabbit cartoons were released amid a cloud of mutual accusations made by Warners and MGM animators regarding corporate and artistic espionage. See Joe Adamson, *Bugs Bunny: Fifty Years and Only One Grey Hare*

(New York: Henry Holt, 1990), 140–45, 191. See also Gary Marmorstein, *Hollywood Rhapsody: Movie Music and Its Makers, 1900 to 1975* (New York: Schirmer Books, 1997), 358.

3. Richard S. Tedlow, *The Watson Dynasty: The Fiery Reign and Troubled Legacy of IBM's Founding Father and Son* (New York: HarperBusiness, 2003).

4. The symphony was described in an IBM house organ at the time; a description and the songbook are reproduced on the IBM corporate archives website www.ibm.com/ibm/history. I am grateful to Martin Fridson for obtaining and providing me with a copy of the original document from the IBM archives.

5. The best-known essay on the subject is Chuck Jones, "Music and the Animated Cartoon," *Hollywood Quarterly* 1 (1946), reprinted in *Hollywood Quarterly: Film Culture in Postwar America, 1945–1957*, ed. Eric Smoodin and Ann Martin (Berkeley: University of California Press, 2002), 69–76. See also Prendergast, *Film Music*, 180–209.

6. Even among practitioners of enlightened, reconstructed musicology this perception of musical relationships between "high" and "low" forms (in the traditional sense) as a particular mode of union that lies outside the range of normative musical discourse remains largely unquestioned. See, e.g., Walser's arguments concerning the legitimacy of heavy metal virtuosity (throughout *Running With the Devil*) and Ken McLeod, "Bohemian Rhapsodies: Operatic Influences on Rock Music," *Popular Music* 20 (2001): 189–203. Especially telling in the latter case are the unidirectional developmental and teleological implications of "influences" in the title. Compare also the author's conclusion, which refers to works that "bridge" the "seemingly unassailable gulf" between opera and rock.

7. Joseph Kerman, *Concerto Conversations* (Cambridge, MA: Harvard University Press, 1999), 6–8.

8. See Walser, *Running With the Devil*, 44–45.

9. Daniel Goldmark, *Tunes for 'Toons: Music and the Hollywood Cartoon* (Berkeley: University of California Press, 2005), 129; Goldmark addresses other aspects of both cartoons (pp. 110–11). For the review, see James Agee, *Agee on Film: Criticism and Comment on the Movies*, ed. Martin Scorsese (New York: Random House, 2000), 210.

10. In an interview with Boston's AM 1670 (December 6, 2000), the Toys' lead singer Barbara Harris related that the producers and songwriters, Sandy Linzer and Denny Randell, asked her to front the songs. She replaced the former lead singer Barbara Parritt, who switched to back-up. Linzer and Randell felt that Harris was the only one with a sufficiently "commercialized" voice (the group had been singing on street corners in New York). This and other interviews are excerpted in the Harris biography by Joe Viglione, available online at http://wm02.allmusic.com (accessed August 2, 2007).

11. The song's structure here reflects something already evident in ("real") classical music, in which, as Charles Rosen argued, musical elements suggestive of "folk" origins are confined to metrically square moments usually outside the developmental trajectory of movements. See his *The Classical Style* (New York: W. W. Norton, 1972), 334–37.

12. As a medievalist, I would venture that a meaningful analogy might be drawn between the song's naively sylvan idyll and an older lyric form, the

fourteenth-century Italian madrigal, a pastoral genre that emphasized fabricated innocence in its choice of words and topic, and characteristically included a contrasting poetic-rhetorical unit positioned outside the narrative strophes. I don't mean to suggest that Linzer and Randell were aware of such a model. I draw the comparison to illustrate the relevance of analytical methods usually reserved for "art music," historically considered, to "other" musics, historically considered, and at the same time to underscore the arbitrariness by which certain generic forms have been assigned to the former category.

13. Harris's vocal background, in fact, was as a church gospel singer in rural North Carolina, and then in the church of her aunt, a "pastor" in Queens, New York. Linzer and Randell penned several songs for the Four Seasons, one of which even bore the classical register title "Opus 17."

14. Cf. Middleton's discussion of songs that exceed the limits of convention in *Studying Popular Music,* esp. 51–54.

15. See, e.g., the examples translated in William D. Paden, ed., *The Medieval Pastourelle,* 2 vols. (New York: Garland Publishing, 1987).

16. Cf. Andreas Capellanus, *The Art of Courtly Love,* trans. John Jay Parry (New York: Columbia University Press, 1960), 150.

17. See Joseph Lanza, *Elevator Music,* 99.

18. Cf. Flinn, *Strains of Utopia,* 135–36.

19. Andy Ellis, "Quest for Fire: Carlos Santana on Spirit Guides, Rainbow Music, and Passionate Guitar," *Guitar Player* (August 1999): 74–89.

20. *Rolling Stone* (July 8, 1999): 144.

21. *Rolling Stone* (March 16, 2000): 41.

22. Quoted in Ellis, "Quest for Fire," 82.

23. *Rolling Stone* (March 16, 2000): 42.

24. Gabler, *An Empire of Their Own,* 227–28.

25. The Columbia period is not mentioned in Wakeman's biography, which is based on Lewin's own autobiographical note. See "Albert Lewin," in *World Film Directors,* ed. John Wakeman, vol. 1 (New York: H. W. Wilson: 1987), 657–61.

26. See Ronald Rodman, "Tonal Design and the Aesthetic of Pastiche in Herbert Stothart's *Maytime,*" in *Music and Cinema,* ed. Buhler, Flinn, and Neumeyer (Hanover, NH: University Press of New England, 2000), 187–206, esp. 198–203.

27. Hebbel's text reads: *Die Blumen, so hoch sie wachsen / Sind blass hier, wie der Tod; / Nur eine in der Mitte / Steht da im dunkeln Roth* [The flowers that grow so high / here are pale as death; / only one in the middle / stands there in dark red]. The flower's red derives, according to the poem's final stinger, from drinking *Menschenblut* (human blood), rendering it all the more appropriate for Dorian's cruel and murderous descent.

28. "Verrufene Stelle" is of course hardly "charming"; indeed, its fantastic morbidity rendered it not merely unpleasant but unperformable for Clara when she began featuring excerpts from *Waldszenen* in concerts during the 1850s. See Nancy B. Reich, *Clara Schumann: The Artist and the Woman* (Ithaca, NY: Cornell University Press, 1985), 274–75.

29. Marmorstein, *Hollywood Rhapsody,* 250.

30. Lewin's honorific "Sir" was perhaps a reference to the medieval *Sir Tristrem* version of the Tristan story, published by Sir Walter Scott in 1804 (and no doubt familiar to Lewin from his intensive study of nineteenth-century British poetry).

31. James Agee found the addition of the old man an egregious flaw in the film: "I can't see . . . why Dorian's sinning . . . should culminate in a couple of visits to a dive where an old man plays Chopin" (*The Nation*, March 10, 1945). Reprinted in James Agee, *Agee on Film*, 136.

32. Compare the more obvious racial representation in the Tom and Jerry feature, *Zoot Cat*. See also Goldmark, *Tunes for 'Toons*, 99–106.

33. Flinn, *Strains of Utopia*, discusses the musical quotations in this film in detail (118–33).

34. *The Dialogues of Plato*, ed. B. Jowett, 4 vols. (Oxford: Oxford University Press, 1967), 1:103.

35. The song here shares this shamanistic aspect with other Queen productions that transform audiences into receptors, passive agents of the group's voice. The most familiar example of this phenomenon is their rhythmic chant number "We Will Rock You," which, along with "We Are the Champions," has become a staple of mainstream and decidedly macho, heteronormative sporting events. This mode of performance, in which a "spirit" is passed from celebrant to congregation via a shared musical text, is reminiscent of Near Eastern and Semitic call-and-answer liturgies. In live performances Mercury occasionally engaged the audience in responsorial Islamic chant. "Bohemian Rhapsody" includes a reference to the Koran (*Bismillah*, "In the name of Allah").

36. The megasong's unusual—monumental—proportions no doubt contributed to its ready acceptance as a repertoire of future classics.

37. *Rolling Stone* (January 9, 1992): 13–14. When *A Night at the Opera* was first released, Jon Pareles's review in *Crawdaddy* (April 1976): 77–78, called it an "avalanche of overdubs."

38. See Kevin J. H. Dettmar and William Richey, "Musical Cheese: The Appropriation of Seventies Music in Nineties Movies," in Dettmar and Richey, *Reading Rock and Roll: Authenticity, Appropriation, Aesthetics* (New York: Columbia University Press, 1999), 316–18.

39. Kembrew McLeod, "A Critique of Rock Criticism in North America," *Popular Music* 20 (2001): 47–60, considers the complicity of professional rock criticism and historiography in the transmission of a circumscribed notion of authenticity.

40. Jacky Gunn and Jim Jenkins, *Queen: As It Began* (New York: Hyperion, 1992), 94. The implicit note of competition sounded in the remark is perhaps not surprising. Many will hear in the overdubbed a cappella opening of the song the "Sun King" sound of the Beatles' album of several years earlier, *Abbey Road*. Indeed, if the role of "classic" falls to those works standing as exempla for those that follow, the Beatles' concept albums of the mid- to late 1960s stand on rock's Parnassus, apparently creating for those musicians who followed a Bloomian anxiety of influence similar to that which many scholars have attempted to read into the careers of post-Beethoven symphonists. For instance, from the beginning of work on *Night at the Opera*, Mercury maintained that "this will be our Sergeant Pepper."

41. Ken McLeod, "Bohemian Rhapsodies: Operatic Influences on Rock Music," *Popular Music* 20 (2000): 189–203, makes these cases in his analysis of the song's contents and style, which he links—from the standpoint of opera, and presumably because of the song's apparent references to Mozart—to eighteenth-century *opera buffa* (193).

42. For a description of the circumstances surrounding the production and release of "Bohemian Rhapsody" written "in cooperation with Queen," (that is to say, authorized), see Gunn and Jenkins, *Queen*, 92–97. Useful interviews with colleagues from the early period of Queen's success are available on the (unauthorized) DVD *Becoming Queen* (Passport Video). Relevant quotes are also contained in Mick St. Michael's picture book *Queen: In Their Own Words* (London: Omnibus Press, 1992).

43. Walser, *Running With the Devil*, 130.

44. The two performers are discussed in Mark Booth, *Camp* (London: Quartet Books Ltd., 1983), 162–72. Performative aspects of glam extend beyond the props, of course, and intersect with a number of historical performance modes, especially those based on exaggeration of emotion, forms of excess, "deviance," and the performer's identification with the work's own narrative. Compare, for example, Frith's discussion of Piaf, Bowie, Almond, and others in *Performing Rites*, 170–71.

45. Cf. the similarly obscure surface of "A Whiter Shade of Pale": Procul Harum's Keith Reid, in one of the *Melody Maker* interviews (published June 3, 1967: 10–11), said, "I think an artist's conception of what he creates has nothing to do with what someone else gets out of it."

46. Gunn and Jenkins, *Queen*, 94.

47. His association with the fandango in the song could stem from any number of sources and might reflect them all: Mozart ("Non più andrai"), Puccini (act 4 of *La Bohème*), or Procol Harum's "A Whiter Shade of Pale." The battle between the forces of darkness and light in the "opera" chorus recalls in its concept and syntax the finale of *Don Giovanni*.

48. If "Bohemian Rhapsody" is a "parody" (a mock opera in Freddie's words), it is (at least) doubly so, in its essential identification with the overtly parodistic Strauss work. See Herbert Lindenberger, *Opera in History from Monteverdi to Cage* (Stanford: Stanford University Press, 1998), 240, who cites Adorno's remark that "the closer opera gets to a parody of itself, the closer it is to the principle most inherent to it."

49. See Margaret Reynolds, "Ruggiero's Deceptions, Cherubino's Distractions," in *En Travesti: Women, Gender Subversion, Opera*, ed. Corinne E. Blackmer and Patricia Juliana Smith (New York: Columbia University Press, 1995), 145.

50. E.g., Wayne Koestenbaum, *The Queen's Throat: Opera, Homosexuality and the Mystery of Desire* (New York: Vintage Books, 1993). Koestenbaum's experience, as he describes it, was largely acted out in a fetishistic appreciation of recorded music. Mercury, by all accounts, often sat at the piano and sang entire scenic units from operas by heart, voicing all roles.

51. Leonora's response to the poison echoes in the implications of fever and disease (shivers and aches)—a verismo and melodrama staple—in Freddie's second solo strophe.

52. Robert Pullen and Stephen Taylor, *Montserrat Caballé: Casta Diva* (Boston: Northeastern University Press, 1994), 198–99; on Caballé's personal acquaintance with Mercury, see 289, 304–5, 318.

53. It was also the name of the recording label that first signed the pre-Queen version of the group, Smile, and was a significant producer of opera recordings.

54. Concerning the aesthetic Pan and his attributes, see Richard Taruskin, *Text and Act* (New York: Oxford University Press, 1995), 140–41. The characterization of Nijinsky is taken from Ramsay Burt, *The Male Dancer: Bodies, Spectacle, Sexualities* (London: Routledge, 1995), 85.

55. *Dionysus in '69* circulated widely as a photographic essay (New York: Farrar, Straus and Giroux, 1970) and—perhaps less widely—as a film by Brian de Palma.

56. According to a videotaped interview with the song's producer, during the creation of "Bohemian Rhapsody" the members of the group and studio staff simply waited for Mercury to tell them what to do, play, or sing, and then followed his directions; this confirms that Freddie, and not Brian May, conceived the guitar riffs. See *Queen: Magic Years. Volume One* (VHS, 1987: MPI Home Entertainment MP 1690).

57. A standard translation like "I am filled with godlike joy" doesn't quite capture the corporeal resonance of the god's stirring his "Glieder" (limbs) or that of "Lust" as both joy and desire.

58. Dettmar and Richey, "Musical Cheese," 317, quoting Linda Hutcheon.

CONCLUSION

1. In its playful piano introduction and the sliding, chorused guitars of the transitional sections, "Lazing on a Sunday Afternoon" makes reference to Chico Marx's on-screen piano presentations that feature "tripping" along the keys and monumental glissandi, respectively. Both gestures found their way into Bugs Bunny's performance in *Rhapsody Rabbit*, even if Bugs's persona was modeled primarily on Groucho.

2. *Queen: The Interview Collection Volume I: Freddie Mercury* (Collector Direct/Baktabak CBAK 4057). The interview was recorded in Detroit in 1977, while the band was on tour.

3. My reading differs fundamentally from the one proposed by Lawrence Kramer, *Musical Meaning*, 137–38.

4. Gregory Ulmers, "A Night at the Text: Roland Barthes's Marx Brothers," *Yale French Studies* 73 (1987): 38–57, 46.

5. Ibid., 54.

6. See Kramer's representation of the postmodern engagement with "unoriginal" music in his *Musical Meaning*, 261–87.

7. It is perhaps significant in this context that the next scheduled Badguy game release will be titled *Overture*. On the "thematic and expressive continuity" between "art" literature, "art" cinema, and the "mediocre" genre of video games, see Aaron Smuts, "Are Video Games Art?" in *Contemporary Aesthetics* 3 (2005), available online at www.contempaesthetics.org (accessed March 17, 2007).

Selected Bibliography

Abbate, Carolyn. "Outside Ravel's Tomb." *Journal of the American Musicological Society* 52 (1999): 465–530.

———. *Unsung Voices: Opera and Musical Narrative in the Nineteenth Century.* Princeton, NJ: Princeton University Press, 1991.

Abrams, M. H. *Natural Supernaturalism: Tradition and Revolution in Romantic Literature.* New York: W. W. Norton, 1971.

Ackermann, Peter, and Herbert Schneider, eds. *Clara Schumann: Komponistin, Interpretin, Unternehmerin, Ikone.* Hildesheim: Georg Olms Verlag, 1999.

Adams, John. *Symphony of Six Million: A Novelization by John Adams of the Fannie Hurst Screen Story. An RKO Radio Picture.* New York: A. L. Burt Company, 1932.

Adamson, Joe. *Bugs Bunny: Fifty Years and Only One Grey Hare* (New York: Henry Holt, 1990).

Adorno, Theodor W. *Essays on Music.* Ed. Richard Leppert. Berkeley: University of California Press, 2002.

———. *Minima moralia: Reflections from Damaged Life.* Trans. E. F. N. Jephcott. London: New Left Books, 1974.

———. "The Radio Symphony." In Paul Lazarsfeld and Frank Stanton, *Radio Research 1941.* New York: Duell, Sloan and Pearce, 1941.

———, and Hanns Eisler. *Composing for the Films.* London: Athlone Press, 1994.

Agee, James. *Agee on Film: Criticism and Comment on the Movies.* Ed. Martin Scorsese. New York: Random House, 2000.

Altman, Rick. "Deep-Focus Sound: *Citizen Kane* and the Radio Aesthetic." *Quarterly Review of Film and Video* 15 (1994): 1–33.

———, ed. *Genre: The Musical.* London: Routledge and Kegan Paul, 1981.

Arce, Hector. *Groucho.* New York: G. P. Putnam's Sons, 1979.

Auiler, Dan. *Hitchcock's Notebooks.* New York: HarperCollins, 1999.

Bachelard, Gaston. *The Poetics of Space*. Trans. Maria Jolas. Boston: Beacon Press, 1994.

Bakhtin, Mikhail. *The Dialogic Imagination: Four Essays by M. M. Bakhtin*. Ed. Michael Holquist. Trans. and ed. Caryl Emerson and Michael Holquist. Austin: University of Texas Press, 1981.

Baldwin, Barry. *Studies in Aulus Gellius*. Lawrence, KS: Coronado Press, 1975.

Barrier, Michael. *Hollywood Cartoons: American Animation in Its Golden Age*. New York: Oxford University Press, 1999.

Belmer, Scott F. *20th Century Rock and Roll: Psychedelia*. Burlington, Ontario: Belmo, 1999.

Berger, Anna Maria Busse. *Medieval Music and the Art of Memory*. Berkeley: University of California Press, 2005.

Berkowitz, Joel, ed. *Yiddish Theatre: New Approaches*. Portland, OR: Littman Library of Jewish Civilization, 2003.

Bernstein, Charles. *My Way: Speeches and Poems*. Chicago: University of Chicago Press, 1999.

Biancorosso, Giorgio. "Film, Music and the Redemption of the Mundane." In *Bad Music: The Music We Love to Hate*, ed. Christopher Washburne and Maiken Derno, 190–211. New York: Routledge, 2004.

Biber, Douglas, and Edward Finegan, eds. *Sociolinguistic Perspectives on Register*. New York: Oxford University Press, 1994.

Blackmer, Corinne E., and Patricia Juliana Smith. *En Travesti: Women, Gender Subversion, Opera*. New York: Columbia University Press, 1995.

Bluestone, George. *Novels into Film*. Baltimore, MD: Johns Hopkins Press, 1957.

Bogard, Travis. *Contour in Time: The Plays of Eugene O'Neill*. New York: Oxford University Press, 1972. Rev. ed., 1988.

Booth, Mark. *Camp*. London: Quartet Books Ltd., 1983.

Bourdieu, Pierre. *Distinction: A Social Critique of the Judgement of Taste*. Trans. Richard Nice. Cambridge, MA: Harvard University Press, 1984.

———. *Outline of a Theory of Practice*. Trans. Richard Nice. Cambridge: Cambridge University Press, 1977.

Brooks, Peter. *The Melodramatic Imagination: Balzac, Henry James, Melodrama, and the Mode of Excess*. New Haven, CT: Yale University Press, 1976.

Broun, Heywood Hale. "At Play on Neshobe Island." *Architectural Digest* (June 2002): 124–32.

Brown, S. Royal. "Hitchcock's *Spellbound*: Jung vs. Freud." *Film/Psychology Review* 4 (1980): 35–58.

———. *Overtones and Undertones: Reading Film Music*. Berkeley: University of California Press, 1994.

Buhler, James, Caryl Flinn, and David Neumeyer, eds. *Music and Cinema*. Hanover, NH: University Press of New England, 2000.

Burt, Ramsay. *The Male Dancer: Bodies, Spectacle, Sexualities*. London and New York: Routledge, 1995.

Butler, Lance St. John. *Registering the Difference: Reading Literature through Register*. Manchester: Manchester University Press, 1999.

Cahn, Steven J. "'Kol Nidre' in America." *Journal of the Arnold Schoenberg Center* 4 (2002): 203–18.

Calcagno, Mauro. "'Imitar col canto chi parla': Monteverdi and the Creation of a Language for Musical Theater." *Journal of the American Musicological Society* 55 (2002): 383–431.

Capellanus, Andreas. *The Art of Courtly Love.* Trans. John Jay Parry. New York: Columbia University Press, 1960.

Carey, Melissa, and Michael Hannan. "Case Study 2: *The Big Chill.*" In *Popular Music and Film,* ed. Ian Inglis, 162–77. London: Wallflower Press, 2003.

Carpenter, Thomas H., and Christopher A. Faraone, eds. *Masks of Dionysus.* Ithaca, NY: Cornell University Press, 1993.

Carringer, Robert L. *The Jazz Singer.* Madison: University of Wisconsin Press, 1979.

Carruthers, Mary. *The Book of Memory: A Study in Medieval Culture.* Cambridge: Cambridge University Press, 1990.

Carter, R. A., and W. Nash. "Language and Literariness." *Prose Studies* 6 (1983): 123–41.

Charters, Ann. *Kerouac.* London: Picador, 1980.

Chion, Michel. *Audio-Vision: Sound on Screen.* Ed. and Trans. Claudia Gorbman. New York: Columbia University Press, 1994.

———. *The Voice in Cinema.* Trans. Claudia Gorbman. New York: Columbia University Press, 1999.

Clague, Mark. "Playing in 'Toon: Walt Disney's *Fantasia* (1940) and the Imagineering of Classical Music." *American Music* 22 (2004): 91–109.

Code, David J. "Hearing Debussy Reading Mallarmé: Music 'après Wagner' in the *Prélude a l'après-midi d'un faune.*" *Journal of the American Musicological Society* 54 (2001): 493–554.

Cohen, Sarah Blacher, ed. *From Hester Street to Hollywood: The Jewish-American Stage and Screen.* Bloomington: Indiana University Press, 1983.

Colley, Ann C. *Nostalgia and Recollection in Victorian Culture.* New York: Saint Martin's Press, 1998.

Collins, Christopher. *Reading the Written Image: Verbal Play, Interpretation, and the Roots of Iconophobia.* University Park: Pennsylvania State University Press, 1991.

Collins, Paul. *The Stylus Phantasticus and Free Keyboard Music of the North German Baroque.* Aldershot, England: Ashgate, 2005.

Cook, Nicholas. *Analysing Musical Multimedia.* Oxford: Clarendon Press, 1998.

———, and Mark Everist, eds. *Rethinking Music.* Oxford: Oxford University Press, 1999.

Crafton, Donald. *The Talkies: American Cinema's Transition to Sound, 1926–1931.* Berkeley: University of California Press, 1999.

Crawford, Dorothy Lamb. "Arnold Schoenberg in Los Angeles." *Musical Quarterly* 86 (2002): 6–48 .

Curtis, James. *James Whale: A New World of Gods and Monsters.* London: Faber and Faber, 1998.

Dahlhaus, Carl. *Realism in Nineteenth-Century Music.* Trans. Mary Whittall. Cambridge: Cambridge University Press, 1985.

Dante Alighieri. *De vulgari eloquentia*. Ed. Pier Ricci. Florence: F. Le Monnier, 1968.

Darby, William, and Jack Du Bois. *American Film Music: Major Composers, Techniques, Trends, 1915–1990*. Jefferson, NC: McFarland, 1990.

Daubney, Kate. *Max Steiner's "Now Voyager": A Film Score Guide*. Westport, CT: Greenwood Press, 2000.

Davison, Annette. *Hollywood Theory, Non-Hollywood Practice: Cinema Soundtracks in the 1980's and 1990's*. Aldershot, England: Ashgate, 2004.

Deleuze, Gilles. *Cinema 1: The Movement-Image*. Trans. Hugh Tomlinson and Barbara Habberjam. Minneapolis: University of Minnesota Press, 1986.

DeNora, Tia. *After Adorno: Rethinking Music Sociology*. Cambridge: Cambridge University Press: 2003.

Dettmar, Kevin J. H., and William Richey, eds. *Reading Rock and Roll: Authenticity, Appropriation, Aesthetics*. New York: Columbia University Press, 1999.

Donnelly, K. J., ed. *Film Music: Critical Approaches*. New York: Continuum Publishing Group, 2001.

Douglas, Susan J. *Listening In: Radio and the American Imagination*. New York: Random House, 1999.

Doyle, Jennifer, Jonathan Flatley, and José Esteban Muñoz, eds. *Pop Out: Queer Warhol*. Durham, NC: Duke University Press, 1996.

Doyle, Peter. *Echo and Reverb: Fabricating Space in Popular Music Recording 1900–1960*. Middletown, CT: Wesleyan University Press, 2005.

Draughon, Francesca. "Dance of Decadence: Class, Gender, and Modernity in the Scherzo of Mahler's Ninth Symphony." *Journal of Musicology* 20 (2003): 396–404.

Durgnat, Raymond. *A Long Hard Look at "Psycho."* London: British Film Institute, 2002.

Dyer, Richard. "The Talented Mr. Rota." *Sight and Sound* 14 (September 2004): 42–45.

Elsaesser, Thomas. "Le cinéma d'après Lumière: Rereading the 'Origins' of the Filmic Image." In *The Practice of Cultural Analysis: Exposing Interdisciplinary Interpretation*, ed. Mieke Bal, 60–74. Stanford: Stanford University Press, 1999.

———. *Metropolis*. London: British Film Institute, 2000.

Erdmann, Hans, and Giuseppe Becce. *Allgemeines Handbuch der Film-Musik*. 2 vols. Berlin and Leipzig: Schlesinger'sche Buch-u. Musikhandlung, 1927.

Feisst, Sabine M. "Arnold Schoenberg and the Cinematic Art." *Musical Quarterly* 83 (1999): 93–113.

Feld, Stephen. "From Schizophonia to Schismogenesis: On the Discourses and Commodification Practices of 'World Music' and 'World Beat.'" In *Music Grooves: Essays and Dialogues*, ed. Charles Keil and Steven Feld, 257–89. Chicago: University of Chicago Press, 1994.

Fink, Robert. *Repeating Ourselves: American Minimal Music as Cultural Practice*. Berkeley: University of California Press, 2005.

Flinn, Caryl. *Strains of Utopia: Gender, Nostalgia, and Hollywood Film Music*. Princeton, NJ: Princeton University Press, 1992.

Floros, Constantin. *György Ligeti: Jenseits von Avantgarde und Postmoderne.* Vienna: Verlag Lafite, 1996.

Focillon, Henri. *The Life of Forms in Art.* New York: Zone Books, 1992.

Fowler, Roger. *Linguistic Criticism.* 2nd ed. Oxford: Oxford University Press, 1996.

Frith, Simon. *Performing Rites: On the Value of Popular Music.* Cambridge, MA: Harvard University Press, 1996.

Gabbard, Krin. *Jammin' at the Margins: Jazz and the American Cinema.* Chicago: University of Chicago Press, 1996.

Gendron, Bernard. *Between Montmartre and the Mudd Club: Popular Music and the Avant-Garde.* Chicago: University of Chicago Press, 2002.

Genette, Gérard. *Narrative Discourse: An Essay in Method.* Trans. Jane E. Lewin. Ithaca, NY: Cornell University Press, 1980.

Ginsberg, Allen. *Collected Poems 1947–1980.* New York: Harper Perennial, 1988.

Girard, René. *Violence and the Sacred.* Trans. Patrick Gregory. Baltimore: Johns Hopkins University Press, 1977.

Glinsky, Albert. *Theremin: Ether, Music and Espionage.* Urbana: University of Illinois Press, 2000.

Gold, Michael. *Jews Without Money.* Repr. New York: Carroll and Graf, 1996.

Goldmark, Daniel. *Tunes for 'Toons: Music and the Hollywood Cartoon.* Berkeley: University of California Press, 2005.

———, Lawrence Kramer, and Richard Leppert, eds. *Beyond the Soundtrack: Representing Music in Cinema.* Berkeley: University of California Press, 2007.

Gorbman, Claudia. "Film Music." In *Film Studies: Critical Approaches,* ed. John Hill and Pamela Church Gibson, 41–48. Oxford: Oxford University Press, 2000.

———. *Unheard Melodies: Narrative Film Music.* Bloomington: Indiana University Press, 1987.

Gottlieb, Jack. *Funny, It Doesn't Sound Jewish: How Yiddish Songs and Synagogue Melodies Influenced Tin Pan Alley, Broadway, and Hollywood.* Albany: State University of New York, 2004.

Gracyk, Theodore. *Rhythm and Noise: An Aesthetics of Rock.* Durham, NC: Duke University Press, 1996.

Griffiths, Paul. *György Ligeti.* London: Robson Books, 1983.

Groos, Arthur, and Roger Parker, eds. *Reading Opera.* Princeton, NJ: Princeton University Press, 1988.

Gunn, Jacky, and Jim Jenkins. *Queen: As It Began.* New York: Hyperion, 1992.

Halliday, M. A. K., A. MacIntosh, and P. Strevens. *The Linguistic Sciences and Language Teaching.* London: Longman, 1964.

Hickman, Roger. *Reel Music: Exploring 100 Years of Film Music.* New York: W. W. Norton, 2006.

Hilton, Timothy. *The Pre-Raphaelites.* London: Thames and Hudson, 1970.

Hirschkop, Ken, and David Shepherd, eds. *Bakhtin and Cultural Theory.* Manchester: Manchester University Press, 1989.

Hoberman, J. *Bridge of Light: Yiddish Film Between Two Worlds.* New York: Museum of Modern Art: Schocken Books, 1991.

Holford-Strevens, Leofranc. *Aulus Gellius.* London: Duckworth, 1988.

Hurst, Fannie. *Anitra's Dance*. New York: Harper and Brothers, 1934.

Idelsohn, A. Z. *Jewish Music in Its Historical Development*. New York: Henry Holt, 1929.

Jakobson, Roman. *Language in Literature*. Cambridge, MA: Harvard University Press: 1987.

Jameson, Fredric. *Postmodernism, or The Cultural Logic of Late Capitalism*. Durham, NC: Duke University Press, 1991.

Jauss, Hans Robert. *Toward an Aesthetic of Reception*. Trans. Timothy Bahti. Minneapolis: University of Minnesota Press, 1982.

Jay, Gregory S. *T. S. Eliot and the Poetics of Literary History*. Baton Rouge: Louisiana State University Press, 1983.

Johnson, Julian. *Who Needs Classical Music? Cultural Choice and Musical Value*. Oxford: Oxford University Press, 2002.

Jost, François. "The Voices of Silence." In *The Sounds of Early Cinema,* ed. Richard Abel and Rick Altman, 48–65. Bloomington: Indiana University Press, 2001.

Kagan, Norman. *The Cinema of Stanley Kubrick*. New York: Continuum Publishing Company, 1996.

Kalinak, Kathryn. "The Fallen Woman and the Virtuous Wife: Musical Stereotypes in *The Informer, Gone With the Wind,* and *Laura.*" *Film Reader* 5 (1982): 76–82.

———. *Settling the Score: Music and the Classical Hollywood Film*. Madison: University of Wisconsin Press, 1992.

Karlin, Fred. *Listening to Movies: The Film-Lover's Guide to Film Music*. New York: Schirmer Books, 1994.

Kerman, Joseph. *Concerto Conversations*. Cambridge, MA: Harvard University Press, 1999.

Kermode, Frank. *The Classic: Literary Images of Permanence and Change*. Cambridge, MA: Harvard University Press: 1983.

Kloppenburg, Josef. *Die dramaturgische Funktion der Musik in den Filmen Alfred Hitchcocks*. Munich: Wilhelm Fink Verlag, 1986.

Koestenbaum, Wayne. *The Queen's Throat: Opera, Homosexuality and the Mystery of Desire*. New York: Vintage Books, 1993.

Kolker, Robert, ed. *Alfred Hitchcock's "Psycho": A Casebook*. Oxford: Oxford University Press, 2004.

Koppelman, Susan. *The Stories of Fannie Hurst*. New York: The Feminist Press at the City University of New York, 2004.

Kramer, Lawrence. *Classical Music and Postmodern Knowledge*. Berkeley: University of California Press, 1995.

———. *Musical Meaning: Toward a Critical History*. Berkeley: University of California Press, 2002.

———. *Why Classical Music Still Matters*. Berkeley: University of California Press, 2007.

Krims, Adam. *Rap Music and the Poetics of Identity*. Cambridge: Cambridge University Press, 2000.

Lanza, Joseph. *Elevator Music: A Surreal History of Muzak, Easy-Listening, and Other Moodsong*. New York: Picador USA, 1995.

Leckie-Tarry, Helen. *Language and Context: A Functional Linguistic Theory of Register*. London: Pinter Publishers, 1995.

Lee, Martin A., and Bruce Shlain. *Acid Dreams: The Complete Social History of LSD*. New York: Grove Press, 1985.

Leech, Geoffrey, and Michael Short. *Style in Fiction: A Linguistic Introduction to English Fictional Prose*. London: Longman, 1981.

Levin, David J. "Is There a Text in This Libido? *Diva* and the Rhetoric of Contemporary Opera Criticism." In *Between Opera and Cinema*, ed. Jeongwon Joe and Rose Theresa, 121–33. New York: Routledge, 2002.

Levine, Joseph A. *Synagogue Song in America*. Crown Point, IN: White Cliffs Media, 1989.

Lexmann, Juraj. *Theory of Film Music*. Frankfurt: Peter Lang, 2006.

Locke, Ralph P. "Constructing the Oriental 'Other': Saint-Saëns's 'Samson et Dalila.'" *Cambridge Opera Journal* 3 (1991): 261–302.

Leydon, Rebecca. "Hooked on Aetherophonics: *The Day the Earth Stood Still*." In *Off the Planet: Music, Sound, and Science Fiction Cinema*, ed. Philip Hayward, 30–41. London: John Libbey Publishing, 2004.

Lhamon, W. T., Jr. *Jump Jim Crow: Lost Plays, Lyrics, and Street Prose of the First Atlantic Popular Culture*. Cambridge, MA: Harvard University Press, 2003.

Lindenberger, Herbert. *Opera in History from Monteverdi to Cage*. Stanford: Stanford University Press, 1998.

London, Kurt. *Film Music*. Trans. Eric S. Bensinger. New York: Arno Press, 1970.

Macan, Edward. *Rocking the Classics: English Progressive Rock and the Counterculture*. Oxford: Oxford University Press, 1997.

MacCabe, Colin. *The Eloquence of the Vulgar: Language, Cinema, and the Politics of Culture*. London: British Film Institute, 1999.

Manguel, Alberto. *Bride of Frankenstein*. London: British Film Institute, 1997.

Marks, Emerson R., ed. *Literary Criticism of Sainte-Beuve*. Lincoln: University of Nebraska Press, 1971.

Marks, Martin Miller. *Music and the Silent Film: Contexts and Case Studies 1895–1924*. Oxford: Oxford University Press, 1997.

Marmorstein, Gary. *Hollywood Rhapsody: Movie Music and Its Makers 1900 to 1975*. New York: Schirmer Books, 1997.

Maurice, Alice. "'Cinema at Its Source': Synchronizing Race and Sound in the Early Talkies." *Camera Obscura* 49 (2002): 31–71.

Marx, Groucho. *The Groucho Letters: Letters From and To Groucho Marx*. New York: Da Capo Press, 1994.

McClary, Susan. *Feminine Endings: Music, Gender, and Sexuality*. Minnesota: University of Minnesota Press, 1991.

McLeod, Kembrew. "A Critique of Rock Criticism in North America." *Popular Music* 20 (2001): 47–60.

McLeod, Ken. "Bohemian Rhapsodies: Operatic Influences on Rock Music." *Popular Music* 20 (2001): 189–203.

Mellor, Anne K. "Making a 'Monster': An Introduction to *Frankenstein*." In *The Cambridge Companion to Mary Shelley*, ed. Esther Schor, 9–25. Cambridge: Cambridge University Press, 2003.

Middleton, Richard. *Studying Popular Music*. Philadelphia, PA: Open University Press, 1990.

Miller, J. Hillis. *Ariadne's Thread: Story Lines*. New Haven, CT: Yale University Press, 1992.

Miller, James. *Flowers in the Dustbin: The Rise of Rock and Roll, 1947–1977*. New York: Simon and Schuster, 1999.

Moore, Allan F. *The Beatles: Sgt. Pepper's Lonely Hearts Club Band*. Cambridge: Cambridge University Press, 1997.

———. *Rock: The Primary Text: Developing a Musicology of Rock*. Buckingham, PA: Open University Press, 1993.

Moorefield, Virgil. *The Producer as Composer: Shaping the Sounds of Popular Music*. Cambridge, MA: MIT Press, 2005.

Morgan, Robert P. "Circular Form in the Tristan Prelude." *Journal of the American Musicological Society* 53 (2000): 69–103.

Móricz, Klára. "Sensuous Pagans and Righteous Jews: Changing Concepts of Jewish Identity in Ernest Bloch's 'Jézabel' and 'Schelomo.'" *Journal of the American Musicological Society* 54 (2001): 439–91.

Morrison, Michael A. *John Barrymore: Shakespearean Actor*. Cambridge: Cambridge University Press, 1997.

Naremore, James. *More Than Night: Film Noir in Its Contexts*. Berkeley: University of California Press, 1998.

Nasta, Dominque. *Meaning in Film: Relevant Structures in Soundtrack and Narrative*. Berne: Peter Lang, 1991.

Neumeyer, David. "Melodrama as a Compositional Resource in Early Hollywood Sound Cinema." *Current Musicology* (1995): 61–94.

———. "Source Music, Background Music, Fantasy and Reality in Early Sound Film." *College Music Symposium* 37 (1997): 3–20.

Nicosia, Gerald. *Memory Babe: A Critical Biography of Jack Kerouac*. New York: Grove Press, 1983.

Ottoson, Robert. *A Reference Guide to the American Film Noir: 1940–1958*. Metuchen, NJ: The Scarecrow Press, Inc., 1981.

Paden, William D., ed. and trans. *The Medieval Pastourelle*. 2 vols. New York: Garland Publishing, 1987.

Page, Christopher. *Voices and Instruments of the Middle Ages: Instrumental Practice and Songs in France, 1100–1300*. London: J. M. Dent and Sons Ltd., 1987.

Paglia, Camille. *The Birds*. London: British Film Institute, 1998.

Patrick, James. "Charlie Parker and Harmonic Sources of Bebop Composition: Thoughts on the Repertory of Jazz in the 1940s." *Journal of Jazz Studies* 2 (1975): 3–23.

Pattison, Robert. *The Triumph of Vulgarity: Rock Music in the Mirror of Romanticism*. New York: Oxford University Press, 1987.

Pausanias. *Description of Greece*. Trans. W. H. S. Jones and H. A. Ormerod. 4 vols. Cambridge, MA: Harvard University Press, 1918.

Pearlman, Sandy. "Van Dyke Parks New Release." *Crawdaddy* 13 (February 1968): 43.

Pearson, Roberta. *Eloquent Gestures: The Transformation of Performance Style in the Griffith Biograph Films*. Berkeley: University of California Press, 1992.

The Performance Group. *Dionysus in '69.* New York: Farrar, Straus and Giroux, 1970.

Pfann, Walter. "'Hat er es denn beschlossen . . .': Anmerkungen zu einem neuen Verständnis der 'Symphonie Pathétique.'" *Die Musikforschung* 51 (1998): 191–209.

Powrie, Phil. *French Cinema in the 1980s: Nostalgia and the Crisis of Masculinity.* Oxford: Clarendon Press, 1997.

Prendergast, Roy M. *Film Music: A Neglected Art.* 2nd ed. W. W. Norton: New York, 1992.

Prettejohn, Elizabeth, ed. *After the Pre-Raphaelites: Art and Aestheticism in Victorian England.* New Brunswick, NJ: Rutgers University Press, 1999.

Puecker, Brigitte. *Incorporating Images: Film and the Rival Arts.* Princeton, NJ: Princeton University Press, 1995.

Pullen, Robert, and Stephen Taylor. *Montserrat Caballé: Casta Diva.* Boston: Northeastern University Press, 1994.

Quinn, Justin. "Coteries, Landscape and the Sublime in Allen Ginsberg." *Journal of Modern Literature* 27 (2003): 193–206.

Rabkin, Eric S. *The Fantastic in Literature.* Princeton, NJ: Princeton University Press, 1976.

Ravitz, Abe C. *Imitations of Life: Fannie Hurst's Gaslight Sonatas.* Carbondale: Southern Illinois University Press, 1997.

Ray, Robert. "Impressionism, Surrealism, Film Theory." In *Film Studies: Critical Approaches,* ed. John Hill and Pamela Church Gibson, 65–74. Oxford: Oxford University Press, 2000.

Raykoff, Ivan. "Hollywood's Embattled Icon." In *Piano Roles,* ed. James Parakilas, 329–57. New Haven, CT: Yale University Press, 1999.

Rebello, Stephen. *Alfred Hitchcock and the Making of Psycho.* New York: Saint Martin's Press, 1990.

Reed, Teresa L. *The Holy Profane: Religion in Black Popular Music.* Lexington: University of Kentucky Press, 2003.

Reich, Nancy B. *Clara Schumann: The Artist and the Woman.* Ithaca, NY: Cornell University Press, 1985.

Reid, T. B. W. "Linguistics, Structuralism, and Philology." *Archivum linguisticum* 8 (1956): 28–37.

Richards, Annette. *The Free Fantasia and the Musical Picturesque.* Cambridge: Cambridge University Press, 2001.

Rogin, Michael. *Blackface, White Noise: Jewish Immigrants in the Hollywood Melting Pot.* Berkeley: University of California Press, 1996.

Rosar, William H. "Music for the Monsters: Universal Pictures' Horror Film Scores of the Thirties." *The Quarterly Journal of the Library of Congress* 40 (1983): 390–421.

Rose, Andrea. *The Pre-Raphaelites.* Ann Arbor Michigan: Borders Press, 1997.

Rose, Tricia. *Black Noise: Rap Music and Black Culture in Contemporary America.* Hanover, NH: Wesleyan University Press, 1994.

Rosen, Charles. *The Classical Style: Haydn, Mozart, Beethoven.* New York: W. W. Norton, 1972.

———. *Romantic Poets, Critics, and Other Madmen.* Cambridge, MA: Harvard University Press, 1998.

Ross, Andrew. *No Respect: Intellectuals and Popular Culture.* New York: Routledge, 1989.

Rózsa, Miklós. *A Double Life: The Autobiography of Miklós Rózsa.* New York: Hippocrene Books, 1982.

Segal, Rachel. "Franz Waxman: A Musical Innovator." *The Cue Sheet* 22 (2007): 11–22.

Seldes, Gilbert. *The Seven Lively Arts.* New York: Harper and Brothers, 1924.

Sharot, Stephen. "Judaism and Jewishness." In *Modern Jews and Their Musical Agendas,* ed. Ezra Mendelsohn, 188–202. New York: Oxford University Press, 1993.

Sheppard, W. Anthony. "An Exotic Enemy: Anti-Japanese Musical Propaganda in World War II Hollywood." *Journal of the American Musicological Society* 54 (2001): 303–57.

Shiloah, Amnon, and Erik Cohen. "The Dynamics of Change in Jewish Oriental Ethnic Music in Israel." *Ethnomusicology* 27 (1983): 227–52.

Singer, Ben. "The Nickelodeon Boom in Manhattan." In *Entertaining America: Jews, Movies and Broadcasting,* ed. J. Hoberman and Jeffrey Shandler, 23–27. Princeton, NJ: Princeton University Press, 2003.

Singer, Irving. *Three Philosophical Filmmakers: Hitchcock, Welles, Renoir.* Cambridge, MA: MIT Press, 2004.

Sisman, Elaine. *Mozart: The "Jupiter" Symphony.* Cambridge: Cambridge University Press, 1993.

———. "Pathos and Pathétique: Rhetorical Stance in Beethoven's C-Minor Sonata, Op. 13." *Beethoven Forum* 3 (1994): 81–105.

Skal, David J. *Screams of Reason: Mad Science and Modern Culture.* New York: W. W. Norton, 1998.

Slobin, Mark. *Chosen Voices: The Story of the American Cantorate.* Urbana: University of Illinois Press, 1989.

———. *Tenement Songs: The Popular Music of the Jewish Immigrants.* Urbana: University of Illinois Press, 1982.

———. *Yiddish Theater in America: David's Violin (1897) and Shloyme Gorgl (189-).* New York: Garland Publishing, 1994.

Smart, Mary Ann. *Mimomania: Music and Gesture in Nineteenth-Century Opera.* Berkeley: University of California Press, 2004.

Smith, Stephen C. *A Heart at Fire's Center: The Life and Music of Bernard Herrmann.* Berkeley: University of California Press, 1991.

Smoodin, Eric, and Ann Martin, eds. *Hollywood Quarterly: Film Culture in Postwar America, 1945–1957.* Berkeley: University of California Press, 2002.

Smuts, Aaron. "Are Video Games Art?" *Contemporary Aesthetics* 3 (2005); available online at www.contempaesthetics.org.

Sobchack, Vivian. "Lounge Time: Postwar Crises and the Chronotope of Film Noir." In *Refiguring American Film Genres: History and Theory,* ed. Nick Browne, 129–70. Berkeley: University of California Press, 1998.

Sontag, Susan. *Against Interpretation and Other Essays.* New York: Picador USA, 2001.

Strauss, Jonathan. *Subjects of Terror: Nerval, Hegel, and the Modern Self.* Stanford: Stanford University Press, 1998.

Straw, Will. "Characterizing Rock Music Culture: The Case of Heavy Metal." In *On Record: Rock, Pop, and the Written Word,* ed. Simon Frith and Andrew Goodwin, 97–110. New York: Pantheon Books, 1990.

Stump, Paul. *The Music's All That Matters: A History of Progressive Rock.* London: Quartet Books Ltd., 1997.

Sullivan, Jack. "*Psycho:* The Music of Terror." *Cineaste* 32 (Winter 2006): 20–28.

Summit, Jeffrey A. *The Lord's Song in a Strange Land: Music and Identity in Contemporary Jewish Worship.* Oxford: Oxford University Press, 2000.

Szatmary, David. *A Time to Rock: A Social History of Rock and Roll.* New York: Schirmer Books, 1996.

Tagg, Philip. *Fernando the Flute: Analysis of Musical Meaning in an Abba Megahit.* 3rd ed. New York: Mass Media Musicologists' Press, 2001.

Tamarkin, Jeff. *Got a Revolution! The Turbulent Flight of Jefferson Airplane.* New York: Atria Books, 2003.

Tarkovsky, Andrey. *Sculpting in Time: Reflections on the Cinema.* Trans. Kitty Hunter-Blair. Austin: University of Texas Press, 1996.

Taruskin, Richard. *Defining Russia Musically.* Princeton, NJ: Princeton University Press, 1997.

———. "The Golden Age of Kitsch." *New Republic* (March 21, 1994): 28–38.

———. *Text and Act.* New York and Oxford: Oxford University Press, 1995.

Taylor, Timothy D. *Strange Sounds: Music, Technology, and Culture.* New York: Routledge, 2001.

Tedlow, Richard S. *The Watson Dynasty: The Fiery Reign and Troubled Legacy of IBM's Founding Father and Son.* New York: HarperBusiness, 2003.

Théberge, Paul. *Any Sound You Can Imagine: Making Music/Consuming Technology.* Hanover, NH: Wesleyan University Press, 2005.

Thompson, Stephanie Lewis. *Influencing America's Tastes: Realism in the Works of Wharton, Cather and Hurst.* Gainesville: University Press of Florida, 2002.

Todorov, Tzvetan. *The Fantastic: A Structural Approach to a Literary Genre.* Trans. Richard Howard. Ithaca, NY: Cornell University Press, 1975.

Tomlinson, Gary. *Metaphysical Song: An Essay on Opera.* Princeton, NJ: Princeton University Press, 1999.

Touré. "DMX Reigns as the Dark Prince of Hip Hop." *Rolling Stone* (April 13, 2000): 82–91.

Trotter, David. "Stereoscopy: Modernism and the 'Haptic.'" *Critical Quarterly* 46 (2004): 38–58.

Tsur, Reuven. *What Makes Sound Patterns Expressive? The Poetic Mode of Speech Reception.* Durham, NC: Duke University Press, 1992.

Ulmers, Gregory. "A Night at the Text: Roland Barthes's Marx Brothers." *Yale French Studies* 73 (1987): 38–57.

Wakeman, John, ed. *World Film Directors.* Vol. 1. New York: H. W. Wilson, 1987.

Walser, Robert. *Running With the Devil: Power, Gender, and Madness in Heavy Metal Music.* Hanover, NH: Wesleyan University Press, 1993.

Webster, James. "The *Creation*, Haydn's Late Vocal Music, and the Musical Sublime." In *Haydn and His World,* ed. Elaine Sisman, 57–102. Princeton, NJ: Princeton University Press, 1997.

Weiskel, Thomas. *The Romantic Sublime: Studies in the Structure and Psychology of Transcendence.* Baltimore, MD: Johns Hopkins University Press, 1976.

Weiss, Allen S. *Breathless: Sound Recording, Disembodiment, and the Transformation of Lyrical Nostalgia.* Middletown, CT: Wesleyan University Press, 2002.

Whitely, Sheila. *The Space Between the Notes: Rock and the Counter-Culture.* London: Routledge, 1992.

Whitfield, Stephen J. *In Search of American Jewish Culture.* Hanover, NH: Brandeis University Press, 1999.

Whitney, John. *Digital Harmony: On the Complementarity of Music and Visual Art.* Peterborough, NH: Byte Books, 1980.

Williams, Alan. "Historical and Theoretical Issues in the Coming of Sound to the Cinema." In *Sound Theory, Sound Practice,* ed. Rick Altman, 126–37. New York: Routledge, 1992.

Worton, Michael, and Judith Still, eds. *Intertextuality: Theories and Practices.* Manchester: Manchester University Press, 1990.

Yates, Frances. *The Art of Memory.* London: Routledge and Kegan Paul, 1966.

Yousef, Nancy. "The Monster in a Dark Room: *Frankenstein,* Feminism, and Philosophy." *Modern Language Quarterly* 63 (2002): 197–226.

Zak, Albin J. III. *The Poetics of Rock: Cutting Tracks, Making Records.* Berkeley: University of California Press, 2001.

———. *The Velvet Underground Companion: Four Decades of Commentary.* New York: Schirmer Books, 1997.

Žižek, Slavoj. *Tarrying with the Negative: Kant, Hegel, and the Critique of Ideology.* Durham, NC: Duke University Press, 1993.

Zumthor, Paul. *Essai de poétique médiévale.* Paris: Éditions du Seuil, 1972.

Index

Abbate, Carolyn, 247n44, 249n64, 263n13, 271n51, 279n69
Adams, John. See *Symphony of Six Million*
Addinsell, Richard, 4, 249n62. See also *Warsaw Concerto*
Adler, Jacob, 89, 90, 91
Adorno, Theodor: on contrafacts, 128, 269n25; on parody, 284n48; on radio, 62–63; on Wagnerian leitmotif, 116; web metaphor of, 117–18. See also *Composing for the Films*
aesthetic value, 1, 3, 5, 7, 27, 31, 54, 117, 140, 142, 148; of poetry, 13, 29; in rock, 130. *See also* authenticity
Agee, James, 67, 205, 283n31
Alexander Nevsky, 173
Allen, Steve, 162, 264n21
Altman, Rick, 182, 183; mise-en-bande concept, 20
ambience effects: Phil Spector, 115, 264n24; Raveonettes, 115; visual analogies, 136, 270n44. *See also* reverberation
American Idol, 210
Anders als die Andern, 226–27
Andrei, Frederic, 61
Andrews, Dana, 158
androgyny, 230
animation, and avant-garde, 199, 281n5. *See also* anime
anime, 49, 239
Anna Magdalena Bach Büchlein, 206
Antheil, George: *Ballet mécanique*, 172; and Bernard Herrmann, 38, 40, 171;

Fifth Symphony, 276n29; Fourth symphony, 171; waltzes, 172
Apartment, The, theme from, 212
Aristotle: *Ethics*, 98; *Poetics*, 16; *Politics*, 233
Arnoux, Alexandre, 176–77
ars praedicandi, medieval, 207
Astaire, Fred, 261n74
Attali, Jacques, 250n74
authenticity, in rock music: 131, 223, 224, 261n4, 265n26, 283n39

Bach, C. P. E., 156
Bach, Joh. Seb.: arrangements by the Swingle Singers, 133–35, 136, 141; and the Doors, 125; and film, 118, 119–20, 159, 200, 201; in "A Lover's Concerto," 202; in "A Whiter Shade of Pale," 109, 116, 122, 133–35, 136, 137, 261n5, 270n38
Bach, Wilhelm Friedemann, 125
Bachelard, Gaston, 58, 59, 63
Bakhtin, Mikhail: on the carnivalesque, 16, 244n16; on the chronotope, 39, 138, 147; on dialogic zones, 40, 250n79, 272n77; and genre, 44; and myth, 143
Bar kochba, 80, 81
Baroque music: and rock music, 116–17, 127, 264n20, 265n34; and soul music, 138; temporality in, 117, 265n34; as wallpaper music, 274n89. *See also* Bach, Joh. Seb.
Baroques (group), 265n34

Barrymore, John, 91
Barthes, Roland, 245n26; on comedy, 236, 237; on inversion, 16
Bashir, Martin, 31
Bass, Saul: titles for *Psycho*, 40; titles for *Vertigo*, 167
Battleship Potemkin, 173, 235, 236
Beach, Rex, 259n54
Beast with Five Fingers, The, 35, 203
"beat" generation, 111, 117, 157, 264n21. *See also* Ginsberg, Allen; Kerouac, Jack
Beatles: concept albums of, 283n40; live performances of, 138–39; use of looping, 166, 275n15. *See also* "Lucy in the Sky"; "Revolution No. 9"; "Strawberry Fields Forever"
Bebung, and eighteenth-century affect, 128, 268n20; and rock, 138
Becce, Giuseppe, 29
Beethoven, Ludwig van, 18, 32, 84, 131, 220, 242n9
Beinex, Jean-Jacques, 61
Bellini, Giovanni, 141
Benchley, Robert, 79
Berg, Alban, 191
Bergman, Ingrid, 168
Berlioz, Hector, 209, 236
Bernstein, Charles, 263n19
Bernstein, Elmer, 164
Berry, Chuck, 131
Besseler, Eugenie, 55, 75
Big Chill, The, 146, 148, 152–55
Biggs, E. Power, 133
bilabial phonemes: in "Bohemian Rhapsody," 243n8; in disco, 65; expressive register of, 13–14; and memory, 243n7; in surf music, 14–15
Birds, The: sound and music, 165, 169, 170, 183, 275n24; visual elements, 169–70, 242n7, 276n25
Black Cat, The, 254n29
Blake, William, 111, 113, 262n12
Boer War, 141, 144–45
"Bohemian Rhapsody" (song), 222–32, 233, 243n8, 244n10, 283n35; covers of, 222; gender in, 225, 228–30; as mock opera, 226, 229, 284n48; overdubs in, 225; production of, 284n42, 285n56; reception, 223; Richard Strauss in, 227, 228–31, 284n48; in *Wayne's World*, 222, 223, 231–32. *See also* Mercury, Freddie
"Bohemian Rhapsody" (video), 224–25; costuming, 225; gesture, 226–27; piano in, 222, 224, 225, 226
Born to Kill, 163, 275n12

Bourdieu, Pierre, 41, 42, 251nn81,86
Bowles, Paul, 25, 247n41
Boyer, Charles, 165
Brahms, Johannes: in "Love of My Life," 214–16; in *Detour*, 221
Bride of Frankenstein, 158, 187–95, 197, 279nn64,66–67, 280nn76–77,81
Britton, Joe, 75
Brooker, Gary, 125, 137, 269n36; and the Swingle Singers, 134; vocal timbre of, 109, 270n48. *See also* "Whiter Shade of Pale, A"
Brooks, Peter, 37, 54, 55, 82, 84, 90, 104, 253n21, 254n25. *See also* melodrama
Brown, Ford Madox: *The Last of England*, 143–44, 272n71
Brown, Royal S., 19, 81, 245n23, 250n76, 254n29, 276n30, 278n52
Browning, Tod, 160
Bruch, Max, 81, 85, 256n8, 258n36
Bugs Bunny, and the Marx Brothers, 221, 285n1. See also *Rhapsody Rabbit*
Buñuel, Luis, 168
Buxtehude, Dietrich, 128

Caballé, Montserrat, 229, 230, 285n52
Cale, John, 162
camera angles, 20, 87
camp, 7, 16, 66, 225, 242n10, 280n78, 284n44
Campbell, Thomas: *The Soldier's Dream*, 149–50, 150fig., 273n81
cantors, Jewish, 75, 80, 103, 257n18. See also *Jazz Singer, The*; *Sons of Liberty*
Captain Blood, 44, 45, 58
Carey, Melissa, 152, 153
Carmen, 253n15
Carroll, Lewis, 122–23
cartoons, animated. See *Cat Concerto, The*; *Fantasia*; *Merrie Melodies*; *Rhapsody Rabbit*
Casablanca, 85, 86, 104, 247n39
Caspary, Vera: *Laura*, 45, 251n83, 274n2
Cat Concerto, The, 197–98, 204–5, 221, 280n2; Chopin in, 198; reviews of, 205
"Cat Food," 153, 262n6
Chaikovsky, Pyotr Ilich.: B♭-Major Piano Concerto, 202, 203; in Erdmann's *Handbuch*, 51, 57, 254n31; and melodrama, 54; *Pathétique* Symphony (in films), 21, 30, 59–60, 61–63, 254n31; in popular music, 128, 131; *Romeo and Juliet* Fantasy Overture (in films), 30, 51, 52, 53, 54–55, 56, 57, 76, 78, 88, 97, 254nn29,35, 253n16; *Swan Lake*, 184

Chaplin, Charles, 32–33
Chaucer, Geoffrey, 11, 130, 153, 208, 247n45
chazan. See cantors, Jewish
chien andalou, Un, 168
"Childhood," 31, 32
Chion, Michel: on *acousmêtre,* 222, 264n25; on *Psycho,* 175–76; on *The Informer,* 83; on *The Jazz Singer,* 79, 176–77, 277n42
Chopin, F.: C-Minor Prelude (Manilow), 17, 35; D-Minor Prelude (in films), 198, 201, 217, 218–19, 219 *example,* 220, 283n31; as heroic, 203, 249n62
chromaticism, 51, 100, 114, 275n15: in film scores, 40, 46, 68, 160, 161, 162, 163, 171, 173, 184, 195, 253n16; Manilow's, 210
chronotopes, 138, 139; acoustical, 157; of film noir, 250n77; and nostalgia, 147, 148, 151, 155; of the road, 39; visual, 68, 145. *See also* Bakhtin, Mikhail
cinematicism: in Ginsberg's poetry, 112; in Hurst's writings, 93, 94, 97, 259nn54,60; in popular music, 17, 24, 34, 38, 39, 40, 63, 64, 65, 105, 126, 129, 138, 139, 140, 160, 207, 211, 212, 213, 246n36; in Respighi, 127
Cinerama, 165
circularity, 165, 166, 167, 168, 169, 275n23. *See also* loops
Citizen Kane, 66–67, 255n42, 270n44, 279n58
classic, the: in consumer goods, 28; Eliot on, 27–28; Gellius on, 31, 32; hearing of, 31; imaginative, 5, 6; origins of notion, 31
classic register, 26, 27, 29, 30, 33, 34, 39, 47, 105, 129, 282n13. *See also* register of the classic
clavichord: expressiveness of, 128; invoked in rock music, 154
Clive, Colin, 200
Close Encounters of the Third Kind, 61
Code, David, 114, 263n20
Cohn, Harry, 89
Colley, Ann, 144
Communards, 65
Composing for the Films, 116, 190, 247n38, 254n37. *See also* Adorno, Theodor; Eisler, Hanns
concerto: invocations in popular music, 32, 33, 36, 38, 199, 202, 203, 204, 206, 208, 209, 210, 212; and pianist's hands, 203, 219; power chords, 36, 202, 204, 210; verbal resonance of,

198, 199–200, 215–16. *See also* piano keyboard
Conniff, Ray, 128, 136
Cook, Nicholas, 3, 171
cookbook register, 49, 50, 52
Copland, Aaron, 49, 25–26, 33
Cordell, Denny, 153, 154
Cosmopolitan, 81
Country Girl, The, 272n75
Crawdaddy, 130, 264n26, 283n27
Crawford, Joan, 61, 254n32
Crowther, Bosley, 275n12
Crystals, 114, 115, 209
Culy, Christopher, 50
Curtiz, Michael, 86

Dahlhaus, Carl, 52
Dalí, Salvador, 168, 275n22
Dangerous Moonlight, 36, 203, 204, 249n62. See also *Warsaw Concerto*
Dante, 4, 11, 13, 14, 16, 22, 27, 120, 244n10, 245n25, 247n45
Dark Victory, 68
Daubney, Kate, 21, 246n31
Davis, Bette, 17, 42, 59, 68; close-ups of, 60, 61, 62, 254n32. See also *Now, Voyager*
Day at the Races, A, 234
Day the Earth Stood Still, The, 50, 160, 167, 168 *example,* 252n3, 275n18
death: aesthetics of, 141, 184, 269n34; and cover art, 132; monumentalized, 130, 132, 160, 184, 192; in rock journalism, 130–32; romanticized, 129, 132, 269n28; sacrificial, 37; and sexuality, 124, 159, 268n11; and war, 130, 145–46, 153
"Death on Two Legs," 233–34, 235
Debussy, Claude, 83, 109, 114, 163, 169, 184, 188, 226, 275n23
deep focus, 89, 135–36, 165, 180
Deleuze, Gilles, 4, 242n7, 246n33
de Man, Paul, 184
DeNora, Tia, 19
de Palma, Brian, 285n55
Dessau, Paul, 85
Detour, 221
Die Hard, 255n41
Dietrich, James, 184–85
disco music, 63–66
Diva, 61
DMX: Christian imagery of, 37; timbres of, 36. *See also* "What's My Name"
Don Juan, 178
"Don't Leave Me This Way," 64–65
Doors, The, 124–25, 127–29, 149, 214, 262n10

doo-wop, 18
Dreyfuss, Richard, 200, 202
Dr. Jekyll and Mr. Hyde, 90, 91
drug use: and listening, 110, 111–13,
    128, 153, 154, 262n9, 269nn24,34;
    and "picturesque" experience, 126,
    153, 163; post-psychedelic, 162–63,
    164; recreational, 265n34, 269n27;
    representations of, 153, 262n8. *See
    also* psychedelia
Du Bois, W. E. B., 260n60
Dudgeon, Elspeth, 277n37
Dukas, Paul, 190, 279n69
du Maurier, Daphne, 90
Dumont, Margaret, 237–38, 239
Durgnat, Raymond, 277n35
Dyer, Richard, 142, 143, 268n17

Eagling, Wayne, 230
ecstasy (ecstasis), 266n41; in Chasidic Ju-
    daism, 80; and film, 79, 119, 175,
    277n35; in Ginsberg's poetry, 112,
    262n12, 263n14
Edison, Thomas, 90, 120, 168; kineto-
    scopes of, 170
Eisenstein, Sergei, 248n47, 277n35. See
    also *Alexander Nevsky; Battleship
    Potemkin;* montage
Eisler, Hanns, 62–63, 238, 280n73. See
    also *Composing for the Films; Hang-
    men Also Die*
Electric Prune, 267n8
electronic instruments, in film: nova-
    chord, 159; ondes martenot, 158, 174,
    191; theremin, 50, 158, 159, 160, 161,
    163, 168, 174, 275n18, 277n45; trau-
    tonium, 169, 170. *See also* Theremin,
    Leon
Elfman, Danny, 174
Eliot, T. S., 4, 248n47, 250n75; on the
    classic, 27–28, 32; and Groucho, 28,
    41; and hearing, 29, 31, 121
Ellington, Duke, 252n7
Eminem, 249n60, 274n8
"End, The," 127
Enter the Dragon, 48
Erdmann, Hans, 20; *Allgemeines Hand-
    buch der Film-Musik,* 29–30, 51, 57,
    60, 70, 77, 78, 248n54, 252n13,
    254n31, 255n48
ether (aether): as poetic concept, 112–13,
    116; association with sound technolo-
    gies, 115, 174, 177–78, 192
"Eve of Destruction," 280n1

Fahey, John, 132, 166
Faith, Percy, 64

Fake, 49
Fantasia, 118, 119–20, 266n42, 267n8;
    reception, 251n86
fantastic, the: in Carroll, 122–23; in film,
    68, 158–60, 164, 166, 167, 170, 172,
    176, 181, 184, 185, 186, 188, 190,
    191, 192, 194, 195, 218, 219, 220,
    277n37; in painting, 140; as register,
    61; in rock, 110, 116, 117, 122–24, 127,
    137, 149, 154, 157, 161, 162, 262n8,
    267n8. *See also* Todorov, Tzvetan
fantasy (fantasia), in eighteenth-century
    music, 127, 128, 268n18
Ferrante and Teicher, 211–12
film music: as genre, 105; and "mean-
    ing," 19, 20, 21, 24, 44, 46, 53,
    152–53, 171, 245nn24,26; and narra-
    tology, 19, 245n24, 278n51; and semi-
    otics, 18, 245nn23,24
films: as texts, 13, 19, 232
films, silent: music for. *See* Kinotheks
film scores: cue sheets for, 102; historical
    models for, 81–82, 84, 102, 104, 105;
    horror, 36, 184, 249n64; mickey-
    mousing in, 83, 172, 193; overtures in,
    68, 69, 71, 72, 255n44; popular music
    in, 3, 75–76, 223, 231–32, 152–55;
    and register, 15, 21, 42, 45, 47, 48,
    49–52, 53; science fiction, 50, 167,
    252n3. *See also* title sequences in film;
    specific film titles
film sound: close-ups, 181; hyperrealism,
    141; and radio, 178, 179, 278n50;
    sound effects, 20, 152, 183, 194; spa-
    tial implications of, 63, 148, 153, 181,
    185, 173, 279n58; Vitaphone technol-
    ogy, 52, 89, 178, 179, 278n47. *See
    also* Altman, Rick; Chion, Michel
film stock, 89, 180, 181
Fink, Robert, 274n89
Firth, J. R., 15
Fisher, Matthew, 109, 117, 124, 125,
    127, 129, 132–34, 155, 156, 269n36.
    See also "Whiter Shade of Pale, A"
Fleming, Victor, 68
Flinn, Caryl, 142, 245n24, 265n31,
    272n75, 283n33
Forbstein, Leo: *Sons of Liberty,* 86–87,
    104, 258n38
Ford, John, 48, 83. See also *Informer,
    The*
Forster, E. M, 59, 236
Four Seasons, 207
Frankenstein (film), 176, 187. *See also*
    Shelley, Mary Wollstonecraft
Freaks, 160–61, 179
Friml, Rudolf, 82

Frith, Simon: on cinematic listening, 246n36; on critical language, 2, 241n3; on identification, 284n44; on ideologies of listening, 247n37; on somatic response, 249n61
Fuzzbox, 222

Gabbard, Krin, 79–80, 277n42
Gable, Clark, 181
Garfield, John, 61
Gassmann, Remi, 169
Gellius, Aulus, 31, 32, 33, 239, 240
Genette, Gérard, 19, 20, 278n51
Gershwin, George: C♯-Minor Piano Prelude, 48; "Summertime," 252n7
gestures. See melodrama; piano keyboard
Giannini, Vittorio, 199
"Gimme Some More," 34, 38–41
Ginsberg, Allen, 7, 111–13, 114, 115, 116, 117, 118, 119, 120, 262n12, 263nn14,19, 264n21
Girard, René, 37
girl groups. See "Lover's Concerto, A"; "I Hear a Symphony"
glam rock, 225, 284n44
Goethe, J. W., Werther, 121, 141, 146, 149, 272n74
Gold, Michael, Jews Without Money, 99–100
Goldfaden, Abraham, 96, 97, 99, 102, 103, 259n59. See also musical theater, Yiddish; theater, Yiddish
Goldfaden, Samuel, 80
Goldmark, Daniel, 205
Golem, The, 186–87, 190
Gone With the Wind (film), 67–70, 71, 72; Tara theme, 69–70
Gone With the Wind (novel), 67
Good Earth, The, 216
Gorbman, Claudia, 19–21, 152, 153, 245nn24,32, 246n33, 247n39
Gordin, Jacob, 90, 96, 103. See also theater, Yiddish
Gottlieb, Jack, 260n61
Gracyk, Theodore, 269n27
Graduate, The, 100, 252n9
Grapes of Wrath, The, 49
Green Dolphin Street (film), 36
"Green Dolphin Street" (song), 36
Greenwich, Ellie, 114, 115
Grieg, Edvard, 95, 204
Griffiths, Paul, 256nn53–54

Hall, Mordaunt, 181
Hallelujah, 79, 257n14
Halliday, M. A. K., 15

Hammond organ. See "Whiter Shade of Pale, A"
Handel, Georg Friedrich, 69–70, 255n48
hands, severed, 35, 100, 101, 203, 204
Hangmen Also Die, 190–91
Hannan, Michael, 152, 153
Harris, Barbara, 281n10, 282n13
Hatfield, Hurd, 201
Haydn, Joseph, 195
Heat, 162
Hedgcock, William, 183, 194
Hegel, Georg Wilhelm Friedrich, 192
"He Hit Me (It Felt Like a Kiss)," 115, 209
Herek, Stephen, 197
Hermes: in "Bohemian Rhapsody," 226, 229, 230, 231; dilemma of, 196
"Heroin," 162–63, 164
Herrmann, Bernard, 4; and Antheil, 171–72; classic register of, 40; collaboration with Hitchcock, 169, 173; waltzes of, 167, 168, 169, 172–73. See also Birds, The; Citizen Kane; Day the Earth Stood Still, The; Psycho (1960), sound and music; Psycho (1998), sound and music; Vertigo
Hickman, Roger, 276n30, 280n76
hip-hop music. See rap music
Hitchcock, Alfred: collaboration with Herrmann, 169, 173; fetish motifs of, 167–68; on pure cinema, 168. See also Birds, The; Psycho (1960); Rebecca; Spellbound; Vertigo
Hoffmann, E. T. A., 32, 35, 131, 267n8
Holly, Buddy, 115
"Hollywood rocket" (musical gesture): in disco, 63–66; in silent film practice, 51–56; in sound films, 47, 56, 58, 60, 62
"House of the Rising Sun," 233
Houston, Thelma, 65
How I Won the War, 132
Humoresque, 61, 197. See also Hurst, Fannie
Huppertz, Gottfried, 194–95
Hurst, Fannie: Anitra's Dance, 94–97, 96 example, 259n60; cinematic sensibility of, 92–94, 95–96, 259n54; "Humoresque," 81, 91, 92, 99; Imitation of Life, 92; and melodrama, 88, 93, 95, 96–97, 235, 236; musical experience, 92, 96; on popular success, 259n52; reception of, 259n51; "Russia Free," 94; screen adaptations of, 92; "Sob Sister," 92, 93; story for Symphony of Six Million, 88, 91, 93, 95, 259n56, 260n64; Yiddishkeit in, 92, 97. See also Symphony of Six Million
"Hustle, The," 64

Hutcheon, Linda, 143, 146, 272n75, 285n58
Huxley, Aldous, 113, 128, 262n12
Huysmans, Joris-Karl, 216, 220, 262n9

IBM, 198–99; *IBM Songbook*, 199; *IBM Symphony*, 199, 281n4
Idelsohn, A. Z., 76, 77, 259n59
"I Hear a Symphony," 196, 202, 203; cinematicism in, 211, 212–13; concert music in, 210–13; harmonic progression of, 213; rhetorical aspects of, 206; rhythmic content of, 212; soundscape of, 210; structure of, 281n11
"I'm in Love with My Car," 231
Informer, The (film), 48–49, 82–84, 85, 103, 187, 279n58, 280n73
Informer, The (novel), 83–84, 258n34
inspiration: artistic, 119, 222; ethical, 31; morbidity, 131; muses and, 237–38; poetic, 113
Intermezzo, 197
"I.O.U.," 64
Iron Butterfly, 223
Ishiwatari, Daisuke, 239, 240
Isley Brothers, 196

Jackson, Michael, 4; classic register in, 31–33; moon walk of, 56
Jakobson, Roman, 57
James, Henry, 55, 236, 258n48
Jameson, Frederic, 142, 146, 152, 271n63
Jan and Dean, 14, 244n11
jazz: bebop, 264n21; in *The Jazz Singer*, 78, 79, 80, 177, 277n42; saxophone, 45, 47–49
Jazz Singer, The, 51, 52–58, 74, 75–80, 86, 89, 103, 253nn17,19, 278n50; human voice in, 75, 176, 277n42; and kinothek practice, 30; *Kol nidre* in, 53, 54, 56, 76 *example*, 80, 86, 273n78, 277n42; as melodrama, 54–56; nostalgia in, 273n78; *Romeo and Juliet* in, 51, 52–53, 56, 57, 88, 97, 253n18; silent portions of, 74, 180; *Symphonie espagnole* in, 76, 77 *example*, 256n8; synchronized sound in, 176, 177, 178–79. *See also* Silvers, Louis
Jefferson Airplane, 122–24, 262n8, 267n4
Jewish music: ethnographic study of, 76–77; in kinotheks, 77. *See also Jazz Singer, The; Kol nidre*; musical theater, Yiddish; *Symphony of Six Million*; theater, Yiddish
Jews: and assimilation, 56, 74, 75, 99, 256n7, 259n60; ethnic distinctions

among, 76–77, 78, 79, 256n3, 257n21; in Hollywood, 54, 74, 89, 90, 258n37; as theatre owners, 89, 104. *See also* musical theater, Yiddish; theater, Yiddish; Yiddishkeit
Joel, Billy, 18
John, Elton, 225
John of Garland, 16, 68
Johnson, Julian, 1–3, 5, 8, 31, 39, 50, 59, 128, 191, 241n3
Jolson, Al, 7; African-Americanisms of, 75, 78–79, 257n14; "Blue Skies," 52; reception of, 79, 179; use of blackface, 257n14. See also *Jazz Singer, The*
Joyce, James: *Finnegan's Wake*, Marx Brothers in, 41

Kafka, Franz, 90, 102
Kalinak, Kathryn, 44, 46, 47, 48, 50, 53, 274n4
Kant, Immanuel, 263n12. *See also* sublime, the
Karloff, Boris, 36; as Frankenstein's monster, 176, 187, 189, 192; in *The Old Dark House*, 183
Kasdan, Lawrence, 146
Kaukonen, Jorma, 123
Kaun, Bernard, 48
Keats, John, 112–13, 115
Kerman, Joseph, 202
Kermode, Frank, 28, 244n19
Kern, Jerome, 101, 104, 260n74
Kerouac, Jack, 162, 262n10; cosmic imagery of, 264n21; and *Fantasia*, 266n42; *Satori in Paris*, 268n8
King Crimson, 153, 261n6; and Wagner, 110, 124, 130, 158
King Kong, 46, 66, 68–69, 164, 176, 184, 187, 188
Kinkeldey, Otto, 30
Kinotheks, 20, 29–30, 50, 51, 52, 57, 69, 77, 248n54
Kiss, 18
kitsch, 7, 139, 141, 142, 149, 150, 152, 263n19
Koestenbaum, Wayne, 284n50
Kol nidre, 76 *example*, 256n4; commercial circulation of, 85, 87–88; in *The Jazz Singer*, 54, 56, 79–80, 85, 86, 176, 177, 277n42; Schoenberg on, 85, 87, 256nn7–8; in *Sons of Liberty*, 86–87; in *Symphony of Six Million*, 91, 98; in Yiddish theater, 103–4
Korngold, Erich Wolfgang, 44, 45, 47, 58, 251n3
Koyaanisqatsi, 199
Kozloff, Max, 70, 71, 256n54

Kramer, Lawrence, 238, 245n24,
    285nn3,6
Krims, Adam, 241n4, 248n57
Kubrick, Stanley. See *2001: A Space
    Odyssey*

Lacan, Jacques, 243n4
Lalo, Edouard, *Symphonie espagnole*, 73,
    76, 77 *example*. See also *Jazz Singer,
    The*
Lanchester, Elsa, 176, 192
Landini, Francesco, 17
Lang, Fritz, 164, 165, 166, 190, 191,
    194, 275n22, 277n34
language. *See* linguistics; register;
    vernacular
Lansbury, Angela, 201
Laura (film), 42, 44–46, 47, 52, 58, 59,
    76, 163, 251n83, 252n7, 253n16,
    274n2; the fantastic in, 158, 166
"Laura" (song), 45, 94, 212
"Lazing on a Sunday Afternoon," 234,
    285n1
Led Zeppelin, 126–27, 243n8
Leff, Leonard, 90
Le Franc, Martin, 78
Léger, Fernand: *Ballet mécanique*, 166,
    168
Legrand, Christiane, 134, 141
Leigh, Janet, 250n78
len-a-tone process, 158, 274n24
Lennon, John, 132, 267n4
Lennox, Annie, 156
Lenoir, Jean, 165, 275n13
Leonard, Robert Z., 181
Leoncavallo, Ruggiero: *Pagliacci*, 227
Leone, Sergio, 159
Lévi-Strauss, Claude, 19
Lewin, Albert E., 216–20, 282n25,
    283n30. See also *Picture of Dorian
    Gray, The*
Liberace, 33
Ligeti, György: *Atmosphères*, 71–72,
    256n54
"Light My Fire," 124–25, 268n14
Liliom, 190–91, 280n78; "carousel
    song" in, 165, 275n13; electronic in-
    struments in, 191; time in, 166; title se-
    quence of, 164–65
linguistics: situational, 2; structural, 22.
    See also register
Linzer, Sandy, 281n10, 282nn12–13
listening, cinematic, 7. *See also* cinemati-
    cism in popular music
Liszt, Franz: C♯-Minor Hungarian Rhap-
    sody, 198, 204–5, 205 *example*, 206,
    221

Local Hero, 255n41
Locke, Ralph, 242n9, 256n5
loops, 36, 166, 167, 171, 275n15. *See
    also* circularity
Lost Weekend, The, 158, 163, 252n11
"Love of My Life," 214–16
"Lover's Concerto, A" 17, 196, 203–9;
    Bach in, 202, 208; introduction, 203
    example; Liszt in, 204–5, 206; melody
    and harmony, 213; in *Mr. Holland's
    Opus*, 200–201, 202; pastoralism in,
    207–8, 209, 281n12; poetics of, 210;
    vocal technique in, 206, 281n10,
    282n13
"Love's Theme," 64
Lowe, John Livingston, *The Road to
    Xanadu*, 41
LSD, Ginsberg's experiment with, 111
Lucas, George. See *Star Wars*
"Lucy in the Sky," 267n4, 275n15
Ludwig, Friedrich, 29, 30, 248n52
Lumière brothers, 165, 166, 168, 170,
    176
Lyons, Leonard, 41

MacCabe, Colin, 245n25
Machaut, Guillaume de, 11
Mad Love, 35
madrigals, medieval, 282n12
Mahler, Gustav, 81
Mallarmé, Stéphane, 114, 264n20
Manilow, Barry, 17, 35, 210
Man With the Golden Arm, The, 164
Manzarek, Ray: and the Doors, 124–25,
    127, 129, 214; *The Poet in Exile*,
    262n10
Markovitsch, Joseph, *Kol nidre*, 103, 104
Marks, Martin, 248n54
Martin, George, 109, 114
Marx, Chico: immigrant persona of, 236;
    in *A Night at the Opera*, 24, 236, 237;
    pianistic style of, 205, 285n1
Marx, Groucho, 42; and Bugs Bunny,
    221, 285n1; and Eliot, 28–29; and
    Joyce, 41, 42; in *A Night at the Opera*,
    24, 237–38
Marx, Harpo: and Liszt, 221; in *A Night
    at the Opera*, 236; persona of, 237, 238
Marx Brothers: Barthes on, 236, 237; in-
    fluence on Joyce, 41; and melodrama,
    235; mythemic registers of, 237; Queen
    and, 231, 233, 234–35, 239; social cri-
    tique by, 235; and vaudeville, 24, 224,
    234; Woolcott and, 41, 251n83. See
    also *Night at the Opera, A*
Mascagni, Pietro, *Cavalleria Rusticana*,
    227

"mass" media, 4–5
Matrix, The, 255n41
Matthews, Dave. *See* "Love of My Life"
Maurice, 59
May, Brian, 231, 285n56
Maytime (film), 217
Maytime (operetta), 82
Mazower, David, 103, 104
McCartney, Paul, on "White Rabbit," 267n4
McClary, Susan, 52
McClure, Michael, 262n10
"Mea culpa," 267n8
medievalia, in twentieth-century media, 267n8
melodrama: in film, 54–56, 82–84, 90–91, 235, 253nn21–23; and gesture, 54, 227; in rock music, 224. *See also* Brooks, Peter; Hurst, Fannie
Melody Maker (trade paper), 109–10, 129, 133, 157, 273n86
Meltzer, Richard, 265n26
Melvin, Harold, and the Blue Notes, 64–65
memory: and language, 243n7; medieval representation of, 242n8; and register, 26; spatial, 63. *See also* Mnemosyne
Mendelssohn, Felix, *Spring Song,* 188
Mercer, Johnny, 45
Mercury, Freddie, 7, 222–23, 225, 226–27, 229, 238, 270n38, 285n56; and ballet, 230; *Barcelona,* 229; on the Beatles, 283n40; and Caballé, 229, 230, 285n52; and excess, 223; and *Guilty Gear* (video game), 239; as Hermes, 226, 229–31; Islamic background, 283n35; "I Want to Break Free" (video), 230; as Pan, 230; as rhapsode, 222. *See also* "Bohemian Rhapsody"; Queen
Merrie Melodies, theme music, 66
Mescall, John, 195
Messiaen, Olivier, 174
Metropolis, 194–95, 259n55, 275n22
Meyer, Leonard, 16, 206
Middleton, Richard, 6, 241n4, 242n9, 261n5, 265n33, 269n37, 270n48, 282n14
Milestone, Lewis, 25
Million Dollar Movie, 70
Mills, Stephanie, 64
mise-en-bande. *See* Altman, Rick
Mnemosyne, 5, 238, 239
modernism: literary, 11, 93, 114, 259n51, 264n20; in media, 162, 170; musical, 1, 48, 116, 170, 171
Moeller, Philip, 180
Monkees, 109

montage (technique), 199; and Eisenstein, 172, 173, 235, 237; and Hitchcock, 170, 172, 173
Moonlight Sonata (film), 198
Moore, Allan F., 242n9, 262n8, 265n34, 275n15; on genre terms, 261n1, 264n21; on the "sound box," 114, 270n46
More, Thomas, 117
Morricone, Ennio, 159
Morris, Sarah Jane, 65
Morris, William, 139, 140, 143, 144
Morrisey, Paul, 162, 163
Morrison, Jim, 125, 128, 129, 262n10, 269n27
Motown, 200, 201, 202, 206, 209, 213
Mozart, W. A., 61, 284nn41,47
Mr. Holland's Opus, 197–201, 202
multiplanar effects: acoustical, 182, 278; in multimedia, 174, 211, 220; visual, 101, 170, 276n25. *See also* stereoscopy
Mummy, The, 82, 184–86, 279n70
muses, classical, 238
musical theater, Yiddish, 96, 97, 99, 100, 102–4, 260n72; genres of, 261n75. *See also* theater, Yiddish

Nerval, Gérard de, 35
Neumeyer, David, 82, 83, 84, 274n6
Newman, Alfred, 47, 253n20
Newman, Paul, 212
"Night and Day," 59–60
Night at the Opera, A (Marx Brothers), 24, 228, 233, 234, 235, 236, 237
Night at the Opera, A (Queen), 224, 231, 233, 234, 283nn37,40; and *Guilty Gear* (video game), 239
Nijinsky, Vaslav, 230
"No One Ever Tells You," 115
Nordau, Max, 139
nostalgia: acoustical, 7; and death, 143, 145, 147; as formal mode, 142, 145, 147, 148, 151, 273n79; Jameson on, 142, 146, 271n63; in Proust, 143; as psychosomatic experience, 142, 143, 146, 147, 148; and race, 273n78; and sentimentality, 141, 142, 146, 149, 150fig., 152, 215, 235; and utopia, 142, 148, 272n75; visual, 144. *See also* "Whiter Shade of Pale, A"
Novak, Kim, 167
Now, Voyager, 17, 20–21, 30, 40, 59–63, 68, 85, 86, 103, 163–64
Nth Commandment, The, 81
Nugent, Frank, 25, 33, 49, 67

Ockeghem, Johannes, 208, 209
O'Flaherty, Liam, 83

Of Mice and Men, 25–26
Oland, Warner, 75
Old Dark House, The, 184, 277n37;
    sound in, 183, 194
O'Neill, Eugene, 179–80, 278n51
opera: and film music, 29, 81–82, 83, 84,
    102, 217, 218, 270n44, 279n58; and
    Freddie Mercury, 224, 225, 226,
    227–31, 234, 284nn47,50, 285n53;
    gay fans of, 229, 284n50; as immigrant
    culture, 235; and melodrama, 84,
    253n22; pastiche, 257n26; prologues
    in, 227, 228; and rock music, 224,
    281n6, 284n41; self-parody, 284n48;
    Weimar, 139. See also *Night at the
    Opera, A*
opus: verbal resonance of, 197, 282n13
Oswald, Richard, 226
overtures, film, 68, 69, 71, 72, 255n44
"Oyfn Pripetshok," 91, 99, 102

Paderewski, Ignace Jan, 198
Paglia, Camille, 276n25
Parker, Charlie, 45, 47
Parritt, Barbara, 281n10
pastoralism: in film, 68, 69, 188, 190; in
    landscape art, 236; in "A Lover's Con-
    certo," 207–8, 209, 281n12; of madri-
    gals, 282n12; and the picturesque, 126,
    127; register of, 243n9
pastorals, medieval, 208, 209, 282n12;
    register of, 13, 15, 243n9
pathos, cinematic representation of, 61
Peck, Gregory, 168
Pendergrass, Teddy, 65
Pentangle, 271n60
Performance Group, *Dionysus in '69*,
    230, 285n55
Perkins, Anthony, 171
Pfann, Walter, 254n35
Philles Records, 114, 115
piano keyboard: and sheet music art,
    101; and visual gestures, 201, 203,
    204–5, 218, 219, 226. See also con-
    certo
Picture of Dorian Gray, The (film), 198,
    201, 203, 216–21, 283n30
Picture of Dorian Gray, The (novel), 131,
    217, 219, 220
picturesque, the, 117, 125–27, 128, 153,
    154, 163, 217
picturizations, of novels and stories, 88,
    90, 92, 93, 197, 259n51
poetics: of death, 192; historical, 6, 11,
    12, 13, 15, 16, 22, 68, 113, 243n9; of
    listening, 111, 141, 264n21; in popular
    music, 36, 206, 207, 208, 209, 210; of
    space, 58, 59, 63

polyphony, fifteenth-century, 35, 78–79,
    208–9
popular music: academic study of, 3, 6,
    241nn4,5, 242n9; meaning in, 19, 110,
    227, 275n15; as "text," 246n32. *See
    also specific genres*
Pop-Up Videos, 223
Porter, Cole, 59, 60
power chords. *See* concerto
Preminger, Otto, 42, 164, 212, 252n7.
    See also *Laura*
pre-Raphaelite art, 139–42, 143–45,
    271n60
Procul Harum. *See* "Whiter Shade of
    Pale, A"
Program music, spatial effects in, 209
Prokofiev, Sergey: *Alexander Nevsky*, 173
psychedelia: and individual experience,
    117, 128, 153, 157, 262n6,
    269nn27,34; and poetry, 111, 264n20;
    reaction against, 162–63, 273n86; and
    rock music, 14, 116, 122, 125, 126,
    128, 161, 162, 164, 214, 265n34,
    267n8
Psycho (1960), sound and music, 165,
    169, 170–76, 250n76, 276n30; as rap
    sample, 34, 38–41; waltz, 173 *example*
Psycho (1960), visual elements, 34, 38–40,
    119, 167, 170–73, 175, 266n40
Psycho (1998), 173–75
psychosis, in film music, 50, 158–59,
    160–61, 162, 163, 168, 171, 172,
    252n11, 278n45
Psych-Out, 161
Puecker, Brigitte, 276n34

Quattro, Suzy, 225
Queen: in live performances, 225; and
    the Marx Brothers, 224, 233, 234–35,
    239, 285n1; as Smile, 285n53. *See also*
    "Bohemian Rhapsody"; *Day at the
    Races, A*; Mercury, Freddie; *Night at
    the Opera, A*

Rabkin, Eric, 139
radio: association with ether, 177–78;
    critiques of, 63, 131; radio-miking,
    214. *See also* film sound
Rains, Claude, 86
Raksin, David, 32, 159. See also *Laura*
Randell, Denny, 281n10, 282nn12–13
Rank, J. Arthur, 231
Raphaelson, Sampson, 53, 77, 79, 86
rap music, 248n57; cinematic aspects of,
    34, 36, 38–39, 40, 60, 105, 249n60;
    and register, 33–34; repetition in, 39;
    sampling in, 33, 34–35, 248n58; theo-
    sophical, 36, 249n66

Ravel, Maurice: *Bolero*, 123
Ray, Robert, 248n47
Raykoff, Ivan, 249n62
Rebecca, 90, 159, 193
register, 6, 47, 252n5: expressive, 12, 13,
    15, 17, 22, 45–46, 53, 86, 99, 100,
    243n5; in language and literature, 13,
    14, 19, 23, 24, 27, 29, 57, 95, 100,
    119, 122, 164, 198, 207, 227, 231,
    243nn4,8,9, 244n10, 245n25; in lin-
    guistic theory, 12, 15–16, 22, 30,
    244n13; registration and reregistra-
    tion, 12, 22, 23, 25, 33, 34, 43, 47, 50,
    56, 246n35. *See also* classic register;
    register of the classic; registers,
    expressive
register of the classic, 26, 27, 28, 30, 34,
    39, 56, 101, 105, 247n44. *See also*
    classic register
registers, expressive: in film music, 21,
    24, 26, 29, 30, 42, 50, 51–52, 56, 57,
    61–62, 66, 68–70, 85, 86, 101, 159,
    163, 174, 193, 252nn3,7, 254n31; in
    nineteenth-century music, 17, 51; in
    popular music, 16–17, 32–41, 64, 65,
    125, 130–31, 204, 206, 223, 225, 226,
    231, 239; visual, 45, 60–61, 66, 67,
    71, 101, 204, 207
Reid, Keith, 109, 110, 117, 122, 130,
    131, 137, 151, 214, 263n12, 270n38,
    284n45. *See also* "Whiter Shade of
    Pale, A"
Renbourn, John, 271n60
Respighi, Ottorino, 127, 268n17
reverberation, 115, 123, 136, 245n21
"Revolution No. 9," 166
rhapsodes, 221–23; Plato's Ion, 222
Rhapsody Rabbit (cartoon), 75, 221,
    285n1; Agee on, 205; Liszt in, 198
rhetoric: pedagogical, 196; rhetorical fig-
    ures, 203
Rhymes, Busta, 34, 38–40. *See also*
    "Gimme Some More"
Richards, Annette, 125, 126, 127, 131,
    268n18
Riehl, Heinrich Wilhelm, 7–8
Riemann, Hugo, 95
Rochlitz, Friedrich, 154
Rocket Ship, 190, 279n70
rock journalism, 130, 131–32. *See also*
    authenticity; *Crawdaddy*; *Melody
    Maker*; *Rolling Stone*
Rogin, Michael, 75
"Roll Over, Beethoven," 131
Rolling Stone, 35, 130, 131, 132,
    138–39, 215, 223, 265n34
Rolling Stones, 109

Romanticism: concept of inspiration,
    113; and film music, 40, 43, 50,
    246n31; and rock music, 129, 131,
    162, 269nn27–28
Romberg, Sigmund, 82
Ronettes, 114–15
Rose, Tricia, 39, 248n58, 249n63,
    250n74
Rosen, Charles, 32, 128, 281n11
Ross, Andrew, 269n31
Ross, Diana, vocal nuances of, 211, 213.
    See also "I Hear a Symphony"
Rosse, Herman, 194
Rossetti, Christina, 144
Rossetti, Dante Gabriel, 139–40, 271n57
Rota, Nino, 126–27, 268n17
Rózsa, Miklós, 278n44. See also *Lost
    Weekend, The*; *Spellbound*
Rush, Richard, 161

Sabatini, Rafael, *Scaramouche*, 228
Sade, Marquis de, 267n8
Saint, Eva-Marie, 212
Sainte-Beauve, Charles Augustin, 27, 28
Saint-Saëns, Camille, *L'Assassinat du
    duc de Guise*, 188
Sala, Oskar, 169
sampling, musical, 40. *See also* rap music
Santana, Carlos. *See* "Love of My Life"
Saville, Victor, 36
Savino, Domenico, 57
Schaeffer, Pierre, 177, 264n25
Schifrin, Lalo, 48–49
Schillinger, Joseph: *Airphonic Suite*, 178
Schoenberg, Arnold, 42, 43, 54, 73, 76,
    81, 85, 87, 158, 216, 253n20,
    256nn7–8, 258n36. See also *Kol nidre*
Schubert, Franz, *Ave Maria*, 188
Schumann, Robert: *Waldszenen*, 217–18,
    219, 282nn27–28
science: mad, 118, 119, 190, 192, 200,
    266n38; Victorian, 123
"Seaside Rendezvous," 234
Seldes, Gilbert, 79, 233, 235, 257n13
self, subjective, loss of, 38, 250n71
Selznick, David Oliver, 67, 82, 86, 88,
    90, 98, 255n44
semiotics, in study of media, 18–19, 21,
    22, 245n23
sensory experience: and musical descrip-
    tion, 78–79; in synaesthesia, 211,
    251n86, 262n9. *See also* synaesthesia
sentimentality. *See* nostalgia
sexuality, and expressive register, 47–50,
    51, 52, 61
Shakespeare, William: in Jewish theater,
    89, 96; in popular music, 207

Shapiro, Peter, 64
Shaw, John Byam, *The Boer War*, 144–45, 145*fig.*
Shaw, Julie, 31
Shearer, Douglas, 181
Shelley, Mary Wollstonecraft: in *Bride of Frankenstein*, 189, 192; *Frankenstein*, 118, 187, 266n38
sickness, registers of, 130, 131
Silvers, Louis, 74: and Judaism, 54, 73, 75–76, 77–78; and Schoenberg, 54, 253n20. See also *Jazz Singer, The*
Simon and Garfunkel, "59th Street Bridge Song," 270n40
Simone, Lela, 218
Sinatra, Frank, 164
Sisman, Elaine, 254n33
Sledge, Percy, 137
Slick, Grace, 123, 268n9
Slobin, Mark, 75, 80–81, 100, 101, 102–3, 261n75
Small, Christopher, 250n74
"Smile," 31, 32, 33
Snead, James, 250n74
soap operas: radio, 252n9; television, 49
sociolinguistics, Dante and, 11. See also register
Somerville, Jimmy, 7, 65–66
Song to Remember, A, 203, 249n62
Sons of Liberty, 85–87, 103, 104, 258nn37,38; *Kol nidre* in, 86–87
Sontag, Susan, 242n10
Sony PlayStation, 4, 239
sound box, 136, 203, 211, 270n46
Spector, Phil, 131, 209, 215, 266n37; appreciation of Wagner, 114–15, 116, 117, 118–19, 124, 224, 264n25, 265n37; and ethereal sound, 115, 265n27; monaural acoustical environment, 264n24; percussion, 115; use of ambience effects, 115, 265n24; wall of sound, 114, 115, 119
Spellbound, 158, 160, 163, 168, 252n11, 275n22
Spheeris, Penelope, 222, 231
sphinx, 75, 186, 192
Spielberg, Steven, 61
"Stairway to Heaven," 126–27, 243n8
Stalling, Carl, 255n39
Star Trek, 93
Star Wars, 45, 66, 251n3
Steiner, Gabor, 104
Steiner, Max, 7, 47; cultural background of, 81, 104; on Jewish music, 82, 86, 88, 102; and Kern, 104, 260n74; musical puns, 62, 68, 69; and Selznick, 82; use of anthems, 85, 103–4; on Wagner,

157–58. See also *Casablanca; Dark Victory; Gone With the Wind; Informer, The; King Kong; Now, Voyager; Summer Place, A; Symphony of Six Million*
stereoscopy: aural analogies to, 112, 128, 136, 137, 138, 146, 148, 151, 152, 181, 182, 191, 192; haptic aspects of, 136, 170; visual, 112, 126, 144, 145*fig.*, 165, 170, 185. *See also* multiplanar effects
Stewart, James, 159
Stokowski, Leopold, 119
Stothart, Herbert, 216–21
Strange Interlude, 179, 181–82
Strauss, Richard, 116, 215, 232; *Also Sprach Zarathustra*, 72, 195; *Ariadne auf Naxos*, 227, 228–31, 284n48, 285n57; and Steiner, 81
Stravinsky, Igor: and Herrmann's music, 38, 40, 42, 171; and Waxman's music, 191; in Hollywood, 42, 43
Strawberry Alarm Clock, 161
"Strawberry Fields Forever," 109, 261n2
Streisand, Barbra, 31, 32
Studio 54, 63–64
sublime, the, 113, 114, 229, 254nn33,35, 263nn18–19, 280n82; cinematic representation of, 60–62, 63, 195; mathematical, 61, 113
Sullivan, Jack, 276n30
Sulzer, Johann Georg, 195
Summer Place, A, 47, 48, 64
"Summertime," 48, 252n7
Sunset Boulevard, 162
Supremes. *See* "I Hear a Symphony"
"Surfin' Bird," expressive register in, 14
Swingle, Ward, 137, 270nn40–41
Swingle Singers, 125, 133–35, 136, 140, 141, 149, 151
Swing Time, 261n74
symphonic rock, 110, 222, 223
symphonies, as cultural icons, 198
Symphony in F (Ford Motors), 199
Symphony of Six Million, 81–82, 83, 84, 86, 88, 91, 94, 97–100, 260n74. *See also* Hurst, Fannie
synaesthesia, 211, 216, 220, 251n86, 262n9, 266n42
Szatmary, David, 265n27

Tagg, Philip, 19, 246n32
Tarkovsky, Andrei, 4: *Nostalghia*, 146–49, 151, 272n76; and "zone," 272n77
Taruskin, Richard, 51, 139, 263n13, 285n54

Taylor, Deems, 251n86
Taylor, Timothy D., 241n5, 251n80
"Teen Angel," 131
television shows: *All My Children*, 49; *Dawson's Creek*, 252n9; *Liberace Show*, 33; *Million-Dollar Movie*, 70; novelizations of, 93; *Steve Allen Show*, 162
Thalberg, Irving, 179, 216
theater, Yiddish, 54, 88, 89–90, 91, 99, 102; and "histrionic code," 90, 91; as genre, 105. *See also* musical theater, Yiddish
"Then He Kissed Me," 115
Theocritus, 188
theremin. *See* electronic instruments
Theremin, Leon, 158, 167, 177–78, 192, 275n18, 277n44, 280n75
Thesiger, Ernest, 189
Thomas, Rob, 214
timbre, as marker of register, 24–26, 57
Tinctoris, Johannes, 208
Tinney, Al, 36
title sequences in film, musical and visual elements of, 34, 40, 44–46, 58, 66, 67, 68, 69, 73, 86, 88, 94, 100, 126, 148, 162, 164, 167, 168, 169, 171, 176, 183, 184, 190–91, 194, 198, 212, 250n78, 251n3, 254n29, 255n42, 260n74, 275n13, 279n67. *See also* film scores
Todorov, Tzvetan, 127, 266n38, 267n1, 268n11
Tolstoy, Leo, *War and Peace*, 70
Tom and Jerry. See *Cat Concerto, The*
tombeaux, musical, 247n44
tombs, Egyptian, 184
Top of the Pops, 225
Toys. *See* "Lover's Concerto, A"
Trash, 162
Trashmen, 14
Tsur, Reuven: on expressive utterance, 64, 254n28; on timbre, 24, 57
Tucker, Richard, 80
Tupac, 249n66
2001: A Space Odyssey, 67, 70–72, 255n51, 261n6

Ulmers, Gregory, 236
Uris, Leon, 212
utopias, 117; and dystopias, 117; of girl groups, 209; and nostalgia, 142, 271n63

Van Sant, Gus. See *Psycho* (1998)
Veidt, Conrad, 226–27
Velvet Underground, 162–63, 164, 274nn10–11

Verdi, Guiseppe: *Requiem*, 148; *Il Trovatore*, 229, 284n51
vernacular: ethics, 6; imagination, 5; language, 11–13, 19, 22, 23, 24. *See also* register
Vertigo: sound and music, 159, 165, 168, 171, 275n20; visual elements, 168, 276n25
Vibe (magazine), 251n80
video games, 2, 239–40; aesthetics of, 285n7
Vietnam War, 132, 146, 153
Vigoda, Samuel, 80, 257n18
Village People, 64
Virgil, 16, 27, 28, 120, 209
Vitaphone technology. *See* film sound; *Jazz Singer, The*

Wagner, Richard: and film music, 68, 88, 158, 218; and Ginsberg, 111–12, 113, 114, 116, 117, 118, 264n20; and popular music, 110, 114, 115, 118, 124, 224, 265n37, 269n34, 275n15
Walser, Robert, 225, 261n5, 268n18, 281n6
waltz, 165, 167, 168, 169, 172–73, 221, 275nn15,19,20
Warhol, Andy, 162, 275n12
Warsaw Concerto: 34, 41, 249n62; and DMX, 35, 36–39; reception of, 249n68; register of, 38
Warshawsky, Mark, 99
Watson, Thomas, 198–99
Waxman, Franz, 47, 92, 101, 158, 159, 164, 166, 194, 275n13; and German expressionist cinema, 194; scoring techniques of, 188, 279n66; use of electronic instruments, 158. See also *Bride of Frankenstein; Liliom; Rebecca*
Wayne's World, 222, 223, 231–32; and postmodern irony, 231
Wegener, Paul, 186–87, 189, 279n62
Weiss, Allen, 113–14, 264n20, 269n34
Welles, Orson, 66
"We Will Rock You," 283n35
Whale, James. See *Bride of Frankenstein; Frankenstein; Old Dark House, The*
"What's My Name," 34–38, 39, 40, 41
"When a Man Loves a Woman," 137–38, 271n49
Whitely, Sheila, 261n5, 262n8, 268n19, 269n24, 270n38, 273n86
"White Rabbit," 122–24, 262n8, 267n4
"Whiter Shade of Pale, A" 8, 133 *example*; acoustical depth in, 135–38,

145–46; Baroque elements of, 109–10,
116, 117, 124, 129, 133–35; and
clavichord, 127–28, 131, 138, 149;
fantastic elements of, 117, 122, 137;
and Ginsberg's sublime, 263n12;
Lennox cover of, 156; and nostalgia,
145, 149, 150–51, 155, 268n19; re-
ception of, 124, 129, 130, 132,
138–39, 141; soul elements of, 110,
129, 134, 137; and the Swingle
Singers, 134–35; in *The Big Chill*, 146,
152–53, 154–55
Whitfield, Stephen, 79, 256n2, 257n13
Whitman, Slim, 223
Whitney, John, 167, 168
Wilde, Oscar. See *Picture of Dorian
Gray, The*
Wilder, Thornton, 41
Williams, Alan, 53, 253n17
Williams, John, *Star Wars*, 45, 251n3
Wills, Clair, 244n16
Wilson, B. J., 134. *See also* "Whiter
Shade of Pale, A"
Wilson, Brian, 264n24
Winkler, Max, 248n54

Wise, Robert, 50, 160, 163. See also *Day
the Earth Stood Still, The*
Wisson, Bernard, 174
Wolff, Christian Michael, "Erleichtre
meine Sorgen," 128
Woolcott, Alexander, 41, 251n83
Wordsworth, William, *Prelude*, 113

"Yankee Doodle": in film scores, 85, 86;
in Jewish musical theater, 103. *See also*
Steiner, Max
Yiddishkeit, Steiner's engagement with,
97, 104–5, 260n61. *See also* Hurst,
Fannie; musical theater, Yiddish; the-
ater, Yiddish
Yiddish language, 57
"YMCA," 64
"You Make Me Feel (Mighty Real)," 64

Zak, Albin, 115, 135, 136, 138, 264n24,
265n37, 270n46
Zappa, Frank, 162, 274n10
Zauberin, Die, 96
Zeffirelli, Franco, 126–27
Zumthor, Paul, 243n4